MYTH

DATE DUE

Second Edition

MYTH AND REALITY
A Reader in Education

GLENN SMITH
CHARLES R. KNIKER

Iowa State University

Allyn and Bacon, Inc.
boston   london   sydney   toronto

Library of Congress Cataloging in Publication Data

Smith, Leonard Glenn, 1939-   comp.
   Myth and reality.

   First ed. published in 1972 under title: Myth and
reality : a reader in educational foundations.
   Includes bibliographical references.
   1. Public schools—United States—Addresses, essays,
lectures. I. Kniker, Charles R., joint comp. II. Title.
LA217.S6 1975   371'.01'0973   74-30214
ISBN 0-205-04777-7
Second printing . . . July, 1976

CONTENTS

ACKNOWLEDGMENTS

It takes many people to make a book like this possible and, while we cannot thank all of them specifically, we do want to thank those who were most crucial. Neither edition would have been started without the encouragement of Dean Virgil S. Lagomarcino, and Associate Dean Harold E. Dilts, College of Education, Iowa State University. They have for several years provided an excellent climate for teaching and learning. Wallace C. Schloerke, Coordinator of Student Teaching, and Robert L. Ziomek, Teaching Assistant, Iowa State University, made valuable content suggestions, as did Joan K. Smith, who also contributed original material. Jack Peters, Senior Editor, and Steve Mathews, Education Editor, Allyn and Bacon, Inc., have been most helpful. Several anonymous colleagues to whom they submitted both editions of the manuscript made valuable criticisms. Nancy Murphy, copyeditor for the first edition, and Jane Richardson, copyeditor for this edition, have been friendly, patient, thorough, and exact. James Van Patten, Editor of the *Journal of Thought* and Professor of Education, University of Arkansas, was most cooperative, as were all the other editors, journal representatives and authors represented herein. Finally, we want to thank the many Iowa State University students who read all the articles plus a great many more, for both editions, and whose questions and insights are part of this volume.

PREFACE

In 1972, when this book first appeared, students were celebrating the Age of Aquarius. Critics of schooling, such as A. S. Neill, John Holt, and Jonathan Kozol, were in vogue. Humanizing education, performance contracting, and equal educational opportunity were current jargon.

Some say we are now in an age of nostalgia. Neill is dead, and certain critics have issued reservations about the free school movement. Individualizing instruction and open classrooms are in, busing is out, and accountability is a key issue.

What is happening in the schools? How can we interpret the changes occurring? What will happen next?

We can resort to the standard clichés and say "the pendulum is swinging" or "everything has to change for the better." The first response is less than adequate for the serious student. Our environmental crisis tells us the second is foolish. If we seek help from some textbooks for educational foundations courses, we find glowing accounts of the growth and triumph of public schooling. If we turn to the critics' versions of what schooling is doing to and for children, we learn that it has been either a sinister or a mindless enterprise with few positive accomplishments. We believe that approaching the study of schooling from any of these perspectives results in academic stereotyping, a fatal seriousness, which will promote student disinterest.

Our approach paraphrases the strategy and attitude about studying history suggested by the late Richard Hofstader. He remarked that one should begin with a playfulness about, and piety toward, ideas. By examining basic assumptions about the functions of American schooling, by weighing the distance between what American schooling *is* and what it is *supposed to be,* we believe the study of education can be provocative, exciting, and, yes, enjoyable.

MYTH AND REALITY DEFINED

Stated differently, the purpose of this book is to separate the myths about schooling from the reality that exists.

What is a myth? The dictionary definition closest to our use of the term is: "An ill-founded belief held uncritically, especially by an interested group." However, that definition omits the idea that myths may have been true in another period, or yet contain some truth. We agree with Carl Bereiter that a myth is "a closed system for viewing reality containing elements of truth that prevents the individual from managing to deal with reality."*

In the same article, Bereiter noted that often attempts to get people to accept reality or "face the facts" are messages saying (1) accept my version of reality, (2) reconcile yourself to the status quo, or (3) stop fooling around and get to work. We have tried to avoid inserting our "realities" too much, but we realize that some readers will find our comments, or those expressed by the various writers, to be new myths replacing the old rather than reality. Our hope is that through these readings people may gain some insights on reality.

UNIQUE FEATURES

Toward the above-stated end, we have chosen types of readings that do not appear too often in most other anthologies. Many of the articles describe local school situations, to emphasize what is actually happening at the grass-roots and concrete-pavement levels of instruction today. We have included newspaper reports and journal essays. Senate hearings as well as research studies are in these pages.

There are significant differences between this edition and our first. We were surprised by the number of readers who urged us to include more historical information than we had provided in the introductions to the book sections. A number of historical articles have been added, ranging from liberal interpretations to selections from the "revisionist" camp.

*Carl Bereiter, "Education and the Pursuit of Reality," *Interchange,* Vol. 2, No. 1, 1971, pp. 44–50.

Although most selections are contemporary, we have also included some articles that have "weathered" well, either because they reflect positions that have prevailed or because they were accurate predictions of things to come.

In the last edition we indicated that we had not always sought to balance liberal and conservative points of view, nor to offset an establishment statement with a militant declaration. In this edition we have included a greater variety of opinions and interpretations, though space limitations prevent us from including every significant position. Our intention remains to provide at least some clear indications of major educational issues and alternative positions.

One new section has been added. The focus on the learning environment, the role of the teacher, and accountability made it necessary to include a section on the teacher as a person, as a member of a social organization, and the effectiveness of the teaching-learning process.

ORGANIZATION

The book is organized around five common assumptions about American education. We believe most readers will be stimulated to weigh in their minds what is myth and what is reality in these assumptions.

1. *"The school is the best panacea for America's social ills."*
   Part One traces the development of schooling in American life, with an emphasis upon the many tasks society has assigned to the schools. A variety of voices debate the role of the school in our society and evaluate its past and future functions.
2. *"The school prepares the student for participation in a democratic society."*
   Part Two, "Values Schools Transmit," enumerates professed and actual values that occur in the routine of schooling. Articles on the needs of society and the individual, current curriculum efforts, and the extracurricular events in schools mark this phase of the book.
3. *"The school provides educational opportunity for those who want it."*
   One of the most controversial issues in schooling today is over what constitutes equal educational opportunity, and more specifically, what is a sufficient effort by society to ensure equality. Part Three contains readings usually listed under social class and race in other texts. Although there is ample documentation of the inequities that do exist, a number of selections include descriptions of possible remedies for such injustices.

4. *"Teachers are dedicated professionals who have, for the most part, effectively educated the nation's youth."*
The accountability movement, coupled with teacher militancy, has focused increased attention upon the teacher and the classroom. Part Four explores who goes into teaching, and how effectively we can measure the performance of teachers and students.
5. *"American schools have become progressively better."*
Part Five highlights some current directions schools are exploring. A range of schools, from Summerhill to a Louisiana elementary school, are visited in an attempt to see what changes are occurring in curriculum, instructional aids, and community control. The section ends with a projection of what schooling will be like in the future.

We hope these essays will help students appraise the problems and promises of American schools. If most inquirers, upon reading this book, have increased their ability to separate the myths and realities about the country's educational system, we shall feel we have succeeded. In addition, if some readers can more clearly decide whether or not they want to pursue a teaching career, we shall be doubly rewarded.

PART ONE

SCHOOLING IN AMERICAN LIFE: VOICES IN THE DEBATE

> *"The common school is the greatest discovery of mankind."*
> —Horace Mann

> *"The public schools are the kind of institution one cannot really dislike until one gets to know them well."*
> —Charles Silberman

Looking back at his days in college, a recent graduate wrote a classmate that he had not once been given "a peep at the genitals of originality." The letter was written in the early 1800's. The writer was a friend of Horace Mann, the Massachusetts lawyer and legislator who was to become the leading advocate for public schooling.

Their correspondence reminds us of how differently two people may see the same educational experience. It also informs us that the debate over the purpose and value of American schooling is one of long standing. Then, as now, opinions were advanced that schools were doing too much in certain areas, or not enough in others. It is rare to find anyone who is entirely content with the ways in which schools are operated.

Yet we realize that schools have changed since Horace Mann's day, and the commentaries about schooling do not focus on exactly the same issues. It is important, we feel, to come to some understanding of the reasons that schools were started, and why they have assumed their current shape and status.

A major concern of this portion of the book is with the close, almost exclusive, identification of *education* with *going to school*. During most of our colonial and national experience this was not the case. Until quite recently, an overwhelming majority of people acquired most of their education through a combination of apprenticeship, family, personal interest, church, community, friends, and on-the-job training, with perhaps a short period of school thrown in.

At the beginning of this century, only six percent of American seventeen-year-olds graduated from high school, and less than five percent between the ages of seventeen and twenty-one went to college. Today, over seventy percent of the former age group graduate from high school, and about fifty percent of the people of college age attend college. Almost a third of the total population is involved full-time in American schools as either student, teacher, or administrator. Americans spend over sixty billion dollars each year on elementary, secondary, and collegiate schooling.

Although these statistics suggest, and Gallup polls confirm, that schooling is perceived by many citizens as desirable, if not necessary, there have also been persistent challenges to the form and directions schools have taken. Until recently, many who criticized schools did so on the grounds that schools were not efficient enough, rather than because they were harmful. This meant that school officials worried about the thirty percent who dropped out without diplomas and the eighty percent who decided not to enter or who failed to graduate from college.

But now the question seems to be what schools shall do for the people who stay. And there are a variety of answers.

An interview with Lawrence Cremin begins the readings. His overview contains references to a number of myths that he believes we have held about schooling. Together with the myths, he provides comments about the limitations and potential of American schools in the future.

The selections that follow generally conclude that the schools have granted and can continue to supply great opportunities for those who apply themselves. Another group of articles suggests that schools are destructive of the diversity, independence, intelligence, and inventiveness that we have long regarded as an American characteristic. They suggest reforming various aspects of the schools. The final essays hold that, from their beginnings, schools have been charged with oppressive goals that can only be broken by radical departures.

Readers may well ask of all the writers: What myths do you hold? If you wish to destroy the old, what new myths do you propose? What legitimate function does American schooling have?

A noble gamble, defenders say. A cruel charade, argue its critics. Lawrence Cremin, a leading historian of education, sifts through the myths and realities of American schooling to offer his interpretation of what American schools have done and what they are likely to accomplish.

Readers may ask themselves if they agree with Cremin's feelings about myths. Are there new myths that have replaced the old?

FREEING OURSELVES FROM THE MYTHMAKERS
John Westerhoff and Lawrence Cremin

His [Cremin's] major point is that we are educated and have always been educated by a host of agencies other than the school. These agencies shape the public, its attitudes, and its behavior and must, therefore, come within the purview of those who make educational policy. To ignore them and assume that the schools can somehow transform a regenerate society is to end up a utopian or a fool. That was the big error of the so-called progressive era.

Reading this book made me believe that if our national leaders had had a richer and more accurate history of American education during the last twenty-five years, they would have possessed a much greater range of options for innovation in our American educational system. As it is, the choice of a million dollars for *Sesame Street* versus a million for Head Start never occurred, while our popular theories of sex and drug education over the past two years have continued to assume that if only the school would do something the social order would change. It's about time we took seriously some of the insights we can gain from a historical evaluation of education in American society. This book is a good start.

Westerhoff: Why study history anyway?

From John Westerhoff interviews Lawrence Cremin, *Colloquy,* July–August, 1971, pp. 5–14. Reprinted by permission. Note: This article has been edited, and begins with Westerhoff's reaction to *American Education: The Colonial Experience.*

Cremin: You know the answers usually given: You study history to find out how we got the way we are or to avoid the mistakes of the past. But like most proverbial wisdom, the advice can be contradictory. Some say, "Those who forget history are condemned to repeat it," while others argue, "There is only one thing we learn from history and that is that men never learn from history." I have another notion. The historical mode is the characteristic Western way of understanding the world. Every propagandist knows this. All deliberate and unintentional myth-makers use history to support their myths. History is always being written and told for good and bad purposes by men seeking to influence their contemporaries in one direction or the other. Therefore, a prudent society must support the systematic study of its own history to protect itself from those who would use history for their own benefit.

Westerhoff: But I've heard some of your students goading you with the question: Why are you spending your life writing history in an age when men ought to be making it? What is your reply?

Cremin: We live in a revolutionary time for education, a time when our conceptions of education are inadequate to our needs. Unless we do some radical rethinking, we will be putting Band-Aids on the wrong places and despairing that we cannot solve our problems. The last time our country politically made a major attempt at educational reform, we were so imprisoned by inadequate conceptions of education that we formulated our program with an inadequate understanding of alternatives. We therefore turned to school reforms without ever debating the possibility of using television to meet our needs. One of the major arguments for schooling during the past hundred years was based on the assumption that schools were the only means of teaching masses of children. That's no longer true, but it took *Sesame Street* to persuade us of another possibility. We never even considered the experience of other people, for example, Israel's use of the army, England's use of the open university, Russia's use of youth organizations, or Latin America's use of the radio. Our opportunities are legion. Yet when we embark on educational programs, we don't think of the potential of other resources for education besides schools. We are, therefore, constrained in dealing with our problem. The effort of my three volumes is to create a situation in which no serious person can think about education in a narrow way again.

Westerhoff: How do you, as an historian, define education?

Cremin: I have always insisted upon the importance of a broad investigation of education. That means looking at all the formal and informal agencies which shaped American thought, character, and sensibility as well as the relationship between these agencies and the society itself. Obviously, this projects us beyond schools to a host of other agencies which educate. For example, families, churches, libraries, museums, publishers, benevolent societies, youth groups, agricultural fairs, radio and TV networks, military organizations, law-making bodies, and research institutes. This makes possible our studying the rise of the newspaper in the eighteenth century, the social settlements in the nineteenth, and mass television in the twentieth, and it gives us a new context within which to evaluate the changing role and influence of public and private schools.

But we have to be somewhat clear on what education is as we investigate all these forces in society. I define education as the deliberate, systematic, and sustained effort to transmit or evoke knowledge, attitudes, values, skills, and sensibilities. Now this process is more limited than what the anthropologist calls enculturation or what the sociologist calls socialization, though it obviously includes many of the same elements.

Westerhoff: But for most people isn't deliberate education limited to the schools, while all the other aspects of life illustrate only the tremendous effect of nondeliberate education?

Cremin: Yes, perhaps, but we need to realize that many agencies of education in society are engaged in deliberate education. Nothing is more deliberate and systematic than a one-minute commercial aimed at selling a child a particular toy. I challenge you to find a family—any kind of family—not engaged daily in a sustained effort of intentional education. Nor can you find a church or synagogue, museum, newspaper, TV station, or any other educational institution in a country not engaged in deliberate efforts of education. We have blinded ourselves to the point that we believe the school has effectively taken over the educational efforts of the community. We therefore turn to the schools when we want something taught, without realizing the options that are open to us. At the same time we attempt to teach attitudes in schools without realizing that they are also being taught in other places, perhaps more effectively. Indeed, sometimes it is like trying to fill a crack in a dike which has already broken apart somewhere else.

. . .

At the same time, we need to make the other agencies in society which educate more responsible. We need especially to use television in new ways for new purposes. Perhaps the Federal Communications Commission needs to recognize that it is in many respects the equivalent of a school board if it is to exercise its responsibilities properly. Public education has to be seen as a whole, and that means including museums, libraries, the air waves, and the like in our educational planning. If we ever turn to universal national public service with responsible alternatives (and that is being debated these days) then those programs too must be seen as major educational agencies. We cannot assume that the public schools are equivalent to the education of the public. To say so is not to denigrate the public schools, which are crucially important. It is merely to view education whole and in its entirety.

. . .

The more I study the history of education, the more impressed I am with the disjunction between what the educator thinks he is teaching and what his student learns or chooses to learn from the experience. The history of education is filled with instances of particular groups establishing certain goals, only to have those who come in contact with them use them for different ends. Think of the eighteenth-century Society for the Propagation of the Gospel in Foreign Parts. The colonists used the S.P.G. schools for their own purposes. That should make us humble. It should also make us write the history of education in a way that doesn't assume that the purposes of an institution are always realized even when the institution seems to be doing what it set out to do. To find out what is really going on you have to talk to the client. It is not much good to study only what an institution says it is doing for people.

Westerhoff: It seems as if our professionalized schools have also locked out other kinds of potential education, such as that given by the creative artist, because they don't meet the "professional standards" established by the profession.

Cremin: The schools have tried to include a great deal within their jurisdiction and control. But some of what they take on they do poorly. For example, when the schools took over some forms of vocational training, they academicized it so that the program no longer served its intended purposes. Courses in schools are just not the answer to all our educational needs. But you can't blame the schools entirely. The people have often demanded that the schools provide such programs, not realizing that the schools may not be the best place to meet their educational needs. And often the schools were the only institutions to respond at all—which is to their credit.

Westerhoff: As you look at the history of education, has change always been the gradual process of reform many people would lead us to believe it is?

Cremin: No, change frequently came very rapidly. For example, look at the changes which came with modern technology. The ability of newspapers to print news for large numbers of readers cheaply overnight was very significant. The creation of film made it possible to group large audiences in one place for a single experience. And just reflect on the tremendous effect of television. Those three, in a relatively brief period of history, are perhaps more significant for education than the original invention of the school, and the rather gradual process of reform which has characterized its history.

Then there were other kinds of rapid educational change besides those caused by technology. The first conscription laws (the draft) were probably among the most significant events in educational history, but you do not even find them mentioned in educational histories. The C.C.C. was a fundamental educational invention and the passing of the Servicemen's Readjustment Act transformed American higher education in less than a generation. We are still dealing with the consequences of these political acts and the radical changes they caused in American education.

. . .

Westerhoff: It's obviously a myth to believe that new thoughts make no effect on history. What are some other educational myths we have which hold us captives to new thoughts?

Cremin: Our greatest myth is the association of education with schooling. They simply are not synonymous. Our assumption that they are has been one of the most significant barriers to our responding creatively to our national education needs. Education must always be thought of in terms of configurations of institutions.

A second is the myth that people learn when and what we want them to learn; rather, people learn what they want to learn, when they want it, and in the ways they want to learn it. There is simply no guaranteed correspondence between what we intend to teach and what is learned. We cannot determine ahead of time the full nature of our results.

A third myth relates to the distinction between public and private institutions. We are too prone these days to say that public institutions nurture conformity while private ones liberate, or that one parochializes while the other frees. Now I have found that at any given time, either can do either or both. We must carefully consider each situation and institution in its particularity to discover the degree to which it frees or constrains a particular person. Broad generalization will not help us make necessary decisions. All educational institutions are narrowing as well as liberating, often at one and the same time. On the one hand, they channel you along certain lines and thereby limit your potential. On the other hand, they always increase your potential in one way or another by putting you in touch, either directly or vicariously, with new people and new ideas.

Understanding these and other myths is crucial. We must realize that too frequently in educational circles our debates derive from half truths. When we assert that schools make conformists, we are talking about one thing schools do. They also liberate. To make this distinction clear is a first step toward finding a real solution to the problem which concerns us. Otherwise, we simply replace an old myth with a new one and our problem remains.

. . .

Westerhoff: Throughout your book, you refer to the role of education in the transmission of the culture. Has education in society ever played a significant role in the transformation of culture?

Cremin: It does both all the time. I'm fascinated by the fact that some of our sharpest controversies derive from the classic example of the blind man looking at the elephant. Recall our comments about conformity and freedom. As I've remarked, schools always tend to do both for the same person; they socialize and liberate at the same time. Certainly, schools aim at making conformists—they always do this. At the same time, by taking a child outside his primary contacts they free him from their influence. In seventeenth-century America, education went on largely in the family and church. (And, just as an aside, recall that literacy rates were very high then.) But the thing that impressed me about the eighteenth century was the liberating effect of schools which freed children from their family and church by giving them new experiences. Schools socialize, but that is only half the story; by their very nature, they liberate because they almost always offer alternatives.

At any given time, all the agencies of education are frequently performing both functions. In the seventeenth and eighteenth centuries, the family socialized children into particular values. But I find that it was also the agency through which what the first generation learned was passed on, so that the family was also the agency for the reformation of values and techniques. In the same way, apprenticeship became at once an instrument of social control and a vehicle for social mobility.

One thing that fascinated me about seventeenth-century New England was that the agencies of education were dedicated to the transmission and preservation of Puritan values, including the idea of the "just price." And yet Yankee merchant values won out. How? There are two ways of looking at it. One is to suggest that all the formal agencies of education were on one side, all the informal on the other. The education of the marketplace won out over the education of church, family, schools, and state. Another way to look at it is to affirm that while the church, family, school, and press all continued teaching the "just price," the merchant families became agents for the transmission of a new way of dealing with trade and therefore consciously passed on a different set of values and techniques. The family, therefore, became an effective dynamic against the other institutions of stability.

Westerhoff: I've often wondered, with such a fragmented educational reality, whatever enabled us to become a functioning nation?

Cremin: Some of my students have been suggesting that we have a number of myths, ranging all the way from brotherhood to racism, which have been perpetuated over the generations in this country. They want to know: What are the educational agencies which perpetuate these? When they discover which agencies perpetuate the myths that tear us apart, and which perpetuate the myths that enable us to work together, they'll be able to answer that question. I tell them that I asked that question for many years but looked in the wrong place to solve it. I found the answer in the common school. But as the work of Robert Lynn has demonstrated, the common school was really part of a larger configuration of institutions that ordinarily included the white Protestant family, the white Protestant church, and the white Protestant Sunday school. It worked very well in rural small-town America west of the Alleghenies, and it served its white Protestant sponsors as an effective promoter of social integration and social opportunity. But all the rhetoric on the "common school," my own included, ignored the truth that the public school was not really a common school. All kinds of alternative educational configurations existed. There was, for example, the closed authority system called slavery and its counterpart in the North of the black family, church, and occasionally school. Then there was the Indian reservation. These, along with

Jewish urban ghettos and other ethnic enclaves, existed and rarely intersected with the dominant pattern. The point is that we should not make exaggerated claims for the common school as the single factor in our great melting pot theory of American history, though it obviously contributed much. But that still leaves us with the question: How has our society been enabled to work together? Why haven't we been torn apart? In our search for answers, we need to get beyond half truths and propaganda to genuine historical arguments.

A major point of the first article was that history is often used to defend a group's current action or to persuade people to accept the justness of a new cause. This is aptly illustrated in the following article.

Note how the John Birch Society sees what schools of the past did. Would they agree with Cremin's interpretation? Are they asking the schools to do things that they have done or should do?

THE N.E.A.: DICTATORSHIP OF THE EDUCARIAT
Alan Stang

It seems most Americans spend much of their time these days driving to school to vote down school bond issues. Yet, school taxes go up and up. Workers, beloved by "Liberals," labor to pay them. Retired workers on reduced incomes—whose children were graduated twenty-five years ago—can barely afford to keep their homes. And educators announce that more money is "needed." The Children will suffer from "cultural deprivation," unless the ceilings are carpeted at once.

This year, suffering taxpayers are to be handed the "solution"— and as usual it comes from an organization they should know much

Reprinted by permission from *American Opinion*, March, 1972.

more about: the National Education Association of the United States.

THE N.E.A. PLAN

On January 10, 1972, at a press conference in its national headquarters in Washington, D.C., President Donald E. Morrison of N.E.A. presented its new proposal for school financing. He said that the property tax is unfair because it discriminates against the poor, and reported that Richard Nixon calls it "out of date." And he said that the best solution is for the federal government to increase its school payments vastly. Federal support now amounts to 7.1 percent of the school expenses. It should be increased almost five times, he said—yes, five times—to cover at least one third of the expense.

And this means "more than money," said Morrison. The money must be spent to "attack national priorities in the school program. It shouldn't just be handed to the states."

I asked whether this could lead to a federal takeover of the schools—and he nodded affirmatively. In World War II, he explained, only half the students from the South could pass the sixth-grade test for the draft. Thus, if left to the states, "national goals for education won't be reached. The federal government should establish standards and goals. The federal role has never been what it should be. The state should make the necessary decisions, but the federal government should control."

The large room packed with reporters was perfectly still. Morrison's panegyric to totalitarianism had inadvertently spilled the beans. An N.E.A. President serves for only one year, and poor Donald is apparently not yet proficient at using speech to conceal his purpose. At his right sat the real boss of N.E.A., Executive Secretary Sam M. Lambert, and Lambert rushed to the rescue.

"But states in which federal financing is rising don't show a rise in federal control," Lambert intruded. Exactly which country the N.E.A. Executive Secretary was talking about, I don't know, but of course it wasn't the United States. He explained that the federal government should simply "guarantee a minimum level of education."

I asked Morrison what the new federal money would mean to the current scheme of forced bussing. He answered that parents who refuse to participate say inner-city schools are inferior. If the money were used to make them "quality" schools, these parents would have less reason not to bus.

In other words, the federal money would indeed be used to solidify federal control over every school.

Morrison added that he was "pleased" with the positions of Senators Muskie and McGovern on the matter. He didn't say whether he is pleased that Muskie's school-age children go to private Catholic schools, according to "Liberal" columnist Stewart Alsop, and that McGovern's five children "have gone to the suburban Bethesda-Chevy Chase school, currently with about 3 percent Negro enrollment. . . ." Mutual Network commentator Fulton Lewis III reports that although McGovern boasts he is a resident of the District of Columbia, two of his children "have been transported across the District line to attend Walter Johnson public school (predominantly white) in Bethesda, Maryland."

Forced bussing for racist purposes is of course for us peasants, not for our rulers.

Now, where exactly does the N.E.A. say the new federal money should come from? As you know, the California Supreme Court recently declared the local financing of schools by a property tax to be illegal. There have been similar decisions in federal courts in Texas and Minnesota. Innumerable other such cases are pending. The strategy is to claim that the quality of public education differs markedly from district to district, because of the varying ability or willingness of local taxpayers to support local schools, and that the difference is a violation of the Fourteenth Amendment to the U.S. Constitution. And the N.E.A. enters these cases as *amicus curiae* to call for an end to local financing.

Also seated next to Morrison was Glen Robinson, N.E.A.'s Director of Research, and he explained that the property tax could be replaced simply by increasing the income tax—which would be good news to the billionaires who protect their incomes in tax shelters arranged by friends in Congress. Another possibility, said Robinson, is the so-called "value-added tax," which would be hidden in levies on a product at each stage of manufacture, raising prices on everything we buy, and which would finally be paid by the workers.

Morrison even suggested that the property tax should become a *state* tax to achieve equalization. The state would collect it, taking control from the local community, and finance every child equally.

THE N.E.A. AND POLITICS

Executive Director Morrison also announced that N.E.A.—which is tax-exempt—is forming a "political action committee," which will support candidates in both parties who are "friends of education." Indeed, that support will include not only political "education" and voter registration, but money—a clear violation of federal tax law. The N.E.A. has already spent $10,000 to retain Joseph Napolitan, who will organize the new group, and who ran Hubert Humphrey's advertising campaign in the 1968 election.

Morrison explained that each year five dollars in addition to dues is already being taken from each California teacher for political purposes by way of a payroll deduction—whether the teacher likes it or not—and reminded us that California has 120,000 N.E.A. members. The N.E.A. in New York has $1 million in the political till. And Michigan, for instance, has a similar system.

Somebody asked whether all this might not be a violation of the Hatch Act, since public school teachers are public employees. "Certainly not!" he riposted brilliantly. "Once they get the money, it's theirs."

And along these lines, he said that merger talks on a local level are now being conducted between N.E.A., which has 1,100,000 members, and the American Federation of Teachers, an A.F.L.-C.I.O. affiliate, which has more than 250,000 members. "If Nixon can go to Red China, N.E.A. can meet with A.F.T.," Morrison said.

Also at the press conference, we were handed a *National Foundation Program for Education,* which has been submitted to President Nixon's Commission on School Finance, and which describes the new curriculum it says the federal government should finance in every school. As in almost every other N.E.A. publication, we read of the need to "reorder educational priorities." The "target date" for this reordering, we are told, should be 1976. The new philosophy being sold by N.E.A. looks like this: "Instructional programs aimed at developing the full range of human capacities, not just the intellectual; evaluation for the purpose of improving instruction, not for comparing children . . . these are some of the components of a humane education, an education that gives every individual a personal vision of what he might become rather than forcing him to come up to standards devised in other ways for purposes that are no longer pertinent."

Observe the hostility to teaching *subject matter;* a hostility which has been demoralizing public school students for years, and which originates in the writings of such radicals as John Dewey. Indeed, we are told: "It is not enough for schools to function as sorting agencies. Nor is the complex social fabric served by a populace which has only facts and figures at its command. . . ." We read of a "good life," a good life that "respects individual and group decision-making as inherently human processes, and promises the development of potentials for all."

And according to N.E.A., the federal government must be instrumental in developing all this potential: ". . . This is a call for the national government to join with the state and local school systems to support a nationwide standard of education through a national foundation program." Indeed, we read of the need for "substantial federal intervention to stimulate change." We are told: "The foundation program is a powerful lever for influencing the local educational agencies to undertake programs and reforms they would not otherwise do."

In other words, the local authorities would be told what to teach and how to teach it.

And the federally dominated program would include: "Nursery or prekindergarten for three- and four-year-olds, in a program initially concentrated on children from low-income families." This of course is the heart of the "child development" legislation recently howled down by a storm of protest, and which no doubt will soon be introduced again. The use of the word "initially" means that the N.E.A. wants to take control of *all* children at the age of three.

Later, in his office, I asked N.E.A. Executive Secretary Sam Lambert whether so much concentration of power contained the risk of totalitarianism, no matter who is using it.

He said it didn't and mentioned the Scandinavian countries, England, and France. They have national systems of education, "but no totalitarianism," he said. The two things don't necessarily go together, he said.

Lambert was probably thinking of Sweden—home of Gunnar Myrdal, cited before the Senate Internal Security Subcommittee as a Communist, who along with other conspirators has controlled that country for years. Myrdal's wife, a Swedish Cabinet Minister, has even been named as a tool of Soviet espionage. Indeed, Sweden's Marxist Prime Minister recently recognized North Vietnam—and has been sending aid directly to a Communist enemy killing our sons in the field and torturing others in confinement. France was totalitarianized by Charles de Gaulle, who arranged the expulsion of N.A.T.O. and delivery of part of his own country—Algeria—to the Communists. And the Fabian Marxists tightly control England, where one needs government permission in sextuplicate to blow one's nose. Maybe Sam Lambert doesn't know what totalitarianism means.

"We have a mental complex about private education," Lambert said.

I asked whether he used the word "complex" because he thinks we are sick.

"Yes," Sam Lambert said. He explained that ours used to be an agricultural country, its wealth based on land. Today wealth is based on income, not on land. And school financing must change in recognition of that fact, he said.

I asked whether a change could encourage exactly what he is against: an exodus of children from the public schools. That is possible, he said. If the states take over the property tax, as some suggest, schools will be financed at a sixty percent level—not at one hundred percent. In the Scarsdales and Beverly Hills across the country, people won't be happy if the system is levelled down. In these systems they will opt out. The only answer, said Lambert, is to "upgrade the public schools" by pouring in federal money. You see, he has it all figured out.

Lambert also said that the reading level is "a big problem" in inner-city schools and that school buildings should be used during summers to solve it. I asked whether part of the problem could be caused by the destructive "look-say" method, in which children are taught to "read" not by learning the alphabet, but by memorizing the shapes of words—as if the English language were Chinese.

Sam Lambert snorted. "Look-say" has nothing to do with it, he said. Children couldn't read before it. There were no statistics years ago. Many children left school at the fourth grade.

All of which must be true, of course, just because Lambert says so, but somebody must have been reading all those old *McGuffey Readers*. Indeed, AMERICAN OPINION is willing to bet a Nixon nine dollar bill that the sixth-grade *McGuffey* would be incomprehensible to many "modern" college freshmen. Remember that the *Federalist Papers*, tough going for today's college seniors, were actually published as a popular polemic in a New York newspaper by their authors, who expected the people to read and understand their analysis of the Constitution—which the people did. Adjusting for the growth in population, sales of Tom Paine's *Common Sense* reached the equivalent of 30 million copies in but six months of 1776—an indication of the avid literacy before Sam Lambert's educrats ran things.

And, finally, Lambert didn't mention the reign of terror against teachers in many city schools described by Gary Allen in AMERICAN OPINION for February, 1972, but we did discuss N.E.A.'s new policy of Unification. A teacher used to be able to join her local teachers' association, if she wished; her county association, if she wished; her state association, if she wished; and the National Education Association—if she wished. Under Unification, however, she must join all or none. She no longer has the right to pick and choose. And the pressure upon her to join them all is tremendous. The N.E.A. has now "unified" thirty-five states and wants them all.

Indeed, said Lambert, in some states, such as Michigan, the N.E.A. has arranged an "agency shop," under which dues are taken from the teacher by force—whether she likes it or not—even if she decides to join nothing at all.

I asked Lambert whether an "agency shop" is the same thing as a "union shop." He said it isn't but could not explain why. He assured me that N.E.A. wants not only total Unification but an "agency shop" in every state. It would be "good for the profession," he said.

These are the policies of the men who can see no sign of totalitarianism in America's schools.

THE BACKGROUND

According to N.E.A. itself, the organization began reaching for monopoly control over education from its inception. In its current *Handbook,* N.E.A. President Morrison says this: "The N.E.A. started in 1856 with an organization called the National Teachers Association. At the first meeting in Philadelphia it was suggested that delegates return to their respective states and ask state legislatures to grant them the right to determine what kind of programs were going to prepare teachers, who would enter those programs, who would be licensed to teach, and who would be considered competent enough and ethical enough to continue to teach. . . ."

By 1932, influenced by such Marxists as George S. Counts and William Heard Kilpatrick, N.E.A. had developed the strategy of using ˌthe schools not so much to teach as to manipulate the graduates by means of various psychological techniques. In that year, for instance, N.E.A. said as follows (*Tenth Yearbook,* Department of Superintendence): "Conditioning is therefore a process which may be employed by the teacher to build up attitudes in the child and predispose him to the actions by which these attitudes are expressed."

Conditioning, of course, is one of the techniques experimental psychologists use on rats and dictators use on people.

And, in the same place, N.E.A. also explained that "agencies such as the school must assume responsibilities which in the past have rested upon the home and the community."

The strategy included seizing control over the child by lessening parental influence as much as possible. And the goal was—and is—to use these conditioned graduates of the public schools as the cannon fodder of a revolutionary collectivism.

At the 1934 session of N.E.A.'s Department of Superintendence, Willard E. Givens issued an important report which explained that "many drastic changes must be made. A dying laissez-faire must be completely destroyed and all of us, including the 'owners,' must be subjected to a large degree of social control. A large section of our discussion group maintain that the credit agencies, the basic industries and utilities cannot be centrally planned and operated under private ownership."

So Givens recommended a scheme for "taking these over and operating them at full capacity as a unified national system in the interest of all the people."

What Willard Givens was recommending, in other words, was that the federal government should nationalize just about everything in the United States. In the very next year, 1935, N.E.A. made Willard E. Givens its Executive Secretary, and he ran the organization in that capacity for the next seventeen years.

Perhaps that was why N.E.A. said in 1937 (*Fifteenth Yearbook*, Department of Superintendence): "The present captalistic and nationalistic social system has been supplanted in but one place— Russia—and that change was effected by revolution. Hence the verdict of history would seem to indicate that we are likely to have to depend upon revolution for social change of an important and far reaching character."

Indeed, in 1948 the N.E.A. published *Education for International Understanding in American Schools*, in which we learn that the goal of its boss conspirators is to destroy all national sovereignty and enslave the world's people by force. Sounds hard to believe, doesn't it? Here are the exact words: "... More recently, the idea has become established that the preservation of international peace and order may require that force be used to compel a nation to conduct its affairs within the framework of an established world system. The most modern expression of this doctrine and collective security is in the United Nations Charter."

In order to make this New World Order palatable to Americans, says N.E.A., "the school program must include experiences designed to tap all the sources that go into producing the desired behavior characteristic of the world-minded American. Actual change in behavior is the goal, and any modification in behavior entails changes in attitudes."

Among the mind-modifying tools recommended by N.E.A. was a Russian textbook called *New Russia's Primer* (Houghton Mifflin, New York, 1931), and an inspirational volume entitled *I Want to Be Like Stalin* (John Day, New York, 1947).

And on October 20, 1967, at Sam Lambert's inauguration as Executive Secretary, John I. Goodlad, Dean of the U.C.L.A. Graduate School of Education, said this: "The most controversial issues of the twenty-first century will pertain to the ends and means of modifying human behavior and who shall determine them. The first educational questions will not be, 'What knowledge is of most worth?' but 'What kinds of human beings do we wish to produce?' The possibilities virtually defy our imagination."

When Hitler tried that by breeding "pure Aryans," the world rightly denounced him. Why is the same thing unobjectionable when sponsored by the National Education Association?

THE ORGANIZATION

As we have seen, the N.E.A. is trying to take total control of teachers and is discussing merger with the A.F.T. It is interesting to note that in May, 1937, *The Communist,* official journal of the Communist Party, issued this directive: "The task of the Communist Party must be first and foremost to arouse the teachers to class-consciousness and to organize them into the American Federation of Teachers, which is in the main current of the American Labor movement." Indeed, loyal Communists were told, "every care must be taken to bring together in united front actions all existing teacher organizations. Especial attention must be paid to secure such action with the American Association of University Professors, the National Educational Association and the Guild. Our Party members in these organizations must work actively toward this end."

The late Dr. Bella Dodd wrote in *School of Darkness* (P. J. Kennedy & Sons, New York, 1954): ". . . Before I had left the Union I had been able to lay the basis for affiliation of the Teachers Union with the NEA. In June 1944 I was assigned to speak at a meeting of more than five hundred communist teachers and their friends at the Jefferson School on the new communist perspectives as applied to education. . . . I urged the communist teachers to exercise their influence for unity on all teachers' and citizens' groups."

The Teachers Union was of course being run by the Communists. As she put it: "The executive committee of the Teachers Union always, from the time that I knew it, had a majority of . . . 80 or 90 percent of the executive board who were Communists." Dr. Dodd, who later became an American, was at the time a member of the Executive Committee of the Communist Party, U.S.A.

And exactly as the Communists wanted, its leaders have turned N.E.A. from a professional organization into a union, complete with closed shops, collective bargaining, and strikes. In the Anaheim (California) Secondary Teachers' Association bulletin of February 20, 1970, Executive Director Dr. Lester Julian writes as follows: " . . . The NEA has gone, frankly and openly, to the ranks of former union organizers and hired as their 'Professional Negotiations' consultants teams of personnel knowingly committed to, and experienced in, the organizing of teacher strikes as a common tactical weapon."

At his inauguration in 1967, Sam Lambert described the uses of this weapon: "N.E.A. will become a stronger and more influential advocate of social changes long overdue." Indeed, said Lambert, it "will become a political power second to no other special interest group," and "will organize this profession from top to bottom into logical operational units that can move swiftly and effectively and with power unmatched by any other organized group."

In fact, at the same meeting, former N.E.A. official T. M. Stinnett boasted that "education has gained the power to change society against the will of the politicians. It has become the key to economic progress and to the constant renewal of society. In other words, it is now master as well as servant, and this for the first time in human history."

In other words, N.E.A. has now become more powerful than "the politicians" in Congress. Its handful of leaders has openly claimed the authority to impose what it wants on us, whether our elected representatives vote for it or not. They say so themselves.

It certainly is a lucky thing that Lambert is against totalitarianism.

It is also interesting to note that members of the Student N.E.A., financed by an N.E.A. grant of at least $65,000, have been training at the new Training Institute of the Industrial Areas Foundation, under the guidance of top radical Saul D. Alinsky. Alinsky, of course, is a professional revolutionary, is the author of *Rules for Revolution,* and has actively incited strikes and turmoil in American city after city.

And in 1932, in *Towards a Soviet America,* Communist boss William Z. Foster said of Communist plans for education: "The schools, colleges, and universities will be coordinated and grouped under the National Department of Education and its State and local branches."

Today N.E.A. is pushing for exactly that, by way of a Department of Education to be established in the President's Cabinet, which would take complete control of education, by financing it with billions in federal money.

THE PROPAGANDA

No discussion of the National Education Association would be complete without a look at some of the literature available at its huge, eight-story headquarters in Washington. There is *NEA: Education's Voice in Government,* for instance, in which we learn that the organization wants the President of the United States to proclaim a national holiday in honor of Martin Luther King. No mention is made of such facts as that Hunter Pitts O'Dell, a member of the National Committee of the Communist Party, ran King's organization for years.

In the same document, N.E.A. denounces extremism: "The National Education Association is alarmed at the nationwide attack on the public schools and the teaching profession by extremist organizations. The growing opposition to certain curriculums and to educational policies is recognized by the Association as a thinly veiled political attack on public education itself. The Association urges its affiliates to take concerted action and, if necessary, legal action to defend against such irresponsible attacks."

The N.E.A., of course, has always been against extremism. In 1967, for instance, it brought Dr. Franklin H. Littell to Minneapolis to warn its annual convention about it. Littell has been a member of the executive committee of the notorious Methodist Federation for Social Action—an officially cited Communist Front—in whose *Social Questions Bulletin* Littell went so far as to author an article entitled "A Cell in Every Church," about which Benjamin Gitlow, former General Secretary of the Communist Party, told the Senate Internal Security Subcommittee: "Mr. Littell's organizational proposals on the infiltration of religion follow closely the cell techniques on infiltration described in the thesis on organization of both the Communist Party and the Communist International."

Then there is the N.E.A.'s *Cooperative International Education,* by Willis H. Griffin and Ralph B. Spence, who write: ". . . Commercial television is an example of a counter-educational force in the United States, for example, and the enculturating power of the traditional family is similarly contradicting of new educational goals in a society such as Pakistan." Down with commercial TV! Down with the family!

Pakistan is now headed by a Maoist Red and is no longer an N.E.A. problem.

They also quote Guinea's openly Communist dictator, Sékou Touré, with approval: "Guinea's school system may not remain an alien body in the Guinean revolution. It must achieve its reconversion. . . ."

And, Griffin and Spence explain: ". . . Most societies have channels and procedures for voicing dissent and working for change. When these channels and procedures have been rendered ineffective by 'the establishment,' by special interests, or by corrupt power blocks, extreme and unorthodox measures to achieve change may be required. . . ."

The goal, they tell us, is "a global social system," which can be arranged in the following way: "For the most part, answers to problems of inequalities of resources are being sought within national boundaries. What about the possibilities of finding answers across boundaries, or of redefining boundaries? . . ." Indeed: ". . . Affluent American cities cling to their outmoded governmental units and frequently vote down funds for urgently needed improvements."

Does this mean what it says, that the boundaries of our cities and even our national boundaries are obsolete and should be abolished?

And then there is N.E.A.'s masterpiece, *The Negro American in Paperback*—a list of books recommended for junior and senior high school students. Among the recommended authors in the first edition were Herbert Aptheker, of the Communist Party; W. E. B. DuBois, of the Communist Party; Howard Fast, for years a Communist and winner of the "Stalin Peace Prize"; Philip Foner, of the Communist Party; James J. Green, of the Communist Party; Langston Hughes, of the Communist Party; James E. Jackson, of the Communist Party; Carey McWilliams, who was identified under oath as a Communist; Gunnar Myrdal, officially identified as a Communist; Doxey Wilkerson, of the Communist Party; Richard Wright, of the Communist Party—and Victor Perlo, a Soviet spy.

The list apparently made quite a stir. Soon after publication in 1967, N.E.A. President Braulio Alonso felt the need to defend it as "a magnificent list."

The pressure nevertheless was too great. In 1968, the list was revised. The new list recommends W. E. B. DuBois, of the Communist Party; "Stalin Peace Prize" winner Howard Fast; Philip Foner, of the Communist Party; Shirley Graham, of the Communist Party;

Langston Hughes, of the Communist Party; and, Comrades Carey McWilliams and Gunnar Myrdal.

Indeed, the revised list *adds* the recommendations of Sally Belfrage, a "civil rights worker" who has been an employee of the Soviet Government in Moscow, and whose father, Cedric, a top Eisenhower press officer during World War II, was a Party member in Britain later deported from the United States as a Communist alien; Communist terrorist Stokely Carmichael; Communist artist Frank Cieciorka, among whose works is a widely distributed sketch of the Statue of Liberty and the Goddess of Justice being raped by police officers; radical Communist Tom Hayden, founder of Students for a Democratic Society; guest of honor Ho chi Minh, and author of the statement, "We are all Vietcong"; violent revolutionary LeRoi Jones; violent revolutionary Malcolm X; violent revolutionary James Peck, of the Congress of Racial Equality and Danbury Penitentiary; Arthur Waskow, of the revolutionary Institute for Policy Studies, who was active in laying the groundwork for the turmoil at the Democrat National Convention of 1968; and, Howard Zinn, a Marxist revolutionary.

This is what dues taken from teachers around the country are used to produce. It is interesting to note that *The Communist* of May, 1937, says as follows: ". . . Mass pressure can remove particularly vicious war or chauvinistic propaganda, can win the right of students to classes in sex education, to the inclusion of Negro history in history courses. The latter is a demand which Negro students feel with especial keenness."

THE REVOLUTIONARY RESULT

Exactly how does all this conspiratorial planning and propaganda produce the current turmoil and takeover? In N.E.A.'s *Today's Education* for January, 1969, for instance, we read of a proposal for "mandatory foster homes and 'boarding schools' for children between the ages of two and three whose home environment was felt to have a malignant influence. . . ."

In other words, N.E.A. now wants the power to take two-year-old children away from parents whom N.E.A. doesn't like. Shortly thereafter, as you will recall, we saw the manufactured demand for the "child development legislation" which would begin doing exactly that.

The N.E.A., as you know, is also opposed to homework and grades. The Poor Children find them "demeaning." They encourage nasty competition. The result, of course, is that many students are illiterate—which the N.E.A. blames on their parents' refusal to vote more and bigger bond issues.

In the Eighth Report of the California Senate's Investigating Committee on Education, American diplomat Eric L. Pridonoff testifies as follows of what he saw in post-war Yugoslavia: ". . . The first thing that occurred was the elimination of the grading system. As I later questioned some Soviet officials . . . they said there is a better way to prepare students for a socialized state; in short, eliminate competition and prepare a group of loafers so the State can lead them later on."

But it is of course the turmoil and the threat of violence that parents and students fear more than anything else. In *Today's Education* for September, 1970, N.E.A.'s then-President Helen Bain writes: "I am looking forward to the action programs which will be developed by our Task Force on Student Involvement, action programs which will get students involved in making the decisions that affect their lives. . . . We must give students on all levels some real leadership in how to be effective in bringing about constructive change. . . ."

What does that doubletalk mean? The very next article in the same issue of the N.E.A. magazine is entitled, "Strategies for a Real Academic Revolution," and is adapted from a speech advising college freshmen who are not entirely satisfied with their professors to do as follows: "Is the professor enthralled by his lectures and does he revel in the drama and interpretative nuances of each point he makes? Arrange with other members of the class to applaud the professor after each performance and from time to time to call out, 'Encore! Encore!' . . ."

In other words, the students are told, get "involved" by disrupting the class and making fun of the professor. If that doesn't work, they are advised: "Perhaps the professor is shy or rather too formal to join the company of students as a fellow learner. Then ask a couple of football players to come to class five minutes early to carry out his desk or podium. . . ."

Compare what you have just read with the orders to Party members in *The Communist* of May 1937: "The rebelliousness of school children, directed against a part of the state machinery itself, is something that Communists cannot afford to ignore. This, together with their desire for knowledge and social life, must form the *starting point* for our work among students in the schools."

Communist teachers were told "to arouse in the students a consciousness of what arouses their resentment, accordingly to give their elemental spirit of rebelliousness definite and effective direction and thus to place ourselves at the head of the students. . . ."

THE TEACHERS

Mrs. Carol Applegate has been a high school English teacher for more than eighteen years in the Michigan public schools, and was a member of her local association, the Michigan Education Association and of the National Education Association itself. But in 1968, because of the things we have been discussing here—such as the fact that N.E.A. deducts five dollars from members' salaries for its radical Political Action Council—she decided that these organizations were no longer professional and resigned from the local. And this meant, since Michigan is "unified," that she had resigned from all three.

But in the summer of 1968, the educational totalitarians imposed an "agency shop" clause on the teachers, which meant that Mrs. Applegate was expected to pay the dues, even though she no longer belonged to the organization that had negotiated the contract. And this, by the way, is a clear violation of Michigan state law.

Mrs. Applegate refused. She says she is perfectly capable of negotiating for herself and wants to do so. Did you ever! Where did she go wrong, do you think? Was it something in her childhood?

The totalitarians asked the school board to dismiss her, which it did. After a hearing, Mrs. Applegate was fired. She appealed to the State Tenure Commission, which did no good. Always before there had been only three grounds for dismissal: incompetence, insubordination, and immorality—none of which of course applied in her case. In the free United States (where of course it can't happen) she was being forced to pay a fee in order to hold a job as a public employee.

I played Sam Lambert and asked Mrs. Applegate where she would be without the union. If N.E.A. hadn't fought tooth and toenail for those raises, wouldn't teachers today still be making next to nothing?

"No," Mrs. Applegate said. "Salaries have gone up in all businesses and would have gone up in teaching as well. School boards are composed of businessmen, who are aware of economic conditions."

Perhaps Mrs. Applegate should go back to work as our Secretary of Labor.

Now, what about her fellow teachers? Where do they stand? Mrs. Applegate says that in her school, 50–75 teachers agreed with her but said nothing. "They are afraid, afraid for their jobs and their status." Indeed, Mrs. Applegate is "truly frightened" herself. If N.E.A. seizes total control of all teachers, every system could be struck at once. "The government has banned monopoly in business," she says. "Why not in schools?"

Then there is Mrs. Margaret Maki, who has taught the second to the seventh grades in Adams Township, Michigan, for thirty-one years. Mrs. Maki, too, has belonged to all the necessary unions, but dropped out. She has three years of college, but no degree, and because of M.E.A. pressure was still getting only base pay. Mrs. Maki decided the unions were not worth the dues she had to pay.

But in 1969, the Adams Township Education Association imposed an "agency shop," and when Mrs. Maki refused to pay its dues, because she did not belong to it and it did not represent her, the union forced the school board to fire her—*even though she was within only three months of retirement.*

Isn't she lucky that N.E.A. boss Sam Lambert is against totalitarianism?

"A closed shop is slavery," Mrs. Maki says. Her case is scheduled to come up in March.

And there is Robert Johnson, President of the 1,300-member Detroit Education Association, who says the trouble started about 1965, when D.E.A.'s previous leadership agreed to Unification. The teachers were told that their dues, taken to Washington, would be returned "to make them stronger." The teachers soon discovered that, by means of Unification, M.E.A. and N.E.A. had taken control. For instance, before D.E.A. could go to the State Labor Mediation Board, it had to get permission from M.E.A. and N.E.A. The Michigan Education Association and N.E.A. told the Detroit group how to spend its money. So D.E.A. quit the monopoly, and M.E.A. actually sued, but was forced to settle.

In spite of which, in 1969, the totalitarians managed to impose an "agency shop" on Detroit teachers. Mr. Johnson explains that some of his members have been teaching 25–40 years and were now being told to pay union dues or be fired. The case is now pending in Wayne County Circuit Court.

Exactly how does the National Education Association arrange an "agency shop"? Mr. Johnson thinks M.E.A. and N.E.A. made a deal with the American Federation of Teachers to arrange it. They go to school board members and say, speaking through the mouths of the local associations, "Give us an agency shop to keep out the union." And the royally conned school boards, composed of housewives and businessmen, buy it. Johnson reports that many school board members have since told him, "We didn't know what an agency shop is."

And these are only a few examples. Throughout Michigan, in Southgate and Utica, for instance, hundreds of teachers are involved in suits about their dues. In Fenton, a Seventh Day Adventist, who for religious reasons cannot join a union, is among those being pressured for a payoff.

This is the system—a system of professional dictatorship—that the N.E.A. is trying to impose on all the teachers and school boards in America.

WHAT HAPPENS NOW?

As we have seen, the N.E.A., which says it is opposed to totalitarianism, is agitating to implement Communist William Z. Foster's advice that there be a national Department of Education. Also in strict conformity to Foster, the N.E.A. is trying to nullify local boards, and replace them with fifty subservient branches of that Department. Year after year, local school districts are consolidated and annexed. Forty years ago, there were 127,422 such districts. Ten years ago, there were 35,676. Today there are only 17,218. As you know, a federal district court recently ordered the systems of Richmond, Virginia, and two surrounding counties to merge, so that all the area's children may enjoy the forced blessings of racist bussing. The N.E.A. is for "participatory democracy," of course, and for training children to "make the decisions that affect their lives," but forty years ago there were 423,974 school board members, and today there are only 95,364—which means that today there are 328,610 fewer Americans making decisions about what is done with their educational dollars.

All the remaining districts, except one, are in forty-nine states. The other is in the State of Hawaii. Hawaii has only one school district, one superintendent, and one school board. There is no "participatory democracy." And the Hawaiian system is what N.E.A. is working toward—because, as any dictator knows, *the fewer people there are running something, the easier they are to control.*

Exactly what is happening in Hawaii? In *Today's Education* of January, 1969, the N.E.A. lays it down as follows: "Biochemical and psychological mediation of learning is likely to increase. New drama will play on the educational stage as drugs are introduced experimentally to improve in the learner such qualities as personality, concentration, and memory. The application of biochemical research findings, heretofore centered in infrahuman subjects, such as fish, could be a source of conspicuous controversy when children become the objects of experimentation."

Nine months later, in *Master Plan for Public Education in Hawaii,* partially financed with federal funds, Hawaii's one board of education explained that "it is possible that drugs can be used to improve the intellectual capabilities and capacities of an individual. In comparison to some of the drug problems encountered today that do not provide constructive results, this approach may have profound and beneficial results." Indeed: "The application of biochemical research findings, heretofore centered in lower forms of animal life, will be a source of conspicuous controversy when children become the objects of such experimentation."

Notice how exactly Hawaii's single board of education reproduces the N.E.A.'s mind-control methods in its *Master Plan.* Today, N.E.A. agents are subjecting hundreds of thousands of children around the country to such experiments with drugs. "It's all for the good of humanity," of course, as Heinrich Himmler liked to say.

I asked N.E.A. boss Sam Lambert about the *Today's Education* article, reminding him that it has created quite a stir, but Sam had no idea what I was talking about. He actually asked me for the date of the article and visibly committed it to memory. He did say, "Drugs offer great hope in exceptional cases."

Enter Richard Nixon. As I write, New Jersey's property tax is being declared unconstitutional like the others. It discriminates against The Children. The N.E.A. is braying that there must be more money. Disgusted taxpayers are saying no. So, in his State of the Union speech, President Nixon has promised them relief.

What sort of relief will it be? The property tax will be abolished as the source of school funds. Whoopee! And the "value-added" tax, or something similar, will replace it. Collected by the federal government, it would be sent to the fifty totalitarian state boards N.E.A. is trying to arrange, and combined with state income taxes to finance N.E.A.'s totally uniform—and federally controlled—education.

Which means, of course, that the taxpayers would still be paying for the schools—since even Richard the Archangel cannot manufacture real money—but now they would be paying even more than before, since they would have lost any reasonable control over the money's collection and expenditure. Presently they can vote down school bond issues of which they disapprove. But, in the system being prepared, the taxpayers would have no say at all, just as they have no say about paying their federal income tax. And since most of the money would now be routed via education czars in Washington, they would also have no say about how it should be spent.

The *real* purpose of the National Education Association's phony demands for more money, and the epidemic of decisions declaring the property tax illegal, is to provide a superficially plausible excuse for the federal government to nationalize control of every school, schoolchild, and schoolteacher in America.

By the late 1960's it was quite fashionable to criticize the public schools. Some did it because they felt schools were not strict enough; many because they felt the schools were not open enough. Summerhill was gaining new admirers; Holt and Kozol were the emerging critics. The emphasis was on the failure of the school.

Franklin Parker's chronicle-essay is representative of those who saw then, and who still see, the American school system as a "ladder of opportunity."

Does Parker's evidence convince you of the greatness of the dream of universal education? Have we, as he suggests, become educational exporters rather than educational borrowers?

WHAT'S RIGHT WITH AMERICAN EDUCATION
Franklin Parker

The date is 1787. The occasion: passage of the Northwest Ordinance. The provision: "Religion, morality, and knowledge being necessary to good government and the happiness of mankind, schools and the means of education shall forever be encouraged." Significance: a people, not yet formed into a nation, declare education to be an essential support of free government and set aside western lands for schools and education.

From *Illinois Schools Journal*, Spring 1967, pp. 26–32. Reprinted by permission of the publisher, Chicago State University.

The date is 1789, two years later. The place: Philadelphia. The occasion: the Constitutional Convention. The Constitution is ratified. Nowhere is education specifically mentioned. But ten amendments are passed. The first amendment: "Congress shall make no law respecting an establishment of religion, or prohibiting the free exercise thereof." Significance: church and state separation. Implication: public education will be secular; it will belong to the people and not exclusively to religious bodies. The tenth amendment: "The powers not delegated to the United States by the Constitution, or prohibited by it to the States, are reserved to the States respectively, or to the people." Implication: education will be under state control and support.

The date is 1837. The place: Boston. The occasion: passage of a bill to establish a state board of education. The secretary of the board: a young lawyer and state senator. His name: Horace Mann. His friends tell him not to take the job. The salary is small, the office is new, the board is untried (it failed in New York; why would it succeed in Massachusetts?), businessmen are not convinced about supporting public education, property owners are loathe to tax themselves for free schools. But Andrew Jackson is President and it is the age of the common man; the extension of the franchise, the beginning of new immigration waves, the onset of factories, the rise of cities, the awakening of social conscience. For twelve years Horace Mann labors through the spoken and written word, in reports, magazines, and books. He exhorts, he cajoles, he argues. Better learning and skills, he says, will make better workmen. Better schools, he points out, will make better citizens. In twelve years, he establishes a permanent state board of education, improves school buildings, introduces normal schools for the professional preparation of teachers, creates new school libraries, holds in-service teachers' institutes, and convinces businessmen and property holders to establish free schools for all.

The date is 1852. The place: again Boston. The occasion: passage of a compulsory education act, the first in America to be permanent. Horace Mann had won his fight. Schools for all and compulsory attendance. The pattern is emerging. In a democracy, the people must know and the children must learn. Jefferson had said a people ignorant and free is something that never was and never will be.

The date is 1896. The place: Chicago. The occasion: the establishment of a Laboratory School at the University of Chicago. The man in charge: John Dewey. Chicago in the 1890's was a turbulent city in a decade of ferment. It was a city of two faces, one the brawny thrust for wealth and power; the other, huddled masses, frightened and not yet free. One-third were old-line Americans fattening off a city of one million people linked by rail to the cattle trails of the southwest, and by the Great Lakes to the world's trade. Two-thirds were immigrants and their children, poor and unassimilated, laboring in sweat shops and meat-packing plants. Alive in that city in those days were great forces ready to do mighty battle. The lines were drawn and here was the testing place.

Here had come Francis Wayland Parker to head Cook County Normal School. Fresh from Boston, and fresher still from Quincy Massachusetts, as school superintendent, this bald-headed, bull-headed ex-school teacher, ex-Union Army colonel, had found in post-Civil War study at the University of Berlin the mystique of the nature of childhood as expressed by Heinrich Pestalozzi and more so by Friedrich Augustus Froebel. Beneath Parker's rough exterior lay a tender regard for youth, and a conviction that field trips and nature study could usefully supplement school books, that child growth needs encouragement as plants need watering. It was John Dewey who called Francis Wayland Parker the father of the progressive education movement.

Here too was Jane Addams, Chicago-born lady whose Quaker conscience had been touched when as a young girl of wealth and leisure she had seen with her own eyes on a European trip the hopelessness of those in dire need and impoverishment. She returned to Chicago to work for the immigrant mass, and made her settlement house, Hull House, a cultural bridge for the diverse, uprooted immigrant to cross over a little easier into the new American maelstrom. From Jane Addams and Hull House came the seed of several reforms including the establishment of the Children's Bureau of the Department of Labor.

Here too came the Baptist missionary zeal to revive their defunct Chicago theological seminary at Morgan Park. Marshall Field provided the land, John D. Rockefeller the founding seven million dollars, and William Rainey Harper the presidency of the University of Chicago, third graduate university in America. It was William Rainey Harper, an early leader of the junior college movement, who in 1894 picked the 35-year old John Dewey, enticing him away from the University of Michigan, to head the University of Chicago departments of philosophy, psychology, and pedagogy. It was Harper's idea that John Dewey head a School of Education for the professional preparation of teachers. It was Harper who suggested that Dewey start an experimental elementary and secondary laboratory school.

In Chicago at this experimental school from 1896 to 1904, John Dewey hammered out his educational philosophy. From this experiment came his books: *My Pedagogic Creed, The School and Society,* and *The Child and the Curriculum;* all of them summed up in his important *Democracy and Education,* published in 1916. World War I was in progress and because wars and catastrophes shake people up, Americans, at least intellectual Americans, listened to what Dewey had to say. The very title of his 1916 book was its theme. Democracy requires consent. Consent requires intelligent awareness of problems and issues. Intelligence requires education. Democracy and education were inseparable. And mass democracy required mass education. To teach all youths of all classes ever-widening knowledge, skills, citizenship, and moral behavior in a changing, industrial world, meant broadening the curriculum, group work as well as individual study, and real-life experiences. Seen in the perspective of an industrial America rushing into an uncertain, explosive, technological 20th century, John Dewey's prescriptions had some relevancy, not to all Americans, but particularly to the new intellectual American critics, lately risen from the large middle class. The progressive movement in American education was part and parcel of the progressives in politics, the avant garde artists, the social critics, the trust-busters, and the angry writers left of center.

Trends and events seldom fit into a neat package and American schools, whose doors were opening wider and wider to more and more youths, felt the wave of progressive influence. It was never a tidal wave. Variety, conflicting philosophies, no philosophies at all, pendulum swings from one fad to another have always characterized American education. One trend was sure. We had set our educational course on quantity, numbers, right through high school, and, unheard of elsewhere in the world, relatively easy access to higher education for the average. Our economy could stand it. Indeed, it required it. Labor did not want a flood of youth until 18 or older. The big question was what happens to quality when quantity soars? The people, a few of them, debated, while the quantity trend continued.

The date is 1932. The place: New York. The occasion: a book. The writer: a professor of education at Teachers College, Columbia University. His name: George S. Counts. The title of his book—in the form of a question—*Dare the Schools Build a New Social Order?* The setting: a world depression that hit America hard. Unemployment. Bread lines. Men selling apples on corners. Idle youth. Hungry families. Revolt in the air. Riots in the street. What had happened to the great American Economy? What went wrong?

The progressive educators had some answers. One branch—who like William Heard Kilpatrick (who died February 13, 1965) had concentrated on child welfare and democratic learning—was relatively quiet. Another branch—concerned with education as a lever to social reconstruction—essayed some answers. One of them, Harold Rugg, urged a massive infusion of federal aid to education and a country-wide adult education network for discussion and solution of social ills (see his *The Great Technology*). But George S. Counts, a progressive social reconstructionist, rightly saw the handwriting on the wall. He answered his own question with a sad, resounding "No." The schools dare not build a new social order. Educators were and had been too weak, too mild, too timid to have worked into positions of political power so as to use education as a lever to correct social ills. Progressive educators, he said, could lead America out of the depression and could prevent similar tragedies in the future. But they had not formulated and implemented a comprehensive theory of social welfare. They had not used their intellectual competence on the minds and hearts of youth so as to secure social order.

Counts' call for teachers to seek political power and wield it boldly raised a storm of controversy. Those who agreed with Counts could not agree on the kind of social order which should be established. In the end, it was political power, the Democratic Party, under an innovative leader, Franklin Delano Roosevelt, using primarily economic means, rather than education that combatted the depression. The New Deal reshuffled the wealth through a host of federal agencies, and, some say, it took the defense spending of World War II to really end the Depression. The lesson of 1932 was clear. Reform of aims and content of education, yes. But power the people held and power they alone would delegate through elections to political parties and platforms.

The date is 1957. The place: Russia. The occasion: the launching of Sputnik I. A former war ally but post-war hostile government, barely 40 years in power, which had ruthlessly squeezed industrialization from the backs of Russian peasants, had launched an important projectile and had opened a new age. Not only the space race but the education race was on. Observers pointed out that Soviet education, like that in other European countries, was "tougher" than education in the United States and bore down much more heavily on pure and applied science than did the easy-going American schools. Americans were shocked into realizing that they must have more and better schools, not just because democratic citizenship and intellectual growth required them, but because the nation's security depended on them. The keynote of the times became a search for excellence in education.

We had come smack up against the problem of quantity and

quality, the quest to maintain quantity while improving quality. Sputnik was not the onset of the quest for quality and excellence. It marked the eleventh-hour return to former affirmations, going back to the essentialists (the basic education advocates) of the 1930's and to similar earlier urgings. Never in our history have there been so many rapid changes in American education as in the last ten years. Educational historians who will study our times have their work cut out for them. Nationally, these changes of mammoth proportions are reflected in the federal aid to education acts. On state levels, they are reflected in major revampings of curricular offerings. We are on the move, compelled by competition in hot pursuit.

The date is 1965. The place: Washington, D.C. The scene: the national Congress. The item under discussion: President Johnson's Education Package. What does he call it? "Full Educational Opportunity." What are its basic provisions? What are its innovations?

1. Pre-School Programs in urban and rural slums. In big cities and little towns. This is a pre-school, nursery level enrichment program for children whose families earn less than $2,000 a year. These children have traditionally been the lost ones who later become drop-outs, unemployables, juvenile delinquents, and criminals. The innovation is to begin early, to tackle the problem at its roots, to save the child during the first few years.

2. Aid to elementary and secondary schools in low income school districts. The five lowest income states average $275 per pupil per year expenditure. The five highest income states average more than twice as much or about $600 per pupil per year expenditure. The bill would aid the low income school district in specific ways so as to bring their average closer to the national average spent per pupil per year. Some of these specific purposes would be libraries, instructional material (books, films, AV equipment), and enrichment centers offering special science and foreign language instruction.

   The focus is on schools, private and public, Negro and white, where the proportion of *low* income families makes Federal support appear necessary. The focus is on enrichment programs that are in addition to programs now in effect. The innovation is to break the church-state deadlock which previously blocked federal aid to education bills. The innovation is to neutralize opposition by putting opponents in the uncomfortable position of going on record as being against the poor. The innovation is to build change (i.e., improvement) into the schools while raising their general level.

3. Higher education aid is to be channelled toward scholarships and low interest loans, to strengthen college libraries, to upgrade small colleges, and to improve university extension services to communities. The innovation is to enable students to enter and stay in college while improving college and university services internally for the students and externally for their surrounding communities.

Unlike the progressive social reconstructionists of the 1930's who would use education to remake society, the President's bills would use education as a solvent of social ills, as a cure for economic sores, as an ingredient in social improvement. Where the social reconstructionist would use education as an instrument to gain political power for social ends, the President's bills make use of political consensus to use education as an innovative instrument for social improvement.

What themes emerge from these eight significant events relevant to American Education and the Great Society? I believe our public schools have been adaptable to change. They have been fluid. They have been flexible. They have not molded us to rigidity. I think our schools have adapted reasonably well to the dynamics of cultural cement of citizenship.

Beginning as educational borrowers, we are now an exporter of educational ideas. We borrowed the elementary school from Prussia; the dame school, academy, and college from England; the high school from Scotland; the kindergarten and graduate school from Germany. Some borrowings such as the dame school we have dropped, some like the academy we have transformed into the high school, and some units like the junior high school and the junior college we have invented. We have coupled our school units into a ladder of opportunity for all. In little more than a century of commitment to universal compulsory education, we have used our schools to adapt to changing times.

Our public schools have kept us informed. They have kept us free. Those who first came to these shores knew the Bible. The leaders of the Revolution knew John Locke and Jean Jacques Rousseau. Those who made the Constitution knew the Federalist Papers. Those who built canals and railroads knew transit and rule. Those who built our industries knew mathematics and the lathe. Those who migrated to these shores found in public schools the cement of citizenship.

Bright young people entering teaching need to know that American education is entering a new day. It's bold. It's daring. It's exciting. Technology has caught up with it. It has new tools—teaching machines, educational television, the whole range of audio-visual aids. Curriculum changes are rampant.

New teachers—and old—need to know that American education is coming into its own. It's getting bigger and better. It now involves one out of every four Americans.

What's right with American education? It's becoming professional. It's becoming specialized. It's merging subject matter *and* methods *and* an awareness of the cultural milieu in which it works. Its status is rising. Its esteem is climbing.

What's right with American education and the Great Society? The answer lies with the young people about to enter the teaching profession. They will see and do things we older teachers never dreamed of. If I were young and had to do it all over again, I would be what I am—a teacher—but I would try to be a better prepared one.

Charles Silberman is a journalist who led a foundation team that conducted a three-year investigation
of American schools in the late 1960's. His wife
was part of that team. Although their historical
perspective is much harsher than Parker's, they
agree that schools hold much promise to aid in
developing American society.

For the Silbermans, the "ladders of opportunity" have too often been the "mutilation of opportunity." Readers may ask on what grounds do they
base their optimism. They speak of reforming the
schools, but what reforms do they see occurring in
the near future˜

Mr. Silberman reported many of his group's
findings in *Crisis in the Classroom* (New York:
Random House, 1970) and Arlene Silberman has
written several articles. Their comments are excerpted from testimony before a Senate committee
on equal educational opportunity.

EQUAL EDUCATIONAL
OPPORTUNITY TESTIMONY
Charles and Arlene Silberman

Mr. Silberman: "What the best and wisest parent wants for his own
child," a great American educator once wrote, "that must the community want for all of its children. Any other idea for our schools is
narrow and unlovely; acted upon, it destroys our democracy."

Our democracy is not destroyed, but it is in danger. Not the least
of the reasons is the fact that the community has not wanted for all
its children what the best and wisest parent wants for his own child.
As a result, the public schools are failing dismally in what has always
been regarded as one of their primary tasks. What has distinguished
public education in the United States from education elsewhere, in
fact, has been precisely the expectation that the public schools
would create a sense of unity and national purpose in a society that

Hearings, U. S. Senate Select Committee on Equal Educational Opportunity, 91st Congress,
2nd Session. Part 1A (Washington: U. S. Government Printing Office, 1970), excerpted from
pp. 201–239.

otherwise might be racked by ethnic, religious, and racial conflict. As Horace Mann, generally acknowledged to be the father of the common school, observed a century and a quarter ago, "Education, beyond all other devices of human origin, is the great equalizer of the conditions of man—the balance wheel of the social machinery." Never have we needed the schools to play this role more than now; never has their failure to do so been more ominous for American democracy. If the United States is to fulfill its promise of becoming a truly just and humane society, the schools will have to do an incomparably better job than they are now doing of educating youngsters from minority and lower class homes—Negro Americans, Puerto Rican Americans, Mexican Americans, American Indians, and poor whites in particular, and of educating all children in general.

If the committee is to understand the current crisis, however, it must understand that the failure is not new; it is one the United States has tolerated for a century or more. The public schools have never done much of a job of educating youngsters from immigrant or native lower class homes. While it would be difficult to exaggerate the importance of the wide acceptance and belief in the goal of equal educational opportunity, the goal has never been realized. On the contrary, we have greatly romanticized the role the schools have played in stimulating social and economic mobility for immigrant and poor native-born students. There have been some notable exceptions; but for the ethnic groups who comprised the bulk of the immigration of the middle and late nineteenth and early twentieth centuries, education was not an important means of mobility. Education did not become important to these groups until after they had achieved middle class status.

Why, then, the current crisis? There are two reasons. The first is that education is vastly more important today than it used to be, which means that the schools' failure matters very much more now than it used to. . . . The other . . . is that parents of minority youngsters now recognize the importance of education. Earlier minority groups were more or less indifferent, and sometimes hostile, to the schools, which appeared to threaten the solidarity of the group, which they valued above mobility. Today Negro parents, and increasingly Mexican American, Puerto Rican, and American Indian parents are eager for their children to have the means of mobility and they are angry at the schools' failure to provide it.

What must be understood, however, is the fact that the defects and failures of the schools which educate Negro and other minority youngsters are, in good measure, simply an exaggerated version of what is wrong with schools everywhere. "The most deadly of all possible sins," Erik Erikson suggests, "is the mutilation of a child's spirit." It is not possible to spend any prolonged period visiting public school classrooms, as I have done, without being appalled by the mutilation visible everywhere, in the most prosperous suburbs as well as the most poverty-stricken urban and rural slums: mutilation of spontaneity, of joy in learning, of pleasure in creating, of a sense of self. *The public schools are the kind of institution one cannot really dislike until one gets to know them well* [emphasis added]. Because adults take the schools so much for granted, they fail to appreciate what grim, joyless places most American schools are, how oppressive and petty are the rules by which they are governed, how intellectually sterile and esthetically barren the atmosphere, what an appalling lack of civility obtains on the part of teachers and principals, what contempt they unconsciously display for children as children. I assure you I had not realized this until I began spending day after day, week after week, sitting in public classrooms.

And it need not be! What my studies have demonstrated, beyond any doubt, is that public schools can be organized to facilitate joy in learning and intellectual and esthetic expression and to develop character—in the rural and urban slums no less than in the prosperous suburbs. This is no utopian hope; there are models now in existence that can be followed. The most exciting elementary schools in the United States are to be found in the state of North Dakota—in hamlets like Starkweather and Edmore, with populations of 250 and 400, as well as in cities like Grand Forks, Fargo, and Minto—where, with assistance from the U. S. Office of Education, the University of North Dakota is collaborating with the state department of education to revamp completely the way in which schools are organized and run, and thereby to overcome the unequal educational opportunity which this state has been providing its almost entirely white student population. Unequal opportunity due to the fact that children in that state were scoring well below the national achievement. But there are models to be found, too, in New York City's Harlem; in the black ghettos of Philadelphia; in Tucson, Arizona, in schools serving a predominantly Mexican American population; in Portland, Oregon, in a high school serving a predominantly white working class and lower-middle class neighborhood; and in many other parts of the country.

In short, the public school system can be reformed. What makes change possible, moreover, is that what is mostly wrong with the schools is not due to venality, or indifference, or stupidity, but to mindlessness. What distinguishes my criticism of the public schools from that of a number of other critics, I believe, is at least in part my appreciation of the difficult and sometimes heroic role which teachers play. To be sure, teaching has its share of sadists and clods, of insecure and angry men and women who hate their students for their openness, their exuberance, their color, or their affluence. But the great majority of teachers, principals, and superintendents are decent, intelligent, and caring people who try to do their best, by their lights. If they make a botch of it, and an uncomfortably large number do, it is because it simply never occurs to more than a handful of them to ask why they are doing what they are doing—to think seriously or deeply about the purpose or consequences of education.

It is fashionable, I know, to disparage talk about educational purpose or educational philosophy. To talk about purpose, however, is in no way to be abstract or theoretical. On the contrary, educational purpose or philosophy is exemplified and transmitted in the way schools are organized and run. Education is inescapably a moral as well as intellectual and esthetic enterprise. What educators . . . must recognize is that how teachers teach, and how they act, may be more important than what they teach; the way we do things, that is to say, shapes values more directly and more effectively than the way we talk about them. Children are taught a host of lessons about values, ethics, morality, character and conduct every day of the week, less by the content of the curriculum than by the way schools are organized, the way teachers and parents behave, the way they talk to children and to each other, the kinds of behavior they approve or reward and the kinds they disapprove or punish. . . . Students are taught lessons about the worth and individual humanity of children who belong to different ethnic, racial, and religious groups by the ways in which schools deal with these groups— whether, for example, schools segregate students by race or whether they bring them together in integrated common schools. Indeed, segregated schools teach a lesson about the worth and humanity of black children, and of white children as well—that is far more powerful and far more lasting than all the civic classes, salutes to the flag, and recitals of the Pledge of Allegiance put together.

Thus, I agree completely with the argument which Dr. Kenneth Clark put before this committee last week, namely, that racial segregation is at least as damaging to white children as it is to black children. I do not mean to disparage the evidence that integration raises the academic achievement of black children. What makes integration crucial to this nation's future, however, is not so much what it does to raise academic achievement as what it contributes to the creation of a humane, decent, and united society. That is what the public school's major purpose must be. . . .

Senator Dominick: Mr. Silberman, . . . the thing that this committee is concerned with is the question of what should be done about minority groups. It is generally known, and is perhaps implicit in your statement that the majority of the people on welfare today are white, not black. Mr. Coleman, in his testimony before us Monday, indicated that his investigation of the comparative schools, found that the significant difference in schools was caused by the different backgrounds of the children rather than by tangible classroom variables such as teacher-student ratios or student-classroom ratios. Do you agree that the economic background is the determining factor in education?

Mr. Silberman: I agree, Senator Dominick, that in terms of the things which Professor Coleman measured, the critical factor is not what he called the quality of the school or the inputs into the school, but rather the nature of the student body and the nature of the home environment from which the child comes. What must be recognized and realized, I think, is that Professor Coleman, given the exigencies of time, measured only what could be very easily measured in quantitative terms, which was to say the dollar expenditure per pupil, the number of books in the library, the average size of class, things of that sort. And he found that the results were not related to these kinds of inputs. There is a large body of other research in England and in this country which reports the same kind of findings.

But these are not the critically important differences. The important differences are qualitative, not quantitative. I don't have at my fingertips the average expenditure per pupil in the schools in North Dakota that I am talking about. I am sure they are considerably less than in most of the prosperous suburbs in the East. But what distinguishes those schools is not the size of the class, not the number of books in the library, it is the warm human atmosphere which makes it possible for teachers to deal with each child as an individual rather than standing in front of the classroom trying to teach an entire class as a group. The critical variables have to do with things that are very hard to measure quantitatively.

. . .

Senator Hughes: . . . How can we have a great majority of principals and teachers who want to do their best and then have a system that can be so openly indicted?

Mr. Silberman: Because teachers are victimized by the system of education that we now have every bit as much as the children. Teachers work in surroundings that almost no one else would tolerate. They punch timeclocks like factory workers. They have no privacy. Their conditions are debilitating, to say the least. What is most crucial, however, is that the schools operate on an assumption of distrust. And the most crucial factor is the traditional technique of what some educators disparagingly call "the chalk and talk method," which is to say education in which the teacher stands at the front of the room as a source of all wisdom, all authority, and attempts to teach all children simultaneously, the same thing for the same length of time.

Studies of classroom dialogue, the verbal interaction between students and teachers, indicate that teachers talk anywhere between 60 or 80 percent of the time. All of the children together talk the remainder of the time, and they are talking almost invariably as a response to a question. Given this sort of structure, we define a problem of discipline and control. . . . If the teacher tries to alter this approach, he or she is immediately struck down because the principal way in which a teacher's competence is judged in most school systems is by the degree of control he exercises over the class. So long as the class is quiet, the teacher will never hear a complaint. If there is any noise or movement, regardless of whether that reflects intellectual excitement, the teacher will be criticized. One illustrative example of this, and I will stop. In one school that I know, a sixth-grade science teacher, particularly interested in science, discovered that one of his students was the son of a local butcher. So he acquired from the father the respiratory system from a cow and the next day he had the entire class gathered around him. He had his jacket off, his shirtsleeves rolled up, his hands deep in the respiratory system showing the youngsters how the heart worked and pumped blood to the rest of the body. They were just extraordinarily excited. When he went down to the office for lunch and looked in his mail box, there was a note for him from the superintendent of schools, and the note, to paraphrase—I have a precise quotation in my book—read:

> I looked in your class this morning. Teachers are not supposed to have their jackets removed. If for any reason their jacket must be removed, their shirtsleeves certainly should not be rolled up.

Well, that teacher got the message. . . . And when . . . the structure is changed so that teachers can develop their own creativity, so that they are treated and regarded as professionals with something to contribute on their own, the ordinary average classroom teacher performs in an entirely different way. It is the system in which they are encased that produces the behavior. If you change the way in which schools are organized, you get a very different kind of teacher behavior.

Senator Brooke: Mr. Silberman, you stated that you agreed with Dr. Kenneth Clark that racial segregation in public schools is equally damaging to white children as to black. What are the damages specifically to white children? Mrs. Silberman, would you like to answer that?

Mrs. Silberman: I think the main damage is that white children pick up quite unconsciously a sense of superiority, of their own superiority, which they carry with them all the days of their years unless they then have another experience.

Senator Brooke: Do you distinguish any difference between the damage done to black children and damage done to Puerto Rican children or Indian children?

Mrs. Silberman: A difference in damage? No.

Mr. Silberman: It is hard for me to answer, because I am, I think, more familiar as a result of my earlier work with the damage that has been done to black children in this country than with the damage done to Mexican Americans or American Indians. I suspect that the damage to black children is greater, but that in no way suggests that the damage done to other minorities is not so profound as to be a matter of great concern.

Senator Brooke: What would be the difference, then, specifically? Give me one example of the difference of the damage to Mexican Americans and the damage to a black child.

Mr. Silberman: I think the difference is that racial prejudice runs very much deeper in American life and in western life than ethnic prejudice. Our whole language is suffused with imagery. If we keep someone out of the club, we blackball him. Black is the color we use for funerals. The white lie is the permissible lie, the black lie the unpermissible lie. And this imagery is so deeply rooted in our language and our consciousness, the heritage of slavery, segregation, discrimination is so great, that racial prejudice is almost in the air we breathe. I don't believe that it is possible for any white person to grow up in this country free from prejudice, free from a sense of superiority. I think it is possible for whites to overcome that, to come to grips with their own feelings. It is because this sense of racial superiority and difference is so deeply imbedded in our life and in our institutions and our language that I feel racial segregation is more damaging than ethnic segregation. But I want to emphasize that I am not trying to minimize the damage done to Mexican Americans or Puerto Rican or American Indian children, but simply to suggest that the damage is even greater because of the peculiar circumstances of our own history.

Senator Brooke: It is a question of degree in that regard?

Mr. Silberman: Yes, sir.

. . .

Senator Brooke: You referred in your statement to petty and depressing rules by which our schools were governed. What are you referring to specifically? What sort of rules are you referring to?

Mrs. Silberman: They sound almost too silly to bring before you. I think of one school, for instance, where children must carry their books on their left arm and when the principal was pressed for reasons as to why this rule existed, he was flustered primarily because he really hadn't thought about it much and it exists because it exists. Finally, he said, "That way, they can hold the banister on the stairway and prevent accidents." And I said, "Have there been very many accidents in the other schools where this rule does not obtain?" He had no answer.

I think of another school I visited, which was a junior high school, an eighth-grade class. As the bell rang, these youngsters, some of whom were a strapping 6 feet, 4 inches, had to line up in single file before they could leave the room. When I was interviewing the principal of this particular school, I asked if he could explain that rule to me, as it would be of interest. He said, "Haven't you noticed how narrow our halls are?" I said, "I really hadn't. I noticed as soon as the youngsters left the classroom they dispersed into the hall immediately." His reply was, "Oh? Well, we will have to put more monitors in the hall then, won't we?" So it is things of this ilk that have nothing to do with purpose.

. . .

Senator Randolph: . . . You have said, "The present school system is one that there is a mutilation of opportunity." Would you explain that to me more fully?

Mr. Silberman: I mean that in a twofold sense, sir. In terms of the schooling for all children, there is, as I indicated, a mutilation of the spirit, of joy in learning, and in discovering. The premium in most schools is on conformity, on getting the right grade, on getting the right answer. School becomes for the child a kind of game of trying to dope out what it is that the teacher wants to know, what is the "right answer"—right in the sense of what the teacher wants, which tends to stifle initiative, independent inquiry. . . . Now, the process is far more serious for minority children because it is compounded by a set of sometimes conscious and sometimes unconscious attitudes of prejudice, lowered expectations.

To give you one example of what destroys the spirit of a black student, a youngster I know, a high school junior, was terribly eager to go to college. When he talked to his guidance counselor, the response was, "What? You go to college? Don't make me laugh." When he was insistent, she suggested a few of the poorer southern Negro colleges. His record was poor. He had moved to the community in which I live as a youngster of 10 or 12 from Birmingham, Alabama, and he had not yet made up the deficits. But we knew him. He was a friend of my oldest son, was around the house a good bit, and he struck us as not simply highly motivated, but as having a combination of motivation and articulateness which suggested that there was more here than the grades were reflecting. So we helped get him into an "Upward Bound" program at a local college which was federally financed. As a result, after just the first summer in that program, his grades shot from Fs and Ds to Bs and Cs. By the end of the spring of the following year, he was showing so much promise that the "Upward Bound" officials recommended him for another partially federally financed program, a transitional year program.

There were 500 applicants for this program at Yale; 60 were accepted. He was one of them. When he went to his guidance counselor to ask that the transcript be sent to Yale, she said, "What, you go to Yale? That is crazy. Don't make me laugh." He was accepted. When he came to tell her, she looked up from her papers and said, "Oh," and went back to shuffling her papers. Several weeks later the superintendent of schools heard about it and made a big thing of it in the local newspaper, and when some local civil rights leaders were meeting with the education officials to express some complaints, the answer was, "Look at this youngster, we got him to Yale, that shows what we are doing for him."

After the year at Yale, he is now a student and freshman at one of the finest liberal arts colleges in the country. . . . [But] this sometimes conscious, sometimes completely unconscious prejudice . . . [usually] prevents black youngsters from having the opportunity to learn. Prejudice, and lowered expectations; the other chilling phrase is "They are doing as well as can be expected." This destroys the opportunity for an education.

. . .

Senator Brooke: There is an increasing number of blacks, very respectable body of blacks, who are favoring more and more black schools, black-controlled schools. How do you view this—I won't call it a phenomenon—but how do you view this suggestion?

Mr. Silberman: I view it as a quite natural and almost inevitable response to the failure of the courts, the state and local governments, and federal government to enforce the Supreme Court's mandate of 1954. Having waited sixteen years for the law to be enforced, I think it is understandable that there is some skepticism as to whether it will be, and some attempt, therefore, to search for the solution.

Senator Brooke: Do you think this is a main reason why the blacks are advocating black-controlled schools?

Mr. Silberman: I think this is the major factor that is responsible. I think there are other important factors as well. A search for black identity. Attempt to develop pride in self after all of the centuries of humiliation is a terribly important part of it. But certainly in New York City it was the failure to integrate that first produced the phenomenon. It has then taken on a rationale of its own in terms of pride of identity, in terms of responsiveness of the schools. . . .

In the high school in my own community, Mt. Vernon, New York, which is roughly 40 percent black, 60 percent white, the black proportion has been rising quite rapidly. Five years ago there were severe disorders. There were guards posted all over the school. A new superintendent came in and persuaded the principal to retire, appointed a new principal, who on the first day of school that September announced to the assembled students that he had removed the guards because he trusted the students to maintain order themselves. He managed to convey to the students two things: One, that he liked them and trusted them, that he had empathy for them; and secondly, that he was not any pushover, that he had removed the guards because he wanted to give them a chance to maintain order, that he hoped he would not have to restore them. He also took great pains to establish close relations with the black students who had some kind of leadership among the student body and with the white students who were leaders and asked them to report immediately to him any incidents of racial slurs and tension, so he could try to deal with them.

That school of 3,000 students, which had had to have guards all over the place, had no guards and had no disorder the entire year. And in the spring, when a local radio station ran an annual contest for the most popular high school principal, this man was elected, although this was his first year at the school. The students could send in as many votes as they wanted. Each vote was a 3 x 5 file card with the name. They sent in, with 3,000 students, something like 2.5 million votes, so he was elected the most popular principal in the metropolitan area.

Senator Randolph: How many votes?

Mr. Silberman: 2.5 million. They spent their entire spring vacation going around to every stationery store in town getting contributions of file cards and getting each student to fill out as many as he possibly could. This was the degree of rapport and trust that he had established in a racially very tense community where there had been demonstrations and threats.

He is no longer there. He left in part because of opposition from school board members who wanted much more repressive schools. Two and a half years later he received an offer for superintendency and he left. The school is now chaos. There are guards all over again. There are drugs being sold and used all over the school. There have been firebombings and there have been all sorts of disorders. . . . I think what is crucial is that the whole atmosphere has changed because the administration of the school now takes a very different approach.

I have two examples of what happens under the present system.

In one instance a black student on crutches walked the entire corridor. This is an enormous building. It is a two-story plant with now 4,000 students and it covers a huge acreage. He walked the entire length on crutches. An assistant principal told him there was a school regulation, which no one had ever heard of and to anyone's knowledge had never been enforced before, that students had to walk on the right side of the hall, and so ordered him to go all the way back to the end of the corridor and come back on the right side because he had been on the left side.

Another youngster whom I know came to our house one morning. He had been suspended from school. He came to us because his mother was about to enter the hospital for major surgery and had extremely high blood pressure and he didn't want to upset her. He had been suspended because he was accused of sexually molesting a white girl when she passed his table in the cafeteria. He happened to have been sitting with one of my sons at lunch. I went over to the school to see the deputy principal. He told me, "Oh, there was no question, the girl had witnesses." I asked, "Why didn't you call the boy's witnesses? One of them happened to have been one of my sons." He said, "Well, we knew we didn't have to because she told us he had whispered obscenities in her ear when she had been boarding the school bus at the end of school a month before." In point of fact, the boy was on the wrestling team and so he didn't take the school bus home. The incident could not have happened. Moreover, the parents of the girl seemed to have been mentally unbalanced. A few nights before, they had disrupted a public meeting I attended a number of times to constantly report that their daughter was always being molested. When I said to the deputy principal, "You know that these parents are paranoid or something," he confessed to me that he had suspended the boy to get these parents "off his back." The girl, as he put it, was "a floosey," but he said that she was constantly making accusations, that the last time this happened he had not suspended anyone and the parents had gone to the school board, which had reprimanded him for not acting.

The result is that a boy who had been an A and B student is now getting D and F. This kind of incident occurs in that school over and over again. The result is an atmosphere of distrust and hate that builds up, rather than trust and understanding, and of a breakdown in order which brings more repression, which brings more striking back, which brings more repression, and the cycle just perpetuates itself. And the school board seems to have learned nothing from the earlier experience with the principal, who was able to put the responsibility on the students. . . .

Chairman: Thank you very much. You have given several persuasive examples of how our schools stifle incentive and impose rules upon children which appear to interfere with learning, enthusiasm, self-respect, and all of the rest. A similar indictment was made by . . . others. Is it your testimony that these examples are symptomatic of our entire system more than they are bizarre exceptions which could be used possibly to prove something that doesn't exist as a general matter?

Mr. Silberman: No, sir, I believe they are systematic. I have given some strong examples. They are by no means atypical. They essentially stem from the fact that the schools are not organized to facilitate learning. They are organized to facilitate order, and the result is a whole set of rules and an insistence on silence and lack of motion that we adults find impossible to observe. I would suggest that, as an exercise, the members of this committee attempt to spend an entire day in school and attempt to sit as still and as silently as the students are required to do; you would discover that it would be impossible for them really to do so and they would begin to wonder how children could do it.

. . .

Chairman: What emphasis would you place on early childhood days?

Mr. Silberman: That is a very difficult question to answer. I think I would perhaps place less emphasis than is now being placed on it.

Chairman: You mean in terms of rhetoric?

Mr. Silberman: In terms of rhetoric. My own views have changed over the last several years, but it seems to me that the experience of a substantial number of programs indicates that the gains that are achieved in preschool programs wash out quite rapidly in the schools unless the schools themselves are changed.

Chairman: Is that an indictment of the early childhood efforts?

Mr. Silberman: It is an indictment of the schools, but there is an implicit assumption in the early childhood approach—in the whole emphasis on early childhood education—that the problem is the child and not the school. The reason minority and lower class children fail is that they enter schools lacking certain cognitive and affective skills that middle class children have. I advanced the same argument myself a number of years ago and the solution is to change the child to fit the school. My own studies and my own evaluation of the preschool programs suggests that we might be wiser to put our money into changing the schools to fit the child rather than changing the children to fit the schools.

The interpretations of American schooling offered so far have not satisfied some historians of education. Their research has produced a "revisionist" accounting of the education of American youth.

Michael Katz is a leader in this school of thought, which holds that schools have not been the royal avenues to success so much as they have been protectors of vested interest: "Schools . . . are imperial institutions designed to civilize the natives; they exist to (make) . . . poor children . . . orderly, industrious, law-abiding and respectful of authority."

Such an interpretation forces us to ask such questions as: What are the goals of American schooling? Has the school changed since the Civil War? Should schools be reformed and, if so, how can they be?

CLASS, BUREAURACY, AND SCHOOLS
Michael B. Katz

On a street corner in a Brooklyn slum there stands a modern school, a massive concrete block in the middle of an asphalt playground. Like an ancient fortress, it has long, narrow slits in place of windows. If I were a kid that building would frighten me. So would the windowless school that stands in Harlem. They remind me of the old schools in working-class neighborhoods of London, surrounded by high walls. Those walls testify that the first compulsory schools were alien institutions set in hostile territory. The same point could be made about contemporary educational fortresses in New York; one international feature of educational history that has remained intact is the separation of the school from the working-class community. Sometimes the outward appearance of a school has relevance to the activities that take place within it; that was so in those first compulsory schools in late-nineteenth-century England. It has often been so

Condensed from the introduction to Michael B. Katz, *Class, Bureaucracy, and Schools: The Illusion of Educational Change in America,* published by Praeger Publishers, New York, © 1971, pages xvii–xxvi. Reprinted by permission.

in New York; even the occasional capture of schools by progressives cannot change the assumptions that underlie their architectural design.

Consequently, there is logic in the choice of schools as objects of capture by communities seeking political and social emancipation. For the schools are fortresses in function as well as form, protected outposts of the city's educational establishment and the prosperous citizens who sustain it. In their own way, they are imperial institutions designed to civilize the natives; they exist to do something to poor children, especially, now, children who are black or brown. Their main purpose is to make these children orderly, industrious, law-abiding, and respectful of authority. Their literature and their spokesmen proclaim the schools to be symbols of opportunity, but their slitted or windowless walls say clearly what their history would reveal as well: They were designed to reflect and confirm the social structure that erected them.

There is a great gap between the pronouncement that education serves the people and the reality of what schools do to and for the children of the poor. Despite the existence of free, universal, and compulsory schooling, most poor children become poor adults. Schools are not great democratic engines for identifying talent and matching it with opportunity. The children of the affluent by and large take the best marks and the best jobs.

That fact cannot be explained either by genetics or by theories of cultural deprivation; it is the historical result of the combination of purpose and structure that has characterized American education for roughly the last hundred years. The purpose has been, basically, the inculcation of attitudes that reflect dominant social and industrial values; the structure has been bureaucracy. The result has been school systems that treat children as units to be processed into particular shapes and dropped into slots roughly congruent with the status of their parents. There is a functional relationship between the way in which schools are organized and what they are supposed to do. That relationship was there a century ago, and it exists today. This is why the issues of social class and bureaucracy are central to understanding the public school.

Purely contemporary analysis obscures this point. To appreciate the interweaving of structure and purpose in education it is necessary to study its origin and development. Today's educational structures are historical products; they represent patterns that have become deeply embedded in American society and are enormously resistant to change. The techniques with which the system maintains its equilibrium have themselves become traditions. We have become so accustomed to these ways of responding and to the assumptions enmeshed in existing structures that it is difficult to isolate and examine them clearly. But we gain detachment by looking at their origins. We can in fact pick out the moments when familiar features were new and controversial. We can analyze the interaction of social goals and social forces that entrenched those features in social history and ensured their survival over alternate proposals. . . .

My thesis is that by about 1880 American education had acquired its fundamental structural characteristics, and that they have not altered since. . . .

If the central proposition is accepted, five important questions follow, . . . both implicitly and explicitly. First, did anyone propose alternatives to the structure that emerged? Second, was the establishment of that structure, regardless of alternative proposals, somehow "inevitable"? Third, what have been the interconnections between the major dimensions of that structure, or between its shape, its purpose, and its function? Fourth, why has the structure remained so resistant to reformist thrusts? And fifth, what is the moral of the structure's history for contemporary reform, or, must structural change precede "educational" change?

Acceptance of the proposition that the basic structure of American education has remained unchanged rests, quite obviously, on the definition of "basic." I mean by the term that certain characteristics of American education today were also characteristic nearly a century ago: it is, and was, universal, tax-supported, free, compulsory, bureaucratic, racist, and class-biased. Those features marked some educational systems by 1880; they diffused throughout the rest of the country in a sequence that roughly paralleled urban growth. . . .

I do not deny, or wish to imply that I deny, the introduction of important innovations—for instance, the kindergarten, vocational education, guidance, testing, and various new curricula, to name but a few. These have all made a difference, but they have not touched or altered the structural features I have outlined. It is to me, to use a very crude metaphor, as if the characteristics noted above form the walls of a box within which other sorts of change have taken place. The box is filled with objects that can be moved around and rearranged, but the walls themselves remain solid. Moreover, if I may extend the image for a moment, only objects that can fit within the box can be put there. Thus there is a congruence between the purposes and functioning of innovations that have entered the schools and the structural basis of the educational system itself.

This brief elaboration of my proposition should give meaning to the questions posed above. To take the first: Did anyone propose alternatives to the structure that emerged? Historians too often have conceived of educational history in simple moralistic terms: Good men—reformers of vision, dedication, and courage—proposed in embryo form the school system we now have. Opposing them were selfish, narrow-minded bigots interested in saving money and keeping the working classes down. We now know that this is nonsense, because we can see the consequences of those early proposals and because we find it hard today to accept simple, one-sided explanations of human behavior. But we must also reject the traditional story because of its constriction of historical vision. We must not accept the notion that there was but one educational proposal around which controversy revolved. On the contrary, in the first half of the nineteenth century four different proposals, four alternative modes of organizing public education, competed for acceptance. Each of them rested on a distinct and identifiable set of social values, and the competition among them reflected and expressed wider value conflicts within society. . . . They were, additionally, real alternatives; examples of each did in fact exist. . . .

The second question is largely one of causation. The model that emerged victorious was the one I call incipient bureaucracy, and the question is, Why? Did bureaucracy triumph because it was somehow "inevitable"? It is a question of some importance for social theory as well as for historical inquiry. Perhaps naively, I see one implication to be that bureaucracy *is* inevitable. Given a complex, technological society and a complicated and massive social task like universal schooling, there is no other way of proceeding. Bureaucracy is neither good nor bad in this point of view; it is a social fact, a necessity. If we want schools, hospitals, welfare, or manufactured goods, we must have it, for the alternative is chaos and anarchy. If the logic of that point of view is accepted, then reform directed against the notion and existence of bureaucracy is at best romantic and, in any case, useless. It is better to accept the reality and permanency of bureaucracy and to improve its operation.

But if bureaucracy in education is inevitable, it did not seem so to some men who lived at the time of its creation. This is one moral of the story of alternative propositions. Some men at different points in time, in the nineteenth century and today, have been able to conceive of ways other than bureaucracy for managing the affairs of modern society. It is thus difficult to accept the proposition that bureaucracy is the only means through which social tasks can be accomplished.

In fact, on closer inspection, it appears that bureaucracy is inevitable only when men confront certain problems with particular social values and priorities. It is not industrialization that makes bureaucracy inevitable but the combination of industrialization and particular values. It is because of the mix of setting and priorities, not because of the setting alone, that we have bureaucracy as the dominant form of social organization. . . .

My thesis about bureaucracy suggests an answer to the third question I raised, concerning the interconnections between the dimensions of educational structure or, as we now might phrase it, between bureaucracy and social class. We know that education is bureaucratically organized; we know that it reflects class bias in its purposes and operations. Are the two features independent, at least in their origins if not in their present form? The answer is no. Bureaucracy came about because men confronted particular kinds of social problems with particular social purposes. Those purposes reflected class attitudes and class interests. Modern bureaucracy is a bourgeois invention; it represents a crystallization of bourgeois social attitudes. To its founders, . . . the purposes of the school system and its structure were clearly interrelated. They understood that part of the message they wished to have transmitted, the attitudes they wished formed, would inhere in the structural arrangements themselves rather than in explicit didactic procedures. What they did not admit, although it is hard to see how they could have failed to realize it, was that the bureaucratic structure, apparently so equitable and favorable to the poor, would in fact give differential advantage to the affluent and their children, thereby reinforcing rather than altering existing patterns of social structure. Through bureaucracy, the myth of equal opportunity has been fostered, while the amount of social mobility has been strictly regulated.

Once more we have clues to the answer to the next question: Why has the structure of American education remained impermeable to reformist thrusts? Part of the answer, of course, is that the structure serves powerful interests. It serves the interests of the educators by providing career-lines and regulating entry. They have no intention of permitting its alteration now, and they had none a century ago. . . . The structures serve the interest of affluent groups, too, by working in favor of their children and giving them a disproportionate share of public funds. For those who control the system there has been no point in making fundamental structural alterations.

That is one reason the system has remained unreformed. Another is that very few people, until now, have seriously tried to change it. The reforms that have been proposed at various times, and frequently even enacted, generally consist of moving around the objects in the box, to return to my earlier image. I include in this description the reformers of the progressive period of the late nineteenth century. . . . Additionally, reformers have proceeded with an ineptitude of thought and strategy that has doomed their efforts from the very start. They have ignored the sociological constraints that impede changes within organizations and have lacked the strength or courage to think through the logic of their criticisms. Sometimes they have disturbed the equilibrium of a system for a few years, but in most cases it has reasserted itself, allowing things to continue pretty much in their old way. One clear instance of that was the abortive reform movement of the late 1870's in Boston. . . .

With the foregoing in mind, we can answer what to me seems a critical question confronting contemporary reformers: Must structural change precede educational change? Or is it possible to alter the purposes, biases, and actual functioning of schools without at the same time changing, radically, the structures through which they are organized and controlled? If my reading of history is roughly accurate, the answer to the second question is no. Forms of organizational structure are not and cannot be neutral. The relationships between bureaucracy, class bias, and racism are fixed. They emerged together a century ago, and they have remained essentially unchanged ever since. To attack one without the other would seem to be, if I am right, at best a waste of time and at worst another diversion from the serious need for social and educational reform within American society. . . .

No historian can entirely divorce the categories with which he approaches the contemporary world from those with which he studies the past. Our concerns shape the questions that we ask and, as a consequence, determine what we select from the virtually unlimited supply of "facts." That state of affairs remains submerged and implicit in most historical work. In this case I have chosen to make manifest my questions and my concern. The concern is to provide a perspective that will be helpful in understanding and, I hope, improving urban education today.

Sociological concepts have been indispensable in forming that perspective, and I have used them deliberately and explicitly. The systematic use of concepts and the application of intellectual constructs give explanatory power to history, for they permit the formation of general statements. Too much historical work, however, continues to be remarkably unanalytical. It rests, for instance, on ideas about motivation that are quaint in terms of contemporary behavioral theory. It speaks of institutions and groups as if theories of society, organization, and stratification did not exist. As a consequence, written history usually offers no general statements that can be tested in different settings; it approaches data in a method so unsystematic that its findings cannot be replicated.

In short, there is little on-going, substantive discourse that permits historians to build on one another's work in any but the most primitive sense of adding more facts or extending the chronology backward or forward in time. It seems to me that the time for methodological unconsciousness within history has ended. Narrative history, uninformed by social or behavioral science, is pleasant and sometimes even interesting, but as a way of either advancing knowledge or contributing to substantive intellectual problems it is virtually useless.

Significant problems do not respect disciplinary boundaries; that is true for both intellectual and practical issues. Disciplines are constructs invented for the convenience of academics. They serve a useful function as a way of inducting new research workers into problems and providing an initial orientation to issues, but they should not be taken too seriously. The relations of structure and purpose in organizations, of bureaucracy and social class in education—these are not historical questions or sociological ones or some curious amalgam of the two. They are important intellectual problems that involve the past and the present, and they should be regarded in that light. Social science cut off from its historical base, as Robert Nisbet has elegantly demonstrated in *Social Change and History* (Oxford University Press, 1969), has weaknesses as grave as those of historical writing uninformed by social theory. The same can be said of social reform uninformed by history, which too often rests largely on myth. Myth, in turn, inhibits change by attaching sentimental or unreal value to institutions and forms that should be discarded.

History can serve reform partly by emancipating it from dependency upon an idealized past; it can help develop the strength of will and clear judgment that come from an ability to confront both past and present as they actually exist. . . . For we have many myths about education. We imagine educational arrangements that once were warm, democratic, and communal; we see the schools of long ago as providing a solid training in basic skills and opening up countless avenues of social mobility. We cast a rosy glow over the educational past and too often seek a restoration. But that image is a regressive fantasy and nothing more. . . .

Students as well as scholars and social organizations have voiced reactions about what schools do for and to them. This poem was written by a Canadian high school student.

Such a protest suggests several questions: How often does this happen in schools? Are complaints about conformity exaggerated? Is this indictment against a few or many teachers; all schools or only some? Finally, is the student in this case talking only about school? The person who wrote the poem apparently committed suicide—an act that suggests more intense depression than most people feel about something like school.

ABOUT SCHOOL
R. Mukerji

He always wanted to say things. But no one understood.
He always wanted to explain things. But no one cared.
So he drew.
Sometimes he would just draw and it wasn't anything. He wanted to
    carve it in stone or write it in the sky.
He would lie out on the grass and look up in the sky and it would
    be only him and the sky and the things inside that needed saying.
And it was after that, that he drew the picture. It was a beautiful
    picture. He kept it under the pillow and would let no one see it.
And he would look at it every night and think about it. And when it
    was dark, and his eyes were closed, he could still see it.
And it was all of him. And he loved it.
When he started school he brought it with him. Not to show anyone,
    but just to have with him like a friend.
It was funny about school.
He sat in a square, brown desk like all the other square, brown desks
    and he thought it should be red.
And his room was a square, brown room. Like all the other rooms.
    And it was tight and close. And stiff.
He hated to hold the pencil and the chalk, with his arm stiff and his

R. Mukerji, "About School," *Colloquy*, vol. 3, no. 1 (January 1970), p. 2. Reprinted by permission of United Church Press.

feet flat on the floor, stiff, with the teacher watching and watching.

And then he had to write numbers. And they weren't anything. They were worse than the letters that could be something if you put them together.

And the numbers were tight and square and he hated the whole thing.

The teacher came and spoke to him. She told him to wear a tie like all the other boys. He said he didn't like them and she said it didn't matter.

After that they drew. And he drew all yellow and it was the way he felt about morning. And it was beautiful.

The teacher came and smiled at him. "What's this?" she asked. "Why don't you draw something like Ken's drawing? Isn't that beautiful!

It was all questions.

After that his mother bought him a tie and he always drew airplanes and rocket ships like everyone else. And he threw the old picture away.

And when he lay out alone looking at the sky, it was big and blue and all of everything, but *he* wasn't anymore.

He was square inside and brown, and his hands were stiff, and he was like anyone else. And the things inside him that needed saying didn't need saying anymore.

It had stopped pushing. It was crushed. Stiff.

Like everything else.

An assumption of some critics of education is that failure in schools is accidental, due in part to improper training of teachers, inadequate financing, or overcrowded classrooms. Angrily, Jerry Farber argues that choking conformity is an intentional and pervasive part of schooling.

He proposes some ways students may revolutionize the system. Are his remedies "radical"? Is his assessment accurate? Is he correct when he suggests that how you are taught is more important than what you are taught?

THE STUDENT AND SOCIETY
Jerry Farber

School is where you let the dying society put its trip on you. Our schools may seem useful: to make children into doctors, sociologists, engineers—to discover things. But they're poisonous as well. They exploit and enslave students; they petrify society; they make democracy unlikely. And it's not *what* you're taught that does the harm but *how* you're taught. Our schools teach you by pushing you around, by stealing your will and your sense of power, by making timid square apathetic slaves out of you—authority addicts.

Schooling doesn't have to be this destructive. If it weren't compulsory, if schools were autonomous and were run by the people in them, then we could learn without being subdued and stupefied in the process. And, perhaps, we could regain control of our own society.

Students can change things if they want to because they have the power to say "no." When you go to school, you're doing society a favor. And when you say "no," you withhold much more than your attendance. You deny continuity to the dying society; you put the future on strike. Students can have the kind of school they want—or even something else entirely if they want—because there isn't going to be any school at all without them.

NOTES

(1) "School is Where You Let the Dying Society Put Its Trip on You"

School is a genetic mechanism for society, a kind of DNA process that continually recreates styles, skills, values, hangups—and so keeps the whole thing going. The dying part of society—the society that has been—molds the emerging part more or less in its own image, and fashions the society that will be.

Schooling also makes change possible—evolution, if you like. But here we run into a problem. Although our schools foster enormous technological change, they help to keep social change within very narrow limits. Thanks to them, the technological capacity of society evolves at an explosive rate. But there is no comparable, adaptive evolution in the overall social framework, nor in the consciousness of the individuals who make up society. It isn't just that schools fail to create the necessary social change. They actually restrain it. They prevent it. (*How* they prevent it is the subject of the Notes that follow.)

When I say that schools serve the society-that-has-been, the dying society, I mean just that. It isn't "society" itself that runs our schools. Children and adolescents are a huge segment of society but they don't run schools. Even young adults don't run them. Nor as a general rule do workers. Nor do black people (although a few Negroes do). Nor do the poor in general. By and large our schools are in the hands of the most entrenched and rigidly conservative elements in society. In the secondary and elementary schools, students, of course, have no power and teachers have little power. Administrators possess somewhat more, but the real control comes from those solid Chamber-of-Commerce types—those priests of the American Way—on the school board. They uphold the sovereignty of the past; they are the very avatars of institutional inertia. As for the colleges and universities, California, where I teach, is typical. Higher education is controlled primarily by the business elite, aided by a sprinkling of aging politicos, venerable clergymen and society matrons.[1] And in the rare cases when these trustees and governing boards relax their tight control, they are backstopped by our elected officials, whose noses are always aquiver for subversion and scandal and who

1. Read James Ridgeway's "The Closed Corporation: American Universities in Crisis" (New York, 1968). Ridgeway provides extensive information on the interlocking managements of universities and major corporations, as well as an analysis of the "big-business" aspect of the universities themselves.

are epitomized in that querulous Mrs. Grundy, our current governor.

While schools stifle social change, technological change is, to repeat, another matter. The society-that-has-been, in its slavering pursuit of higher profits and better weapons, demands technological progress at a fantastic, accelerating rate. Universities have consequently become a giant industry in their own right. A few tatters of commencement-day rhetoric still cling to them but it becomes more obvious every day that the modern university is not much more than a Research, Development and Training center set up to service government and industry. And so we have a technological explosion within the rigid confines of our unchanging social institutions and values. Schools today give us fantastic power at the same time as they sap our ability to handle it. Good luck, everybody.

(2) "It's Not *What* You're Taught That Does the Harm But *How* You're Taught"

In fact, for most of your school life, it doesn't make that much difference what subject you're taught. The real lesson is the method. The medium in school truly is the message. And the medium is, above all, coercive. You're forced to attend. The subjects are required. You *have* to do homework. You *must* observe school rules. And throughout, you're bullied into docility and submissiveness. Even modern liberal refinements don't really help. So you're called an underachiever instead of a dummy. So they send you to a counselor instead of beating you. It's still not your choice to be there. They may pad the handcuffs—but the handcuffs stay on.

Which particular subject they happen to teach is far less important than the fact that it is required. We don't learn that much subject matter in school anyway in proportion to the huge part of our lives that we spend there. But what we do learn very well, thanks to the method, is to accept choices that have been made for us. Which rule they make you follow is less important than the fact that there are rules. I hear about English teachers who won't allow their students to begin a sentence with "and." Or about high schools where the male students are not permitted to wear a T-shirt unless it has a pocket. I no longer dismiss such rules as merely pointless. The very point to such rules is their pointlessness.

The true and enduring content of education is its method. The method that currently prevails in schools is standardized, impersonal and coercive. What it teaches best is—itself. If, on the other hand, the method were individual, human and free, it would teach that. It would not, however, mesh smoothly into the machine we seem to have chosen as a model for our society.

It's how you're taught that does the harm. You may only study geometry for a semester—or French for two years. But *doing what you're told,* whether or not it makes sense, is a lesson you get every blessed school day for twelve years or more. You know how malleable we humans are. And you know what good learners we are—how little time it takes us to learn to drive a car or a plane or to play passable guitar. So imagine what the effect must be upon our apt and impressionable minds of a twelve-year-course in servility. Think about it. Twelve years of tardy bells and hall passes; of graded homework, graded tests, graded conduct; of report cards, GPA's, honors lists, citizenship ratings; of dress codes, straight lines and silence. *What is it that they're teaching you?* Twelve years pitted against your classmates in a daily Roman circus. The game is Doing What You're Told. The winners get gold stars, affection, envy; they get A's and E's, honors, awards and college scholarships. The losers get humiliation and degradation. The fear of losing the game is a great fear: it's the fear of swats, of the principal's office, and above all the fear of failing. What if you fail and have to watch your friends move past you to glory? And, of course, the worst that could happen: you could be expelled. Not that very many kids get swats or fail or are expelled. But it doesn't take many for the message to get across. These few heavy losers are like severed heads displayed at the city gates to keep the populace in line.

And, to make it worse, all of this pressure is augmented by those countless parents who are ego freaks and competition heads and who forcibly pass their addiction on to their kids. The pressure at school isn't enough; they *pay* the kids for A's and punish them for D's and F's.

But can you feel any of this? Can you understand what has been done to your mind? We get so used to the pressure that we scarcely are conscious of it without making some effort.

Why does the medium of education affect us so deeply while its purported content—the subject matter—so often slips our minds? This is partly because the content varies from year to year while the form remains more or less the same; but also because the form—a structure of rules, punishments, rewards—affects us directly in a real way, while the subject matter may have no such immediate grasp on our lives. After all, don't we tend to learn best what matters most? Under a coercive system it isn't really the subject that matters; what matters is pleasing the authorities. These two are far from the same thing.

Remember French class in high school (or college, for that matter)? The teacher calls on you, one at a time, to see if you've prepared the questions at the end of Leçon 19. "Marshall," she asks, "*qu'est-ce que Robert allait faire le mardi?*" Marshall doesn't get to respond that he doesn't give a shit—not even in French. Fat chance. While he's in school, he's got to be servile to stay out of trouble. And the law requires him to be in school. He's got to do the questions in Leçon 19 because the teacher said to. He's got to do what the teacher said in order to pass the course. He's got to pass the course to get to college. He's got to get to college because it's been explained to him that he'll be a clod all his life if he doesn't; at assembly they've put up charts showing how many hundreds of thousands of dollars more he'll make in his lifetime if he goes to college. And, of course, there's an immediate reason as well for Marshall to have done his homework. If he hasn't, he'll be embarrassed in front of the class.

The educational medium has a very real hold on his life. Unfortunately, the subject probably does not. So we can't console him for all this dull toil by pointing out that he is at least learning French. Because, of course, he isn't. He'll take two years of French in high school. And when he gets to college, it will be like they never happened. Right? In fact, some acquaintances from Montreal recently told me that English-speaking students there are required to take French every year from the second grade on. And yet, I was told, after ten years of the language, they still haven't learned it.

Or what about Freshman English? What actually gets taught? The purported subject matter is usually writing. But consider, up front, who teaches the course. It's usually some well-meaning instructor or TA whose own writing achievements have reached their zenith in a series of idle and heroically dull papers, written in pretentious faggot-academic for his graduate classes. And how does he teach? What's his method? Well, that depends—because things are changing. Somewhere in some college there is undoubtedly a heavyweight, on the verge of being fired, who is teaching silence to freshmen so that they can hear themselves. Maybe somewhere else a teacher has renounced grading and is letting the students write what they want. Most Freshman English teachers, however, are doing the standard thing. They're demanding and then grading "themes" on capital punishment and on lowering the voting age. They're compelling students to drudge through topic-sentence exercises, outline exercises, library exercises, inference-judgment-report exercises, and a flood of other dreary busy work. They think they know the difference between a B-minus essay and a C-plus essay, and they teach their students to believe in such foolishness. They "correct" their students' work with *ex cathedra* judgments, none of which a student is at liberty to ignore.

In Freshman English, the method teaches you—in case you haven't already gotten the message—that writing is a drag. It's a job you do to please someone else (God knows that writing a theme on The Vanishing Individualist is hardly your own idea of how to spend Sunday night). Writing is school work and "English" is learning how to please your English teacher. What interest there is in the course is provided not so much by your writing experience as by the method. That is to say, you may write something tonight but the payoff, the real excitement, won't come until next week when the papers are handed back and you can find out "what you got." That's what makes it all worthwhile; that's what school writing is all about: pleasing the teacher.

The very essence of Freshman English is that term paper they force out of you. In perfect order, impeccably footnoted, unreal and totally useless—that term paper, that empty form, is pretty much the content of the course: submission—alienation—learning to live a pretend intellectual life, pretend-caring about pretend things.

Sometimes you even get a pretend choice; you're allowed to pick your own topic. But you don't get to make the one choice that would give the whole business some meaning: the choice to write no paper at all. Oh, you *can* make that choice. But then you don't get through Freshman English, which means you don't get through college and, therefore, don't get your hands in the gigantic goodie-box which is programmed to open only upon insertion of a college diploma. Or maybe you even get drafted right away. Yeah, you've got a hell of a choice. And college teachers like to style themselves "seekers after truth." Sure. "Know the truth and the truth shall get you a B." The truth in a freshman term paper is about the same truth a banker can expect from his shoeshine boy.

I'm sorry to sound so snotty about composition teachers. God knows, I've been there too. In my first year I even assigned research papers in Freshman English. I didn't really want to but I did it anyway "to prepare students for their other courses." I prepared them all right. My method was the term paper. What I taught was alienation and servility. Now I try to *un*prepare students for their other courses. I only wish I were better at it.

The medium of schooling, by the way, covers much more than assignments, grading, rules and so on. If *how* you're taught exerts a profound effect, what about the physical environment? What does a classroom teach?

Consider how most classrooms are set up. Everyone is turned

toward the teacher and away from his classmates. You can't see the faces of those in front of you; you have to twist your neck to see the persons behind you. Frequently, seats are bolted to the floor or fastened together in rigid rows. This classroom, like the grading system, isolates students from each other and makes them passive receptacles. All the action, it implies, is at the front of the room.

What would be better? A circle? For a while I used to ask classes to sit in a circle (in rooms where we weren't bolted down). It was much better. But after a time I became depressed about it. It was still awkwardly geometrical; it was still my trip, and they were still dutifully following orders. I felt that if I told them to sit on each other's heads, they'd do it. So next semester I simply took a position in the second seat of the fourth row or thereabouts. I still do this most of the time. Some classes begin to move their chairs around, often within a matter of days, into a sort of loose, pleasant jumble, although they usually maintain a certain pious distance from me, leaving me at the center of a small but unmistakable magic circle. Occasionally, a class is unbelievably faithful to the traditional seating plan. They sit mournfully facing an empty altar and they sprain their necks trying to see me and the other students. I curse and mutter but they hold firm. It's almost as though they're saying, "Screw you, you bastard, you're going to have to *tell* us to move." And I swear to myself I won't. But I usually give in about half way through the semester.

But why those chairs at all? Why forty identical desk-chairs in a bleak, ugly room? Why should school have to remind us of jail or the army? (A rhetorical question, I'm afraid.) For that matter, why are there classrooms? Suppose we started over from scratch. What would be a good place to learn stress analysis? What would be a good place to study Zen? To learn about child development? To learn Spanish? To read poetry? You know, wherever I've seen classrooms, from UCLA to elementary schools in Texas, it's always the same stark chamber. The classrooms we have are a nationwide chain of mortuaries. What on earth are we trying to teach?

The scariest thing about a classroom is that it acts as a sort of psychological switch. You walk into a classroom; some things switch on in you and others switch off. All sorts of weird unreal things start to happen. Any teacher who has tried simply to be real in a classroom knows what I'm talking about. This is so hard to express . . . you walk in and everyone's face is a mask.

Last semester I had the best room yet. Because of overcrowding, one class was in an apartment living room on the edge of campus. The school did its well-meaning best to kill the room, boarding up the door to the kitchen and the can and literally filling the small room with long formica-topped grammar-school tables (the formica itself is a message: furniture has won; you ain't carving no initials in these desks, baby). For a while we floundered miserably but then things got better. Sometimes we sat in a big square. Sometimes we sat on top of the tables; once we crawled under them where it was dark and restful. Sometimes we'd pile up the tables and sit in a bunch on the carpet. Sometimes we'd sit on the grass outside. It was only a very small gain though. Given our conditioning and the overall college context, I could have held that class at the beach, at home, in the Avalon Ballroom. *I* would still be *holding* it; they would still want to rest limply in my hands—good natured, obedient students. Neither they nor I can get out from under our schooling so quickly as we might like.

I think that what we need is not to touch up or modernize classrooms but rather to eliminate them.

(Question for the audience: "Where would we learn?" Answer: "We'd manage.")

(3) "They Exploit and Enslave Students; They Petrify Society . . ."

Let me not be accused of ignoring "what's right with" our schools— to use the patriotic jargon. Schools are where you learn to read, write sort of, and do long division. Everyone knows about that. In college you learn about Pavlov, mitosis, Java Man and why we fought the Civil War. You may forget about Java Man but you get to keep your degree just the same, and it gets you a job. College is also where they discover new medicines, new kinds of plastic and new herbicides to use in Asia. But everybody knows all that. I want to return to the exploit-enslave-and-petrify part.

It's ironic. Radicals dream midnight police raids, or sit around over coffee and talk with glittering eyes about Repression—about those internment camps that are waiting empty. And all the time Miss Jones does her quiet thing with the kids in third grade.

People like to chat about the fascist threat or the communist threat. But their visions of repression are for the most part romantic and self indulgent: massacres, machine guns drowning out La Marseillaise. And in the meantime someone stops another tenth grader for a hall-pass check and notices that his T-shirt doesn't have a pocket on it. In the meantime the Bank of America hands out another round of high-school achievement awards. In the meantime I grade another set of quizzes.

God knows the real massacres continue. But the machine gun isn't really what is to be feared most in our civilized Western world. It just isn't needed all that much. The kids leave Miss Jones' class. And they go on to junior high and high school and college. And most of them will never need to be put in an internment camp. Because they're already there. Do you think I'm overstating? That's what's so frightening: we have the illusion that we're free.

In school we learn to be good little Americans—or Frenchmen—or Russians. We learn how to take the crap that's going to be shoveled on us all our lives. In school the state wraps up people's minds so tight that it can afford to leave their bodies alone.

Repression? You want to see victims of repression? Come look at most of the students at San Diego State College, where I work. They *want* to be told what to do. They don't know how to be free. They've given their will to this institution just as they'll continue to give their will to the institutions that engulf them in the future.

Schools exploit you because they tap your power and use it to perpetuate society's trip, while they teach you not to respect your own. They turn you away from yourself and toward the institutions around you. Schools petrify society because their method, characterized by coercion from the top down, works against any substantial social change. Students are coerced by teachers, who take orders from administrators, who do the bidding of those stalwarts of the status quo on the board of education or the board of trustees. Schools petrify society because students, through them, learn how to adjust unquestioningly to institutions and how to exercise their critical thought only within narrow limits prescribed by the authorities. In fact, as long as a heavy preponderance of a nation's citizens are "good students" and are in some way rewarded for their performance, then dissenters and radical thinkers are no threat and can be permitted to express their opinions relatively unmolested. In the United States, free expression, to the extent that we have it, is a luxury commodity made available by the high standard of living and by the efficient functioning of such disguised forms of repression as schooling.

Schools preserve the status quo in two complementary ways: by molding the young and by screening them. Today almost all of the positions of relative power in the United States are reserved for those who have completed the full sixteen-year treatment, and perhaps a little more. Persons who are unwilling to have their minds and bodies pushed around incessantly are less likely to get through and therefore tend to be screened out of the power centers; the persons who do get through are more likely to accept things as they are and to make their own contributions in "safe" areas. Thus corporations and government agencies insist that executive trainees have a bachelor's degree, often without specifying any particular major. The degree, therefore, doesn't represent any particular body of knowledge. What *does* it represent? A certain mentality.

It is true, though, that an increasing number of rebels and freaks are getting through (as well as a much larger number of essentially adjusted students who try to have the best of two worlds by pretending that they are rebels and freaks). The small but noisy student rebellion of recent years has had the effect of bringing to campus a number of drop-ins—dissidents who would not otherwise be there. One friend of mine is an excellent example. He belonged to a Trotskyist youth group as a teenager but threw that over in 1963 because the civil rights movement seemed to be accomplishing more than his youth group was. He had made a few futile attempts at college but realized that he had absolutely no interest in it and furthermore had no time for it. After a couple of years in Los Angeles, he disappeared into the Southern movement: Alabama, Mississippi, Georgia. For a while I lost track of him. Then, last year, I heard from him again; he had just enrolled in San Francisco State College—where the action is. He is typical of a growing minority of students; he may do more or less what's needed to stay in school but he is more than willing to risk being expelled or failed out (two years ago he was risking his life). It is unlikely that college will disarm him.

As the tensions in our society work their way up to the surface, some overt rebellion appears in many settings; certainly it appears in schools, which offer at least a meeting place and staging ground for young middle-class rebels. May it grow in good health. But, as our college presidents are fond of pointing out, the great majority—the great silent majority—are there "not to make trouble but to get an education" (for "education," read "degree").

What about this majority? What is the mentality which employers depend upon our school system to deliver? What is most likely to emerge from the sixteen-year molding and screening process?

Well, a "good citizen" of sorts—isn't that the way they put it on report cards? Thoroughly schooled and ready for GE or IBM or the State Department, the graduate is a skilled, neat, disciplined worker with just enough initiative to carry out fairly complicated assignments but not so much initiative that he will seriously question the assignment itself. He is affably but fiercely competitive with his peers and he is submissive to his superiors. In fact, as long as he has some respect from his peers and subordinates, he is willing to be almost naked of dignity in the eyes of his superiors; there is very little shit he will not eat if there is something to be gained by it. In asserting himself he is moderate, even timid—except when he exercises the power of a great institution, when he himself is the superior, when he puts on some kind of real or figurative uniform. At that point he is likely to assume the sacerdotal mask that his teachers wore. At that point—when he becomes official—his jaw hardens.

This college graduate is positively addicted to rules of all sorts at every level. In fact, should he help to form some club or group, it will probably have by-laws and officers and will follow parliamentary procedure. Even in games—cards, Monopoly, whatever—he is likely to have a passionate respect for the rules and to get bent out of shape if their sanctity is violated.

Ever since his gold-and-silver-star days he has been hooked on status and achievement symbol systems. He has a hunter's eye for the nuances of such systems in his work, in his leisure life and in the society at large. He carries a series of grade-point averages in his head and they rise or fall with an invitation to lunch, the purchase of a Triumph TR-2, a friendly punch on the arm from his ski instructor or the disrespectful attitude of a bank teller.

Since grade school, also, he has known how to become mildly enthusiastic about narrow choices without ever being tempted to venture rebelliously out of the field of choice assigned to him. His political world, for example, is peopled with Nixons and Humphreys; its frontiers are guarded by McCarthys and Reagans. He himself has had a taste of politics: he was elected sophomore class president in college on a platform that advocated extending snack-bar hours in the evening. Like Auden's "Unknown Citizen": when there is peace, he is for peace; when there is war, he goes. He doesn't expect a wide range to choose from in politics. His chief arena of choice is the marketplace, where he can choose enthusiastically among forty or fifty varieties of cigarettes, without, incidentally, ever being tempted to choose the one variety that will turn him on. His drugs are still likely to be the orthodox ones, the consciousness-contractors: liquor, tranquilizers, a little TV.

He yearns for more free time but finds himself uncomfortable with very much of it. His vacations tend to be well structured. From time to time he feels oppressed and would like to "break out" but he isn't sure what that means. Leaving his family? Starting his own business? Buying a boat? He's not sure.

Let me stop at this point. There is, thank God, a limit to the meaningfulness of such a stereotyped characterization. It hits home in those areas where the college graduate has literally been stereotyped by his upbringing and by the rigid matrix of his schools. But it leaves out what makes him one individual, what makes him real. Doesn't he have a self byond the stereotype? Isn't he unique—splendid—a center of existence? Isn't he, to use Timothy Leary's phrase, a two-billion-year-old carrier of the Light? Of course. But who sees it? His self has been scared into hiding. The stereotype that has been made of him hides his uniqueness, his inner life, his majesty from our eyes and, to a great extent from his own as well. He's got a sure A in Citizenship but he's failing in self-realization (a subject not too likely to appear in the curriculum).

Let's understand, when we consider this college graduate, that harm has been done not only to him but to society as well. There may, after all, be some of us who assume that dehumanization and standardization are no more than the price that an individual pays in return for a smoothly functioning society. But is that true? Is this man really what's good for society?

Social change is not just the radical's hang-up. It's a means of adaptation, of self-preservation. Now, as our technology and our environment change with increasing rapidity, as we acquire ever more awesome resources and more bewildering problems, we need the capacity to recreate our society continually rather than be victimized by it. This, of course, is the sort of thing that gets said a great deal nowadays but what doesn't get said is that we will not meet this need for rebirth without giving up what we now call schooling. A crisis in civilization—and we are in the midst of several—*demands* the radical thought, the radical will and the profound self-confidence which have been schooled out of our college-educated institutional man. His narrow vision and his submissive conformity aren't good for society; they paralyze it. They are a curse on it.

(4) "They Make Democracy Unlikely"

Our schools make democracy unlikely because they rob the people, who are supposed to be sovereign, of their sense of power and of their ability to will meaningful institutional changes.

The democratic ideal—to which even the most conservative college trustees usually give lip service—means government of, by and for the people. It means power in the hands of the people. Our schools, however, remain less suited to this ideal than to an authoritarian society; they are more effective in teaching obedience than in fostering freedom. Our textbooks may teach one kind of political system but the method by which our schools operate teaches another. And the method wins out over the textbooks overwhelmingly.

A more substantial degree of democracy will become likely only when we understand that political freedom is not merely a constitutional matter; it's also a state of mind, which can be either nurtured or blighted in school.

I don't mean to ignore the reasons that already abound to explain that immense gap between our ideals of democracy and the system we see operating. Some people, for example, argue that democracy only works well in small political units and that centralized democratic government of 200 million persons is just not possible. Others insist that the people are and will always remain too stupid and ill-informed to make political decisions. Then there's the very persuasive socialist argument: democracy is just not compatible with capitalism. Even if you grant the socialist proposition, though, the question remains: is democracy compatible with socialism? I think it could be, more or less—but there are problems involved that are not normally recognized in this kind of analysis.

A socialist country where schooling is standardized and coercive might well, in time, develop an electorate as dismal as ours *even though* its constitution provided the most extensive political freedom for the individual and even though it had eliminated class exploitation in the traditional sense. In fact, the resources adhering to a powerful socialist government create a very special danger in this area. That's why the growing student power movement has the greatest importance politically. The more that political radicalism comes to include educational radicalism, the more nearly attainable democratic government will be.

Capitalist or socialist, a democracy cannot possibly function if its citizens are educated to be clever robots. The way to educate children for democracy is to let them do it—that doesn't mean allowing them to practice empty forms, to make pretend decisions or to vote on trivia; it means that they participate in the real decisions that affect them. You learn democracy in school not by defining it or by simulating it but by doing it.

If students and teachers ran their own schools, it would do more for democracy than all the government classes ever taught. But it would have to be just that: true participation in running the schools. Not those little make-believe student governments which govern in about the same way that baby's toy steering wheel drives daddy's car. Not even anything like those "faculty senates," which retain the right to create college policy as long as they don't abuse that right by exercising it.

Also, in considering the effect of schooling on democracy, it's wise to think not only about the overall academic decision-making process but also about day-to-day classroom experience as well. That's at the very heart of the problem. It's in the classroom where you learn that happiness is submission and where you grow used to authoritarianism and coercion. It's in the classroom where you learn how to follow orders mindlessly and how to surrender your sovereignty to an institution.

Incidentally, in discussing this question, I've often heard the objection that teachers legitimately possess authority by virtue of their knowledge and that, therefore, democracy is out of place in the classroom. This argument is a favorite with teachers, so it deserves some attention.

It's true that many teachers possess authority in one particular sense of the word but that does not entitle them to authority in every sense of the word. A teacher's authority rests in his special knowledge or ability, not in his power over students. I may be, say, an authority in ancient history but what has that to do with authority in the sense of a right to enforce obedience, to reward and punish? And the fact that I work for the state of California doesn't amplify my academic authority. If I'm sound in my analysis of Athenian society, the state of California adds nothing. If I'm all wrong the state of California doesn't make me less wrong.

Democracy in school doesn't mean that a class votes on whether two and two make four, even though that seems to be the fear of some teachers. Suppose, for example, my entire history class insists that Rome fell because of its sexual laxity. Suppose we argue. I give my reasons and they give theirs. Then, in desperation, I try to impress them by detailing my academic background but they still insist that they're right. In this (unlikely) situation what relevance would grading have? What would it add to my true authority if I were able to pass, fail, expel, what have you? My value to a class is that I can be of some kind of assistance to them. What they make of it is up to them. I'm a teacher not a cop.[2] Democracy in school doesn't mean that we vote on what's true; it means that education isn't anything which is *done* to somebody.

(5) "Authority Addicts"

It's time to say a few kind words about our coercive schools. They do—more or less—solve an existential problem. They shape time for

2. One counter-argument might be that the authority to pass and fail is necessary, not to coerce knowledge, but to determine a student's fitness to enter a given field or profession. For a discussion of this question and of grading in general, see "A Young Person's Guide to the Grading System" [In Jerry Farber, *The Student as Nigger*, pp. 67–73—Editors.]

us and thus give some meaning, if not to our life, then at least to some segments of it. Do you know what I mean? You study off and on for a final exam, slowly building tension as the date approaches. The night before, you get no sleep; you're in a strange world of glaring lights, notes, coffee cups, piled up books. Whatever other worries you might have are suspended. This task takes precedence; it's something to hold on to. When you approach the classroom, your exhaustion disappears in a fresh wave of tension and nervous energy. This all has to be important, has to be meaningful; anything you stay up all night for and get this worked up about has to mean something. And when you finish the bluebooks, they rest substantial on your desk. It wasn't all a dream; you've got the bluebooks and, eventually, the grade to prove it.

Courses may be pointless and uninteresting. The data may go through you like mineral oil. But at least it is some kind of challenge. And while you're involved in all this, time is off *your* hands and rests in *theirs*—the authorities'. Should you not be attending school, you may feel that you're pissing away time—days and weeks; you may begin to feel very uncomfortable. On your own, you have to face the responsibility for how you spend time. But in school you don't. What they make you do may obviously be a waste but at least the responsibility isn't charged to your account. School in this respect is, once again, like the army or jail. Once you're in, you may have all kinds of problems but freedom isn't one of them.

After you leave school and get a job, you'll find you *need* the job just as you learned to need school. You'll remain an existential minor who needs trustees to spend his time for him.

The schools we have are a cop-out. Why not face the responsibility for what we do with our time? And if we need structures to inform our time, why not find more congenial, more human ones. Why not surround ourselves with tailor-made educational structures rather than torture ourselves to fit the Procrustean set-up we have now.

Besides, things are changing. The leisure-time explosion is removing even the solace of constant work. Leisure calls on the ability to accept autonomy, to be content with internal justification for what you do. The more leisure we have, the more we need to be able to perceive our own needs and then to follow them for no other reason than that we want to.

So where are we headed? Are we going to face the existential problem or run from it? Will we let time fall on our very own hands without trying to kill it. Or will we continue to look for authorities to take the burden of our freedom from us. As we free ourselves from work in the traditional sense, we have the opportunity to lift our heads up and to look around; we become more free to create our lives rather than undergo them.

Drugs, by the way, have some relationship both to school and to the increase in leisure time. A growing number of people have found that smoking a little weed helps them to appreciate the possibilities of unstructured, uninstitutionalized time. Acid and the other psychedelic drugs typically open up possibilities beyond school and beyond the job (dropping out is always dropping *in* to something else). The educational reform movement probably owes a good deal to students and teachers whose drug experiences have made them impatient with the miserable use that schools make of their time.

(6) "If It Weren't Compulsory . . ."

If we want our children locked up all day until they're sixteen, let's at least be honest about it and stop trying to pass imprisonment off as education.

Say, for example, that a mother and father would like their eight-year-old boy out of the house all day and also off the streets. Then I guess they will want there to be some place for him to go. Call it a youth center, a postgraduate nursery or a daytime internment camp. But why does it have to be a school? It should have plenty of room and lots of variety: places to be alone if you want, places to play games if you want, places to build things, and places to learn how to read and do sums—*if you want.*

Learning isn't a duty that we must be flogged into performing; it's our birthright, our very human specialty and joy. Places to learn are everywhere. So are reasons to learn. All we need, occasionally, is a little help from our friends.

We don't need compulsory schooling to force us to read. There are good reasons to read and things all around us that want to be read. And if someone should choose to pass his life illiterate, there are other communications media accessible to him. He'll probably make out fine. He may even be able to teach the rest of us some things that print hides.

It would be well if we stopped lying to ourselves about what compulsory schooling does for our children. It temporarily imprisons them; it standardizes them; it intimidates them. If that's what we want, we should admit it.

There's not much point in going on about this. If you've somehow missed reading A. S. Neill's *Summerhill,* you ought to go out and get it.

Incidentally, with compulsory schooling eliminated, there is no reason to assume that most parents will send their children to public internment centers during the day, or that learning itself will be as dependent upon public institutions as it now is. With compulsory education and all the related red tape out of the way, small groups of parents should be able to make their own arrangements to care for their children and even to satisfy the children's desire to learn. Some areas of learning—nuclear physics, for example—require heavy financial support. But many other areas do not; they provide opportunities for those who want to learn or teach to bypass official institutions. Furthermore, advances in computers, in information retrieval and in communication should soon make it much easier and cheaper than it is now to learn outside of public schools. Technological developments should, before long, give a home resources that are presently available only to a large and well-funded school. Sooner or later, if a child (or adult) wants to learn more about, say, snakes or jet engines, he should be able to tune in, at home, to books, films, learning computers and so on, which he can use as much or as little as he wants. Naturally, if the child chooses not to use the computers and books, that should be his unrestricted right. What I'm getting at is that parents should, before long, be able to develop a formidable alternative to our system of compulsory public elementary schools. As for older children—adolescents—the whole matter is less a parental responsibility and more their own.

(7) "If Schools Were Autonomous and Were Run by the People in Them . . ."

Learning is not something that is done to you.

Suppose we agree that there must be something better than our schools, something better suited to our human potential, our political ideals and our accelerating technology. What then? It is exactly at this point that there is a temptation to make what I believe is the basic educational blunder: Having tried and convicted the present educational system, one then works out in detail his own educational utopia—setting up a blueprint that covers matters such as curriculum, textbooks, administration policy, student-teacher ratio, classroom construction and so on.

From my point of view, however, a good school can't be described very clearly in advance because one essential characteristic of a good school is *the freedom to establish its own direction.* In fact, there may not even *be* such a thing as a good school within our present conception of what "school" means.

To say that learning is not something that is done to you has meaning on more than one level. With respect to the school as a whole, it means autonomy. There should be no dictatorial governing board or other body above the school making its decisions for it. If we are going to continue our policy of public education, this means that the people and their elected representatives will have to accept a new and radical policy: that they must pay for schools without controlling them. What happens, therefore, on a state university campus or on a junior high school campus would be decided neither by the legislature nor by the governor nor by any board of regents or board of education nor by any chancellor or superintendent of schools but only by the persons participating in the school itself. It is true that there would be a kind of power implicit in the fact that the state or community could refuse to pay for the school or could reduce its funds. But that would be the limit. To the extent that a state or city wanted to have a school, it would have to pay for it and leave it alone. Hopefully, the idea of an externally controlled school will in time become a contradiction in terms.

Autonomy in schools would almost certainly create much greater diversity—something that should be very good for us as individuals and as a society. As it is, almost all of our schools, at any given level, are amazingly alike. Given the way they are governed, this is not surprising. But what if schools were autonomous? Naturally there would be standardizing forces. The overall needs of society—the proliferating communications networks—a considerable degree of cultural cohesion—these would tend to restrain diversity in schools. But still, if schools were autonomous, they would show much more variety than they do now. Schooling arrangements in a given neighborhood would more closely reflect the character of the neighborhood. The country's colleges would offer a much wider and more interesting choice. There would be more experimentation and consequently a greater opportunity for one school to learn from the varied experiences of others. Schools might, in fact, begin to look more like a free enterprise system—but an educational rather than an economic one (free enterprise has always made much more sense to me in connection with the production of ideas than with the production of automobiles).

Also, if schools were autonomous, I would expect our rigid system of educational levels to weaken. There might well be large centers where persons of all ages would learn from each other and where the structural divisions would be based on areas of learning rather than on age. School might emerge less as a molding and screening process that usurps the first third of a person's life than as a continuing opportunity for certain kinds of learning and group activity.

Ideas about curriculum would also become much less rigid, since curriculum would be determined not by centralized authority but by the learners' and teachers' own awareness of what is relevant and necessary to them and their society. On one campus you might find a curriculum in light; on another a school of ecstatic pharmacology. Radical movements would develop through schools, not against them. The departmental concept would probably fade. The concept of "curriculum" itself would perhaps become dated.

It's not my intention to predict everything that would result from autonomy in schools. My basic point is simply that autonomy is necessary if we want schools to become places where you can learn without being deadened and intimidated in the process and where adaptive social change is fostered rather than prevented.

To say that learning is not something that is done to you implies the need for more than just autonomy. *Within* the school it means that everyone must have a voice in the decisions that affect him. This kind of arrangement—democracy—doesn't eliminate discord but it does put the responsibility for a school on all of the people in it.

I can't see any reason why either students or teachers should be shut out of the decision-making process. In fact, the supposed conflict between students and teachers doesn't itself seem to be a basic one; it arises rather out of the coercive and judgmental powers that have been held by teachers and out of the slave role that has been forced on students. In an autonomous and noncoercive school, I would expect most disagreements to cut across this tenuous boundary in other directions.

I hesitate to go on about students and teachers. The very categories need to be questioned. The most meaningful distinction may be no more than an economic one: who gets paid for what he does? And when we all get paid for what we do, that distinction will disappear. Suppose that today I teach gymnastics, tomorrow I study Arabic and the next day I participate in an encounter group. In which category do I belong?

Administrator is still another term. Right now it's in bad repute with many of us because administrators are there to do the bidding of some external authority. In an autonomous and democratic school, *administration* would just be people running their own school. A high school administrator, for example, could be either a student or a teacher; he would be more or less a blackboard monitor on a somewhat larger scale. But this category also would be blurred at the very least.

To prevent education from being victimization, it will not be enough to have autonomy and democracy for the school as a whole. One would also want individual groups within a school to be free to develop their own learning structures without being pushed around and standardized by some central administration. However, I want to avoid falling into the trap I described earlier; I want to avoid trying to blueprint an educational utopia in advance. Self-government in practice cannot help but fall short of an ideal and therefore admits of endless approaches. If schools can serve as workshops in self-government, it will be both likely and valuable that they be diverse in this respect.

If schools are free, some of them may choose to renounce a part of their freedom. There may be students who prefer to be dictated to. For all I know there may always be students who want to be graded daily and threatened with probation, dismissal and so on, just as there may always be persons who want to be flogged and will no doubt always find other persons willing to do it. It is certainly not my wish to prevent them.

The freedom I talk about, incidentally, is not merely a matter of "academic" freedom. Schools are not just learning places but communities as well. Many schools are communities in the full sense of the word: people don't just go to them; they live in them. And, in the future, the distinction between "school" and "community" is likely to be much vaguer than it is now. Rochdale, for example, in Toronto, may be a sign of what is to come.

Rochdale is a number of things. To begin with, it's a new 18-story building. The people who live and pay rent in it own it and run it. For some of them it's a very loosely structured place to learn—a sort of experimental college. For others it's just a place to live. There are, furthermore, people who participate in educational activities of Rochdale but who don't live there. Rochdale is also a continuing problem—a place where there is no one to blame things on, where people have to improvise their own structures and to decide what to do with their freedom. Here is a paragraph, titled "The Secret," from one of their pamphlets:

> The secret of dealing with the confusion and uncertainty of Rochdale is to use "we" in place of "they" when referring to the operations of the College. For example, say "what we are going to do with the 17th floor terrace" rather than "what are they going to do, etc." This simple trick clarifies many otherwise ambiguous problems and helps eliminate flatulence.

I hope Rochdale thrives. And even more I hope the idea spreads.[3]

(8) "The Power to Say 'No' "

The people who control colleges are fond of pointing out to students that higher education is a privilege. The implication is that if they don't behave, the privilege will be withdrawn. Similarly, in high school the ultimate threat is expulsion. School is supposed to be some kind of favor that society grants you. The condition for continuing to receive this favor is that you accept it on society's terms.

Sweat shop owners used to tell their workers more or less the same thing. It's astonishing that workers swallowed that line for so long. And it's equally astonishing that most students continue to see schooling as a privilege rather than as a transaction in which they happen to be getting a rotten deal.

When you go to school, you do society an enormous favor; you give it the opportunity to mold you in its image, stunting and deadening you in the process. What you get in return is access to a certain income bracket and the material comforts that go with it. But think what you've given up. Other animals have much of their nature born in them. But you were born with the freedom to learn, to change, to transcend yourself, to create your life—that's your human birthright. In school you sell it very cheap.

I have already tried (in Notes 3 and 4) to show that this rotten bargain isn't even good for society, that it forestalls necessary social change. Unfortunately, the dying part of society, which controls schooling, is also the part least likely to understand the need for profound change. It is the students—the not entirely socialized—who must feel the need for change and who, in trying to transform the society in which they live, become the victims of its self-protective rage.

The power that students have is simply the power not to be students, to refuse a bad bargain, as workers have frequently done—to say "no." If students have power, it is because they have something society needs very badly. Student power is made possible by the dying society's need to remain alive—to preserve itself through its children. Think how our institutions feed on the unformed future. Think even how individuals—those aging businessmen on a college

3. If you're interested in free schools, you ought to read a beautiful essay by Dennis Lee, "Getting To Rochdale," in *The University Game* (Toronto, 1968). The essay originally appeared in *This Magazine Is about Schools* (Winter, 1968).

board of trustees—clutch at immortality by putting their trip on the young. Society *needs* students to retain its identity; they are the only future it has. For this reason, students can demand freedom from exploitation and can get that freedom. They can insist that the continuity they provide society be one that is achieved through rebirth rather than through petrification.

There are a multitude of approaches that students can take toward changing schools. But the one that offers the most hope is the strike or boycott. It is more than a gesture, more than a pressure tactic. It cuts right to the heart of the problem. It refuses a bad bargain; it puts the future on strike. Requests can be denied or put off. Demonstrations can be broken up and the protesters put in jail. But a strike is not really vulnerable to force. When Governor Reagan of California recently promised to keep San Francisco State College open at the point of a bayonet if need be, he failed to understand both the limitations of the bayonet and the power of the student revolution.

High school students are in a more difficult position but this has not stopped them from beginning to use boycotts as well as other forms of noncooperation in order to change their schools. A few high school troublemakers can be expelled or disciplined in other ways. But what does it mean to expel most of the students in a school— especially when you've already compelled them to be there? Also, because these students are so regimented and because they are actually compelled to attend, a high school strike, though very difficult to bring about, is an even more dramatic and powerful action than is a college strike.

I have not yet said anything about the possibility of faculty-student cooperation in changing the nature of school. Such cooperation is difficult; most faculty members are still very much caught up in their roles and, even though they have their own reasons to want to change things, are reluctant to make common cause with students. Faculty, furthermore, are very hesitant to engage in the kind of forceful actions that might endanger their jobs or even their chances for promotion, tenure and so on. Still, there are enough instances of student-faculty cooperation to keep this an important possibility even at present. In order, though, for such cooperation to advance rather than impede student progress, it is essential that students don't wait around for faculty support and that they don't allow professional timidity to rub off on them.

The American Federation of Teachers represents a relatively militant segment of faculty; they have shown themselves, at San Franciso State in particular, to be a possible ally for the student movement. But it must be remembered that the AFT chose to join the students in striking at S.F. State in great part because it was an excellent opportunity to push their own drive for collective bargaining. AFT militancy—to the extent that they possess it—is directed toward rather limited goals. It would be a mistake to assume that the majority of AFT members, in high school or college, are stalwart supporters of the student liberation movement or even that they understand it.

In the long run, if students and teachers can outgrow their feudal relationship, they do indeed have a common cause: the freeing of schools from domination by outside forces. Perhaps the best thing students can do with respect to faculty is, first of all, to emphasize that common cause and to fully support faculty moves for greater self determination and, second, to work ceaselessly to educate teachers, to show them what's lacking in school as it is and to show them what education could be.

Illich shares with Farber a deep concern about the damage schools do; but whereas Farber favors the transformation of the school, Illich hopes to break up the monopoly schools now have as social and economic legitimizers. This "deschooling" of society—that is, downgrading schools as the primary avenue to personal advancement and social acceptability—is perhaps the most radical proposal suggested in this set of commentaries.

Illich's arguments challenge us to ask: Is schooling the central myth of our culture? Are we already seeing, as Cremin indicates, that other agencies more powerfully mold our education? And perhaps the most important question of this section—what *should* be the role of schooling in American life?

THE ALTERNATIVE
TO SCHOOLING
Ivan Illich

For generations we have tried to make the world a better place by providing more and more schooling, but so far the endeavor has failed. What we have learned instead is that forcing all children to climb an open-ended education ladder cannot enhance equality but must favor the individual who starts out earlier, healthier, or better prepared; that enforced instruction deadens for most people the will for independent learning; and that knowledge treated as a commodity, delivered in packages, and accepted as private property once it is acquired, must always be scarce.

In response, critics of the educational system are now proposing strong and unorthodox remedies that range from the voucher plan, which would enable each person to buy the education of his choice on an open market, to shifting the responsibility for education from the school to the media and to apprenticeship on the job. Some individuals foresee that the school will have to be disestablished just

Ivan Illich, "The Alternative to Schooling," *Saturday Review*, June 19, 1971, pp. 44ff. Copyright 1971 Saturday Review, Inc. Reprinted by permission.

as the church was disestablished all over the world during the last two centuries. Other reformers propose to replace the universal school with various new systems that would, they claim, better prepare everybody for life in modern society. These proposals for new educational institutions fall into three broad categories: the reformation of the classroom within the school system; the dispersal of free schools throughout society; and the transformation of all society into one huge classroom. But these three approaches—the reformed classroom, the free school, and the worldwide classroom— represent three stages in a proposed escalation of education in which each step threatens more subtle and more pervasive social control than the one it replaces.

I believe that the disestablishment of the school has become inevitable and that this end of an illusion should fill us with hope. But I also believe that the end of the "age of schooling" could usher in the epoch of the global schoolhouse that would be distinguishable only in name from a global madhouse or global prison in which education, correction, and adjustment become synonymous. I therefore believe that the breakdown of the school forces us to look beyond its imminent demise and to face fundamental alternatives in education. Either we can work for fearsome and potent new educational devices that teach about a world which progressively becomes more opaque and forbidding for man, or we can set the conditions for a new era in which technology would be used to make society more simple and transparent, so that all men can once again know the facts and use the tools that shape their lives. In short, we can disestablish schools or we can deschool culture.

In order to see clearly the alternatives we face, we must first distinguish education from schools, which means separating the humanistic intent of the teacher from the impact of the invariant structure of the school. This hidden structure constitutes a course of instruction that stays forever beyond the control of the teacher or of his school board. It conveys indelibly the message that only through schooling can an individual prepare himself for adulthood in society, that what is not taught in school is of little value, and that what is learned outside of school is not worth knowing. I call it the hidden curriculum of schooling, because it constitutes the unalterable framework of the system, within which all changes in the curriculum are made.

The hidden curriculum is always the same regardless of school or place. It requires all children of a certain age to assemble in groups of about thirty, under the authority of a certified teacher, for some 500 or 1,000 or more hours each year. It doesn't matter whether the curriculum is designed to teach the principles of fascism, liberalism, Catholicism, or socialism; or whether the purpose of the school is to produce Soviet or United States citizens, mechanics, or doctors. It makes no difference whether the teacher is authoritarian or permissive, whether he imposes his own creed or teaches students to think for themselves. What is important is that students learn that education is valuable when it is acquired in the school through a graded process of consumption; that the degree of success the individual will enjoy in society depends on the amount of learning he consumes; and that learning *about* the world is more valuable than learning *from* the world.

It must be clearly understood that the hidden curriculum translates learning from an activity into a commodity—for which the school monopolizes the market. In all countries knowledge is regarded as the first necessity for survival, but also as a form of currency more liquid than rubles or dollars. We have become accustomed, through Karl Marx's writings, to speak about the alienation of the worker from his work in a class society. We must now recognize the estrangement of man from his learning when it becomes the product of a service profession and he becomes the consumer.

The more learning an individual consumes, the more "knowledge stock" he acquires. The hidden curriculum therefore defines a new class structure for society within which the large consumers of knowledge—those who have acquired large quantities of knowledge stock—enjoy special privileges, high income, and access to the more powerful tools of production. This kind of knowledge-capitalism has been accepted in all industrialized societies and establishes a rationale for the distribution of jobs and income. (This point is especially important in the light of the lack of correspondence between schooling and occupational competence established in studies such as Ivar Berg's *Education and Jobs: The Great Training Robbery*.)

The endeavor to put all men through successive stages of enlightenment is rooted deeply in alchemy, the Great Art of the waning Middle Ages. John Amos Comenius, a Moravian bishop, self-styled Pansophist, and pedagogue, is rightly considered one of the founders of the modern schools. He was among the first to propose seven or twelve grades of compulsory learning. In his *Magna Didactica*, he described schools as devices to "teach everybody everything" and outlined a blueprint for the assembly-line production of knowledge, which according to his method would make education cheaper and better and make growth into full humanity possible for all. But

Comenius was noι only an early efficiency expert, he was an alchemist who adopted the technical language of his craft to describe the art of rearing children. The alchemist sought to refine base elements by leading their distilled spirits through twelve stages of successive enlightenment, so that for their own and all the world's benefit they might be transmuted into gold. Of course, alchemists failed no matter how often they tried, but each time their "science" yielded new reasons for their failure, and they tried again.

Pedagogy opened a new chapter in the history of Ars Magna. Education became the search for an alchemic process that would bring forth a new type of man, who would fit into an environment created by scientific magic. But, no matter how much each generation spent on its schools, it always turned out that the majority of people were unfit for enlightenment by this process and had to be discarded as unprepared for life in a man-made world.

Educational reformers who accept the idea that schools have failed fall into three groups. The most respectable are certainly the great masters of alchemy who promise better schools. The most seductive are popular magicians, who promise to make every kitchen into an alchemic lab. The most sinister are the new Masons of the Universe, who want to transform the entire world into one huge temple of learning. Notable among today's masters of alchemy are certain research directors employed or sponsored by the large foundations who believe that schools, if they could somehow be improved, could also become economically more feasible than those that are now in trouble, and simultaneously could sell a larger package of services. Those who are concerned primarily with the curriculum claim that it is outdated or irrelevant. So the curriculum is filled with new packaged courses on African Culture, North American Imperialism, Women's Lib, Pollution, or the Consumer Society. Passive learning is wrong—it is indeed—so we graciously allow students to decide what and how they want to be taught. Schools are prison houses. Therefore, principals are authorized to approve teachouts, moving the school desks to a roped-off Harlem street. Sensitivity training becomes fashionable. So, we import group therapy into the classroom. School, which was supposed to teach everybody everything, now becomes all things to all children.

Other critics emphasize that schools make inefficient use of modern science. Some would administer drugs to make it easier for the instructor to change the child's behavior. Others would transform school into a stadium for educational gaming. Still others would electrify the classroom. If they are simplistic disciples of McLuhan, they replace blackboards and textbooks with multimedia happenings; if they follow Skinner, they claim to be able to modify behavior more efficiently than old-fashioned classroom practitioners can.

Most of these changes have, of course, some good effects. The experimental schools have fewer truants. Parents do have a greater feeling of participation in a decentralized district. Pupils assigned by their teacher to an apprenticeship, do often turn out more competent than those who stay in the classroom. Some children do improve their knowledge of Spanish in the language lab because they prefer playing with the knobs of a tape recorder to conversations with their Puerto Rican peers. Yet all these improvements operate within predictably narrow limits, since they leave the hidden curriculum of school intact.

Some reformers would like to shake loose from the hidden curriculum, but they rarely succeed. Free schools that lead to further free schools produce a mirage of freedom, even though the chain of attendance is frequently interrupted by long stretches of loafing. Attendance through seduction inculcates the need for educational treatment more persuasively than the reluctant attendance enforced by a truant officer. Permissive teachers in a padded classroom can easily render their pupils impotent to survive once they leave.

Learning in these schools often remains nothing more than the acquisition of socially valued skills defined, in this instance, by the consensus of a commune rather than by the decree of a school board. New presbyter is but old priest writ large.

Free schools, to be truly free, must meet two conditions: First, they must be run in a way to prevent the reintroduction of the hidden curriculum of graded attendance and certified students studying at the feet of certified teachers. And, more importantly, they must provide a framework in which all participants—staff and pupils—can free themselves from the hidden foundations of a schooled society. The first condition is frequently incorporated in the stated aims of a free school. The second condition is only rarely recognized, and is difficult to state as the goal of a free school.

It is useful to distinguish between the hidden curriculum, which I have described, and the occult foundations of schooling. The hidden curriculum is a ritual that can be considered the official initiation into modern society, institutionally established through the school. It is the purpose of this ritual to hide from its participants the contradictions between the myth of an egalitarian society and the class-conscious reality it certifies. Once they are recognized as such, rituals lose their power, and this is what is now beginning to happen to schooling. But there are certain fundamental assumptions about growing up—the occult foundations—which now find their expression in the ceremonial of schooling, and which could easily be reinforced by what free schools do.

Among these assumptions is what Peter Schrag calls the "immigration syndrome," which impels us to treat all people as if they were newcomers who must go through a naturalization process. Only certified consumers of knowledge are admitted to citizenship. Men are not born equal, but are made equal through gestation by Alma Mater.

The rhetoric of all schools states that they form a man for the future, but they do not release him for his task before he has developed a high level of tolerance to the ways of his elders: education *for* life rather than *in* everyday life. Few free schools can avoid doing precisely this. Nevertheless they are among the most important centers from which a new life-style radiates, not because of the effect their graduates will have but, rather, because elders who choose to bring up their children without the benefit of properly ordained teachers frequently belong to a radical minority and because their preoccupation with the rearing of their children sustains them in their new style.

The most dangerous category of educational reformer is one who argues that knowledge can be produced and sold more effectively on an open market than on one controlled by the school. These people argue that most skills can be easily acquired from skill-models if the learner is truly interested in their acquisition; that individual entitlements can provide a more equal purchasing power for education. They demand a careful separation of the process by which it is measured and certified. These seem to me obvious statements. But it would be a fallacy to believe that the establishment of a free market for knowledge would constitute a radical alternative in education.

The establishment of a free market would indeed abolish what I have previously called the hidden cirriculum of present schooling—its age-specific attendance at a graded curriculum. Equally, a free market would at first give the appearance of counteracting what I have called the occult foundations of a schooled society: the "immigration syndrome," the institutional monopoly of teaching, and the ritual of linear initiation. But at the same time a free market in education would provide the alchemist with innumerable hidden hands to fit each man into the multiple, tight little niches a more complex technocracy can provide.

Many decades of reliance on schooling has turned knowledge into a commodity, a marketable staple of a special kind. Knowledge is now regarded simultaneously as a first necessity and also as society's most precious currency. (The transformation of knowledge into a commodity is reflected in a corresponding transformation of language. Words that formerly functioned as verbs are becoming nouns that designate possessions. Until recently dwelling and learning and even healing designated activities. They are now usually conceived as commodities or services to be delivered. We talk about the manufacture of housing or the delivery of medical care. Men are no longer regarded fit to house or heal themselves. In such a society people come to believe that professional services are more valuable than personal care. Instead of learning how to nurse grandmother, the teen-ager learns to picket the hospital that does not admit her.) This attitude could easily survive the disestablishment of school, just as affiliation with a church remained a condition for office long after the adoption of the First Amendment. It is even more evident that test batteries measuring complex knowledge-packages could easily survive the disestablishment of school—and with this would go the compulsion to obligate everybody to acquire a minimum package in the knowledge stock. The scientific measurement of each man's worth and the alchemic dream of each man's "educability to his full humanity" would finally coincide. Under the appearance of a "free" market, the global village would turn into an environmental womb where pedagogic therapists control the complex navel by which each man is nourished.

At present, schools limit the teacher's competence to the classroom. They prevent him from claiming man's whole life as his domain. The demise of school will remove this restriction and give a semblance of legitimacy to the life-long pedagogical invasion of everybody's privacy. It will open the way for a scramble for "knowledge" on a free market, which would lead us toward the paradox of a vulgar, albeit seemingly egalitarian, meritocracy. Unless the concept of knowledge is transformed, the disestablishment of school will lead to a wedding between a growing meritocratic system that separates learning from certification and a society committed to provide therapy for each man until he is ripe for the gilded age.

For those who subscribe to the technocratic ethos, whatever is technically possible must be made available at least to a few whether they want it or not. Neither the privation nor the frustration of the majority counts. If cobalt treatment is possible, then the city of Tegucigalpa needs one apparatus in each of its two major hospitals, at a cost that would free an important part of the population of Honduras from parasites. If supersonic speeds are possible, then it must speed the travel of some. If the flight to Mars can be conceived, then a rationale must be found to make it appear a necessity. In the technocratic ethos poverty is modernized: Not only are old alternatives closed off by new monopolies, but the lack of necessities is also compounded by a growing spread between those services that are technologically feasible and those that are in fact available to the majority.

A teacher turns "educator" when he adopts this technocratic ethos. He then acts as if education were a technological enterprise designed to make man fit into whatever environment the "progress" of science creates. He seems blind to the evidence that constant obsolescence of all commodities comes at a high price: the mounting cost of training people to know about them. He seems to forget that the rising cost of tools is purchased at a high price in education: They decrease the labor intensity of the economy, make learning on the job impossible or, at best, a privilege for a few. All over the world the cost of educating men for society rises faster than the productivity of the entire economy, and fewer people have a sense of intelligent participation in the commonweal.

A revolution against those forms of privilege and power, which are based on claims to professional knowledge, must start with a transformation of consciousness about the nature of learning. This means, above all, a shift of responsibility for teaching and learning. Knowledge can be defined as a commodity only as long as it is viewed as the result of institutional enterprise or as the fulfillment of institutional objectives. Only when a man recovers the sense of personal responsibility for what he learns and teaches can this spell be broken and the alienation of learning from living be overcome.

The recovery of the power to learn or to teach means that the teacher who takes the risk of interfering in somebody else's private affairs also assumes responsibility for the results. Similarly, the student who exposes himself to the influence of a teacher must take responsibility for his own education. For such purposes educational institutions—if they are at all needed—ideally take the form of facility centers where one can get a roof of the right size over his he d, access to a piano or a kiln, and to records, books, or slides. Schools, TV stations, theaters, and the like are designed primarily for use by professionals. Deschooling society means above all the denial of professional status for the second-oldest profession, namely teaching. The certification of teachers now constitutes an undue restriction of the right to free speech: the corporate structure and professional pretentions of journalism an undue restriction on the right to free press. Compulsory attendance rules interfere with free assembly. The deschooling of society is nothing less than a cultural mutation by which a people recovers the effective use of its Constitutional freedoms: learning and teaching by men who know that they are born free rather than treated to freedom. Most people learn most of the time when they do whatever they enjoy; most people are curious and want to give meaning to whatever they come in contact with; and most people are capable of personal intimate intercourse with others unless they are stupefied by inhuman work or turned off by schooling.

The fact that people in rich countries do not learn much on their own constitutes no proof to the contrary. Rather it is a consequence of life in an environment from which, paradoxically, they cannot learn much, precisely because it is so highly programed. They are constantly frustrated by the structure of contemporary society in which the facts on which decisions can be made have become elusive. They live in an environment in which tools that can be used for creative purposes have become luxuries, an environment in which channels of communication serve a few to talk to many.

A modern myth would make us believe that the sense of impotence with which most men live today is a consequence of technology that cannot but create huge systems. But it is not technology that makes systems huge, tools immensely powerful, channels of communication one-directional. Quite the contrary: Properly controlled, technology could provide each man with the ability to understand his environment better, to shape it powerfully with his own hands, and to permit him full intercommunication to a degree never before possible. Such an alternative use of technology constitutes the central alternative in education.

If a person is to grow up he needs, first of all, access to things, to places and to processes, to events and to records. He needs to see, to touch, to tinker with, to grasp whatever there is in a meaningful setting. This access is now largely denied. When knowledge became a commodity, it acquired the protections of private property, and thus a principle designed to guard personal intimacy became a rationale for declaring facts off limits for people without the proper credentials. In schools teachers keep knowledge to themselves unless it fits into the day's program. The media inform, but exclude those things they regard as unfit to print. Information is locked into special languages, and specialized teachers live off its retranslation. Patents are protected by corporations, secrets are guarded by bureaucracies, and the power to keep others out of private preserves—be they cockpits, law offices, junkyards, or clinics—is jealously guarded by professions, institutions, and nations. Neither the political nor the professional structure of our societies, East and West, could withstand the elimination of the power to keep entire classes of people from facts that could serve them. The access to facts that I advocate goes far beyond truth in labeling. Access must be built into reality, while all we ask from advertising is a guarantee that it does not mislead. Access to reality constitutes a fundamental alternative in education to a system that only purports to teach *about* it.

Abolishing the right to corporate secrecy—even when professional opinion holds that this secrecy serves the common good—is, as shall presently appear, a much more radical political goal than the traditional demand for public ownership or control of the tools of production. The socialization of tools without the effective socialization of know-how in their use tends to put the knowledge-capitalist into the position formerly held by the financier. The technocrat's only claim to power is the stock he holds in some class of scarce and secret knowledge, and the best means to protect its value is a large and capital-intensive organization that renders access to know-how formidable and forbidding.

It does not take much time for the interested learner to acquire almost any skill that he wants to use. We tend to forget this in a society where professional teachers monopolize entrance into all fields, and thereby stamp teaching by uncertified individuals as quackery. There are few mechanical skills used in industry or research that are as demanding, complex, and dangerous as driving cars, a skill that most people quickly acquire from a peer. Not all people are suited for advanced logic, yet those who are make rapid progress if they are challenged to play mathematical games at an early age. One out of twenty kids in Cuernavaca can beat me at Wiff 'n' Proof after a couple of weeks' training. In four months all but a small percentage of motivated adults at our CIDOC center learn Spanish well enough to conduct academic business in the new language.

A first step toward opening up access to skills would be to provide various incentives for skilled individuals to share their knowledge. Inevitably, this would run counter to the interest of guilds and professions and unions. Yet, multiple apprenticeship is attractive: It provides everybody with an opportunity to learn something about almost anything. There is no reason why a person should not combine the ability to drive a car, repair telephones and toilets, act as a midwife, and function as an architectural draftsman. Special-interest groups and their disciplined consumers would, of course, claim that the public needs the protection of a professional guarantee. But this argument is now steadily being challenged by consumer protection associations. We have to take much more seriously the objection that economists raise to the radical socialization of skills: that "progress" will be impeded if knowledge—patents, skills, and all the rest—is democratized. Their argument can be faced only if we demonstrate to them the growth rate of futile diseconomies generated by any existing educational system.

Access to people willing to share their skills is no guarantee of learning. Such access is restricted not only by the monopoly of educational programs over learning and of unions over licensing but also by a technology of scarcity. The skills that count today are know-how in the use of highly specialized tools that were designed to be scarce. These tools produce goods or render services that everybody wants but only a few can enjoy, and which only a limited number of people know how to use. Only a few privileged individuals out of the total number of people who have a given disease ever benefit from the results of sophisticated medical technology, and even fewer doctors develop the skill to use it.

The same results of medical research have, however, also been employed to create a basic medical tool kit that permits Army and Navy medics, with only a few months of training, to obtain results, under battlefield conditions, that would have been beyond the expectations of full-fledged doctors during World War II. On an even simpler level any peasant girl could learn how to diagnose and treat most infections if medical scientists prepared dosages and instructions specifically for a given geographic area.

All these examples illustrate the fact that educational considerations alone suffice to demand a radical reduction of the professional structure that now impedes the mutual relationship between the scientist and the majority of people who want access to science. If this demand were heeded, all men could learn to use yesterday's tools, rendered more effective and durable by modern science, to create tomorrow's world.

Unfortunately, precisely the contrary trend prevails at present. I know a coastal area in South America where most people support themselves by fishing from small boats. The outboard motor is certainly the tool that has changed most dramatically the lives of these coastal fishermen. But in the area I have surveyed, half of all outboard motors that were purchased between 1945 and 1950 are still kept running by constant tinkering, while half the motors purchased in 1965 no longer run because they were not built to be repaired. Technological progress provides the majority of people with gadgets they cannot afford and deprives them of the simpler tools they need.

Metals, plastics, and ferro cement used in building have greatly improved since the 1940's and ought to provide more people the opportunity to create their own homes. But while in the United

States, in 1948, more than 30 percent of all one-family homes were owner-built, by the end of the 1960's the percentage of those who acted as their own contractors had dropped to less than 20 percent.

The lowering of the skill level through so-called economic development becomes even more visible in Latin America. Here most people still build their own homes from floor to roof. Often they use mud, in the form of adobe, and thatchwork of unsurpassed utility in the moist, hot, and windy climate. In other places they make their dwellings out of cardboard, oil-drums, and other industrial refuse. Instead of providing people with simple tools and highly standardized, durable, and easily repaired components, all governments have gone in for the mass production of low-cost buildings. It is clear that not one single country can afford to provide satisfactory modern dwelling units for the majority of its people. Yet, everywhere this policy makes it progressively more difficult for the majority to acquire the knowledge and skills they need to build better houses for themselves.

Educational considerations permit us to formulate a second fundamental characteristic that any post-industrial society must possess: a basic tool kit that by its very nature counteracts technocratic control. For educational reasons we must work toward a society in which scientific knowledge is incorporated in tools and components that can be used meaningfully in units small enough to be within the reach of all. Only such tools favor temporary associations among those who want to use them for a specific occasion. Only such tools allow specific goals to emerge in the process of their use, as any tinkerer knows. Only the combination of guaranteed access to facts and of limited power in most tools renders it possible to envisage a subsistence economy capable of incorporating the fruits of modern science.

The development of such a scientific subsistence economy is unquestionably to the advantage of the overwhelming majority of all people in poor countries. It is also the only alternative to progressive pollution, exploitation, and opaqueness in rich countries. But, as we have seen, the dethroning of the GNP cannot be achieved without simultaneously subverting GNE (Gross National Education—usually conceived as manpower capitalization). An egalitarian economy cannot exist in a society in which the right to produce is conferred by schools.

The feasibility of a modern subsistence economy does not depend on new scientific inventions. It depends primarily on the ability of a society to agree on fundamental, self-chosen, anti-bureaucratic and anti-technocratic restraints.

These restraints can take many forms, but they will not work unless they touch the basic dimensions of life. (The decision of Congress against development of the supersonic transport plane is one of the most encouraging steps in the right direction.) The substance of these voluntary social restraints would be very simple matters that can be fully understood and judged by any prudent man. The issues at stake in the SST controversy provide a good example. All such restraints would be chosen to promote stable and equal enjoyment of scientific know-how. The French say that it takes a thousand years to educate a peasant to deal with a cow. It would not take two generations to help all people in Latin America or Africa to use and repair outboard motors, simple cars, pumps, medicine kits, and ferro cement machines if their design does not change every few years. And since a joyful life is one of constant meaningful intercourse with others in a meaningful environment, equal enjoyment does translate into equal education.

At present a consensus on austerity is difficult to imagine. The reason usually given for the impotence of the majority is stated in terms of political or economic class. What is not usually understood is that the new class structure of a schooled society is even more powerfully controlled by vested interests. No doubt an imperialist and capitalist organization of society provides the social structure within which a minority can have disproportionate influence over the effective opinion of the majority. But in a technocratic society the power of a minority of knowledge capitalists can prevent the formation of true public opinion through control of scientific know-how and the media of communication. Constitutional guarantees of free speech, free press, and free assembly were meant to ensure government by the people. Modern electronics, photo-offset presses, time-sharing computers, and telephones have in principle provided the hardware that could give an entirely new meaning to these freedoms. Unfortunately, these things are used in modern media to increase the power of knowledge-bankers to funnel their program-packages through international chains to more people, instead of being used to increase true networks that provide equal opportunity for encounter among the members of the majority.

Deschooling the culture and social structure requires the use of technology to make participatory politics possible. Only on the basis of a majority coalition can limits to secrecy and growing power be determined without dictatorship. We need a new environment in which growing up can be classless, or we will get a brave new world in which Big Brother educates us all.

PART TWO

VALUES
SCHOOLS
TRANSMIT

"The basic moral and spiritual value in American life is the supreme importance of the individual personality . . . In educational terms, this value requires a school system which, by making freely available the common heritage of human association and human culture, opens to every child the opportunity to grow to his full physical, intellectual, moral, and spiritual stature. . . . By exploring and acknowledging the capacities of each child, education seeks to develop all his creative powers, to encourage him to feel that he can do things of value, that he belongs, and that he is wanted. It discourages every tendency toward despotism. It assigns no superior moral status, but rather a more definite moral responsibility, to the strong and the able. It endeavors to arouse in each individual a profound sense of self-respect and personal integrity."
—Educational Policies Commission,
National Education Association

"Today it embarrasses many teachers to be reminded that all sorts of values are transmitted to students, if not by their textbooks then by the informal curriculum—seating arrangements, the school bell, age, segregation, social class distinctions, the authority of the teacher, the very fact that students are in a school instead of the community itself. . . . Yet the formal curriculum continues to be presented as though it were value-free. . . ."
—Alvin Toffler, *Future Shock*

Individualized instruction. Open education. Values clarification. Flexible scheduling. The "discovery" method. Humanized learning.

This vocabulary, current in today's schools, suggests that students are being given unique opportunities to pursue their own interests and develop their personal values.

Although these concepts are admirable, and it is to be hoped that they will be accomplished, we should not overlook what is at the heart of the public school. The fundamental purpose of a government-supported system of education is to build a unified citizenry. One public is to be built from many "publics." As sociologist Patricia Sexton has observed, "All societies use the schools for ideological instruction, to transmit core values to the young and teach order and loyalty to the society."[1]

America has been no exception to this design. On the national level, we have witnessed a number of historical statements by prominent groups on the values that they expected and demanded the schools to transmit. Interestingly, most were developed within a decade or two following the end of our large military confrontations. Apparently, the major wars have caused Americans to reexamine and reshape their country's priorities. For example, encouraged by a large financial prize offered by the American Philosophical Society in 1796, major thinkers called for a national system of education. One essayist wanted schools to produce "republican machines."

In 1918 the National Education Association's Commission on the Reorganization of Secondary Education issued its recommendations, *Cardinal Principles of Secondary Education.* Citing poor international relations, an increasingly complex economic order, the immigrant problem, and more available leisure time, the Commission urged health courses and promotion of "worthy home-membership, worthy use of leisure, and ethical character" as needed concerns of the schools.

Six years after World War II ended, another NEA body asked schools to promote "moral and spiritual values." Its list of values began with "the supreme importance of the individual personality," and included moral responsibility, brotherhood, the pursuit of happiness, and the belief that institutions are the servants of mankind.

It seems clear, then, that the American school has been asked repeatedly to transmit values. Patriotism and some sort of "civic religion" have been high on the list. Certainly, order and obedience have ranked near the top. Textbooks show that hard work is deemed important. Stories from the *McGuffey Readers* and Dick and Jane have taught us that "good" will be rewarded and "wrong" punished.

Because schools have been asked to do certain tasks does not mean that they have succeeded or even tried. At some points, schools have also taken more credit than they have deserved for altering the course of American life. The sifting of myths from realities in the

1. P. Sexton, *The American School: A Sociological Analysis* (Englewood Cliffs: Prentice-Hall, 1967), p. 6.

matter of values schools transmit becomes an important and frustrating mission.

The first two articles in Part Two provide more historical insights into past moral education and give us some indication of where we are now as a society.

The majority of the articles in this section concentrate upon value instruction in the formal curriculum. We see how general goals are set, and how specific textbooks can be eliminated; how volatile issues such as religion and drug use are handled; and how values-education is being developed.

As Illich and Farber suggested in Part One, the incidental routines of schooling may be more important than the academic skills passed on. Several selections focus on such concerns as cafeteria rules, dress codes, and student rights.

Whereas most articles concentrate on one value under limited conditions, the Levy and Stacey article addresses itself to one topic (sexism) in the total school context. This article, and those which close Part Two, show the consequences of our past value-instruction, and suggest ways in which graduates of the future might be different.

The central question raised in Part Two is: Can the schools be as democratic as they claim to be? Stated differently: Can the student be socialized without being indoctrinated? Or still another way: How can the needs of the individual be balanced against the needs of the community and do justice to both?

What constitute the "core values" of today's society? Are they so different from the "middle-class" values of yesterday and the Puritan values of the day before yesterday?

Some readings will challenge prospective teachers to ponder: Will I be able to use an unpopular book, or join a controversial group? How sure can I be that I am not indoctrinating my students?

Finally, we have almost assumed that the schools do transmit values. Can we prove that they have?

For a host of reasons, Americans in growing numbers seem to want schools to emphasize moral education. Fraser's and Lynn's article is a reminder that moral education in the public schools has a long history. Considering some of the reasons cited for the need of instruction in morals, one wonders how much progress the nation has made since the days of the *McGuffey Readers*.

The authors' most pressing question is: Should we attempt to build a common morality in our pluralistic culture? And, although they do not raise it directly, they also question whether it is even possible to teach morals.

HOW MORAL
IS MORAL EDUCATION?

James W. Fraser
and Robert W. Lynn

There is more than one way of taming unruly school children. That was the conclusion reached recently by a New York state legislator and published in *The New York Times,* April 28, 1972. It was unfair, he decided, for "students who have robbed, mugged, assaulted, or been lured into drug use to receive their diplomas along with students of strong moral fiber." His remedy? A bill that would require all high school students in New York state to pass "citizenship and character-development requirements to qualify for diplomas." Without such "punitive leverage," the school administrators have no way of dealing with troublemakers. Meanwhile, opponents of the bill worried about the morality of this sort of moral education. It would not be the first time that an invasion of human rights has been justified by appeals to "law and order." Such a legislative act could be a handy bludgeon in the hands of a school principal who wanted to silence civil rights activists.

Fortunately, the bill never became the law of the state. Yet that defeat does not mean the idea has been buried. Not at all. Its author

From James W. Fraser and Robert W. Lynn, *Colloquy,* May–June, 1973, pp. 6–9. Reprinted by permission.

is only one among many Americans, past and present, who have concluded that the true business of the public school is the making of moral Americans. This is an idea whose lineage can be traced back at least one hundred and fifty years.

In the 1830's and 1840's, when the shape of the present-day public school system was becoming evident in New England and elsewhere, nearly all educators assumed the importance of moral education. Let's sound the roll call for just a few of these people. At the head of the list is Horace Mann, the illustrious architect of the Massachusetts school system. "It may be an easy thing to make a Republic," Mann declared, "but it is a very laborious thing to make Republicans." The public school was to take on that "laborious thing" and to make the white children of all classes into citizens of the Republic. (These educators shared the basic racism of most Americans; Blacks and Indians were largely ignored in any discussion of the commonness of the people, even by abolitionists such as Horace Mann.) See Horace Mann, "Twelfth Report," in Lawrence A. Cremin, *The Republic and the School* (New York: Teachers College Press, 1957), p. 92.

The same urgent need to "make" Americans was felt in other parts of the country. Out on the edge of the Western frontier, various denizens of Ohio were working hard in the cause of moral education. William H. McGuffey was starting to compile his famed set of Little Readers. Now generally regarded as a nostalgic bit of Americana, McGuffey Readers were then offered as a means of instructing a people about their memory and destiny. In his estimate the public school was not merely for the common folk; it was to be a school which was common to all white people, whether they were great or unknown, rich or poor, Yankee or immigrant.

Meanwhile, a young seminary professor by the name of Calvin E. Stowe (later to be well known as the husband of Harriet Beecher) was mounting a citizens' crusade for moral education. In "On the Education of Immigrants" (*Transactions of the Fifth Annual Meeting of the Western Literary Institute,* Cincinnati: Western Literary Institute, 1836), Stowe states "It is not merely from the ignorant and vicious foreigner that the danger is to be apprehended. To sustain an extended republic like our own, there must be a *national* feeling, a national assimilation; and nothing could be more fatal to our prospects of future national prosperity, than to have our population become congeries of clans, congregating without coalescing and condemned to contiguity without sympathy."

According to Stowe, "the only way to produce . . . this harmony of national feeling and character is to bring our children into the same schools and have them educated together." The Sunday schools could help in the making of Americans. (Indeed, some of Stowe's students at Lane Theological Seminary ran a Sunday school for German-speaking immigrants in Cincinnati.) Finally, however, the "public schools should be our best schools," so "that all the children of the Republic may be educated together." Otherwise "the evils of a clannish feeling" which the "judicious and patriotic Washington clearly foresaw" would tear asunder the fragile unity of the young country.

McGuffey, Stowe, and company had few doubts about using religion in the making of Americans. "The Bible [read] without dogmatic comment," said Calvin Stowe, "should be the textbook of religion and morals in all our institutions of education, from the primary school to the university and professional seminary." Without the Bible and "the religion which purifies and preserves us," there could be no hope of forming one public out of many clans and cultures. And apart from the public school there was no way of cultivating a sense of *belonging* to a new people, God's altogether New Israel with its own shared memories of the past and its hopes for a glorious future to come.

It may seem like a long leap from Stowe, McGuffey, et al. in the 1830's to the Progressive education movement which flowered in the early decades of the twentieth century. At first glance the thought of John Dewey and his fellow Progressives bears little resemblance to the outlook of the earlier generation. Dewey was bitterly opposed to the "devotional" reading of the Bible in the public school classroom. His work in philosophy represented an effort to develop a more contextual ethic than the static, conventional morality so evident in the McGuffey world. In fact, many Progressives looked upon the Little Readers as an unhappily rich incarnation of the inadequacies of the old-fashioned school which they were now trying to transform into a new institution.

But for all of their quarrels with their predecessors, these Progressives also subscribe to the fundamental credo of early nineteenth-century America. The task of forming a common public through common schools was still central to the work of the educator. John Dewey stated the faith as well as anyone in his *School and Society:* "When the school introduces and trains each child of society into membership within such a little community, saturating him with the spirit of service, and providing him with the instruments of effective self-direction, we shall have the deepest and best guarantee of a larger society which is worthy, lovely, and harmonious." What is important, in other words, is the sense of *belonging,* of being a part of the

American public. Therein lay the Progressives' clue to moral education. Morality is not taught by memorizing Bible verses or abstract, textbook maxims. Rather, let the children learn by working together on common projects. Include all youngsters in a class discussion so that they will not feel left out. If a public school staff wants to teach immigrants something about Columbus and the lore of this pioneer democracy, then help the students to put on a Columbus pageant which incorporates their handmade costumes and dances. "The patriotic value of such exercises," John Dewey commented, "is greater than the daily flag salute or patriotic poem, for the children understand what they are supposed to be enthusiastic about, as they see before them the things which naturally arouse patriotic emotions."

These are only a few of the byways explored by the Progressives in their pursuit of a genuinely moral education. Not all of these educators were agreed about the proper means of achieving that sought-after experience of belonging. Yet in their emphasis upon this clue to moral education they were at one with each other, as well as with the generation of the 1830's. During the heyday of Progressivism in the years leading up to World War I, this company of persons—as much as Horace Mann, William H. McGuffey or Calvin E. Stowe—were working for better schools, because better schools would build a more unified Republic. The public would become a reality as each child was inducted into the society—its past and its future.

John Dewey's life spanned ten decades. Born in a time when the McGuffey Readers were enormously popular, he lived through the Progressive era and into a third period in which none of the old certainties seemed to hold quite so true. Shortly after World War I, Dewey began to speak wistfully of the "eclipse of the public," a diminishing sense of solidarity and belonging together. Perhaps it is this "eclipse of the public" which has led to so much confusion, not only in the school but in much of society. As Lawrence Cremin said in a *Colloquy* interview (see July–August 1971 issue): "I think that we face a social crisis today which is sharply reflected in education. What's happening is that we are calling into question many of our cherished values, attitudes, beliefs and actions."

This crisis is the source of much of the anxiety and frustration that marks so many of the current educational debates. There is apparently no longer any compelling agreement either about what the schools should do, or on the more profound question of who we are as a people.

Even those who advocate sweeping changes in American education often find themselves divided when they become specific about their hopes for a new school. Consider, for a moment, a story recently told by the historian Michael B. Katz in his *Class, Bureaucracy and Schools:* "Seven poor mothers, disgusted with the treatment of their children," finally decided to run one of their number for membership on the city school board. Among other things they called for volunteer campaign workers from a nearby university and from the political party. The temporary alliance began to fall apart when the two groups discovered their differences. The platform of the candidate included "the reintroduction of report cards and corporal punishment; she opposed sex education." In contrast, the reformers from the university hoped for something utterly different in the classroom. They "put happiness and warm human relations above subjects, skills, and classroom order." But the liberation of the child was not the first order of business for the ghetto parents. They were fighting for a school which would equip the children for jobs in the larger world. Happiness and freedom could come later.

This incident is a painful one for *Colloquy* readers, for it reminds us of the cruel disappointments experienced by the school reform movement of the late 1960's. It should also jar us into recognizing the thinness of the current debate about moral education. Both sides in this little dispute could claim the mantle of the moral educator. What could be more moral, the supporters of the parents might ask, than giving oppressed children access to a job and a chance for survival in the future? The counter-question comes quickly: What could be more moral than the liberation of the children's human potential right now—not in some indefinite tomorrow, but today?

Yet neither side comes to grips with the most fundamental issue involved in moral education. Is there a larger public worthy of the allegiance of these youngsters? Is it enough for well-trained youth, once their schooling is ended, to be inducted into a society of technocrats who build—without seeming purpose or morality—only bigger and better means of self-destruction? Or can one speak of the liberation of the child without also contemplating the liberation of the society? In short, both sides offer a version of moral education which is highly individualistic; both advance arguments that reflect the continuing erosion of a shared sense of the public.

What then is to be done? A program for national character education as in the McGuffey Readers would be much more repressive now than it was in the nineteenth century. However naively it was done in the past, such an enterprise could now be used, as the comments of the New York state legislator indicated, to crush dissent and to force conformity in a nation less and less able to command allegiance. There is nothing moral about that kind of moral education.

A plurality of groups might seem to be the only answer, but this is hardly an inviting option. If there is no common morality and memory among the people in this nation, what will keep them together at all? What will deliver us from that specter which haunted Stowe in the 1830's, "the evil of clannish feelings"? Perhaps a nation of semiautonomous factions "condemned to contiguity without sympathy" is the best one can hope for. Perhaps only a revolutionary change will ever again allow the American people to be a public.

This leads to the most poignant of all questions to emerge from the 1960's: Should the American people remain united at all?

Arizona educators are worried that some citizens already have a disproportionate amount of control over public education. Using the issue of accountability (that schools and teachers should be held more responsible for outcomes in student performance), one group appears to have become dictators of what and how classroom teachers teach.

Who should determine the goals of a local school district? How much "free speech" can be allowed in public schools, by teachers or students?

"ACCOUNTABILITY" AS A SMOKE SCREEN FOR POLITICAL INDOCTRINATION IN ARIZONA

M. M. Gubser

The worst that educators have had to fear thus far from the concept of "accountability" has been that it be used as a red herring to divert attention from the main question of adequate educational finance. School boards, legislatures, and governmental agencies and officials

Reprinted by permission of the author and the *Phi Delta Kappan*, September, 1973, pp. 64, 65.

who have been loath to spend enough money on education to achieve satisfactory results have been among the first to champion performance-based systems. Frequently accountability has been employed not to increase instructional quality but to excuse cuts in already meager educational budgets. In Arizona, however, accountability has acquired a much more insidious connotation.

For the past four years individuals and organizations representing extreme conservative viewpoints have intensified their attacks on Arizona's public school curriculum. They have placed their representatives on state boards of education and state curriculum commissions. Ultraconservative legislators have been used to introduce legislation seeking to inflict super-patriotic values upon the schools by statutory edict. In three years, the state department of education has increased in size by over 100%, providing Arizona's self-styled ultraconservative superintendent of public instruction with an agency having considerable power to affect the course of public education in Arizona.

Much of the strategy of those who would use the schools to indoctrinate rather than educate has been predicated upon the adoption of some system of "instructional accountability." The state board of education has appointed "basic goals" commissions to develop guiding philosophies by listing performance objectives in four curricular areas: social studies, U.S./Arizona history, health, and science. Commissions in 15 other subject areas are planned for the future. The goals developed by these commissions will constitute the basic course of study for particular subject areas. The goals will be used as criteria for statewide text and supplementary book selection and for "deletion of offensive and controversial passages" in present instructional materials.

Appointed by conservative state board of education members, subject area commissioners have included housewives and mothers, the wives of conservative Republican party officials, wives and secretaries of conservative state legislators, and husbands of some of these secretaries, in addition to a handful of educators. The political orientation of these commissioners is readily evident in the list of objectives which they have submitted for state adoption to the board of education.

The U.S. history commission would require teachers to teach that "the U.S. remains the envy of the civilized world and the last best hope of mankind." The social studies course of study indicates that private property is the basis of all our political rights and that "strict interpretation of constitutional provisions is necessary" to preserve American society. Thrown in for good measure is the old chestnut that "America is a republic, not a democracy." The contributions of blacks, Chicanos, and Indians to national and southwestern culture have been completely ignored.

A course of study has also been developed for health education. It eliminates instructional objectives which include anything but the most mechanical references to sex. Venereal disease is hardly mentioned. Mental health is regarded as a "spiritual" problem.

The science commission has been less controversial, yet scarcely any of the objectives it lists for the science curriculum have escaped criticism by some recognized scientific authority. Most frequently noted is the fact that the science report carefully avoids objectives which mention the Darwinian theory of evolution, and that objectives appear locked into the fact-and-rote approach to teaching science.

In addition to setting up the commission goals and objectives, Arizona's state department of education has begun strict enforcement of a 1971 statute which requires that all high school graduates complete a course in "the essentials and benefits of the free enterprise system." An older law requiring instruction in "American history and values" has received new impetus. So specific have been the requirements for teaching "American values" that in the state's largest district less than 10% of all students from grades 7 through 12 now take any coursework which relates to the world outside the U.S.

Many Arizonans were amazed when with little discussion and great haste the legislature passed a statute mandating the state board of education to "develop, establish, and direct the implementation of a continuous uniform evaluation system of pupil achievement in relation to measurable performance objectives in basic subjects" by June 30, 1975. This statute provides the mechanism to establish state-determined achievement requirements for children in local districts with little input from their parents, local boards, educators, or taxpayers concerned with the specific needs of their local situations.

To ensure that teachers do not deviate from the behavioral objectives and goals of the state-prescribed curriculum, the state board of education approved performance recertification to become effective July 1, 1974. Pupil performance will be a fundamental criterion in rating teachers upon their eligibility for recertification. A standardized test measuring instruction in "free enterprise" has already been prepared. Others are being constructed to test students on concepts acquired in U.S. history and other subjects. A model system for performance-based recertification will be tested in several Arizona public school districts over the 1973–74 academic year.

To combat these encroachments on academic freedom, state educators this year formed the Arizona Coalition on Educational Policy, a group representing more than 30 professional and lay organizations. A "Bill of Rights for Education" was proposed to replace existing sections of Arizona law with statements guaranteeing to public school teachers and students freedom from political indoctrination. Local districts would be promised the right to participate in determining curriculum for local schools.

Reaction to the ACEP's proposal was strong and swift. A group calling itself the Arizona Citizens for Parental Rights immediately introduced through conservative Arizona legislators a "Parents' Bill of Rights." This bill would have severely limited any experimentation with "progressive" methods and curriculum, including open classrooms, values clarification, and many social studies programs. "Psychological services" were expressly forbidden, as was any instruction which would "alter the attitudes of Arizona students." One of the leading supporters of the bill said at a public hearing that "we are going after programs inspired by pornographers and persons who have been linked with the Communist conspiracy."

The Arizona legislature soundly defeated the Parents' Bill of Rights. But the state board of education revived the dead measure in a new policy statement which plagiarized much of the defeated bill, word for word. As a creature of the legislature, the state board is now under fire by lawmakers of both parties, who are charging that actions of the legislature have been furtively circumvented.

All of this has been accomplished under the guise of "accountability" for public instruction. It may be the beginning of a national trend. California's Governor Ronald Reagan, in a recent address, cited Arizona's developing educational situation as a model for his and other states. The nationally syndicated, ultraconservative radio program, *Lifeline,* sponsored by oil millionaire H. L. Hunt, has urged school patrons throughout the country to press for legislation and a curriculum patterned after that adopted in Arizona. In Georgia a situation remarkably similar to Arizona's has developed over the past year. Texas has now legislated performance-based teacher education and criterion-referenced instruction.

It is becoming evident that performance-based certification and performance-based salary schedules may provide some of the controls necessary to ensure that teachers do not deviate from state-prescribed procedures and official courses of study. Shared funding may well afford the resources necessary for state educational agencies to achieve mastery over what and how materials are presented to local school districts.

The *New York Times* has noted that "Arizona educators are most . . . fearful of a future where teachers are told which courses to teach, what textbooks to use, and what materials to stress—all by the state board of education and with the threat of noncertification hanging over their heads." It is doubtful that such a future would be Arizona's alone.

Elite power groups are not the only ones who change school curricula. As Clifford Hardy indicates, state textbook committees and local school district groups have banned certain books and edited others.

The basic question behind this and other censorship questions is one of allowing alternative views to be stated. What kind of people, do you imagine, stood on opposing sides of whether or not to use *Body Language?* If you were a teacher using a controversial text, what defense would you use?

A persistent question of this article, and this part remains: How are the requirements of free inquiry to be balanced against the dominant values and wishes of the community?

CENSORSHIP
AND THE CURRICULUM
Clifford A. Hardy

Legislation recently passed by the Tennessee Senate would prevent textbooks from presenting as scientific fact the various theories concerning man's origin. This legislation would stipulate that the

From *Educational Leadership,* October, 1973, pp. 10, 11, 13. Reprinted with permission of the Association for Supervision and Curriculum Development and Clifford A. Hardy. Copyright © 1973 by the Association for Supervision and Curriculum Development.

Book of Genesis' explanation, as well as Darwin's and other theories of man's origin, be presented as theories rather than as scientific fact. The action is similar in nature to a recent California ruling whereby textbooks are being modified by the insertion of conditional statements concerning evolution.[1]

While these events and others that will doubtless follow in their wake may seem harmless enough to many, perhaps evoking only amusing memories of the Scopes trial and little else, there are implications of a serious nature that perhaps should be considered. Since these changes have been brought about generally by forces external to the scientific and academic communities at a time when the specter of censorship in the form of intimidation of newsmen, news sources, and network television is on the rise, perhaps we should give pause to consider the ever-present problem of censorship and the school curriculum.

There have been numerous and powerful advocates of censorship in every age. While the advocates operate in different ways, there are recurring patterns that tend to emerge. In this regard, Sloan has suggested that:

> Today's censors still exhibit one or more of the four traditional characteristics of the censor: they espouse *secrecy*, attempt to *edit* that with which they disagree, and/or make themselves judges for what is morally or politically acceptable for society.[2]

TEXTBOOK SELECTION

Perhaps in no other area have all of these characteristics been expressed more than in the area of textbook selection in the social studies. The persistent efforts of a handful of persons can often result in the banning of a particular text or in its alteration or modification. In this regard, Nelson and Roberts have provided a detailed and interesting case study illustrating how the character of a textbook can be transformed through alteration. The brief example to follow, drawn from their study of a Texas State Textbook Committee hearing, represents the kind of subtle alteration that along with several other changes resulted in the substantial modification of a geography text adopted by that state.

1. Laurel N. Tanner and Daniel Tanner. "Charles Darwin Needs Clarence Darrow." *Educational Leadership* 30 (6): 579; March 1973.

2. George W. Sloan. "Censorship in Historical Perspective." *Top of the News* 22: 271; April 1966.

Original Version: "Because it needs to trade, and because it needs military help, the United States needs the friendship of countries throughout the world. But to keep its friends, a country must help them, too."

Changed to: "The United States trades with countries in all parts of the world. We are also providing military help to many nations. In addition, the United States aids many countries in other ways."[3]

While instances of censorship can be treated as isolated cases, the pressure of textbook censorship is not a welcome event when one considers the time and money spent on emphasizing the inquiry approach to social studies during the past decade. Unfortunately, the adoption of sterile, safe textbooks may create a climate of self-imposed censorship that can run counter to the values of the inquiry method as well as inhibit in various other ways the teaching of social studies by the process approach.

While English teachers have traditionally borne the brunt of book-banning attempts, there seems to be little "rhyme or reason" to this type of censorship. Apparently nearly every book of consequence, including such classics as *Gone with the Wind, Huckleberry Finn, 1984, To Kill a Mockingbird,* and *The Grapes of Wrath,* has fallen victim to the censor at one time or another. The conclusion that few books have indeed escaped the would-be censors' wrath seems to be highlighted by the fact that:

> In the files of the National Council of Teachers of English are reports of efforts to ban *Robin Hood,* because he advocates sharing the wealth and is therefore Communistic; *The Scarlet Letter,* because it deals with adultery; *The King and I,* because it mentions a concubine; a short account of the life of Plato, because he advocated something like free love; the *Odyssey,* because this book from the ninth century B.C. is "non-Christian."[4]

While this kind of censorship has often affected the school library in a general way, it can also be felt in quite specific ways, as in the case of the recent banning of the best-seller *Body Language* by a New York school board. Concerned with nonverbal communication and used in an elective "communications" course, the book was banned by a review committee following the complaint of a local citizen. In addition to the banning of *Body Language,* the school principal was apparently "instructed by the committee to draft a

---

3. J. Nelson and G. Roberts. *The Censors and the Schools.* Boston: Little, Brown and Company, 1963, p. 130.

4. H. Norris. "Should We Censor What Adolescents Read?" *The PTA Magazine* 50: 11; March 1965.

policy assigning textbook selection and curriculum solely to board members."[5]

INFLUENCE ON SCIENCE

While the effect of censorship in the area of humanities should be evident, its effect on the science curriculum has perhaps been less noteworthy. However, with the advent of the kind of action mentioned at the beginning of this article concerning the treatment of evolution in science textbooks, several factors should be kept in mind. The first and perhaps most important would question the effect that this kind of censorship might have upon the science curriculum in general and student learning in particular.

Few educators need to be reminded of the fact that since 1956 the National Science Foundation has contributed vast sums to support major curriculum projects primarily in science and mathematics. This is, of course, in addition to the large amounts contributed by private organizations and the U.S. Office of Education toward the goal of improving course content in the sciences. The outgrowth of this work and expenditure has resulted in the development of the PSSC physics, the CHEM Study chemistry, and the BSCS biology materials, in addition to various other projects with similar aims, objectives, and methods. As a by-product, many of the objectives, methods, and unifying ideas from these courses have been incorporated into several of the so-called traditional textbook approaches in science.

It should be kept in mind that each of the curriculum projects mentioned has been centered around certain unifying or organizing themes. For instance, one of the principal organizing themes for the BSCS biology materials is the concept of evolution. As such, evolution plays a central role in organizing, unifying, and clarifying the content of modern biology.[6] At this point, the question must come into play as to whether or not it is sound learning practice to begin isolating the organizing element of modern biology, namely evolution, in order to present it as a discrete isolated theory, and in order to place it in competition, so to speak, with other discrete isolated theories.

While this approach may be applauded by some, the fact that it

5. "N. Y. School Board Bans Body Language." *Library Journal* 98: 1332; April 15, 1973.
6. J. Marshall and Ernest Burkman. *Current Trends in Science Education.* New York: Center for Applied Research in Education, 1966, p. 39.

might represent a serious step backward toward the discreteness of the subject-centered curriculum should at least be given consideration. An interesting action in this regard can be seen in a recent decision by the Texas State Board of Education to remove two BSCS biology textbooks from the state-approved list, in addition to the requiring of all textbooks treating evolution to insert a preface to the effect that "evolution is presented not as a fact, but as a theory."[7]

Finally, it should be remembered that whether a censorship action is local in nature, as in a recent Connecticut case where an entire chapter was removed from the local high school physiology text,[8] or whether an action is statewide in nature, students in other parts of the country may well be affected. It appears to be the case that the textbook industry is too often vulnerable both directly and indirectly to censorship efforts. With this in mind, educators should more than ever work to oppose censorship, or at the very least work to assure that any textbooks or curriculum changes are, as much as possible, in accord with sound learning theory and teaching method.

7. Tanner, *op. cit.*
8. "Physiology Text Mutilated; Depicts Sexual Reproduction." *Library Journal* 98: 1331; April 15, 1973.

On the surface, the "creationist" battle in California may appear to be a silly struggle over an antiquated issue. Upon reflection, we can view it as a powerful example of various "publics" vying to have the schools present their versions of the truth. Moreover, since the California texts will be adopted in other states, the decision reached challenges the myth that local school boards wield much curriculum control.

Recalling the strategies used by board members, pressure groups, and media coverage, the reader may ask: Is this a just way, or the best way, to determine academic curricula?

SCIENTISTS VERSUS FUNDAMENTALISTS: THE CALIFORNIA COMPROMISE

Donald H. Layton

The California State Board of Education was embroiled during much of the past year in a controversy over science texts for the state's elementary school children. The issue has been: How shall man's origins be presented in elementary science textbooks? Reminiscent of the 1925 "monkey trial" of teacher John T. Scopes, the discussions pitted many eminent scientists against a group of articulate religious fundamentalists. Most observers agree that implications of the debates transcend the boundaries of the Golden State and may portend developments elsewhere.

The controversy arose during the course of the board's discussions of textbook adoptions scheduled to take effect in the fall of 1974. Unlike many other states, California has statewide adoption of elementary school books. This means that local school districts select texts from among those on a list approved by the State Board of Education. Technically, books not on the list cannot be used as major textbooks. This procedure has had the advantage of standardizing book usage throughout the state as well as effecting major economies in state purchases of textbooks.

Reprinted by permission of the author and the *Phi Delta Kappan*, June, 1973, pp. 696, 697

The state board began to consider new science texts for elementary schools last summer. In anticipation of these deliberations, the board had approved a resolution in 1969 that the creation theory (that is, special or divine origin of man) be ranked alongside evolution in the state's science framework. This framework was intended to specify content of subsequent science texts selected by the board.

However, in subsequent months the board's textbook screening committee, the Curriculum Commission, ignored the board's mandate and screened out books which presented the creation theory. Only books with evolutionary accounts of man's origins were thus presented for the board's final consideration. A spokesman for the Curriculum Commission stated that he did not think that the inclusion of both theories had been made mandatory by the board.

Last fall the board found itself in a quandary. Should it approve the books recommended to it by its Curriculum Commission, which included only evolutionary versions of man's origins, or should it insist that alternative presentations of special creation also be incorporated? In the past the board had not involved itself in matters of curriculum specifics; this was felt to be the province of qualified scholars, not of the laymen on the board. (Besides this jurisdictional problem, the board's difficulty was further complicated by the fact that not all four of nine new appointees agreed with the 1969 decision.)

After hearing much conflicting testimony at its November meeting, the board met to determine its course of action last December. A motion that the creation account be included in all elementary science texts failed to receive the required six votes.

The board then moved to a compromise resolution offered by one of its members. This motion called for elimination of "scientific dogmatism" in the teaching of evolution (nothing was said about special creation in the motion). Dogmatic statements about evolution were to be changed to conditional statements. It was further specified that science books discuss "how," not ultimate causes, and that questions yet unresolved in science be presented to the student to stimulate interest and inquiry processes. The motion carried unanimously.

In January a board member again brought up the topic of special creation. He recommended that all elementary science books contain a reference to the possibility of special creation in addition to evolutionary theory. The motion failed by a 6-3 vote. In February, another member of the board moved that the science books be edited "to provide examples of unresolved questions in science as a means of stimulating the inquiry process, including a theory of creation." This motion failed by one vote.

The volatile textbook issue was apparently settled in March. The board approved editorial revisions in the science texts labeling evolution as theory instead of fact. No mention of special creation was ordered.

The pending textbook decisions of the board stimulated impassioned debate throughout California last fall. Most of the state's scientific community, including 19 of its Nobel laureates, argued that only evolutionary statements ought to be presented in elementary science books. The scholars generally stated that there was no scientific evidence to support the notion of "special creation," and contended that textbook discussions of origins ought to be based only on evidence uncovered by studies in geology, paleontology, astronomy, and other branches of science. They subscribed to the view that man evolved from lower life forms over tens of thousands of years.

In pressing their claims, California scientists were supported by the prestigious National Academy of Sciences. In a rare involvement in a state issue, the academy adopted a resolution pointing out that "religion and science . . . are separate and mutually exclusive realms of human thought whose presentation in the same context leads to misunderstanding of both scientific theory and religious beliefs." Insertion of religious views "will almost certainly impair the proper segregation of the teaching and understanding of science and religion nationwide."

The evolutionists were also joined by important segments of the state's press. The *Los Angeles Times* editorialized:

> . . . [I]n dealing with science, the rules of science must apply. The theory of special creation is a belief that can be respected. But it is not science, and it has no place in a science textbook. Efforts to put it there must be resisted and denied by the State Board of Education.[1]

In opposition, the religionists or fundamentalists argued that the textbooks ought to include an alternative to evolution. This alternative, they argued, was special creation—creation by design—with its implications of supreme intelligence undergirded by belief in God.

One of the staunchest supporters of this point of view was Dr. John R. Ford, a San Diego physician, active Seventh-Day Adventist, and vice president of the state board. In a September statement to

1. "Science and the Creation Theory," *Los Angeles Times*, November 16, 1972, p. II-6.

the board, Ford said, "Children are taught only one idea today: that the universe, life, and man are simply 'accidents' that occurred by fortuitous chance without cause, purpose, or reason." Believing this to be an untestable hypothesis, Ford asserted that he would "at the same time propose that the same identical scientific data . . . will support equally well (if not more so) the hypothesis that these origins occurred by design with cause, purpose, and reason."

Ford added that he sought only "to have any and all discussions in the [science] materials be connoted as unresolved theories and further that two contrasting possibilities—*chance* and *design*—be discussed side by side without bias for one over the other."

Last fall numerous California religious bodies rallied to the support of Ford and like-minded members of the board. In November California's Southern Baptists urged the board to abide by its decision to add the biblical view of creation to the science textbooks. The resolution was passed unanimously by 950 delegates to the Baptists' state convention. Many other churchmen in the state, including Mormons, Nazarenes, Pentecostals, and Church of Christ members, gave support in varying degrees to the mention of the biblical account of creation in the science texts.

The board's unanimous action in December to eliminate "scientific dogmatism" from the texts seemed to meet the objections of those who believe scientific observations about origins are tentative. Many statements asserted as facts were ordered changed to conditional in the books. One sentence asserting that "life began in the seas," for instance, was changed to read, "Most scientists believe that life may have begun in the sea. Thus scientists can only speculate about the character of early life forms."[2]

The board's actions were not received enthusiastically by other groups engaged in the California debates. Most fundamentalists were still unhappy that the creation theory will not appear in the texts; conditional statements about evolution do little to allay their basic objections to what they see as a serious omission. Many scientists also disapproved of the board's compromise. Arthur Kornberg, a Stanford biochemist and Nobel prizewinner, said, "Conditional statements are appropriate when multiple theories have been proposed and none of these can be eliminated by the existing scientific evidence. No alternative to the evolutionary theory of the origins of man exists today which gives an equally satisfactory explanation of the biological facts."

2. Edward B. Fiske, "Should God Have Equal Time?" *New York Times,* December 17, 1972, p. E-7.

In any event, the science textbooks, with perhaps some "scientific dogmatism" eliminated, will go to three million California youths beginning in September, 1974. California is the nation's largest textbook market, accounting for 10% of all national sales. Given this fact, chances are that children in a number of other states will be reading the same account of man's origins as do their counterparts in California.

America will frequently demand that its schools solve the problems of its youth (without mentioning that they are adult problems too). The increase in drug abuse education is one recent example.

Joanne Zazzaro reviews a number of curricular aids in this area. Speculating on the effectiveness of these efforts, she forces us to analyze the often-held belief that providing information will lead to the cure of a problem.

The poll at the end of the article raises yet another question: Knowing the limitations of drug education programs, administrators still favor them. Why?

DRUG EDUCATION: IS IGNORANCE BLISS?
Joanne Zazzaro

"I remember this one ex-addict. She talked about how degraded her life had been. But you should have seen her—she was gorgeous."

"I got all excited about trying heroin from the movie we watched. It looked good to me, and everybody knows you can't get addicted the first time around."

Sound like something out of *True Confessions?* Unfortunately, the comments aren't fictionalized. They come straight from the mouths of two students taught in traditional drug education courses. And they hint that the traditional approach, however well-meaning, has flopped.

Indeed, convincing evidence shows that school drug education programs actually turn kids on to drugs by rousing their curiosity.

Item: Speculating that drug education in recent years has been "counterproductive by stimulating rebellion and raising interest in the forbidden," the National Commission on Marihuana and Drug Abuse just called for a moratorium on all drug education programs in schools.[1]

Item: Following completion of a 10-week lecture course intended to expose the dangers of drugs, selected junior high students in Ann Arbor, Mich., worried less about drugs and significantly increased their use and sale of marijuana and LSD.[2]

Item: In a recent evaluation of drug education programs done for the Department of Health, Education and Welfare, approximately 75 percent of the surveyed youth and adults stated that current drug education programs don't prevent drug use. Schools and teachers were considered to be among the least effective presenters of drug education by youngsters of high school age.[3]

Item: Of 220 drug abuse films and audiovisuals evaluated by the National Coordinating Council on Drug Education, only 16 percent were rated "scientifically and conceptually acceptable." The films used most frequently in schools come from NCCDE's "unacceptable" or "restricted" lists.[4]

Item: Finding nothing to recommend about school drug education programs and materials, the National Education Association's Task Force on Drug Education explained that "the majority of drug education programs are superficial and educationally poor. Some of the programs, because of false statements made by misinformed or uninformed educators, could very well have contributed to the increase in drug use in this society."

The list could go on and on, of course, but the point is painfully

1. "Drug Use in America: Problem in Perspective," Second Report of the National Commission on Marihuana and Drug Abuse, March 1973: U.S. Government Printing Office, Washington, D.C. 20402, $2.60 (stock number 5266-00003).

2. "Teaching Facts About Drugs: Pushing or Preventing?" By Richard B. Stuart, Preprint from *Journal of Educational Psychology:* Family and School Consultation Project, 209 South 4th Ave., Ann Arbor, Mich. 48104, $1.75.

3. "Evaluation of Drug Education Programs," Macro Systems, Inc., June 1972: National Technical Information Service, U.S. Department of Commerce, 5285 Port Royal Rd., Springfield, Va. 22151, $15.95 (three volumes, order numbers PB-213 649. PB-213 650, PB-213 651).

4. "Drug Abuse Films," Third Edition: National Coordinating Council on Drug Education, 1211 Connecticut Ave., N.W., Washington, D.C. 20036, $5.

clear: Drug education may cause more harm than good. At the very least, it hasn't worked the way schoolmen expected.

Neither conclusion seems too surprising when you consider how drug education programs have been conceived, conducted and evaluated. Simply put, they were designed—hastily and often in response to community pressure—on the idealistic premise that students educated about the dangers of drugs would have enough sense to quit or never begin using drugs.

But as the National Commission on Marihuana and Drug Abuse points out, that was "wishful thinking." Just as knowing about the relationship between lung cancer and cigarette smoking hasn't spurred smokers to kick the habit, so, too, knowing about overdoses and chromosome damage hasn't convinced kids to steer clear of drugs. Nor is it likely to. Programs focused strictly on preventing drug use, the commission adds, probably will never be effective.

Still, most school drug courses take a classic prevention approach: Tell students the straight facts about drugs, mainly through classroom lectures or presentations. (Overt preaching and scare tactics got axed long ago.) Use plenty of films and printed materials. Invite clergymen, narcotics agents, and ex-junkies to visit schools and describe the evils of drugs. Pound in the message that abstention assures life, liberty and the pursuit of happiness.

Well, the message apparently missed its mark—drug-taking has increased since schools undertook their intensive, expensive drug abuse campaign in the late Sixties. Part of the reason kids turned a deaf ear: the gnawing suspicion that use of some illegal drugs has advantages no one bothered to mention.

And therein lies a tale. Let the national commission tell it. "Prevention programs may proclaim goals which stress the prevention of high-risk drug use, or of drug dependence, or use of particular drugs, but in practice they must try to curtail *all* illicit drugs [lest they tacitly condone some]. . . . They suggest that all use patterns are equally harmful because all are likely to evolve into undesirable behavior. From the program's point of view, such an argument may not seem an exaggeration. . . . From the point of view of many recipients, however, the 'all use is equally dangerous' approach undermines the credibility of the information."

Even programs that attempt to achieve complete objectivity leave much to be desired, the commission adds. Though they remove all traces of value judgment from descriptions of drug risks and attractions, often giving both sides of the issue, they may encourage more experimentation than they discourage. "Even a simple, objective statement of costs and attractions could arouse curiosity," explains the commission. "In fact, any prevention program which focuses specifically on drugs and drug use will introduce the idea of consumption to the naive among its recipients."

To the naive and fairly sophisticated alike, certain aspects of drug education (not to mention drug-taking) seem appealing. No matter how gruesome ex-addicts say their junkie lives were, for example, in person they often appear "groovy" compared to school teachers. They're good talkers, tend to dress in the latest styles, and come across as "cool." Indeed, that a former addict is alive to tell about his drug experience proves to some kids that "you can turn off drugs any time you want."

Then there's the titillating explicitness of drug education materials—how many students might like to experience a high just like the one reached by a person shooting up heroin in a drug film? If a student doesn't know how to mainline heroin, more likely than not the film will give him adequate visual instruction. One of the films reviewed and panned by the National Coordinating Council on Drug Education, in fact, contains a sequence the council considers "an excellent demonstration of how to prepare and inject heroin."

Other less obvious but equally powerful reasons why drug education may turn kids on come from Richard B. Stuart, University of Michigan sociologist. He conducted the fact-oriented drug education experiment in Ann Arbor that showed increased use and sale of marijuana and LSD among the better educated subjects who worried least about drug dangers. Among other things, Stuart found that age of the teacher (adult or peer) and specific course content had little bearing on the experiment's outcome. He concluded that classroom instruction definitely broadens students' knowledge about drugs, and that an interaction between high knowledge and low worry leads to increased drug-taking.

In addition to providing enough information to get students started on drugs, says Stuart, drug education may exacerbate drug use by:

1. leading students to think of themselves as potential drug users merely by being included in drug education programs.
2. desensitizing students through repeated discussion of drug concepts. "The more times you talk about drug-taking," speculates Stuart, "the less worrisome it well may become."
3. providing students with facts which overcome the prejudices that had been inhibiting use. Kids' false ideas about the negative consequences of drugs actually serve as barriers to use, Stuart explains. Students may become disinhibited when they find out

that a lot of the bad things they once believed about drugs fall
into the "crazy or stupid" category.
4. including inaccurate or biased information which can destroy the
credibility of the basic educational message.

Stuart might have added another sticky point: Once upon a time
students were deceived about the effects of marijuana and other
low-risk drugs. Now they don't trust any drug information dispensed
in school, even if it's free of exaggeration, half-truth and value
judgment.

All of these reasons speak eloquently for killing off facts-only,
preventive drug education programs in schools. But what are the
alternatives? Unfortunately for schoolmen, the answer depends on
who you're listening to. And if you listen carefully, you may detect
the same kind of confusion, conflict and lack of direction that put
"old" drug education programs out in left field.

Says the HEW study: Accept the fact that drug-taking is woven
into youngsters' total lifestyle and that limited drug use, especially
smoking marijuana, won't hurt anyone. (More than 73 percent of
youth claim they know all about drug consequences but use drugs
for fun, pleasure or to satisfy curiosity.) Abandon drug education as
a single-issue concept, concentrating instead on human problems
such as inability to make decisions, solve problems, and get along
with parents, teachers and peers. Identify drug-users and non-users,
then present different materials to each. For drug-users, try "intervention programs" using rap sessions, group and individual counseling, and parent and community involvement. "By de-emphasizing a
'message to be conveyed' approach and departing from traditional
classroom situations," notes the study, "rap sessions and encounter
groups are most likely to lead to meaningful personal decisions as a
result of group interaction and understanding."

Says Richard Stuart: Instead of spending money on drug education, put the funds into programs to increase teacher accountability;
provide more innovative, constructive curriculum materials; boost
students' academic achievement levels; and so on. Drug use, after all,
is not a matter of individual deviance but a response to a variety of
"systemic failures ranging from boring, dreadfully conducted school
experiences to punitive family experiences to general social chaos
and dislocation." Attempts to use schools to control socially related
behaviors such as drug use only detract from their basic purpose.

Says the national commission: Declare a moratorium on all
drug education programs in schools, at least until the ones already in operation have been evaluated and have proven both

realistic and helpful. [That's unlikely to happen. After reviewing hundreds of school approaches, the commission concluded that "no drug education program in this country, or elsewhere, has proven sufficiently successful to warrant our recommending it."] Urge state legislatures to repeal all statutes requiring drug education in the public schools.

Continues the commission, in what may seem incongruous with a moratorium: Rather than concentrating resources and efforts in persuading or "educating" people not to use drugs, emphasize other means of obtaining what users seek from drugs—means that foster and instill the necessary skills for coping with the problems of living. Information about drugs and their disadvantages should be incorporated into more general programs, stressing benefits with which drug taking is largely inconsistent. Other programs should focus on providing goals and activities for drug-prone youth or on encouraging a sense of purpose and self-esteem rather than on the presence or absence of a drug.

More: Get away from programs oriented solely toward drugs. Education should integrate drug information into broader mental hygiene or problem-solving courses. "In this way, the overall objective of encouraging responsible decision-making can be emphasized, without placing the teacher in the position of defending drug policy or of persuading students to comply with it."

The commission's implication, of course, is that presenting drug facts in a context that makes them meaningful probably will increase their long-term impact. Whether that's true or simply another case of wishful thinking won't be known until schools now trying to blend drug information into more general courses thoroughly evaluate their programs.

But Lee Strandberg, University of Colorado pharmacy instructor, sides with the commission. To avoid the overkill found so commonly in drug education, he's setting up an experimental program for the Boulder Valley Public Schools that will sack separate drug education courses and slip the materials into a student's regular classwork. Aimed at middle school and junior high students, the program will incorporate drug information into business education, physical education, mathematics, music, science and social studies.

In math, for example, students may be given figures on heroin addiction and asked to determine how much each addict spends per year to maintain his habit. In music they may learn the role drugs played in the acid-rock craze of the Sixties.

Other educators point out that physical education courses offer opportunities to mention the effects of cigarettes, alcohol and other drugs on physical fitness; biology courses, physiological effects of drugs; family relations courses, the impact of compulsive drug use on interpersonal relations; social studies, the historical and social implications of drug-using behavior.

To be sure, drug education can be integrated into almost any part of the curriculum. And schools can (many already have) design programs to help kids develop positive self-concepts, establish meaningful relationships, practice decision-making skills, and clarify values. And teachers can be better trained to keep their personal opinions about drugs to themselves. And drug-prone youth can receive special attention. And youth of all ages can be involved in developing information materials, planning drug education programs, and even teaching their peers.

But will any of this work? Don't get your hopes up. Federal outlays alone for drug education, information and training totaled an estimated $67.6 million in Fiscal 1972, and look what they've brought—conclusions from at least two federal studies that the money purchased a Pandora's box.

Perhaps the national commission comes closest to providing an answer when it states: "The best response the school system can make to drug use is not more and better drug education, narrowly defined, but education improved generally. Education is the career which this nation designates for its young. For some of them, though, it is a meaningless one."

Isn't that what Richard Stuart implies when he recommends dropping drug education from schools? And, heretical as it may seem, isn't that an admission that, when it comes to drug education, ignorance may be bliss?

DUMP DRUG EDUCATION? NOT ON YOUR LIFE

Convincing schoolmen that drug education may be a bummer won't be easy. As results of this month's opinion poll show, a majority of administrators want drug education programs to remain in schools. They don't think the programs have flopped or that states should repeal drug education laws. In fact, they intend to proceed with any expansion plans that might have been contemplated before the National Commission on Marihuana and Drug Abuse took a swipe at drug education and recommended a moratorium.

Yet—here's the corker—nearly half of the schoolmen polled readily admit that drug education may lead to experimentation. And even larger numbers apparently believe something's wrong with drug education, or 76 percent wouldn't have had to—or be planning to—re-evaluate their programs.

How to explain the inconsistency? Unfortunately, nothing close to a rationale surfaced in respondents' remarks about the poll. The only comment that cropped up occasionally was one indicating "suspicion" of federal reports in general, especially those issued during periods of national budget-cutting.

Reported an Iowa superintendent: "We usually do what we think is right for our district, without paying much attention to Presidential commissions. Very few recommendations that come from such commissions can be expected to meet the needs of small, large and in-between schools."

Could it be that schoolmen are saying: "Yes, we believe drug education may cause some harm, but we'd rather not have Big Brother tell us what to do about it"? If that's the case, maybe the drug education picture isn't as bleak as it appears.

How Administrators Voted

1. Do you agree with conclusions of the National Commission on Marihuana and Drug Abuse that:
a) school drug education programs have flopped? *23%* Yes *77%* No
b) state legislatures should repeal all statutes mandating drug education in public schools? *32%* Yes *68%* No
2. Does your district plan to follow the commission's recommendation to declare a moratorium on any additional funding or expansion of school drug education programs? *18%* Yes *65%* No *17%* Do not have drug education
3. Have the commission's recommendations spurred you to consider re-evaluating your drug education program? *36%* Yes *24%* No *40%* Have already done so
4. Finally, do you consider valid the commission's speculation that current drug education programs may actually stimulate students' interest in and experimentation with drugs? *44%* Yes *56%* No

This opinion poll survey, based on a 5% proportional sampling of 14,000 school administrators in 50 states, brought a 24% response.

"Values clarification" (the process of providing strategies for students to analyze and determine their own values) is "in" at teacher workshops and in-service sessions. However, Kniker and Hash point out that values clarification is only one approach to values education. A wide spectrum of materials bears evidence of this.

Readers may ask themselves: Which approach do I favor? Would I oppose any "camp" if it was adopted in my school district? And the basic question: Is it really possible to treat the subject of personal values in the public schools?

CHOOSING VALUE CURRICULA: A SURVEY OF FOUR VALUE CAMPS

Charles R. Kniker and Virginia Hash

Values education has arrived. Or so it appears when a superintendent calls to inquire whether you know of anyone he might hire who is certified in values clarification. Or so it seems when *My Weekly Reader* and J. C. Penney's *Forum* magazine for educators offer values strategies for teachers. Or so it may be when a government study indicates values education programs may be among the most effective techniques for reducing hard drug usage.[1] Perhaps in some areas it may even be old hat. One administrator reports that students have become "glazed" by the battery of attitude tests and strategies being tried in his district.

The immediate concern of this article is the examination of four "camps" of values curriculum. Through an analysis of their general goals, educational assumptions, and teaching strategies, we hope to help readers evaluate more wisely those curricular aids which will be most appropriate for their educational situations.

1. "The Learning-About-Values Discovery Kit," *My Weekly Reader,* American Education Publications, 1971. Penney's *Forum,* Spring/Summer, 1972. *PREP Report #36,* "Drug Education" (Washington, D.C.: U.S. Department of Health, Education and Welfare, n.d., circa, 1972).

Some readers might be satisfied with a mere listing of various values curricula; that is, those materials which deal exclusively with values topics. We want to offer more than a collection of references for two reasons. First, certain approaches to values education appear to be disarmingly simple. Far too often we have seen too many teachers with too little preparation use too many gimmicks, and end with too many failures. Values confusion rather than values clarity resulted. Second, the term "values clarification" has become synonymous with values education. This is only one of many approaches, and that term has been too loosely applied. Thus, we feel it is time to compare "values clarification" with other approaches.

We have chosen to omit such curricular items as social studies texts that have units on values in American life. Also, in our opinion, media kits devoted to values issues deserve a separate article.

Using the factors cited above—general goals, educational assumptions, and teaching strategies, the writers have identified four types of values curricula widely available today. They are: the values indoctrination camp, the values systems camp, the guidance camp, and the values clarification camp.

The term "camps" suggests that these independently constructed programs form philosophical and pedagogical clusters. "Camps" also implies that these confederacies display diversity. One camp may contain the work of commercial publishers and foundation grantees and reflect an interesting variety of geographical participants and historical ancestors.

THE VALUES INDOCTRINATION CAMP

Although the common interpretation of the word indoctrination is a derogatory one, Webster's first definition is "to instruct in the rudiments or principles of learning." This camp believes certain values are fundamental to any learning, and seeks to ensure that students will acquire these values.

With this understanding, we could consider *The Aesthetic Education Program* for primary grades a values indoctrination curriculum because it aims "to create within individuals an aesthetic sensitivity."[2] Although it uses a variety of creative sensory exercises, it builds specific affective skills and attitudes. Many drug education programs would fall into this camp, too, because of their goals to change attitudes and nurture anti-drug behavior.

2. _____, "Welcome to the Five Sense Store: The Aesthetic Education Program," a promotional brochure of the Viking Press, circa 1973, p. 2.

We seek here to concentrate upon those curricula which openly seek to improve moral behavior. Typically, they open with an essay about the decline in the country's morals that can only be averted by a return to "eternal truths," or at least the life-style of our colonial forebears. Such values as a belief in God, a regard for America as the best example of a Judeo-Christian civilization, and respect for authority and property are highlighted.

The Thomas Jefferson Research Center of Pasadena, California, illustrates this camp. It has distributed a booklet, *Cure for Crisis,* which sounds many of these themes.[3] Frank Goble, President of the Center, encourages teachers to structure leadership building sessions. Frequent references to successful businessmen or political figures are used. Goble finds a psychological rationale for this in the work of Abraham Maslow, who contended that students can benefit from studying the lives of "self-actualized" persons.[4] Helping students to set realistic goals is another frequently mentioned goal.

This curriculum assumed that the teacher will be a dominant figure in classroom interaction. The student is seen as a somewhat mischievous receptacle to be filled with insight. Teachers' manuals urge instructors to lecture, organize panels, show films, and "experiment."[5] Many stories about American heroes, past and present, that end with obvious moral lessons, typify the curriculum. For example, the teacher is encouraged to use the story of John Adams' defense of some British soldiers in 1770, despite his attack on the British system, as a symbol of what a good American does; namely, acts on principle first.[6] The suggested resources do not include those (one thinks of *1776*) which could show another side of the Massachusetts lawyer.

In summary, the values indoctrination camp is geared to the transmission of specific values and involves a minimum of "input" from the students.

THE VALUES SYSTEMS CAMP

On first glance the second camp is quite similar to the first. Statements in some publications are couched in terms of the negative flow of national events, and proclaim that hopefully their programs will

3. Frank Goble, "Cure for Crisis," Thomas Jefferson Research Center, Pasadena, California, 1971. The Center issues a monthly newsletter.

4. *Ibid.,* pp. 8, 9, and 14–18 especially.

5. Virginia Trevitt, *The American Heritage* (Santa Barbara, California, McNally and Loftin Publishers, 1964), pp. 3, 206–259.

6. *Ibid.,* pp. 78, 79.

provide such benefits as decreased "vandalism, narcotics usage, participation in criminal acts, and indulgence in antisocial antics."[7] In the same promotional bulletin, the Character Education Project (CEP) of San Antonio, Texas, funded largely by the Lily Endowment, indicated its general intent was "to assist in setting up educational programs directed to the development of socially useful, self-fulfilling citizens of sound character."[8]

Like the indoctrination group, this camp offers lists of acceptable virtues. CEP, whose materials currently range from kindergarten through junior high, proposed fourteen components of good character, including honesty, generosity, tolerance, and making creditable use of time and talents.[9] Steck-Vaughn's *Human Values Series,* based on the psychological findings of Rucker, suggests eight values themes: affection, respect, power, wealth, enlightenment, skill, well-being, and rectitude.[10]

The educational assumptions and classroom activities that this camp favors are different than those of the indoctrination advocates. Much more stress is placed on the student's rational powers. Often statements appear that underscore the importance of developing the analytical abilities in students who will be the citizens of tomorrow.[11] Despite this concern there is still a heavy reliance upon the teacher's role as a provider of materials and leadership.

A key to analyzing this camp is found in its literature, which insists that values discussions be systematically arranged and conducted. Steck-Vaughn's objectives indicate that students are to develop their skill in values analysis. They begin by defining values, then locate them in the stories, and finally relate the same values in personal and peer situations. A spontaneous approach to values education, discussing it when it happens, is viewed as too haphazard, pedagogically.

Unlike the indoctrination group, this camp assumes that their values lists will be starting points and not ends in themselves. Proponents want students to form their own conclusions about the mean-

7. _____, "Introducing . . . Character Education Project" (San Antonio, Texas: American Institute for Character Education, 1972), p. 1.

8. *Ibid.,* p. 3.

9. Character Education Project, *Living with Me and Others* (San Antonio, Texas: American Institute for Character Education, 1971), pp. 6, 7. This is a third grade or level C book.

10. _____, *About You and Me* (Austin, Texas: Steck-Vaughn Company, 1973), p. 1. Teacher's edition of the second grade text.

11. Lawrence Metcalf (ed.), *Values Education* (Washington, D.C.: National Council for the Social Studies, 1971), is typical of the books for teachers which emphasize the importance of rationality. Another proponent of the high value of rationality is Michael Scriven. See "Values and the Valuing Process," June 21, 1971, ERIC ED 059 932.

ing of honesty in their lives, for example. So, although there may be a tendency in this curriculum to elicit right answers, there is also the acknowledgement that individuals may come to a variety of conclusions.

Stories about fictional boys and girls illustrated in a Norman Rockwell style are a favorite teaching tool. As Steck-Vaughn states, "Still another purpose of these readers is to provide specific examples of moral standards and ethical behavior that are compatible with the democratic view."[12] A story entitled "Ramon Makes Friends" details the first day experiences at school of a son of a professional baseball player. What happens in the classroom and on the playground are to encourage discussions about respect and skill.[13]

Another technique frequently used is the open-ended story. Several curricula provide photographs or sketches of incidents, such as one of two playful boys who have knocked over a lamp. A story about their dilemma on how to explain the accident follows.[14]

One report on the effectiveness of this approach indicated that teachers who used it were very enthusiastic about the results.[15] According to the report, teachers had observed less cheating on exams, improved personal interaction among students, and a decline in vandalism.

THE GUIDANCE CAMP

Characteristic of the two previous camps is their heavy reliance on such traditional values as honesty, courage, and respect. In the guidance camp such terms are avoided. Techniques and resources are used specifically to help each student become more socially and emotionally mature, more self-actuated, and more aware of himself as a unique, potentially capable individual.

Typical curricula in this area are *Developing Understanding of Self and Others* (DUSO), *Human Development Program* (HDP), *Motivation Achievement Program* (MAP), and *Search for Meaning*. A closer investigation of the HDP developed by Harold Bessell and Uvaldo Palomares and published by Human Development Training

12. _____, *Seeking Values* (Austin, Texas: Steck-Vaughn Company, 1973), pp. 7, 8. Teacher's edition of the fourth grade text.
13. *Ibid.*, pp. 154–161.
14. Joan M. Sayre, *Teaching Moral Values Through Behavior Modification* (Danville, Ill.: Interstate Printers and Publishers, 1972), pp. 22, 23.
15. Character Education Project, "Report of the First National Evaluation Conference of the Character Education Project," American Institute for Character Education, 1972.

Institute will serve to illustrate the goals of a guidance camp advocate. In its broadest outline, this is "a curriculum designed to improve communications between the teacher and the child." [16] Using a set of well-defined lesson plans, this program focuses "on three main areas of experience or themes: *Awareness* (knowing what your thoughts, feelings, and actions really are), *Mastery* (knowing what your abilities are and how to use them), and *Social Interaction* (knowing other people)."[17]

Another program, MAP, published by combined Motivation Education Systems, Inc., proposes a thematic organization of ideas and concepts including: sharing, successes, strengths, values, creative life, management, and reinforcement.[18] These six phases are specified in terms of behaviorial objectives.

This camp provides direction and assistance to the teacher as evidenced by extensive printed curriculum guides. Flip charts, posters, puppets, recordings, as well as comprehensive lesson plans enable both the experienced and inexperienced teacher to be more effective in guiding and encouraging children's development in the affective domain.

Search for Meaning is one example.[19] It has been organized to provide a logical and sequential approach toward an examination of values. Three distinct units, each comprehensive, have been designed and it is urged that these be followed in an orderly fashion, from the first through the third, although not all need be included in one year's work.

Typically, each curriculum in this camp is based on some form of group interaction activity with a great deal of verbal interchange. Perhaps none have the arrangement so clearly defined as does the HDP, with its Magic Circle. The importance of children and teacher sitting in a circle is emphasized because of the belief that it is important to see each other. Thus, they can learn to identify and react to nonverbal communication as well as to what they hear.

It is the teacher's responsibility in all programs to introduce the daily, or weekly, discussion topics, often called experiences, and to see that all have an opportunity to talk and to be heard. "One of the cardinal features of the Magic Circle is that the teacher is always

16. Harold Bessell and Uvaldo Palomares, *Methods in Human Development: Theory Manual* (El Cajon, California: Human Development Training Institute, 1970), p. 1.
17. *Ibid.*, p. i.
18. Combined Motivation Education Systems, Inc., *Motivation Achievement Program* (Chicago, Ill.: Achievement Motivation Program, 1971).
19. Center for Learning, *Search for Meaning* (Dayton, Ohio: Pflaum/Standard, 1974). Junior High level.

courteous, children are spoken to by name, thanked by name, and always responded to in a polite manner. Children experience themselves as being taken seriously as people, and they are, because that is what courtesy is all about."[20]

In summary, this approach provides directed learning activities aimed toward helping an individual develop an increased awareness of himself and his relationships to and with others. Planned experiences and materials emphasize the dynamic relationship of feelings, goals, and behaviors.

VALUES CLARIFICATION CAMP

The function of information is to inform.
To inform what?
To inform your values.[21]

These words by Louis E. Raths point out in a general way the focal point of the values clarification camp. Whereas the three camps already discussed are product or concept-oriented, this approach is process-oriented. Leaning heavily on the thinking of John Dewey, Raths focuses on how people come to hold and how they change certain beliefs and establish certain behavior patterns. Valuing, according to Raths, is composed of: 1) choosing one's beliefs and behaviors; 2) prizing one's beliefs and behaviors; and 3) acting on one's beliefs. These three main areas have been further refined into seven subprocesses.[22] "The goal of the values clarification approach is to help students utilize the above seven processes of valuing in their own lives, to apply these valuing processes to already formed beliefs and behavior patterns and to those still emerging."[23]

The significance, worth, and dignity of each individual is emphasized in all aspects of this camp. An additional point is that one does not force his own values on others. Words such as openness, accep-

20. Bessell and Palomares, *Methods in Human Development*, p. 10.

21. Merrill Harmin, Howard Kirschenbaum, and Sidney B. Simon, *Clarifying Values Through Subject Matter* (Minneapolis: Winston Press, Inc., 1973), p. 1.

22. Louis Raths, Merrill Harmin, and Sidney Simon, *Values and Teaching* (Columbus, Ohio: Charles E. Merrill, 1966), pp. 27–30. In summary, the seven processes of valuing are: values must be freely chosen; thoughtful consideration must be evident; real alternatives in choices must be present; values will have a positive connotation; values will be publicly affirmed; values show evidence of expenditure of resources; and values will be part of a person's life-style.

23. Sidney Simon, Leland W. Howe, and Howard Kirschenbaum, *Values Clarification: A Handbook of Practical Strategies for Teachers and Students* (New York: Hart Publishing Co., Inc., 1972), p. 20.

tance, and respect are all found frequently in the literature. The values clarification process is aimed at helping each individual integrate his or her choices of values into the pattern of his or her own life. Each person can be helped to become more positive, more enthusiastic, and prouder about his or her personal beliefs, purposes, and attitudes when they are chosen freely, prized, and acted upon. The person is trusted to lead his or her own life in a personally responsible manner.

It is the contention of Raths that "children who are helped to use the valuing process will behave in ways that are less apathetic, confused, and irrational."[24] Since each person is his own authority, the teacher-student relationship is one of mutuality rather than of the leader-follower type. However, the modeling behavior of the teacher cannot be overlooked or underemphasized. The teacher must set the example as someone who also prizes, chooses, and acts. The modeling of good listening skills, verbal reinforcement, and active participation in classroom valuing strategies are seen as necessary elements in helping children learn to use the process of valuing. It has already been pointed out that the main component of this approach is not the content of a person's values but the process of valuing.

Many clarifying strategies have been compiled in *Values Clarification*.[25] Each strategy is described in a standard format: 1) the purpose, which relates to one or more of the processes of valuing; 2) a detailed procedural description; and 3) notes and tips for the teacher. It is repeatedly emphasized that there is no single right way to use these strategies and there is no hard and fast sequence of strategies to follow. Rather, users are urged to change, adapt, and develop their own strategies appropriate to their specific situations.

Another process system for self-examination, *Search for Values,* for senior high students, provides for a number of activities to be kept in a diary.[26] With minimal cues, each person examines his personal meaning and relationship to such concepts as time, competition, authority, personal space, commitment, relationships, and images. Since basic trust and integrity are assumed, individuals exercise free choice in discussing, or not discussing, their personal findings with others in their group.

24. Raths, *Values and Teaching,* p. 11.
25. Simon, *et al., Values Clarification.*
26. Center for Learning, *Search for Values* (Dayton, Ohio: Pflaum/Standard, 1972). For senior high students. By diary approach, we mean that a series of activities, many done on ditto sheets, are collected by students in a notebook. Although there are opportunities in class for the students to express their reactions to the activities, and although they may decide to turn in the diary, they reserve the right not to do so.

Briefly, then, the values clarification camp attempts to help persons understand and apply a series of valuing processes to their own lives in order that they might build their own unique values system.

CONCLUSION

Surveying the four types of curricula indicates to the writers that each has its strengths and weaknesses, advantages as well as disadvantages. Our position is that individual teachers and local administrators are in the best position to determine which single curriculum or combination of curricula would be most appropriate for their situation. We have tried to avoid giving our imprimatur to one camp.

In general, we do find significant differences between the camps. The first three are product-oriented, either in terms of specific values, or in terms of a life-style, while the fourth, values clarification, is process-oriented. The latter almost reaches the point which states "I don't care what your values are, just so you know how you arrived at them."

Some teachers may be more comfortable with the clear-cut delineations of values and lesson plans in the first two camps. Both these camps, as noted, seem to be hard-pressed to avoid "right answers," despite using such techniques as open-ended stories. The guidance camp is not free from this tendency, either, although it offers a different vocabulary of right answers. Despite the language of building self-worth, and the beauty of individual differences, many activities still want children to adjust to the group. In the hands of some teachers, this has been used to subtly manipulate children who have challenged the teacher's authority.

Although we maintain that these categories are valid, we must also point out that individual curricula have blended strategies from several camps. For example, a text by Carl Elder, *Making Value Judgments,* is organized around traditional moral issues—whether or not to smoke, drink—but incorporates many value-clarifying strategies.[27]

Obviously, we could not evaluate all materials now on the market. We only hope we have provided an adequate and accurate system of analysis that will help in the assessment of value curricular materials for use in schools. We invite your comments on the validity

27. Carl Elder, *Making Value Judgments: Decisions for Today* (Columbus, Ohio: Charles E. Merrill, 1972).

of our criterion, along with suggestions for expanding and refining it, should you deem it worthwhile.

Finally, we are listing more complete data on values curricula below to encourage study on this emerging curricular area.

RESOURCES FOR VALUE CURRICULUM

General

William G. Carr (ed.), *Values and the Curriculum* (Washington, D.C.: National Education Association, 1970), 1201 16th St., N.W., 20036. Stock No. 381-11936. The Fourth International Curriculum Conference explored values implicit in the educational systems, the processes by which human beings acquire values, and the ways in which curricula might be modified to include explicit and implicit values education.

Thomas B. Roberts, *Seven Major Foci of Affective Experience: A Typology for Educational Design, Planning, Analysis, and Research* (De Kalb, Ill.: University of Northern Illinois, 1972), abstract. Roberts suggests that personal awareness, creative behavior, interpersonal awareness, subject orientation, specific content, affective styles of teaching/learning, and the role of the educator should be the foci for evaluating a curriculum and designing one's own affective activities. (ERIC number Ed 063 215.)

Publishers of Values Materials

Achievement Motivation Program, 111 East Wacker Drive, Suite 510 Chicago, Illinois, 60601. The W. Clement and Jessie V. Stone Foundation prepared the "On Stage: Wally, Bertha, and You" program for primary grades; "About Me" for intermediate students; and "The Motivation Advance Program" (MAP) for junior high/senior high levels.

American Guidance Service, Inc, Publishers' Building, Circle Pines, Minnesota, 55014. DUSO D-1 and D-2 *Developing Understanding of Self and Others* kits, for the lower-primary and upper-primary grades, which were developed under the leadership of Don Dinkmeyer, are available from this firm.

American Institute for Character Education, P.O. Box 12617, San Antonio, Texas, 78212. This foundation supported the Character Education Project, which has developed the following materials: (K) "Happy Life Series"; (E) "Living With Me" and "Our Rights and

Responsibilities"; (JH) "Decisions I Must Make—About Me" and "Decisions I Must Make—About Me and School."

Charles E. Merrill Publishing Co., 1300 Alum Creek Drive, Columbus, Ohio, 43216. See the footnotes for a sample of the books they have published in this field.

College Entrance Examination Board, 888 7th Avenue, New York, New York, 10019. H. B. Gelatt, Barbara Varenhorst, and Richard Carey, *Deciding*. It is a kit for the secondary level.

Educational Research Council of America, Rockefeller Building, Cleveland, Ohio, 44113. Primarily they produce guidance materials, but see "The Learning to Decide Program" for grades four, five, and six.

Human Development Training Institute, 1081 E. Main Street, El Cajon, California, 92021. The Human Development programs range from kindergarten through sixth grade.

The Interstate Printers and Publishers, 19—27 N. Jackson, Danville, Illinois, 61832. Interstate publisher of *Teaching Moral Values Through Behavior Modification* by Joan Sayre. For the intermediate level.

McNally and Loftin, Publishers, P.O. Box 1316, Santa Barbara, California, 93102. Publishers of *The American Heritage* by Virginia Trevitt.

My Weekly Reader, Education Center, Columbus, Ohio, 43216. "The Learning-About-Values Discovery Kit" and "How I Feel" are marketed by this Xerox subsidiary.

Pflaum/Standard, 38 W. 5th St., Dayton, Ohio, 45402. This firm produces the *Dimensions of Personality* series for elementary students, the *Search for Meaning* kit for junior high usage, and the *Search for Values* materials for the high school level.

Science Research Associates, Inc., 259 E. Erie St., Chicago, Illinois, 60611. Their *Focus on Self-Development Series* is beamed at the elementary level. They have produced other value-related curriculum materials which are appropriate for upper grades.

Steck-Vaughn Publishing Company, P.O. Box 2028, Vaughn Building, Austin, Texas, 78767. *The Human Values Series* has materials for the K-6 grade levels.

Thomas Jefferson Research Center, 1143 N. Lake Ave., Pasadena, California, 91104. In addition to materials cited in the footnotes, Frank Goble has written *The Third Force,* which examines educational implications of Maslow's findings.

The Viking Press, 625 Madison Ave., New York, New York, 10022. In *The Aesthetic Education Program,* themes include aesthetics in the physical world; aesthetics and arts elements; and aesthetics and the creative process.

Values are not only encountered in the formal curriculum. They also emerge in the day-to-day and hour-by-hour routines of the school.

Those who believe schools do not deal with values, those who hope that schools teach students to think for themselves, and those who hold that people leave school as autonomous individuals to be corrupted by other agencies may reassess their positions after reading the following article.

The following suggestions, seriously proposed by a New York teacher and approvingly published by a respected national educational journal, raise serious value questions. How many schools follow this spirit of control, if not the specific steps, advocated by Joel Santoro? Granted the school's responsibility to provide a safe environment, is this the price that must be paid?

CONTROL AND DISCIPLINE IN SCHOOL CAFETERIAS

Joel T. Santoro

Organization, control and discipline in school cafeterias is a job that can be handled most effectively by teachers. It is also a task that is viewed as distasteful, since at many times it becomes more exhausting than teaching itself. This assignment will never be easy, but with the proper techniques, the situation can be improved.

Certain physical aids are extremely necessary. A clear-sounding portable microphone is a "must" for effective control of any large group. The teacher can move among the students, instantly adjust the volume, take the instrument out of doors, and easily have it repaired.

Another aid is the division of the cafeteria into approximately four sections. This can be accomplished by numbering the tables or taping large numbers opposite designated sections. By dividing the area in this way, dismissal at the close of the period is facilitated,

Joel T. Santoro, "Control and Discipline in School Cafeterias," *Clearing House,* vol. 40, no. 3 (November 1965), pp. 152–154. Reprinted by permission.

since one section at a time can be released and the area checked for cleanliness and order.

Next, a clear, short definition of cafeteria rules can be posted in several visible places. Having something tangible to point to seems to help. When a rule is violated, have the student read it back so there is no ground for complaint when appropriate measures are taken if the problem reoccurs. Here are a few examples that may be of help:

1. Do not run in aisles.
2. Obtain passes before leaving cafeteria.
3. Take a seat when the whistle is blown.
4. Eat ice cream in the cafeteria only.
5. Empty garbage into receptacles.

The signs can be made in the art department or by gluing one and one-half inch plastic letters to a heavy piece of poster paper.

A whistle, used in conjunction with the microphone, may be used to signal students to their seats before daily announcements. If blown more than several times during the period the whistle will become ineffective. Overuse, a common mistake, becomes annoying, and soon no one listens.

Last of all, be sure that the cafeteria clock is synchronized with the school master clock. It is wise to dismiss students by sections at the close of the period—generally a few minutes early, to avoid a clash with the next lunch period.

Controls for the cafeteria have to be established with the administration. One administrator, assigned to handle chronic problem cases, should pass through the cafeteria daily, to help set a proper tone. Through early planning and scheduling, an effective method of immediately curbing uncooperative students is to request a lunch detention room. Obtaining volunteers to supervise this room will be difficult, but on a rotation basis the assignment is tolerable and the cafeteria situation always improves.

Administrators must place in charge one teacher with authority commensurate to the large responsibility at hand. They must also avoid placing in supervisory positions custodians, aides, parents, or other well-meaning individuals who do not have the proper training and authority. Such people have been tried in many metropolitan schools and have not proven effective. Teachers know the students, understand the supervisory problem, and are more apt to possess the skills to deal with and prevent discipline problems.

Assuming most of the preceding suggestions are in effect, let's look at a typical daily procedure from entrance to exit and consider some techniques of control and discipline.

Every day must have a similar pattern from start to finish, consistent with a prearranged organizational plan. Entering the cafeteria is the first phase of the pattern. Students should form an orderly line and wait to pick up their food. Immediately have those who attempt to sneak ahead, push, or create a disturbance go to the end of the line. Do not hesitate! Act at once and the days to come will be automatically easier, once students recognize that poor conduct will be dealt with firmly. Keeping those lines moving and in order prevents confusion from the start. Maintaining another line with trays for those who bring a lunch from home speeds the serving a great deal.

When the students are in the cafeteria and eating, very little "horse-play" or unnecessary traffic occurs. As the actual eating of lunch is completed, the "fooling" and jostling about begin. There are specific techniques that, if utilized by the professional staff, can be effective in curbing these difficulties.

The raising of the voice is the most effective tool the teacher has. Use a strong voice whether a student is next to you or ten tables away. Remember, this is not a classroom of 25 students but a cafeteria of possibly 500 talking boys and girls. Use a powerful voice and be heard!

Another useful thing is a whistle, used only by the teacher in charge to seat students once a period for announcements, and once for dismissal. On a whistle signal, students should be seated. Make this clear from the first day or when the time comes for an emergency announcement, fire drill instructions, or some message, order will be difficult to obtain.

A method of enforcing cafeteria regulations is to assign one or more teachers to a section of the cafeteria for which they are responsible. Teachers must not all stand together, but should constantly move around their section, talking to students and keeping order. Teachers should make a conscious effort to learn the names of students. It is much easier to correct students and prevent problems when youngsters are known on a first name basis.

Students will test the rules; so enforce the determined regulations. Immediate discipline might range from having a student pick up several pieces of paper to lunch detention. If possible, avoid letting the detention room become a crutch for problems. Get used to handling them yourself, since most schools cannot spare the staff to organize a lunch detention room anyway. Setting up what is called a "manners table" within the cafeteria can substitute for a detention room. By placing a sign saying "Manners Table" over several tables set aside in one corner of the cafeteria, a convenient area for disruptive students can be established. Discipline cases can eat there or remain seated for the entire lunch period. Be careful not to overload these tables or the method will not succeed, because it will become impossible to contain all the problem students in one small section.

On occasion a silent lunch can be given to quiet things down, but this becomes more of a strain on the teachers and its results are negligible. An uncooperative group can be improved by first having them report to the auditorium for 15 minutes and then dismissing them for lunch. The shorter lunch period automatically reduces the time available for horseplay.

At the end of the period, dismissal can be a hectic time, and a definite system goes a long way to alleviate confusion and congestion at exits. Start by blowing the whistle approximately five minutes before the bell and seat all students. When this is accomplished, teachers can check their sections and the cafeteria can be looked over for cleanliness and order. The section which is in order first can be dismissed, then one section at a time. Good timing will have the cafeteria cleared just as the next lunch class begins to enter, and the regulation of sections for dismissal will reduce the accident potential on crowded stairways.

Whatever the methods used in the cafeteria for its many phases, always be consistent and follow a well-organized routine. The assignment will always be difficult, but it certainly can be handled effectively with a good staff and careful organization.

That schools may represent the interests of conformity, control, and censorship is further illustrated by the personal appearance or "dress" codes
that are still a widespread phenomenon. Controversies have been reported in the press all over the
country recently. Typical of these is the account of
what happened in Maquoketa, Iowa, a midwestern
town of 6,000 people.

ANATOMY OF A TOWN
VS. LONG HAIR
Gordon Gammack

Maquoketa, Ia.—A mood of smoldering fury has engulfed Maquoketa
over resistance to a ban against long hair in the public schools. That's
the issue on the surface. But there are those who sense also the wrath
of a no-longer-silent majority against rebellious, non-conforming
youth and disrespect for authority. In the midst of all this the Iowa
Civil Liberties Union, considered subversive by many Maquoketans,
has become the whipping boy. The controversy started when William
Brooks, principal of Maquoketa Community High School, sent a
letter to parents warning that hair covering boys' ears and below the
collar line at the neck would not be tolerated.

There was nothing new about this code. What made it especially
provocative was that it was issued in the face of a United States
District Court ruling written by Iowa Judge William C. Hanson, in
the case of Susan Sims vs. the Colfax (Iowa) Community School
district that the Constitution guarantees "a student's free choice of
his appearance." At the high school's opening assembly, about nine
boys showed up with hair violating the code. The number isn't
precise because several dropouts seeking readmission were involved.
The facts are that four students with long hair remain out of school
and the storm center is 15-year-old Kevin Allen because his mother,
Mrs. Kenneth (Darlene) Allen, sought and obtained the intervention
of the Iowa Civil Liberties Union. She has become the target of
extensive hostility. She says she has received a barrage of ugly phone

Gordon Gammack, "Anatomy of a Town vs. Long Hair" *Des Moines Register*, September
20, 1970, T1+. Copyright 1970. Reprinted by permission.

calls, has been subjected to obscene gestures as she walks along the streets, and has been shunned by clerks when she goes shopping. It is crystal clear that the school authorities have the backing of the overwhelming majority in Maquoketa, at least ten to one, probably. The five-member Board of Education backs Principal Brooks unanimously.

The strongest opposition to Brooks seems to come from within his own faculty, and some of the teachers, claiming that the school officials and public are taking a courts-be-damned attitude, are outspoken. Says Richard Wolf, history, English and humanities instructor and also Democratic chairman in Jackson County: "This equation they have developed is dangerous—Long hair equals drug addiction equals peaceniks equals Communism."

Wolf says that some of the backers of the hair code have "total contempt for the law of the land. These are the same people who mouth law and order," he continues. "I find law and order coming out of their mouths as valid as love out of the mouth of a street walker."

Like so many storms, this one developed in relative serenity. Early in August, the "dress code" of Principal Brooks was discussed at a meeting of school board members and school administrators. Attitudes were more resilient than they are now. One school board member, Mrs. Ross River, an unbending supporter of the boys' hair code, challenged a Brooks' directive that girls wear stockings. Stockings are both hot and expensive, she said, and Brooks replied that "this is easy to amend."

Superintendent of Schools Melvin Sikkink, who now maintains that Judge Hanson's rule in "the Colfax case" doesn't apply to the Maquoketa situation, said then that at summer seminars he attended it was brought out that most court cases have held that hair length is none of the school's business. And Gaylord Willman, long-time principal of the junior high schools, said, "Your dress code is illegal. You are going to lose every case that goes to court. You can't force a majority thing on a minority."

The polarization seems to have come with the intervention of the Iowa Civil Liberties Union and Principal Brooks may have provoked some of the hostility a year ago. He had asked Robert Melvold, publisher of the Maquoketa Newspapers, for permission to write a weekly column about school affairs and Melvold agreed. Brooks wrote in a column:

"Just who or what is this Iowa Civil Liberties Union?" he started. "Where does this so-called champion of the people get the right to tell the public schools how to handle students? 'I.C.L.U. WARNS

SCHOOLS VS. LONG HAIR RULES!' Big deal! They really sound tough! A teacher or administrator says something to a student and if this student doesn't happen to like it, he yells 'Foul' or 'Iowa Civil Liberties Union' and a couple of two-bit shyster lawyers come crawling in and scream that we are violating this poor child's freedom. What freedom? The schools are trying to educate students. We are attempting to help bring these students up to that certain age when they are supposed to be mature enough to make their own wise decisons. How can we possibly do this when every time we turn around, some nut hollers, 'You can't do that.' "

The attacks on the Civil Liberties Union are viewed with both sadness and amusement by Agnes Evans, high school journalism and English teacher, who will retire in four years. She says that most people in Maquoketa completely misunderstand the Civil Liberties Union and don't realize it has been supported vigorously by such men as Dwight Eisenhower and a host of other conservative leaders. Back in the 1940's she was a zealous I.C.L.U. member and was on a committee that fought against unjust dismissals of teachers. "Teachers were being dismissed without reason, without being warned that they were doing anything displeasing," she recalls. "Much of the controversy sprang from gossip and personal dislikes. Especially in the humanities, teachers make statements that are rather involved and a pupil will pick up a word and when he repeats it at home, a parent misunderstands and a teacher becomes suspect. Until the 1950's teachers had no security in this state."

Mrs. Evans—a Republican and a member of the Daughters of the American Revolution—says of the Maquoketa hair controversy, "People who are well enough educated, good enough citizens and are fair enough, want to support the law. Many don't realize that the courts have spoken."

There was a stormy public hearing, attended by 400, over the hair code. There was a reference to Joseph Johnston, Iowa City attorney representing the Civil Liberties Union, "coming out from under a rock" to attend the meeting and the revelation that he is a member of the Iowa Legislature proved to be something of a shock to townspeople. When Johnston said that the purpose of the Civil Liberties Union is to protect Constitutional rights, a Maquoketa businessman, Ben Hulsen, said the organization "ought to get a better press agent" because "it appears they only defend those in shady operations."

Mrs. Allen says she sought help of the I.C.L.U. because she didn't have the funds to hire a private attorney. Her husband has been a coronary invalid for 12 years. She has three sons at college—two studying to be teachers at the University of Northern Iowa—and she works part time to support the family. "This is the first time I've ever taken a stand on anything," she says. "But I think it is so important. People should be able to question rulings like this without being considered a Communist or a rabble-rouser. I've been called a permissive parent, no discipline whatever, but I've probably broken as many yardsticks over the boys' little fannies as any mother. The love and respect of my son and my husband mean more to me than this whole community. These town people have checked all the church rolls and decided I'm a heathen because I don't belong to a church. Organized religion has become so big, an individual is lost in the shuffle. I have my own personal relationship with God. I am a Christian. I know I am."

Mrs. Allen has been gratified by the support she has received—especially from Sue River, daughter of the school board member and a freshman at Carleton College who spoke out against the hair code at the public hearing and told Mrs. Allen, "I'm with you all the way." And Mrs. Allen received a letter, signed by two teachers, who praised her for standing up against "embittered and frustrated people infected with fear and irrationality. . . . Hate may be stronger than love, but love is more enduring."

Some Maquoketa community leaders have found it difficult to take a middle ground and some businessmen even suspected of being critical of school authorities reportedly have suffered business sanctions. Publisher Melvold has opened his pages to every possible expression and editorially urged the long-hairs to conform pending a conclusive ruling. Yet, he is criticized by Principal Brooks for giving the controversy "too much attention."

The clergy has been involved, too. Mrs. Allen is especially distressed over the reference by the Rev. Jerry B. Walcott (Methodist) to "a mangy looking character from nowhere." Her son, she says, bathes and shampoos his hair daily. Said the Rev. Mr. Walcott: "Even though Mr. Brooks' action to dismiss long hairs until they clean up and come back to the human race is supposedly illegal, I will be most disappointed if the school board does not give him full backing all the way."

Superintendent Sikkink says he is satisfied that Judge Hanson's ruling in the Colfax hair case does not apply because "it applied to one student, a female; we're dealing with boys and that's quite different right there. Just look at the difference between men's and women's hair all over the country."

Said Judge Hanson: "School hair rules are reasonable and thus Constitutional only if the school can objectively show that such a rule does in fact prevent some disruption or interference of the school system." Civil Liberties Union supporters stress that at Maquoketa the boys with long hair were suspended before classes started, thus depriving the schools of claims that long hair was disruptive.

One school board member, William Lamb, was high school principal before Brooks and now is in business. He says: "Whenever you open the door, there's hardly room to find a stopping place. How far do rights extend? Authority is being challenged everywhere these days. The public hasn't caught up with this liberal thinking. Maybe the public doesn't want to catch up."

Says Mrs. River: "I don't prefer to call it a hair issue because it is not really that. It's a matter of do we have rules and regulations or don't we. One judge's ruling doesn't make a law."

One of the most controversial figures in the Maquoketa rhubarb is Gary Holst, who came from the St. Louis area this year to teach shop. At the public hearing some observers thought he favored putting the "ugly heads" of the long haired boys into the machines of his shop but he says, "No, no, no, I don't think I said that. Anyway, what I meant was that with their long hair, their heads might be caught in the machines." Holst thinks the number of boys wanting long hair is inconsequential. "We're talking about two or three out of 500. If you're talking about 30, 40 percent, you've got something different. I can't see bucking the establishment. Outside forces are involved in this. Someone, somewhere is putting a little pressure on someone." Was he referring to something subversive, Communist-inspired? "I've seen things that have been," he replied.

Teacher Wolf says there are undercurrents of violent hatred in Maquoketa and a feeling against college campus militants of "shoot 'em; kill 'em." And he sees much of the bitterness caused by rifts within the family. "In every single case here where we have a really vociferous opponent, it's because of their home situation. These people have been threatened at home. Their children are rejecting them. The children are going through this traumatic declaration of independence and all this bitterness seems to follow right out of it."

Through all of this, little attention has been paid to one section of Judge Hanson's opinion: "There has undoubtedly been too much said if not written concerning long hair or unusual hair styles. Mankind's experience has demonstrated that in this area of fashion, fads constantly come and go as the pendulum unceasingly swings from extreme to extreme. Thus, no doubt, the proper characterization of the current controversy over students' hair is that of the proverbial tempest in a teapot."

The two previous articles may imply that virtually nothing has been done regarding student rights in schools. That impression would be erroneous. High schools have relaxed dress codes, and quasi-official underground student papers exist at the high school and junior high level.

Some efforts even reach to the elementary level. *Scholastic Magazine* has provided materials to teachers and students to encourage discussion on "free speech" and student rights.

The reactions cited in this newspaper account pose such questions as: Was this too "advanced" for the elementary level indicated? Is this an accurate interpretation of "free speech"?

(Editors' note: We were unsuccessful in our efforts to gain permission to reprint *Scholastic Magazine's* materials, which its editors did emphasize had a follow-up article on the responsibilities of students.)

RAKE STORY ON RIGHTS OF 5TH GRADERS
James Ney

Davenport, Ia.—Some Davenport elementary school principals and parents are upset about a recent insert in the magazine "Scholastic Young Citizen"—aimed at fifth-graders—which told pupils they have constitutional rights as "persons."

Carl Dresselhaus, director of elementary education, said last week that the Davenport Community School District is considering dropping its subscription to the elementary education supplement at the end of the current year because it carried the article.

CITES HARM

He said less than half the school district's elementary schools use "Young Citizen" in conjunction with social studies. But after a

From *Des Moines Register*, April 29, 1973. Reprinted by permission of the *Register*.

discussion of the Scholastic insert with principals of the schools using it, Dresselhaus said, "The consensus was that the article could do nothing but hurt the cause of what we are trying to teach boys and girls."

The article, "Have You Got Rights?" was brought to Dresselhaus' attention by members of his staff and parents who questioned its place in educational materials for students of fifth-grade age.

"We try to promote positive values and we feel this article doesn't do that," said Dresselhaus.

The insert, in booklet form, tells fifth-graders:

"You can wear your hair as long as you wish and how you wish if it isn't a danger to your health and safety or the health and safety of others."

"You may also wear whatever you want. And you can't be kept from taking part in school clubs, music groups, or sports because of how you dress or wear your hair. However, you must use good sense!"

"The laws of most states say that you must 'show respect' for the U.S. flag. But suppose, because of your own religious or personal beliefs, you do not believe in such salutes. You need not take part. You may sit or stand quietly or be allowed to leave the room during the pledge."

"Your desk and your locker are yours and they are private. In some cases, no one should look in them. But they CAN be searched—for a good reason. And you must be told the reason."

The booklet also details students' rights to freedom to print what they want, freedom of assembly, and to petition. It tells students that before they are punished they have a right to know what they have done wrong, and also tells students their rights when suspension or expulsion are being considered.

NOT MATURE

Dresselhaus said students of fifth-grade age are not mature enough to receive such information, but that the booklet would be appropriate for older students.

"It makes it difficult for the home and school to develop citizenship because students of the fifth-grade age are not mature enough to develop the responsibility that is needed," he said.

He said he feels the article "doesn't promote the home and school situation."

"You've got to watch what is given to these youngsters," he said.

The subscription to "Young Citizen" is continuing for the remainder of the year, he said. "After this, I'm sure the principals are looking closely at each issue," he said.

He emphasized that Scholastic "has been a useful publication in the schools here" and has been used for a number of years.

Dresselhaus said the editors of the publication apologized for the article when he objected, and that they told him they had "erred" in printing it.

How thoroughly biased the school culture and society in general are is documented in this study of sexism. Levy and Stacey promise to do more than just spotlight wrongs; they propose "directions for future analysis and activity."

Were you aware of the extent of prejudice that they found? Do you agree with their assessment of previous reform efforts? How valid are their strategies for the future?

SEXISM IN THE ELEMENTARY SCHOOL: A BACKWARD AND FORWARD LOOK
Betty Levy and Judith Stacey

The purpose of this article is twofold. First, it presents a feminist case against the elementary school. It does so by summarizing the existing documentation in this area. Since most of this literature has been presented in liberal, equal rights terms, the typical response to

Reprinted by permission of the authors and the *Phi Delta Kappan*, October, 1973, pp. 105–109, 123.

it has been limited to patching up inequities. For this reason, a second purpose of this article is to show the limits of a liberal approach to sexism and to suggest directions for future analysis and activity.

The elementary schools present us with a facade of equal education for boys and girls: Classes are coeducational and the curriculum appears to be the same for both sexes. Developmentally, children are at a stage where sexuality is "latent" according to Freud, and where the focal concern, according to Erikson, is the development of skills and competencies and the learning of adult tools and methods. Sex-typing would appear to be a relatively minor concern or occurrence.

Nevertheless, sex-typing occurs in the elementary school. It permeates all aspects of the curriculum, classroom organization, the structure of the school, teacher behavior with children, and the extracurricular milieu. Furthermore, although this traditional sex-typing is detrimental for both sexes, it is particularly damaging for girls.[1] Rigid designation of one set of interests and behaviors to only one sex limits the potential of each. But compared to males, females are the oppressed group in our society, and the roles and characteristics assigned to females are less positive and less desirable than those assigned to males.

Unfortunately, even feminists have often overlooked the fact that schools exist in part to perpetuate various roles which maintain our sexist society. That is why the inequalities are not removed on first expose. Whether schools "make a difference" in dramatically changing the life chances of the poor, of minority groups, or of women, schools do "make a difference" in that they remain effective agents of social control, perpetuating the existing class, racial, and sexual divisions in our society. In documenting the ways in which schools maintain existing sex distinctions, we must remember the conflict between liberal ideology ("schools should treat all children alike") and the more conservative reality that schools in fact prepare youngsters for social stratification.

To concretize what is meant by roles which are functional to a sexist society, consider some selections from an oft-quoted children's book (Darrow's *I'm Glad I'm a Boy. I'm Glad I'm a Girl*) which makes explicit the roles girls and boys are supposed to play:

1. Betty Levy, "The School's Role in the Sex-Role Stereotyping of Girls: A Feminist Review of the Literature," *Feminist Studies,* summer, 1972, pp. 5–23; and Judith Stacey, Susan Bereaud, and Joan Daniels, *And Jill Came Tumbling After: Sexism in American Education* (New York: Dell, 1974).

Boys have trucks. Girls have dolls. Boys are doctors. Girls are nurses. Boys are presidents. Girls are first ladies. Boys fix things. Girls need things fixed. Boys build houses. Girls keep houses.[2]

Here the assumed complementarity of the sex roles is flawed by the blatant inequality of the roles presented.

The message of Darrow's book is dramatically reinforced by the standard academic curriculum. A particularly offensive example of overt sex-typing is "Alpha One," a relatively new phonics program for kindergartners and first-graders being used in many Long Island and New York City school districts. It has been estimated that 8,000 classrooms around the nation are using this expensive multimedia approach to reading instruction,[3] which seems to teach more about sex roles than it does about phonics. In the Alpha One program, each letter of the alphabet is assigned a personality and a gender. The 21 consonants, known as "the letter boys," are male; the five vowels are female, each with something wrong with her. When "Little Miss A" appears, the boys exclaim: "Oh, no. Oh, no. It can't be true. Not with so much work to do. A girl. A girl. Oh, go away. A girl's no good for work or play." Little Miss A sneezes "ah-choo all day." Little Miss E is so weak she can hardly walk, and Little Miss I has an incurable itch. The boys address these last two respectively: "It looks like we are stuck again. We much prefer to work with men." "Little Miss I, you're a sight. Just looking at you is a fright." And to make male domination absolutely clear, Mr. R bullies the girls into giving up their names when they stand at his side—an unintentional paradigm for matrimonial tradition!

Alpha One is being marketed as a cute, innovative approach to language arts. Without evaluating its effectiveness in teaching reading, we think its sex role message could hardly be more harmful.

A number of descriptive studies have documented sex-stereotyping in elementary school readers. One of the most thorough studies was conducted by a Princeton, New Jersey, group called the Women on Words and Images.[4] This group surveyed 134 books used in New Jersey schools. The books represent 18 major textbook companies, including those that have developed urban, multi-ethnic series. The same old sex roles appear even in the "newer" series. In terms of

2. Whitney Darrow, *I'm Glad I'm a Boy. I'm Glad I'm a Girl.* (New York: Simon and Schuster, 1970).
3. Annabelle Kerins, "Vowels Are Seeking Lbrtn Frm th Cnsnnts," in *Report on Sex Bias in the Public Schools* (New York Chapter of the National Organization of Women, 1972), p. 21.
4. *Dick and Jane as Victims* (Princeton, N.J.: Women on Words and Images, 1972).

sheer quantity, boys and men are present in the readers overwhelmingly more than girls and women. The 6:1 discrepancy between male and female biographies is particularly striking. Women appear in 25 different occupations, men in 147. Furthermore, men appear in a wide range of jobs, whereas women are limited to traditionally female pursuits such as teacher, nurse, telephone operator, and secretary. In addition to being sex-typed, many of the jobs portrayed were also demeaning (such as fat lady in a circus), and unrealistic for most girls (such as queen, witch, acrobat). A content analysis indicated that, in "active mastery" stories, where the main character exhibited cleverness, problem-solving ability, bravery, acquisition of skills, and adventurousness, males were the protagonist four times as often as females. By contrast, girls were more often portrayed as passive and dependent, restricting their goals, practicing domesticity, being incompetent, and being victimized or humiliated by the opposite sex. Some of the dialogue in the stories is as blatantly sexist as in Alpha One. For example, in "The Day We Made the Electro-Thinker," Albert says to Annabelle, "It is no secret. We are willing to share our great thoughts with mankind. However, you happen to be a girl" (*Ventures,* Book 4, Scott Foresman, 1965).

It is often said that schools reflect social reality. Concerning sexism, schools are not presenting the status quo; they are actually presenting a distorted view of it. Quite often males and females presented in the school readers are like few people we know. Jan Pottker compared the sex ratio of the occupations in the readers to U.S. Department of Labor statistics. She found that there are more women working in a greater variety of jobs in the labor force than the readers indicate.[5] Although women are disproportionately present in low-level and traditionally "women's work" jobs, the school readers are actually more sexist than the social reality they are supposed to describe.

Feminists first looked at readers because it was easy to ascertain how primers and story books could foster sex roles. Many of us thought that "neutral" math books couldn't be sexist too. But when math books are analyzed with a feminist eye, it is clear that they are as sexist as their reader cousins.[6] In quantitative and qualitative terms, they favor boys over girls and men over women. Word problems and illustrations reproduce the familiar stereotypes. Girls cook,

5. Janice Pottker, "Female Sex-Role Stereotypes in Elementary School Readers," master's thesis, University of Maryland, 1971.
6. Marsha Federbush, "The Sex Problems of School Math Books," in *And Jill Came Tumbling After,* by Stacey et al., op. cit.

sew, and look on as boys climb, race, and fly to the moon. The career situation in math books is the same as in readers: Women have few of them. On the rare occasions in which women are shown as capable of managing anything more than a white wash, they are in stereotyped, unattainable, or undesirable roles. Men, of course, have seemingly endless occupational vistas, appearing as policemen, circus performers, astronauts, farmers, scientists, etc.

Math books put people into roles associated with numbers. For math book authors. the most obvious activities for girls are jumping rope, or going to the store to buy this much fabric or that much flour to serve their sewing and cooking "instincts." Boys need X amount of wood or Y amount of paint for their creative, constructive projects. More subtly, the word problems often deliver the same messages: "Susan could not figure out how to. . . ," "Jim showed her how to. . . ." Or more blatantly, " 'I guess girls are just no good in math,' said Joe." This all-too-popular notion may be part of a self-fulfilling prophecy. By the intermediate years, certainly, math begins to be typed as a boy's subject.

The "new math" has nothing new to teach about sex roles. Set theory readily adapts itself to the sexist status quo. When math book authors arrange people into sets, they segregate them by sex and depict the sexes in the expected groupings; women are in sets of nurses, housewives, etc.; men are sets of doctors, pilots, and the like.

Science books continue the tradition. Girls appear in them mainly to record, observe, and applaud the accomplishments of the boys. Boys are doers; they have control over their environment. Even when boys and girls appear to be doing the same thing, subtle distinctions are made. In one elementary science text, boys and girls are both experimenting with pinwheels. The boys are blowing theirs to make them spin; the girls are waiting for the wind to make theirs go.

Social studies texts are even more explicitly sexist. Because primary social studies curricula focus on such themes as the family, community helpers, and work, the opportunities for sexism are enormous. Once again we find the stereotyped careers and traits. In one picture book in which children are asked to match people with their work instruments, a woman is supposed to be matched with a shopping cart!

So far we have summarized the case that sexism permeates the formal elementary school curriculum. Feminists have gone on to explore and expose other common mechanisms of sex-role reinforcement. One such mechanism is segregated classes and activities. A number of primary grades have been "experimenting" with sex-segregated classes.[7] The all-boy classes in one such experiment emphasized large-muscle activity, team games, building, repairing, and other tasks "ordinarily performed by father," and arts and crafts with wood, rock, clay, and other "male" materials. The all-girl classes included activities such as "dressing up like mother and playing house," and playing with crayons, paper, and pasting materials. Although the authors noted that "in the mixed group which stressed masculinity, the girls seemed to enjoy the program as much as the boys," they did not discuss the varied needs of individual children or the rigid role definitions being imposed on girls and boys.

Within unsegregated classes, certain activities, such as cooking and sewing, are encouraged primarily for girls; other activities such as woodwork and mechanical work are encouraged primarily for boys. Physical education and playground activities are frequently sex-segregated. In instrumental music, percussion and brass are perceived as masculine, while girls are encouraged to play the violin and flute. As children move through elementary school, certain subjects such as English come to be regarded as "girls' subjects" while math and science are perceived as "boys' subjects." Studies find that children's perceptions of the sex-appropriateness of school activities become progressively more rigid as they advance up the grades.[8]

Other mechanisms are more subtle. When teachers separate girls and boys for seating, lining up, hanging up coats, and so on, they unwittingly call attention to sex distinctions and sex roles. The choice of monitors also teaches sex roles: "Girls water the plants; boys move the chairs."

Traditional sex roles are also reinforced by the authority structure of the school itself. Whereas 85% of all elementary school teachers are women, 79% of all elementary school principals are men. Simply by observing which sex is in which position in the school, children may learn the differential status of men and women in our society.

Even in "free schools," where there is no conscious attempt to sex-type, the policy of allowing children to follow their own interests usually results in condoning the pervasive sex-typed activities and interests the children have learned outside the schools. Effective open classrooms, while basically noninterventionist, still require children to master certain basic skills. But intervening to require choices

7. "Boys Are Different," *The Instructor*, December, 1970, pp. 50–54.

8. Althea Stein and Janis Smithells, "Age and Sex Differences in Children's Sex-Role Standards About Achievement," *Developmental Psychology*, vol. 1, no. 3, 1969, pp. 252–59.

and activities that are free of sex-typing has not yet become an important concern of the open classroom. In a workshop for teachers conducted by one of the authors in November, 1972, teachers would intervene in role-playing situations to ensure that a child would read a book or to prevent disruptive behavior. Teachers would also protect the child's right to "free choice" in other activities. So the boys worked with electrical equipment and girls drew butterflies. The teachers participating in this workshop came with the avowed purpose of "understanding and changing our own sexist behavior with children." Thus even though they were committed to eliminating sexism in their own practice, this objective had low priority in their operational values.

Teacher/pupil interaction is another area characterized by traditional sex-typing. Teachers behave differently with boys and girls in ways that reinforce masculine and feminine roles.[9] Teachers tend to discipline boys more often and more harshly than girls. They tend to praise boys more than girls, particularly for achievement, and to spend more instructional time with the boys. Girls tend to be rewarded for good (i.e., conforming) behavior or else to be ignored. In the long run, the double-barreled message that girls get—in home and at school—to be dependent, passive, quiet, and "good"--is detrimental to their self-esteem and to their intellectual development. The mixed message that boys get—at home to be aggressive, independent, achieving (i.e., to "be a man") and at school to be obedient and quiet—creates different pressures for boys. If boys can reconcile and live up to these dual standards, they tend to become high achievers and successful chauvinists. If they can't, they often rebel, act out, or become low achievers and unsuccessful chauvinists.

As a matter of fact, many teacher behavior studies tend to be sexist themselves; e.g., their major concern is with what happens to boys in elementary schools. Patricia Sexton, among others, has expressed concern that elementary schools are "feminizing" boys— that is, training them to be docile, obedient, and conforming.[10] There has been little concern that schools are "feminizing" girls—that is, training them to be docile, obedient, and conforming—since that has traditionally been the expected set of behaviors for little girls.

Of course, sex-typing is also learned through the surrounding milieu of toys, television, and child-rearing practices. The world of

9. Pauline Sears and David Feldman, "Teacher Interaction with Boys and Girls," *The National Elementary Principal*, November, 1966, pp. 30–37.
10. Patricia Sexton, "Schools Are Emasculating Our Boys," *Saturday Review*, November, 1966.

toys is the familiar world of stereotypes. One study found that 1) "masculine" toys are the most varied, expensive, complex, active, and social, whereas 2) "feminine" toys are the most simple, passive, and solitary.[11] The same study found that while boys and girls receive an equal number of gifts, 73% of boys' gifts are toys, compared with 57% for girls. Girls often get clothes, jewelry, cosmetics, and furniture instead of toys. Observing in toy departments during Christmas shopping, no field worker saw even one scientific toy purchased for a girl. They found that adults spend more time picking boys' toys than girls' toys, perhaps because there are more to choose from and because there are more fixed notions of what to buy for girls. One doctor's kit, marketed for boys, had a stethoscope with amplifying diaphragm, miniature microscope, blood pressure tester, etc. The corresponding nurse's kit, marketed for girls, came equipped with a nurse's apron, cap, plastic silverware, plate, sick tray, and play food. In these two kits, the professional recruitment for boys is straightforward, whereas the homemaker recruitment for girls is more subtle.

Children often spend as much time watching television as they do in school. Clearly, regular television programming for children and adults is characterized by rampant sexism. What is especially disturbing is that the same is true for educational television. Until feminist groups began a vigorous protest, even "Sesame Street" was as misogynist as James Bond. Hardly any characters were female; those few were in stereotyped roles. After much protest and monitoring by NOW and other feminist groups, tokenism has come to the program, but there have been few substantial changes. Although there are a few more female puppets, the new additions—a cheerleader, a hysterical show contestant (Sally Screamer), and a monster woman (Arlene Frantic)—are hardly in the liberated direction. And while the live female to male ratio is now 3:7 instead of 1:4, these three often appear in the stereotyped housewife role. (Susan, for example, seems to be infatuated with laundry.)

Many observers concede the harmful effects of the media, but argue that they are relatively unimportant because children learn most of their values at home. Even if this is so, the situation in the home concerning sex roles is no better, at least not if child-rearing manuals are any indication. Dr. Spock, the Confucius of American child care, spent many decades counseling mothers to stay home and nurture their children's sex-role identities. Even in his 1970 book, *Decent and Indecent,* Spock spoke favorably of "feminine drives":

11. "A Report on Children's Toys," *Ms.,* December, 1972, p. 57.

In bringing up our children—boys as well as girls—I think we should be enthusiastic about their maleness or femaleness as attributes to be proud of, enjoyed, emphasized, rather than taken for granted or even denied as they so often are today. A boy should know that his father enjoys his company in a special way because they can talk about cars or carpentry or sports. Even a small boy should feel that his mother appreciates his manly help in carrying things for her, opening doors, running errands, fixing things.

A girl needs from her father compliments on the attractiveness of her appearance, on her skill in feminine occupations, and particularly on her thoughtfulness and helpfulness.

Most of all a girl needs a mother who shows enthusiasm for playing the role of woman herself—with verve and style. . . .

Dr. Spock has come under feminist scrutiny and has since revised his views somewhat, but the professional literature of child development remains reactionary on sex roles. A recent study of the major texts on child development shows that traditional gender roles remain a major article of faith in the training of child-care experts. [12]

Thus far we have presented the first level of feminist criticism of elementary education. The second level is to point out that these messages have harmful effects. Studies of children's vocational aspirations, for example, indicate that children learn quite early what roles society expects of them. William Looft in 1971 asked a group of first- and second-graders, "What would you like to be when you grow up?" The boys' list totaled 18 different occupations, including doctor, dentist, scientist, pilot, astronaut, policeman, and football player. The girls' list totaled eight different occupations, all sex-typed, nurse and teacher being the most common. Interestingly, when asked, "What do you think you *really* will do when you grow up?" the children often changed their answers. Many of the boys switched to other vocations. Many of the girls switched to housewife and mother or else downshifted their choices; e.g., one girl who had said she wanted to be a doctor changed to "store lady."[13] These findings are corroborated by Lynne Iglitzin's studies in 1971 and 1972. [14] She found that fifth-grade children see most jobs and their own aspirations as being defined by sex. What all such studies reveal is that both boys and girls learn quite early to aspire to sex-typed

12. Zelda Klapper, "The Impact of the Women's Liberation Movement on Child Development Literature," *American Journal of Orthopsychiatry*, October, 1971, pp. 725–32.

13. William R. Looft, "Sex Differences in the Expression of Vocational Aspirations by Elementary School Children," *Developmental Psychology*, September, 1971, p. 366.

14. Lynne B. Iglitzin, "A Child's-Eye View of Sex Roles," *Today's Education*, December, 1972, pp. 23–25.

occupations. For girls even sex-typed aspirations are dreams which fall aside when they are asked to "be realistic." Then they see themselves doing what society has sanctioned women to do—clean house and raise children.

In addition to learning their roles early, children of both sexes experience conflict over such rigidly imposed expectations. Ruth Hartley's interviews with 8- to 11-year-old boys supported the hypothesis that boys in our culture are under greater pressure to conform to stringent sex role norms than are girls.[15] The girl labeled "tomboy" is less ostracized than the boy considered "sissy." It's a smart girl who wants to do boy things, but the boy who aspires to female pursuits is thought to be engaged in a kind of "status slumming." Boys in Hartley's study have to be able "to fight in case a bully comes along, run fast, play rough games, take care of themselves, and know what girls don't know." They said that grown-ups expect boys to "be noisy, get dirty, mess up the house, get into more trouble than girls do, and not to be cry-babies." They think men must be "strong, able to protect women and children in emergencies, able to fix things, able to get money to support their families, and be in charge of things."

Considering the weight of the perceived male burdens, one might wonder why boys are so anxious to measure up. A quick look at the boys' concept of the female role satisfies our curiosity. The boys say that girls have to "stay close to the house, play quietly, keep clean, and be gentler than boys, and they cry when they are scared or hurt." The boys see adult women as "indecisive, afraid of many things, tired a lot, staying home most of the time, squeamish, and not very intelligent." In effect, women are incompetent and a bother: "Women haven't enough strength in the head or in the body to do most jobs." With such caricatures in his head, the young boy scrambles to become an athletic he-man and to suppress his tender feelings.

Girls, meanwhile, are under a different sort of pressure. The conflict they experience is between "femininity" and achievement. Matina Horner has conducted several much-reported studies of this conflict in college women. Grace Baruch is currently replicating this work with grade school children.[16] Her study of fifth-grade youngsters shows that the conflict between "femininity" and success begins to develop early. She gave the fifth-graders in her study this

---

15. Ruth Hartley, "Sex-Role Pressures and the Socialization of the Male Child," *Psychological Reports,* no. 5, 1959, pp. 457–68.

16. Grace K. Baruch, "Sex-Role Attitudes of Fifth-Grade Girls," in Stacey et al., op. cit.

cue: "Anne (or John) has won first prize in the science fair for her (his) exhibit on car engines." She then asked the youngsters to write a story about Anne (or John). Imagery indicating a fear of success was present in 29% of the girls' and 25% of the boys' stories. This doesn't sound very different, but a closer look reveals the expected distinctions. Those boys who indicated conflict about success generally feared revenge from an unsuccessful competitor. But the girls in this category exhibited the same mechanisms of denial, fear of rejection, or fear of negative consequences that Horner had found in her college-age sample. Girls wrote such stories as:

> Sue and Mary Ellen got very jealous and started being very mean to Anne. They thought they should win because they took the courses for it and Anne didn't. The fair manager called and said that they had made a mistake and Anne won second prize. They made friends again even though Anne was disappointed.

But more striking, even when the girls did not show outright fear of success, they were less often without conflict. Many of the girls' stories (and none of the boys' stories), showed an attempt to cope with a conflict situation or to appease others by sharing their success. A typical "coping" story was:

> Everybody thought that Anne would not win because car engines are boys' things, but there was not any law about doing it on car engines so she tried her hardest and won.

A sample "sharing" tale was:

> Anne: "Oh boy. I know just what I'm going to do with this dollar I won on car engines at the science fair. I'm going to get candy for all the other girls." She tells Sally.
>
> Sally: "Oh, that's so nice of you, Anne."

Although these behaviors are not undesirable in themselves, their use in this context is self-denying for the successful girls. Another way of stating it is that 75% of the boys' stories showed no qualms about success compared with 50% of the girls' stories.

A third level of feminist involvement in the schools has been to try to change stereotyped curricula and attitudes. Parent/teacher consciousness-raising groups have formed, old curricula have been rejected, new books and materials have been written, and legal actions have challenged sex-discriminatory practices in schools. A prefeminist study in a different context highlights both the promise and some of the barriers to an interventionist approach. In the 1959 post-Sputnik era, Paul Torrance investigated children's attitudes towards science.[17] Groups of fourth-, fifth-, and sixth-graders were given a collection of science toys to explore. Each child was then asked to rank each member of the group according to the value of her or his contribution. Meanwhile, experimenters tabulated the actual number of ideas initiated, demonstrated, and explained by each child. They found that the boys were ahead on all counts. Not surprisingly, then, the boys' contributions were valued more by both sexes. In fact, many girls shrank from participating, saying, "I'm a girl. I'm not supposed to know anything about science." The experiment was repeated the next year after teachers and experimenters had intervened, attempting to convince the girls that science was appropriate for them too. This time the performance of the girls improved remarkably, and there was no significant difference between the performance of the girls and the boys. But one thing had not changed: Both boys and girls valued the contributions of the boys more highly. Sexism runs deep. Short-term intervention can affect outward behavior, but it does not seem to shake internalized values such as low self-esteem and stereotypic expectations.

Thus far we have summarized the feminist "case" against the elementary schools. We think the weight and scope of the evidence is more than persuasive. Elementary school education is sexist indeed.

Let us now consider briefly some typical responses to feminist criticism. First, there is the "classical chauvinist" response. The upfront chauvinist flatly denies the validity of the feminist charges. He bases much of his argument on biological and divine destiny, asserting that women are naturally different from and subordinate to men, and reassuring himself that "true" women like it better like that anyway. When he is confronted by the foregoing data on sexual inequities in the schools, he nods his head at the familiar patterns and says proudly, "Yes, we encourage our little girls to be feminine and our boys to be masculine. After all, *vive la différence.*"

A more subtle conservative response is the "Hortense Alger" approach, which reaffirms the popular American myth that hardworking individuals succeed in an open society: "If a woman really wanted to make it, she could." Although Hortense is "hip" enough to reject an exclusive homemaking role for herself, she denies the existence of the social forces which keep other women in their place. She refuses to realize that the same system which tolerates her hard-won success as a token female requires that the majority of

17. E. Paul Torrance, *Rewarding Creative Behavior: Experiments in Classroom Creativity* (Englewood Cliffs, N.J.: Prentice-Hall, 1965.)

women accept subordinate status. In schools little Hortense, the pride of her teachers, is encouraged to develop her talents and not to fritter away her time playing dolls with the other little girls. She grows up to be the male-identified women who liberates neither herself nor her sisters.

The most frequent responses to feminist criticism are liberal and reformist, perhaps because the feminist "case" itself comes largely from a liberal perspective. One transitional version is the patronizing "under-the-rug" approach: "Yes, yes, dear, we know you're upset. We'll put up a few more posters with women in them" and "We'll add 'and girls' to the notice inviting boys to participate in the science fair."

For those educators who are not satisfied by trivial changes, there is the "even-Steven/even-Stella" model: Redress the grievances by balancing everything out. While this liberal, equal rights approach is productive in eliminating some of the grosser aspects of discrimination, it is limited by viewing "equality" as "sameness." It tends, therefore, to avoid such knotty problems such as "compensatory" programs for girls or "different" programs for boys and girls which might open up opportunities for both.

The more serious limitation of the liberal response is its tendency to assume that to point out the inequality is to define the solution. Liberals jump from *examples* of sexism to *eliminating those examples,* and thus avoid the difficult tasks of analyzing thoroughly what sexism is all about or seeking solutions which change the *underlying causes* of sexist practices. For instance, where girls are discriminated against in all aspects in athletics, a typical response has been to allow a few girls on previously all-boy teams. This response does not speak to the need for physical training for everyone or to the effects of the highly competitive aspect of most sports on the participants. It does not speak to the issue of how children feel about their bodies or of how children can be helped to test out their physical strengths and limits.

Recently introduced sex education courses perpetuate the same old notions concerning sex roles. They do not openly explore heterosexuality and homosexuality as legitimate human options; nor do they explore ways for people to enjoy their sexuality more.

Similarly, the feminist protest against sexism in readers has sent a few liberal school boards scurrying for "nonsexist" books from the "Little Miss Muffett Fights Back" reading list. School boards in such cities as New York; Detroit; Washington, D.C.; Evanston, Illinois; and Wellesley, Massachusetts, have begun to set new "nonsexist" guidelines for textbook selection. The problem here is that even many of the new feminist readers are reformist at best. Typically, they resort to mere "role reversal"—the boys pass out cookies and the girls play doctor—without exploring what truly androgynous roles for people would be. Moreover, this quickie reader-supplement action feeds right into the current educational obsession with standardized reading levels.

"Even-Stella" proponents struggle to hire more women administrators in schools, but not to challenge the general authority structure of the schools or to open up the school's decision-making structure to all those groups—students, parents, teachers, etc.—who are affected by it. Like-minded struggles to get more girls into the honors track operate to support tracking itself rather than to challenge this discriminatory, elitist, and invalid system of grouping children for "learning."

We do not mean to put down reforms. We welcome the efforts as well as many of the changes. But we are concerned that the rush to solve (read: "do away with in a hurry") the problem of sexism in schools has led many to grab at palliative measures which deflect energies from the more basic struggle. To document the problem is to describe symptoms, not to prescribe a cure. We feel that the symptoms have been sufficiently presented to call attention to the issue. We are fearful that unless more analytic work is done the response will amount to a form of "symptom management" rather than cure. The first stage of documenting complaints, which this article has inventoried, should be over. It is time to move toward analyzing and struggling for the sorts of changes which will facilitate a genuinely liberating education for all of our children.

Statements made by these pageant contestants come as no surprise, considering the evidence provided in previous articles. After all, they are school graduates.

Are the Martin article and Milgram experiment (the next selection) extreme examples of society's products? Think: How often have I sold out, buckled under, kept quiet? Granted I cannot blame the school for all of my actions, for what can I hold it responsible? Did it adjust me socially, as intended?

THE UNTAINTED WORLD
OF OUR MISS AMERICAS
Judith Martin

Atlantic City, N.J.—"Anybody here over 35?" shouted Bert Parks as he gave an extra wiggle to his hips.

"Yaaay" came back the answer from the crowd gathered in Convention hall last week to watch the Miss America pageant.

They had come to cheer *their idea of what youth should be like* and 50 girls tried all week to personify that idea.

Miss America girls do not smoke, drink, date, discuss controversial topics or go around unchaperoned during the pageant—the winner agrees to behave that way for a year—and they are very polite to their elders.

They support their government, condemn dissent, and set their goals on spending a year or two in traditional female occupations— modeling or elementary school teaching—until the right man comes along.

Miss America of 1970, Pamela Anne Eldred of Detroit, Mich., gave a press conference Sunday in which she said she was a spokesman for her generation and she made a statement about the establishment: "I feel that the people who were voted into office must have the intelligence to know what to do and that everybody should have faith in them."

As a spokesman, she said she does not object when the pageant officials refuse to let her speak on certain subjects. "I feel that they are older and wiser than I am and I can always learn something especially from someone who is older. If I am told I can't do something, I am told for a reason and I don't challenge it."

"God love you," said a state pageant official from Michigan.

Other pageant officials, the audience and the judges all talked about how comforting it was to see this girl and the others like her. They called them "true representatives of American youth."

For a few magic days the drug scene, the sexual revolution, and the civil rights, anti-war, female liberation and student protest movements seemed to them to have been just bad dreams or as they kept saying "a tiny minority of kooks."

Miss America told her admirers that the Vietnam war was right because otherwise the government never would have gotten into it.

Miss Minnesota, Judith Claire Mendenhall, a runner-up to the title, told them that women shouldn't try to run things "because they are more emotional and men can overcome their emotions with logic."

Miss Virginia, Sydney Lee Lewis, won a talent award for a speech in which she condemned student reform movements but lauded her generation for things like "conceiving the rally for decency."

The theme of this year's pageant was "The Sound of Young." There was much talk in it about the new sound and then one talent winner sang "Get Happy" and another played "Bumble Boogie" on the piano.

"Each generation has its own translation of young, and this generation's is a search for the golden rainbow of peace and understanding," said Parks to introduce Miss America 1969, Judi Ford, who wore a Ginger Rogers white pleated chiffon dress and danced the kind of number which used to be the finale of motion picture musical comedies of the 40's. The pastel chiffon dresses with sequined tops, which girls wore with 18-button length white cotton gloves in the evening dress competition, had to be specially made. So did the one-piece, solid color, no-cut-outs bathing suits, which are no longer stocked commercially. Spiked heeled, pointed-toed shoes dyed to match were worn with the bathing suits.

Evening culottes were permitted during the talent competition but most of the girls favored sequined drum majorette type of costumes. Several chose mid-knee cocktail dresses just a shade longer than the new habits of a group of nuns, who attended the preliminary competition one night.

Make-up was used in the shows to create the kewpie doll look of decades ago—bright red lipstick, blue eye shadow and hair teased into bee-hives with wiglets of curls added.

Offstage, however, the girls were more contemporary with shoulder length hairstyles and little wool dresses which gave them the look of 50 Tricia Nixons.

The judges said they were gratified at what they saw and had a hard time picking a winner. "It renews my faith in youth," said Hollywood make-up man Bud Westmore, a judge, whose wife was Miss California of 1952.

"We have a complete misconception of what is going on when we see the New York hippies who don't wash," said Leon Leonidoff, another judge, who has been staging Radio City Music Hall spectaculars since 1932. "This country is wholesome and healthy." His wife is a former Miss New Jersey and he has been going around all week offering contracts to his favorite contestants.

"We really haven't got a thing to worry about," said Judge Jane Pickens Langley, who describes herself as "singer, artist and philanthropist."

"These aren't the girls you hear about because there is never any scandal attached to them," said Judge Zelma George, executive director of the Cleveland Job Corps Center for Women. "Someone should do a master's thesis on them."

"You don't hear about them later because basically they are not ambitious," said writer Joan Crosby, a judge. "They want to be good wives and mothers."

No one seemed to know, however, why most of the past Miss Americas have been divorced at least once.

The pageant officials expressed their delight with the way Miss America 1970 handled reporters' questions Sunday.

Topics on which she smiled and said, "I really couldn't voice an opinion—I don't know enough about that," included drugs, nudity in the theater, unisex fashions, student unrest, what the priorities of America should be, and whether or not 18-year-olds should have the vote. She also stated that she was happy about the moon shot "which proves that the United States is a great country" and that her goal in life is "to be a nice person."

Her mother, Mrs. William B. Eldred, who broke in once just after the crowning to tell Miss America "you are no expert" said that she and her daughter feel alike on all topics. "There is no generation gap," said Mrs. Eldred.

Miss America's one moment of confusion was when she was

asked where her father works. He is an employee of Chrysler, and loyalty to the pageant's sponsors, one of which is Oldsmobile, is an important quality of Miss America.

Miss America 1969 said that during her year, love of Toni hair products, Pepsi Cola and Oldsmobile became a spontaneous part of her.

The past and present Miss Americas looked very much alike—both with blonde bouffant hairdos, green eyes, pale skin and wide smiles. They are both, said Bert Parks, "composites of positive wonders."

"All Miss Americas are," he said.

As indicated throughout this section, one of the persistent verbal commitments in American experience has been to the value of personal independence. Stanley Milgram suggests that our professed belief in the primacy of individual conscience be treated as another myth.

We hold the schools responsible for teaching cognitive skills. Should they be held more accountable for affective changes?

Finally, do Milgram's experiments prove that Americans are more addicted or *as* addicted to authority as Germans—or some other national group? Can this be legitimately called an experiment?

IF HITLER ASKED YOU TO ELECTROCUTE A STRANGER, WOULD YOU?

Philip Meyer

In the beginning, Stanley Milgram was worried about the Nazi problem. He doesn't worry much about the Nazis anymore. He worries about you and me, and, perhaps, himself a little bit too.

Philip Meyer, "If Hitler Asked You To Electrocute a Stranger, Would You?" *Esquire,* February 1970, pp. 72–73+. Reprinted by permission of Esquire Magazine © 1970 by Esquire, Inc.

Stanley Milgram is a social psychologist, and when he began his career at Yale University in 1960 he had a plan to prove, scientifically, that Germans are different. The Germans-are-different hypothesis has been used by historians, such as William L. Shirer, to explain the systematic destruction of the Jews by the Third Reich. One madman could decide to destroy the Jews and even create a master plan for getting it done. But to implement it on the scale that Hitler did meant that thousands of other people had to go along with the scheme and help to do the work. The Shirer thesis, which Milgram set out to test, is that Germans have a basic character flaw which explains the whole thing, and this flaw is a readiness to obey authority without question, no matter what outrageous acts the authority commands.

The appealing thing about this theory is that it makes those of us who are not Germans feel better about the whole business. Obviously, you and I are not Hitler, and it seems equally obvious that we would never do Hitler's dirty work for him. But now, because of Stanley Milgram, we are compelled to wonder. Milgram developed a laboratory experiment which provided a systematic way to measure obedience. His plan was to try it out in New Haven on Americans and then go to Germany and try it out on Germans. He was strongly motivated by scientific curiosity, but there was also some moral content in his decision to pursue this line of research, which was, in turn, colored by his own Jewish background. If he could show that Germans are more obedient than Americans, he could then vary the conditions of the experiment and try to find out just what it is that makes some people more obedient than others. With this understanding, the world might, conceivably, be just a little bit better.

But he never took his experiment to Germany. He never took it any farther than Bridgeport. The first finding, also the most unexpected and disturbing finding, was that we Americans are an obedient people: not blindly obedient, and not blissfully obedient, just obedient. "I found so much obedience," says Milgram softly, a little sadly, "I hardly saw the need for taking the experiment to Germany."

There is something of the theater director in Milgram, and his technique, which he learned from one of the old masters in experimental psychology, Solomon Asch, is to stage a play with every line rehearsed, every prop carefully selected, and everybody an actor except one person. That one person is the subject of the experiment. The subject, of course, does not know he is in a play. He thinks he is in real life. The value of this technique is that the experimenter, as though he were God, can change a prop here, vary a line there, and see how the subject responds. Milgram eventually had to change a lot of the script just to get people to stop obeying. They were obeying so much, the experiment wasn't working—it was like trying to measure oven temperature with a freezer thermometer.

The experiment worked like this: If you were an innocent subject in Milgram's melodrama, you read an ad in the newspaper or received one in the mail asking for volunteers for an educational experiment. The job would take about an hour and pay $4.50. So you make an appointment and go to an old Romanesque stone structure on High Street with the imposing name of The Yale Interaction Laboratory. It looks something like a broadcasting studio. Inside, you meet a young, crew-cut man in a laboratory coat who says he is Jack Williams, the experimenter. There is another citizen, fiftyish, Irish face, an accountant, a little overweight, and very mild and harmless-looking. This other citizen seems nervous and plays with his hat while the two of you sit in chairs side by side and are told that the $4.50 checks are yours no matter what happens. Then you listen to Jack Williams explain the experiment.

It is about learning, says Jack Williams in a quiet, knowledgeable way. Science does not know much about the conditions under which people learn and this experiment is to find out about negative reinforcement. Negative reinforcement is getting punished when you do something wrong, as opposed to positive reinforcement which is getting rewarded when you do something right. The negative reinforcement in this case is electric shock. You notice a book on the table, titled, *The Teaching-Learning Process,* and you assume that this has something to do with the experiment.

Then Jack Williams takes two pieces of paper, puts them in a hat, and shakes them up. One piece of paper is supposed to say, "Teacher" and the other, "Learner." Draw one and you will see which you will be. The mild-looking accountant draws one, holds it close to his vest like a poker player, looks at it, and says, "Learner." You look at yours. It says, "Teacher." You do not know that the drawing is rigged, and both slips say "Teacher." The experimenter beckons to the mild-mannered "learner."

"Want to step right in here and have a seat, please?" he says. "You can leave your coat on the back of that chair . . . roll up your right sleeve, please. Now what I want to do is strap down your arms to avoid excessive movement on your part during the experiment. This electrode is connected to the shock generator in the next room.

"And this electrode paste," he says, squeezing some stuff out of a plastic bottle and putting it on the man's arm, "is to provide a good contact and to avoid a blister or burn. Are there any questions now before we go into the next room?"

You don't have any, but the strapped-in "learner" does.

"I do think I should say this," says the learner. "About two years ago I was at the veterans' hospital . . . they detected a heart condition. Nothing serious, but as long as I'm having these shocks, how strong are they—how dangerous are they?"

Williams, the experimenter, shakes his head casually. "Oh, no," he says. "Although they may be painful, they're not dangerous. Anything else?"

Nothing else. And so you play the game. The game is for you to read a series of word pairs: for example, blue—girl, nice—day, fat—neck. When you finish the list, you read just the first word in each pair and then a multiple-choice list of four other words, including the second word of the pair. The learner, from his remote, strapped-in position, pushes one of four switches to indicate which of the four answers he thinks is the right one. If he gets it right nothing happens and you go on to the next one. If he gets it wrong, you push a switch that buzzes and gives him an electric shock. And then you go to the next word. You start with 15 volts and increase the number of volts by 15 for each wrong answer. The control board goes from 15 volts on one end to 450 volts on the other. So that you know what you are doing, you get a test shock yourself, at 45 volts. It hurts. To further keep you aware of what you are doing to that man in there, the board has verbal descriptions of the shock levels, ranging from "Slight Shock" at the left-hand side, through "Intense Shock" in the middle, to "Danger: Severe Shock" toward the far right. Finally, at the very end, under 435- and 450-volt switches, there are three ambiguous X's. If, at any point, you hesitate, Mr. Williams calmly tells you to go on. If you still hesitate, he tells you again.

Except for some terrifying details, which will be explained in a moment, this is the experiment. The object is to find the shock level at which you disobey the experimenter and refuse to pull the switch.

When Stanley Milgram first wrote this script, he took it to fourteen Yale psychology majors and asked them what they thought would happen. He put it this way: Out of one hundred persons in the teacher's predicament, how would their break-off points be distributed along the 15-to-450-volt scale? They thought a few would break off very early, most would quit someplace in the middle and a few would go all the way to the end. The highest estimate of the number out of one hundred who would go all the way to the end was three. Milgram then informally polled some of his fellow scholars in the psychology department. They agreed that very few would go to the end. Milgram thought so too.

"I'll tell you quite frankly," he says, "before I began this experiment, before any shock generator was built, I thought most people would break off at 'Strong Shock' or 'Very Strong Shock.' You would get only a very, very small proportion of people going out to the end of the shock generator, and they would constitute a pathological fringe."

In his pilot experiments, Milgram used Yale students as subjects. Each of them pushed the shock switches, one by one, all the way to the end of the board.

So he rewrote the script to include some protests from the learner. At first, they were mild, gentlemanly, Yalie protests, but, "it didn't seem to have as much effect as I thought it would or should," Milgram recalls. "So we had more violent protestation on the part of the person getting the shock. All of the time, of course, what we were trying to do was not to create a macabre situation, but simply to generate disobedience. And that was one of the first findings. This was not only a technical deficiency of the experiment, that we didn't get disobedience. It really was the first finding: that obedience would be much greater than we had assumed it would be and disobedience would be much more difficult than we had assumed."

As it turned out, the situation did become rather macabre. The only meaningful way to generate disobedience was to have the victim protest with great anguish, noise, and vehemence. The protests were tape-recorded so that all the teachers ordinarily would hear the same sounds and nuances, and they started with a grunt at 75 volts, proceeded through a "Hey, that really hurts," at 125 volts, got desperate with, "I can't stand the pain, don't do that," at 180 volts, reached complaints of heart trouble at 195, an agonized scream at 285, a refusal to answer at 315, and only heart-rending, ominous silence after that.

Still sixty-five percent of the subjects, twenty- to fifty-year-old American males, everyday, ordinary people, like you and me, obediently kept pushing those levers in the belief that they were shocking the mild-mannered learner, whose name was Mr. Wallace, and who was chosen for the role because of his innocent appearance, all the way up to 450 volts.

Milgram was now getting enough disobedience so that he had something he could measure. The next step was to vary the circumstances to see what would encourage or discourage obedience. There seemed very little left in the way of discouragement. The victim was already screaming at the top of his lungs and feigning a heart attack.

So whatever new impediment to obedience reached the brain of the subject had to travel by some route other than the ear. Milgram thought of one.

He put the learner in the same room with the teacher. He stopped strapping the learner's hand down. He rewrote the script so that at 150 volts the learner took his hand off the shock plate and declared that he wanted out of the experiment. He rewrote the script some more so that the experimenter then told the teacher to grasp the learner's hand and physically force it down on the plate to give Mr. Wallace his unwanted electric shock.

"I had the feeling that very few people would go on at that point, if any," Milgram says. "I thought that would be the limit of obedience that you would find in the laboratory."

It wasn't.

Although seven years have now gone by, Milgram still remembers the first person to walk into the laboratory in the newly rewritten script. He was a construction worker, a very short man. "He was so small," says Milgram, "that when he sat on the chair in front of the shock generator, his feet didn't reach the floor. When the experimenter told him to push the victim's hand down and give the shock, he turned to the experimenter, and he turned to the victim, his elbow went up, he fell down on the hand of the victim, his feet kind of tugged to one side, and he said, 'Like this, boss?' Zzumph!"

The experiment was played out to its bitter end. Milgram tried it with forty different subjects. And thirty percent of them obeyed the experimenter and kept on obeying.

"The protests of the victim were strong and vehement, he was screaming his guts out, he refused to participate, and you had to physically struggle with him in order to get his hand down on the shock generator," Milgram remembers. But twelve out of forty did it.

Milgram took his experiment out of New Haven. Not to Germany, just twenty miles down the road to Bridgeport. Maybe, he reasoned, the people obeyed because of the prestigious setting of Yale University. If they couldn't trust a center of learning that had been there for two centuries, whom could they trust? So he moved the experiment to an untrustworthy setting.

The new setting was a suite of three rooms in a run-down office building in Bridgeport. The only identification was a sign with a fictitious name: "Research Associates of Bridgeport." Questions about professional connections got only vague answers about "research for industry."

Obedience was less in Bridgeport. Forty-eight percent of the subjects stayed for the maximum shock, compared to sixty-five percent at Yale. But this was enough to prove that far more than Yale's prestige was behind the obedient behavior.

For more than seven years now, Stanley Milgram has been trying to figure out what makes ordinary American citizens so obedient. The most obvious answer—that people are mean, nasty, brutish and sadistic—won't do. The subjects who gave the shocks to Mr. Wallace to the end of the board did not enjoy it. They groaned, protested, fidgeted, argued, and in some cases, were seized by fits of nervous, agitated giggling.

"They even try to get out of it," says Milgram, "but they are somehow engaged in something from which they cannot liberate themselves. They are locked into a structure, and they do not have the skills or inner resources to disengage themselves."

Milgram, because he mistakenly had assumed that he would have trouble getting people to obey the orders to shock Mr. Wallace, went to a lot of trouble to create a realistic situation.

There was crew-cut Jack Williams and his grey laboratory coat. Not white, which might denote a medical technician, but ambiguously authoritative grey. Then there was the book on the table, and the other appurtenances of the laboratory which emitted the silent message that things were being performed here in the name of science, and were therefore great and good.

But the nicest touch of all was the shock generator. When Milgram started out, he had only a $300 grant from the Higgins Fund of Yale University. Later he got more ample support from the National Science Foundation, but in the beginning he had to create this authentic-looking machine with very scarce resources except for his own imagination. So he went to New York and roamed around the electronic shops until he found some little black switches at Lafayette Radio for a dollar apiece. He bought thirty of them. The generator was a metal box, about the size of a small footlocker, and he drilled the thirty holes for the thirty switches himself in a Yale machine shop. But the fine detail was left to professional industrial engravers. So he ended up with a splendid-looking control panel dominated by the row of switches, each labeled with its voltage, and each having its own red light that flashed on when the switch was pulled. Other things happened when a switch was pushed. Besides the ZZUMPHing noise, a blue light labeled "voltage energizer" went on, and a needle on a dial labeled "voltage" flicked from left to right. Relays inside the box clicked. Finally, in the upper left-hand corner of the control panel was this inscription, engraved in precise block letters:

SHOCK GENERATOR TYPE ZLB
DYSON INSTRUMENT COMPANY
WALTHAM, MASS.
OUTPUT: 15 VOLTS—450 VOLTS

One day a man from the Lehigh Valley Electronics Company of Pennsylvania was passing through the laboratory, and he stopped to admire the shock generator.

"This is a very fine shock generator," he said. "But who is this Dyson Instrument Company?" Milgram felt proud at that, since Dyson Instrument Company existed only in the recesses of his imagination.

When you consider the seeming authenticity of the situation, you can appreciate the agony some of the subjects went through. It was pure conflict. As Milgram explains to his students, "When a parent says, 'Don't strike old ladies,' you are learning two things: the content, and, also, to obey authority. This experiment creates conflicts between the two elements."

Here is a partial transcription from one of the experiments. The naïve "teacher" is a heavyset, worried-looking man with prematurely grey hair. He is wearing a polo shirt. He is very polite. He has just pushed the 180-volt lever. A hidden camera is recording the performance.

Learner (who, from the teacher's point of view is heard but not seen, an offstage voice): Ow, I can't stand the pain. Don't do that. . . .

Teacher (pivoting around in his chair and shaking his head): I can't stand it. I'm not going to kill that man in there. You hear him hollering?

Experimenter: As I told you before, the shocks may be painful, but—

Teacher: But he's hollering. He can't stand it. What's going to happen to him?

Experimenter (his voice is patient, matter-of-fact): The experiment requires that you continue, Teacher.

Teacher: Aaah, but, unh, I'm not going to get that man sick in there . . . know what I mean?

Experimenter: Whether the learner likes it or not, we must go on, through all the word pairs.

Teacher: I refuse to take the responsibility. He's in there hollering!

Experimenter: It's absolutely essential that you continue, Teacher.

Teacher (indicating the unused questions): There's too many left here, I mean, Geez, if he gets them wrong, there's too many of them left. I mean who's going to take the responsibility if anything happens to that gentleman?

Experimenter: I'm responsible for anything that happens to him. Continue please.

Teacher: All right. (*Consults list of words.*) The next one's "Slow—walk, truck, dance, music." Answer, please. (*A buzzing sound indicates the learner has signaled his answer.*) Wrong. A hundred and ninety-five volts. "Dance." (*Zzumph!*)

Learner: Let me out of here. My heart's bothering me! (*Teacher looks at experimenter.*)

Experimenter: Continue, please.

Learner (screaming): Let me out of here, you have no right to keep me here. Let me out of here, let me out, my heart's bothering me, let me out! (*Teacher shakes head, pats the table nervously.*)

Teacher: You see, he's hollering. Hear that? Gee, I don't know.

Experimenter: The experiment requires. . . .

Teacher (interrupting): I know it does, sir, but I mean—hunh! He don't know what he's getting in for. He's up to 195 volts! (*Experiment continues, through 210 volts, 225 volts, 240 volts, 255 volts, 270 volts, delivered to the man in the electric chair, at which point the teacher, with evident relief, runs out of word-pair questions.*)

Experimenter: You'll have to go back to the beginning of that page and go through them again until he's learned them all correctly.

Teacher: Aw, no. I'm not going to kill that man. You mean I've got to keep going up with the scale. No sir. He's hollering in there. I'm not going to give him 450 volts.

Experimenter: The experiment requires that you go on.

Teacher: I know it does, but that man is hollering in there, sir.

Experimenter (same matter-of-fact tone): As I said before, although the shocks may be painful. . . .

Teacher (interrupting): Awwww. He—he—he's yelling in there.

Experimenter: Start with "Blue," please, at the top of the page. Continue, please, Teacher. Just go ahead.

Teacher (concentrating intently on list of words in front of him, as if to shut everything else out): "Blue—boy, girl, grass, hat." *(Buzz indicates answer.)* Correct. "Night—day, sky, job, chair. *(Buzz)* Wrong. The answer is "day." Two hundred and eighty-five volts. *(Zzumph!)*

Learner: Ohhhuhhoohhh!

Experimenter: Continue, please.

Teacher: "Fat—man, lady, tub, neck." Answer, please. *(Buzz)* Wrong. The answer is "neck." Three hundred volts. *(Zzumph!)*

Learner: Ohhh. I absolutely refuse to answer any more. *(Shouting urgently, now)* Let me out of here. You can't hold me here. Get me out. Get—me—out—of—here.

Experimenter: Continue. The next word is "Green," please.

Teacher: "Green—grass, hat, ink, apple." *(Nothing happens. No answering buzz. Just gloomy silence.)*

Teacher: I don't think he is going to answer.

Experimenter: If the learner doesn't answer in a reasonable time, about four or five seconds, consider the answer wrong. And follow the same procedures you have been doing for wrong answers. Say "Wrong," tell him the number of volts, give him the punishment, read him the correct answer. Continue, please.

Teacher: "Green—grass, hat, ink, apple." Answer, please. *(More silence. Teacher just sits there.)*

Experimenter: Go on with the procedure, please, Teacher.

Teacher: Three hundred and fifteen volts. The answer is "ink." *(Zzumph!)*

Learner: Ohh. Ooohh.

Teacher (relieved to hear response): Next one. . . .

Learner: I absolutely refuse to answer.

Teacher: You got to. You get a shock if you don't answer. *(Experiment continues with learner refusing to answer, and, finally, failing even to grunt or groan. At 375 volts, the teacher stands up. Has he had enough? Will he break off the experiment? Will he disobey?)*

Teacher: I think something's happened to that fellow in there. I don't get no answer. He was hollering at less voltage. Can't you check in and see if he's all right, please?

Experimenter (same detached calm): Not once we've started. Please continue, Teacher.

Teacher (sits down, sighs deeply): "Cool—day, shade, water, paint." Answer, please. Are you all right in there? Are you all right?

Experimenter: Please continue, Teacher. Continue, please. *(Teacher pushes level. Zzumph!)*

Teacher (swiveling around in his chair): Something's happened to that man in there. *(Swiveling back)* Next one. "Low—dollar, necklace, moon, paint." *(Turning around again)* Something's happened to that man in there. You better check in on him, sir. He won't answer or nothing.

Experimenter: Continue. Go on, please.

Teacher: You accept all responsibility.

Experimenter: The responsibility is mine. Correct. Please go on. *(Teacher returns to his list, starts running through words as rapidly as he can read them, works through to 450 volts.)*

Teacher: That's that.

Experimenter: Continue using the last switch on the board, please. The four-fifty switch for each wrong answer. Continue, please.

Teacher: But I don't get no anything!

Experimenter: Please continue. The next word is "White."

Teacher: Don't you think you should look in on him, please.

Experimenter: Not once we've started the experiment.

Teacher: But what if something has happened to the man?

Experimenter: The experiment requires that you continue. Go on, please.

Teacher: Don't the man's health mean anything?

Experimenter: Whether the learner likes it or not. . . .

Teacher: What if he's dead in there? (*Gestures toward the room with the electric chair.*) I mean, he told me he can't stand the shock, sir. I don't mean to be rude, but I think you should look in on him. All you have to do is look in the door. I don't get no answer, no noise. Something might have happened to the gentleman in there, sir.

Experimenter: We must continue. Go on, please.

Teacher: You mean keep giving him what? Four hundred fifty volts, what he's got now?

Experimenter: That's correct. Continue. The next word is "White."

Teacher: (*now at a furious pace*): "White—cloud, horse, rock, house." Answer, please. The answer is "horse." Four hundred and fifty volts. (*Zzumph!*) Next word, "Bag—paint, music, clown, girl." The answer is "paint." Four hundred and fifty volts. (*Zzumph!*) Next word is "Short—sentence, movie. . . ."

Experimenter: Excuse me, Teacher. We'll have to discontinue the experiment. (*Enter Milgram from camera's left. He has been watching from behind one-way glass.*)

Milgram: I'd like to ask you a few questions. (*Slowly, patiently, he dehoaxes the teacher, telling him that the shocks and screams were not real.*)

Teacher: You mean he wasn't getting nothing? Well, I'm glad to hear that. I was getting upset there. I was getting ready to walk out.

(*Finally, to make sure there are no hard feelings, friendly, harmless Mr. Wallace comes out in coat and tie. Gives jovial greeting. Friendly reconciliation takes place. Experiment ends.*)[1]

Subjects in the experiment were not asked to give the 450-volt shock more than three times. By that time, it seemed evident that

1. © Stanley Milgram 1965.

they would go on indefinitely. "No one," says Milgram, "who got within five shocks of the end ever broke off. By that point, he had resolved the conflict."

. . .

[F]or most subjects in Milgram's laboratory experiments, the act of giving Mr. Wallace his painful shock was necessary, even though unpleasant, and besides they were doing it on behalf of somebody else and it was for science. There was still strain and conflict, of course. Most people resolved it by grimly sticking to their task and obeying. But some broke out. Milgram tried varying the conditions of the experiment to see what would help break people out of their state of agency.

"The results, as seen and felt in the laboratory," he has written, "are disturbing. They raise the possibility that human nature, or more specifically the kind of character produced in American democratic society, cannot be counted on to insulate its citizens from brutality and inhumane treatment at the direction of malevolent authority. A substantial proportion of people do what they are told to do, irrespective of the content of the act and without limitations of conscience, so long as they perceive that the command comes from a legitimate authority. If, in this study, an anonymous experimenter can successfully command adults to subdue a fifty-year-old man and force on him painful electric shocks against his protest, one can only wonder what government, with its vastly greater authority and prestige, can command of its subjects. . . ."

PART THREE

PATTERNS
SCHOOLS REINFORCE

"Schools free children to rise to the level of their natural abilities."
—Committee for the White House
Conference on Education, 1960

"In its desegregation decision of 1954, the Supreme Court held that separate schools for Negro and white children are inherently unequal. This survey finds that, when measured by that yardstick, American public education remains largely inequal in most regions of the country, including all those where Negroes form any significant proportion of the population."
—Coleman Report

Schools exist in a political, social, and economic matrix—and almost everywhere in the world there are serious tensions over whether money, power, and status are correctly distributed. This is certainly true in America and the schools are very much caught up in the debate. Part of this is due to our long-standing habit of assuming that schools would meliorate social tensions. Horace Mann, Henry Barnard, and other nineteenth-century "founders" of our current school system certainly thought this would be the case. But in the last ten years a number of social scientists, educators, and journalists have charged that the schools have failed and are failing to offer anything like equal opportunity, treatment, or results to children from varied backgrounds. Teachers and administrators, most of whom want to be fair and intend well, are caught in the crossfire of this political and psychological struggle.

The readings in this section illuminate some of the questions involved in the whole issue of "equality" as it relates to schooling. For that matter, so do some of the readings in the other sections. Readers may particularly wish to look at articles by Katz in Part One, and by Michaels, Levy, and Rosenthal in Part Four.

Some of the selections pertain to particular groups in American society whose members (or at least some of them) have grievances to direct toward the schools. We have included the groups that are currently receiving most attention, but there are other minorities—Aleuts, Eskimos, native Hawaiians, American Samoans, Chinese- and Japanese-Americans, to name some—who have not been included for reasons of space.

Many questions thread through the following essays: How just (fair, equitable) is American society? If the distribution of property, status, or power is not right, what would be a suitable distribution? Have the schools done what they should have or did they miss the mark? Can curricular changes (black studies, non-sex-typed texts, etc.) alter social attitudes? How well have political solutions—desegregation, compensatory education—worked? Can the social effects of schools be changed by altering tax-support patterns? Have we used the school system as a scapegoat to avoid facing questions that schools cannot solve? There are other questions but these will perhaps serve to encourage the reader to ask his own.

One final word of explanation is in order. One contemporary debate is not represented directly in these readings. This is the genetics vs. environment question, with a racial and social class twist, as expounded by Jensen, Shockley, Eysenck, and others. The literature on this subject is rather technical and is so voluminous that too much space would be required to present the arguments fairly.

The first six articles in this section are concerned with particular groups—American Indians, Chicanos, blacks, and women—and with proposals for changing attitudes through curricular revisions. The next five essays discuss lower-class and minority group failure in schools and some of the programs that have been proposed and tried. In the last article, Professor Butts argues that critics of the schools have been mistaken in calling for disestablishing schools (see Illich's article in Part One). Schools were never intended to provide economic equality, he says. They were intended to be "the training ground for habits of community."

American Indians have long suffered from discrimination. These excerpts from Senate hearings give graphic examples of an area where our official rhetoric has covered an unpalatable reality. One of the predominant themes that characterize minority groups' efforts to change the schooling patterns offered their children is reflected in the slogan "community control." These brief, edited selections—from the historical descriptions to listings of current statistics—should be a blow to anyone who believes in what Jonathan Kozol labels "the myth of progress."

INDIAN EDUCATION:
A NATIONAL TRAGEDY—
A NATIONAL CHALLENGE
U. S. Senate

A CASE STUDY: CHEROKEE EDUCATION—PAST AND PRESENT

One of the most remarkable examples of adaptation and accomplishment by any Indian tribe in the United States is that of the Cherokee. Their record provides evidence of the kind of results which ensue when Indians truly have the power of self-determination:

a constitution which provided for courts, representation, jury trials and the right to vote for all those over 18 years;

a system of taxation which supported such services as education and road construction;

an educational system which produced a Cherokee population 90 percent literate in its native language and used bilingual materials to such an extent that Oklahoma Cherokees had a higher English literacy level than the white populations of either Texas or Arkansas;

From *Indian Education: A National Tragedy—A National Challenge*, 1969 Report of the Committee on Labor and Public Welfare, United States Senate, special subcommittee on Indian education. 91st Congress, 1st Session. Senate Report No. 91-501 (Washington: U. S. Government Printing Office, 1969).

a system of higher education which, together with the Choctaw Nation, had more than 200 schools and academies, and sent numerous graduates to eastern colleges;
publication of a widely read bilingual newspaper.

But that was in the 1800's, before the federal government took control of Cherokee affairs. The record of the Cherokee today is proof of the tragic results of 60 years of white control over their affairs:

90 percent of the Cherokee families living in Adair County, Oklahoma, are on welfare;
99 percent of the Choctaw Indian population in McCurtain County, Oklahoma, live below the poverty line;
The median number of school years completed by the adult Cherokee population is only 5.5;
40 percent of adult Cherokees are functionally illiterate; Cherokee drop-out rates in public schools is as high as 75 percent;
The level of Cherokee education is well below the average for the State of Oklahoma, and below the average for rural and non-whites in the state.

The disparity between these two sets of facts provides dramatic testimony to what might have been accomplished if the policy of the federal government had been one of Indian self-determination. It also points up the disastrous effects of imposed white control.

Cherokee education was truly a development of the tribe itself. In 1821 Sequoyah, a member of the tribe, presented tribal officials with his invention—a Cherokee alphabet. Within six years of that date Cherokees were publishing their own bilingual newspaper, and the Cherokee Nation was on its way toward the end of illiteracy and the beginning of a model of self-government and self-education.

The Cherokee Indians established a government of laws in 1820 and, in 1927, a constitution patterned after that of the United States. Their nation was divided into districts, and each district sent representatives to the nation's capital, which had a two-house legislative structure. The system compared favorably with that of the federal government and any state government then in existence.

The Cherokee education system itself was just as exemplary as its governmental system. Using funds primarily received from the federal government as the result of ceding large tracts of land, a school system described by one authority as "the finest school system west of the Mississippi River" soon developed. Treaty money was used by

Sequoyah to develop the Cherokee alphabet, as well as to purchase a printing press. In a period of several years the Cherokee had established remarkable achievement and literary levels, as indicated by statistics cited above. But in 1903 the federal government appointed a superintendent to take control of Cherokee education, and when Oklahoma became a state in 1906 and the whole system was abolished, Cherokee educational performance was to begin its decline.

Authorities who have analyzed the decline concur on one point: the Cherokees are alienated from the white man's school. Anthropologist Willard Walker simply stated that "the Cherokees have viewed the schools as a white man's institution over which parents have no control." Dr. Jack Forbes of the Far West Regional Laboratory for Research and Development said that the federal and state schools operated for the Cherokee have had negative impact because of little, if any, parent-community involvement. Several researchers have also commented upon the lack of bilingual materials in the schools, and the ensuing feeling by Cherokees that reading English is associated with coercive instruction.

Alfred L. Wahrhaftig makes the point that the Indian child communicates in Cherokee and considers it his "socializing" language. English is simply an "instrumental" language one learns in school, a place which the Cherokee student sees no value in attending anyway.

In the 1890's Cherokees knew there was a forum for their opinions on how their children should be educated, and they used that forum. Wahrhaftig's study showed Cherokee parents haven't lost interest in their children's education, just faith in a white-controlled system's ability to listen to them and respond. "Cherokees finally have become totally alienated from the school system," he reported. "The tribe has surrendered to the school bureaucracy, but tribal opinion is unchanged."

THE FAILURE OF A NATIONAL POLICY

A careful review of the historical literature reveals that the dominant policy of the federal government toward the American Indian has been one of forced assimilation which has vacillated between the two extremes of coercion and persuasion. At the root of the assimilation policy has been a desire to divest the Indian of his land and resources.

The Allotment Act of 1887 stands as a symbol of the worst aspects of the Indian policy. During the 46-year period it was in effect it succeeded in reducing the Indian landbase from 140 million acres to approximately 50 million acres of the least desirable land. Greed for Indian land and intolerance of Indian cultures combined in one act to drive the American Indian into the depths of poverty from which he has never recovered.

From the first contact with the Indian, the school and the classroom have been a primary tool of assimilation. Education was the means whereby we emancipated the Indian child from his home, his parents, his extended family, and his cultural heritage. It was in effect an attempt to wash the "savage habits" and "tribal ethic" out of a child's mind and substitute a white middle-class value system in its place. A Ponca Indian testifying before the subcommittee defined this policy from the standpoint of the Indian student: "School is the enemy!"

It is clear in retrospect that the "assimilation by education" policy was primarily a function of the "Indian land" policy. The implicit hope was that a "civilized Indian" would settle down on his 160 acres and become a gentleman farmer, thus freeing large amounts of additional land for the white man. But in addition, there has been a strong strain of "converting the heathen" and "civilizing the savage," which has subtly, but persistently, continued up to the present. Two stereotypes still prevail—"the dirty, lazy, drunken" Indian, and, to assuage our conscience, the myths of the "noble savage."

Regretfully, one must conclude that this nation has not faced up to an "American dilemma" more fundamental than the one defined so persuasively for us by Gunnar Myrdal in 1944. The "Indian problem" raises serious questions about this nation's most basic concepts of political democracy. It challenges the most precious assumptions about what this country stands for—cultural pluralism, equity and justice, and integrity of the individual, freedom of conscience and action, and the pursuit of happiness. Relations with the American Indian constitute a "morality play" of profound importance in our nation's history.

The Indian in American Life Today

This nation's 600,000 American Indians are a diverse ethnic group. They live in all fifty states and speak some 300 separate languages. Four hundred thousand Indians live on reservations, and 200,000 live off reservations. The tribes have different customs and mores, and different wants and needs. The urban Indian has a world different from that of the rural Indian.

Fifty thousand Indian families live in unsanitary, dilapidated dwellings, many in huts, shanties, even abandoned automobiles; the average Indian income is $1,500, 75 percent below the national average; the unemployment rate among Indians is nearly 40 percent—more than ten times the national average; the average age of death of the American Indian is 44 years, for all other Americans 65; the infant mortality rate is twice the national average; and thousands of Indians have migrated into cities only to find themselves untrained for jobs and unprepared for urban life. Many of them return to the reservation more disillusioned and defeated than when they left.

Indian Schooling Today

Indian children attend federal, public, private, and mission schools. In the early days of this republic, what little formal education there was available to Indians was under the control of the church. Gradually, however, as the nation expanded westward and Indian nations were conquered, the treaties between the conquering United States and the defeated Indian nation provided for the establishment of schools for Indian children. In 1842, for example, there were 37 Indian schools run by the U. S. government. This number had increased to 106 in 1881, and to 226 in 1968.

This pattern of federal responsibility for Indian education has been slowly changing. In 1968, for example, the education of Indian children in California, Idaho, Michigan, Minnesota, Nebraska, Oregon, Texas, Washington, and Wisconsin was the total responsibility of the state and not the federal government.

In 1968, there were 152,088 Indian children between the ages of 6 and 18. 142,630 attended one type of school or another. Most of these—61.3 percent—attended public, non-federal schools, and 6.0 percent attended mission and other schools. Some 6,616 school-age Indian children were not in school at all. The Bureau of Indian Affairs in the Department of the Interior, the federal agency charged with managing Indian affairs for the United States, was unable to determine the educational status of some 2,842 Indian children.

The Bureau of Indian Affairs operates 77 boarding schools and 147 day schools. There are 35,309 school-age children in these boarding schools, and 16,139 in the day schools. Nearly 9,000 of the boarding-school children are under 9 years old.

Has the federal government lived up to its responsibility? The extensive records of this subcommittee, seven volumes of hearings, five committee prints, and this report, constitute a major indictment of our failure.

Drop-out rates are twice the national average in both public and federal schools. Some school districts have drop-out rates approaching 100 percent. Achievement levels of Indian children are two or three years below those of white students; and the Indian child falls progressively further behind the longer he stays in school; only 1 percent of Indian children in elementary school have Indian teachers or principals; one-fourth of elementary and secondary school teachers—by their own admission—would prefer *not* to teach Indian children; and Indian children, more than any other minority group, believe themselves to be "below average" in intelligence.

A frequent complaint by minority groups is that school textbooks do not fairly represent their culture and history. This results in feelings of rejection and denigration on the part of the minority group members and also deprives the majority from learning the truth. Josephy advances this argument in the following article.

THE FORKED TONGUE IN U.S. HISTORY BOOKS
Alvin M. Josephy, Jr.

In recent years, Indian intellectuals and the editors of *The Indian Historian* conducted a long and detailed study of more than four hundred basic and supplementary American history textbooks used in elementary schools and high schools. They found that almost all of them contained numerous misrepresentations, distortions and ethnocentric anti-Indian interpretations, or—just as bad—omitted any mention at all of Indians, as if they had never existed.

Some samples of what they found:

Reprinted by special permission from *Learning*, The Magazine for Creative Teaching, January 1973. © 1973 by Education Today Company, 530 University Avenue, Palo Alto, California 94301.

- In *The Story of American Freedom,* a basic history textbook used at the time of the study in the California fifth grades, Indians were treated as impersonal obstacles to the white man's progress, like the rocks and trees of the wilderness, or were mentioned only in such context as: "Settlers had gone beyond the Appalachians. The Indians made war upon them. The President had to see that the settlers were protected." There was no explanation that the government had guaranteed the Indians' lands by treaty; that the settlers violated the treaties and were illegal intruders; that the Indians' resistance was defensive; that the government then took the Ohio Valley Indians' lands by fraud, deceit and military might, breaking the treaties and protecting the aggressors rather than their victims.

- In another fifth grade history, *The Story of Our Country,* Indians were also overlooked, save in such general statements as: "The Plains Indians had to be defeated before cattlemen and their families could live in the Great Plains region." In addition to being inaccurate (cattlemen generally only moved onto the plains after the Indians had been defeated and penned on reservations), such history left volumes unsaid about the way the various plains wars started; i.e., the Sand Creek massacre of Cheyenne Indians, the invasion of the treaty-guaranteed sacred Black Hills of the Sioux Indians by Custer and gold miners. In short, the Indians' side of their desperate struggle for their homelands, means of livelihood, freedom and very existence was ignored.

- In a fourth grade reader, *California and the West,* used last year, no individual tribes were mentioned and no attempts were made to present the Indians as living people or give a balanced view of their role in history. The California mission period, which Indians today regard as an era of oppression and tyranny, was characterized only by such sentences as: "The mission priests taught the Indians about Christianity. . . . The padres were very proud of the Indians, and the Indians were very proud of their work." Overlooked was the destruction of Indian tribes and cultures, the herding of Indians into the missions, and the harsh regimentation, slavery and punishments they experienced. Passages on the gold rush period—when genocide was practiced against the California Indians and tens of thousands of them died of disease or were hunted down and slain like wild game—contained no mention whatsoever of the Indians and their fate.

Other Americans who have bothered to look into the Indian record have come up with much the same findings. In 1969 a subcommittee of the U.S. Senate Committee on Labor and Public Welfare reported that in Alaska: "(1) twenty widely used texts contain no mention of Alaska natives at all . . . ; (2) although some textbooks provide some coverage of the Alaskan Eskimo, very few even mention Indians; and (3) many texts at the elementary and secondary level contain serious and often demeaning inaccuracies in their treatment of the Alaskan native."

Another survey in Idaho, the report went on, "found Indians continually depicted as inarticulate, backward, unable to adjust to modern Euro-American culture, sly, vicious, barbaric, superstitious and destined to extinction." In Minnesota, a social studies text used for years in elementary schools depicted Indians as "lazy savages capable of doing little more than hunting, fishing and harvesting wild rice." A study in California confirmed the Indians' own appraisal of history books in that state, noting that in 43 elementary school texts there was barely any mention of the Indian "contribution or of his role in the colonial period, gold rush era or mission period . . . and, when mentioned, the reference was usually distorted or misinterpreted."

Studies made by the Association on American Indian Affairs in New York and by individual researchers like Virgil J. Vogel, an assistant professor of history at Chicago City College, have pointed up the same deficiencies. The association, an Indian-interest group whose board includes both Indians and non-Indians, found that only one of 75 history textbooks was adequate in its treatment of Indians; that is, provided a fair and balanced coverage of their role as participants in American history. Vogel surveyed more than a hundred American histories, many of them major works used as sources by the writers of high school and elementary textbooks, and concluded that, in sum, they defamed the Indians ("The Indian was never so happy as when, in the dead of night, he roused his sleeping enemies with an unearthly yell and massacred them by the light of their burning homes"); disparaged them ("Indians were singularly lacking in inventive ability and in the sense of adaptation"); disembodied them (with phrases like "the Indian menace," "skulking savages" and "human beasts of the forest"); or obliterated them entirely (as in Arthur M. Schlesinger's *The Age of Jackson*, which includes not one word about Jackson's removal policy or the Southeastern Indians' Trail of Tears).

The realization has finally begun to dawn that American society as a whole has suffered from "forked tongue" history books. But the damage to the Indians themselves has been overwhelming. Year after year, the distortions, misrepresentations and failure to tell the whole historical story foster erroneous and stereotyped thinking about Indians and lead to still further misunderstanding, prejudice and contempt. At a time when the Indians of the United States are struggling for self-determination and desperately need non-Indian support for legislation and enlightened attitudes that will permit them to regain control of their own affairs and the right to manage them on a level of equality with all other Americans, they are denied that support by perpetuation of derogatory and untrue images about them. It is no wonder that they are demanding with new passion and urgency that history be set aright.

. . .

And for the first time, Indian pressure for textbook revision is beginning to have an effect on white educators and school systems. North Dakota, Alaska and Montana are among the first states to make genuine efforts to correct texts and issue new ones, prepared either by Indians or with Indian editorial participation.

More significant changes will occur as Indian tribes themselves take over the control and operation of their children's schools and prepare new texts for those classrooms. On the Navajo reservation in Arizona, where this is already beginning to occur, both Indian and white educators have hailed the introduction of Navajo-prepared texts that tell Navajo-related history more fully and accurately than ever before. Similar goals have been announced by the Northern Cheyennes and other tribes.

At Davis, California, the Deganawidah-Quetzalcoatl University, a unique new institution of higher learning operated by and for Indians and Chicanos, is using Indian teachers and teaching materials in such courses as "Pikuni 'Blackfoot' Religion and Philosophy," "The Conflict Between California Indians and Europeans" and "Native American Religion and Philosophy." Even Indians in Leavenworth and other federal penitentiaries are beginning to publish papers filled with articles on Indian history and culture.

In time, as these efforts multiply, the great Indian men and women of the past will emerge from the mists for all Americans, and both the telling of the nation's history and the nation's understanding of itself will be vastly enriched.

Social, political, economic, and educational inequality is not confined to Indians. In southwestern United States are many citizens of Mexican descent who experience subtle or overt discrimination. The following report of recent research documents this problem and describes how "Anglos" retain control in communities even if they are outnumbered. These findings are particularly interesting to compare with Rosenthal's in Part Four.

DISCRIMINATION AGAINST MEXICAN-AMERICANS
Phi Delta Kappan

A vivid and sometimes poignant picture of discrimination against Mexican-Americans in a California community and its school system was disclosed in a recent Stanford doctoral dissertation by Theodore W. Parsons, now assistant professor of education and cultural anthropology at Florida State University.

For three years Parsons studied an agricultural town in central California, called "Guadalupe" in his report, spending 40 days in personal observation of the elementary school where more than half (57 percent) of the nearly 600 pupils are Mexican-Americans.

Some examples of how those of Mexican origin are kept firmly subordinated to the "Anglos" (white Americans of Anglo and other national origins) in both school and community:

1. A teacher, asked why she had called on "Johnny" to lead five Mexicans in orderly file out of a schoolroom, explained: "His father owns one of the big farms in the area and . . . one day he will have to know how to handle the Mexicans."
2. Another teacher, following the general practice of calling on the Anglos to help Mexican pupils recite in class, said in praise of the system: "It draws them [the Americans] out and gives them a feeling of importance."
3. The president of the Chamber of Commerce declared in praise of

the school principal: "He runs a good school. We never have any trouble in our school. Every kid knows his place. . . . We believe that every kid has to learn to respect authority and his betters."

4. The school principal expounded the "grouping" and departmentalized reading programs instituted under his administration: "We thought that the white children would get more out of school if they could work faster and not be slowed down by the Mexicans. We thought the Mexican kids would do better work if they were in classes geared more to their level. We thought that maybe we could give them some special attention. . . .

"Everybody is happy about the grouping programs. . . . The Mexican parents have never said anything, but the kids in school are doing better. . . . I guess the Mexicans are more comfortable in their own group."

5. By admitted subterfuge, the Chamber of Commerce committee sees to it that the artichoke festival "queen" is always an Anglo, with the Mexican candidate in second place as her attendant. An influential citizen told Parsons: "We could never have a Mexican queen represent us at the county fair."

6. Two of the three churches do not accept Mexicans. At the Catholic church, when both groups are assembled for special occasions, the Mexicans sit in the back or stand if seating is inadequate.

Mexicans buy tickets to church affairs but seldom attend because the people "aren't friendly." The one Mexican family who showed up at a barbecue sat alone throughout the afternoon.

7. At school graduation, the Mexicans march in last and sit at the back of the platform. A male teacher explained that this is traditional and "makes for a better-looking stage." Also, the Americans, who have all the parts in the program, can get more easily to the front. He added:

"Once we did let a Mexican girl give a little talk of some kind and all she did was to mumble around. She had quite an accent, too. Afterwards we had several complaints from other parents, so we haven't done anything like that since. . . . That was about 12 years ago."

8. The Mexican cub scout pack was in high excitement at the close of one annual town cleanup drive, when their pile was the highest at the 10 A.M. deadline. At 10:40 the garbage collector's large truck arrived and deposited a big load of trash on the Anglo cub pack's pile. The Anglo pack then was awarded the $50 prize.

9. A light-skinned Mexican high school graduate promptly lost the job as bank teller she had just been engaged to fill when the manager heard her speak to an acquaintance in Spanish. He said he had not realized she was Mexican—it was not bank policy to employ Mexicans.

The school teachers, all Anglo and for the most part indigenous to the area, appeared unanimous in sharing the stereotype of Mexican-Americans—inferior in capacity as well as performance—Parsons reported. So firmly is the pattern in mind that a teacher, in full view of a group of well-dressed, quietly behaved Mexican children, could describe Mexican children as noisy and dirty.

Sociometric tests conducted by Parsons disclosed that even the Mexican children come to share the view constantly held up to them that the Anglos are "smarter" and their good opinion of special value.

"In general, Anglo informants characterized the Mexicans as immoral, violent, and given to fighting, dirty, unintelligent, improvident, irresponsible, and lazy," wrote Parsons.

"Mexican informants often described Anglos as being unsympathetic, aggressive, interested only in themselves, cold, and demanding. . . . Not one of the several hundred people contacted during the field investigation had ever visited a home outside of his own ethnic group."

One of the U.S. Office of Education's programs for preventing school dropouts among Spanish-speaking children is the funding of several bilingual programs. The news releases from the Office of Education have been very encouraging, but Lawrence Wright reported in the November, 1973, *Phi Delta Kappan* that the "capacity for hyperbole in the Office of Education is well developed." The results so far, he reports, are meager. "In Boston last year, out of a school-age Puerto Rican population of perhaps 10,000, a total of 63 graduated from high school." Will bilingual education go the way of other "compensatory" programs described later in this section—lots of promise but few results?

"SEE PEPIN RUN"
Roger Ricklefs

In Viviana Prodromides' Brooklyn, N.Y., classroom, "See Dick run" has given way to a new chant: *"Mira Pepin corre."* When the teacher holds up a rubber ball, the first-graders diligently write down the Spanish words,*"la bola."* Before recess, "Pepin" is looking for the ball and the children are writing in their notebooks: *"Pepin busca la bola."*

This is bilingual education, a fast-growing and highly controversial phenomenon that many educators think will spread to thousands of schools in the next few years. In a bilingual program, a child who speaks little English starts learning in the language he knows best. Instruction in English gradually increases until the child, it is hoped, masters both languages. At the same time, thousands of English-speaking children from Frenchville, Maine, to Cucamonga, Calif., are taking part in the same programs to learn a foreign language at an early age.

According to the U.S. Office of Education, bilingual programs across the nation already enroll 112,000 students, up sharply from 26,000 four years ago, when large federal funding began. The Wash-

From *The Wall Street Journal*, Friday, December 15, 1972. Reprinted with permission of the *Wall Street Journal*. © 1972 Dow Jones and Company, Inc. All rights reserved.

ington agency is pushing for further major expansion—and there is plenty of room. About five million school-aged youngsters (nearly 10% of the total) speak a first language other than English; four million of these speak Spanish.

A HIGH DROPOUT RATE

The bilingual programs strive to alleviate an alarming problem: Millions of children are falling behind because they don't understand what the teacher is saying. Over 57% of the Spanish-speaking youngsters entering New York City high schools drop out before graduation, compared with 46% of the black students and 29% of the whites. Some 86% of the same city's Spanish-speaking children read English below their grade and age level. Other cities report dismal figures too.

These widespread failures contribute heavily to poverty and consequent social problems in adult life, of course. As some see it, the new bilingual programs offer real hope. "Bilingual education offers millions of children the first real chance to break the cycle of failure in the school system and in later life," contends Carmen Perez, director of bilingual education for two New York schools. An Office of Education official adds: "We believe that almost without reservation, kids in the programs are doing better in school than their peers with similar backgrounds who take the regular English program."

As critics see it, however, bilingual education is already full of bureaucratic waste, slows the assimilation of newcomers, perpetuates ethnic divisions and produces only marginal academic improvement. Some contend that the whole trend is really an ethnic power struggle to create teaching jobs for Puerto Ricans and Mexican-Americans—at the expense of "Anglos."

IT'S "HOT AND SEXY"

Says Albert Shanker, president of New York's United Federation of Teachers: "Bilingual education is the hot and sexy thing right now, and there is a good deal of common sense to it. But its real political thrust comes from the creation of a large number of professional job opportunities."

Despite controversy, the programs continue to grow in many languages, including French, Portuguese, Chinese and several Indian languages. Tahlequah, Okla., has a project in Cherokee, and Anchorage offers the Eskimo language of Yuk.

In Woodburn, Ore., a farming and furniture-making town of 7,000 population, the Nellie Muir elementary school enrolls 166 pupils in a Russian-English program. Most of the youngsters are part of a Russian-speaking colony that emigrated from Turkey in the 1950's. But 40 students are local youngsters who mostly didn't know a samovar from a blini when they enrolled. They participate because "their parents recognize the value of a second-language opportunity," says Miguel A. Salinas, director of the school's bilingual projects. The program probably makes Woodburn the only small town in Oregon that must order its reading primers directly from Moscow.

FOR MANY, AN IMPROVEMENT

Many parents say programs like these mean a big improvement in their children's school life. "In this school, my kids felt at home from the very first day," says Margarita Vasquez, who has three young sons in a New York Spanish-English bilingual program. "It's completely different from my own experience," adds the young mother, who moved from Puerto Rico to New York at the age of 12. "In Puerto Rico, I had won prizes in class, but here I felt totally lost and inferior." Like millions of others, Mrs. Vasquez remembers bitterly her early days in mainland schools, where her native language was worthless.

In the school the Vasquez children attend, students are at first divided according to language dominance. Initially, instruction in the nondominant language may be limited to learning that tongue as a second language. Later, the student attends mathematics or social-studies classes taught in the new language. As is common elsewhere, every child in the program is there because his parents requested a bilingual education.

This method works far better than the traditional approach of teaching the youngster English as a second language while keeping him in the regular English-language program, contends Willie Alire, acting deputy director of bilingual programs for the Office of Education. While a child is out of his class learning English, he misses instruction in other subjects, the official notes. Besides, the child fails to understand the English-language instruction he does receive, Mr. Alire says. "If he's lucky, he ends up only a couple of years behind," the official adds.

The bilingual programs also try to build ethnic pride. "This school teaches all about Puerto Rico, and my kids are crazy about it," Mrs. Vasquez says. Indeed, posters for a Puerto Rican "fiesta folklorica" and maps of the island proliferate in the school. Classes stress Puerto Rican history, geography and culture.

In contrast, Mrs. Vasquez remembers Puerto Rican children in her own New York school who were "ashamed of their own language." She recalls: "If you asked them a question in Spanish, they would say they didn't understand." Many members of minority groups, of course, contend that traditional, Anglo-dominated schools commonly make their children feel that their ethnic heritage or language is second-rate.

Critics contend that so far the bilingual programs appear more effective in building ethnic pride than in teaching the Three R's. Even enthusiasts concede that bilingual education alone is rarely enough to close completely the academic gap between poverty-stricken minority students and the typical middle-class "Anglo" school child.

But studies suggest that the bilingual programs can at least help somewhat. For instance, standardized tests show that the typical Spanish-speaking Albuquerque, N.M., fourth-grader in a bilingual program now is reading English "at the third-grade or high-third-grade level," compared with the second-grade level his counterparts attained before the program began, says Carlos Saavedra, bilingual project director in the city's school system.

At the Bridge Street Elementary School in Los Angeles, second-graders in the bilingual program still score in the bottom 43% of the nation in reading English—but that is a jump from the bottom 13% before the program began, says Ramiro Garcia, who heads the school's bilingual program.

As for the English-speaking youngsters in such programs, parents often report encouraging progress. "I figured it would be a lot easier for my children to speak Spanish now than in high school," says Ethel Stephens, who has two young daughters in a Brooklyn bilingual program. Her third-grader already chatters in Spanish with friends at home, and the bilingual instruction hasn't "in the least" hindered progress in other subjects, Mrs. Stephens says.

But the bilingual trend isn't limited to the classroom. With an $890,000 federal grant, the Berkeley, Calif., school system is developing a bilingual television series inspired by "Sesame Street." Officials hope that this will grow into a nationally broadcast daily half-hour show with both English and Spanish portions. Other television projects are also being developed.

Yet this rapid growth of bilingual education may soon generate bitter rivalry over jobs, educators fear. Among other groups, the Spanish-speaking community is increasing pressure to expand bilingual programs rapidly. For instance, Aspira of America, a New York-based organization that tries to further educational opportunity for Puerto Ricans, recently filed a class-action suit in a federal district court in New York. This would force the city's schools to provide bilingual education to all who desired it. Of the 170,000 New York City youngsters whose dominant language isn't English, only 4,000 are reached by current bilingual programs. Aspira contends that equal opportunity is thus denied.

But Aspira concedes that the well-being of children isn't the only issue. "Sure, getting more teaching jobs for Puerto Ricans is a conscious motivation for a lot of people," says Frank Puig, assistant executive director of Aspira's New York affiliate. He believes that getting more jobs would simply redress the current imbalance: Puerto Ricans now account for 26% of New York's public-school students but only 1% of the teachers.

The Puerto Rican demands have generated "very widespread fear," says Mr. Shanker, the leader of the New York teachers' union. "If a school established a new bilingual position, then the current position ceases to exist. The whole concept of job security could become meaningless," he says.

Mr. Shanker says his powerful union would strongly resist any expansion of bilingual programs that would cost present teachers their jobs. Instead, he urges teaching Spanish to present teachers so that they can conduct bilingual classes.

Supporters of bilingual education say the teachers can't possibly master the language in a short enough time. Besides, they insist it is crucial that teachers "share the culture" as well as the language and serve as ethnically similar "role models" for students. This gives Latin Americans a decided edge. Mr. Shanker argues angrily that the idea "that only Puerto Ricans can teach other Puerto Ricans" is "racist through and through," and the battle continues. Conflicts between teacher unions and Spanish-speaking activists have also flared in Hartford, Conn., and other cities.

Another problem is cost. The bilingual programs now cost the federal government $35 million a year, or $312 for each student enrolled. This covers only special expenses of bilingual education like the cost of "second-language" teachers. Local schools pay the rest.

Educators say there is a fair share of waste, including some of the fees paid to outside consultants to evelute individual programs. "Quite commonly an evaluation report will cost the government

$15,000 or $20,000, yet involve only two months of actual man-days," one source says. "And much of this is work done by young kids out of college for $9,000 or $10,000 a year. So you can see what a good deal it can be for a consultant."

So far, the government has paid several million dollars for such reports—some useful and some nearly useless, sources say. "Maybe a project is working and maybe it isn't, but you'd never know from some of these reports," one exasperated Office of Education source says.

An official in the federal agency concedes that the bilingual program hasn't devised adequate evaluation procedures, "partly because we just didn't get around to it." A shortage of good bilingual tests is also a problem, this source says. But a new program of "impact evaluation" will probably go into effect next year, the official adds.

One dimension of the civil rights movement has been a call for greater recognition of the contributions of black Americans. A standard suggestion of the past few years has been for the inclusion of black history in the school curriculum. Black comedian and activist Dick Gregory supports this idea and even extends it to include rearranging the holiday schedule.

THE SHORTEST MONTH
Dick Gregory

February is American history month, it seems, for white America. Banks, schools, public buildings and many offices close twice during February to commemorate the birth of two of traditional American History's most legendary heroes—George Washington and Abraham Lincoln. The Father of our country and the supposed Healer of its

Dick Gregory, "The Shortest Month," *Renewal*, vol. 9, no. 2 (February 1969), pp. 4, 5. Reprinted by permission.

wounds are given their revered and honored place in America's official memory.

February is also a month rich in the history of the black experience in America, although there is no official recognition at the national level. Perhaps that fact partially explains why the nation's wounds are still bleeding profusely.

Frederick Douglass, runaway slave, author, probably the leading voice of the 19th century abolitionist movement, editor of the famed abolitionist newspaper *The North Star,* was born and also died in the month of February. This month saw the birth of Dr. W. E. B. DuBois, prolific writer, noted historian, founder of the NAACP, certainly the father of the current mood among black youth of black identity, black culture and black studies, and Langston Hughes, one of the most renowned black men of letters in this century.

February is both the month of black recognition and black assassination. Hiram Rhoades Revels of Mississippi, the first black United States Senator, took the oath of office in 1870 during the month of February. The wise and courageous spokesman of racial truth in America, Brother Malcolm X, was murdered on February 21, 1965.

An increasing national phenomenon is the demand of black youth that black history be taught in colleges, high schools and grade schools throughout the land. It is primarily a northern phenomenon, since the segregated school system of the South has long provided black youth with black principals, black teachers and a black curriculum. Graduates of all-black southern schools are familiar with the names and accomplishments of black men in America—a history conspicuously eliminated from the supposedly liberal northern educational system.

So there is obviously more to the concept of integration than physical proximity. School buses can "bring students together" to borrow a Nixon phrase, but they are irrelevant to establishing cultural identity and racial pride. The popular phrase "quality education through integration" means more than establishing a physical racial balance in the public schools. It means establishing an educational system which encourages the full integration of the individual human being.

If a black student is fully exposed to his own unique history, not the degrading history of slavery but the noble accomplishments of his ancestors, that student will no longer harbor those feelings of inferiority which the American system has imposed upon him. If the white student is fully exposed to that same black history, he will no longer be able to accept his parents' version of black worth. Such exposure may show the white student who the real "nigger" is.

White folks must study black history to set the record straight. Traditional American history is a slanted version of the story of America. For the black student, black history is only a prelude to a more thorough orientation in black studies. Black studies must relate the entire educational process to the black experience. The only way for the black student to break out of the system in America, which has made him a "nigger" for so long, is to find out who he is and where he came from, so that he himself can determine where he is going. A man without identity is like a tree without roots.

The list of black accomplishments is long indeed. Look at the list of black inventors alone. White America tends only to think of George Washington Carver and peanut butter. But there was also Benjamin Banneker, who made the first clock in America, a wooden "striking" clock, and who laid out the blueprint for the nation's capitol. Henry Blair was the first black man to be issued a patent—first for a corn planting machine and later for a cotton planter.

Dr. Daniel Hale Williams performed the first open heart surgery. Dr. Charles Drew developed the techniques for separating and preserving blood—though he died of injuries received in an automobile accident because a southern hospital would not give blood transfusions to blacks. Jan Matzeliger revolutionized the shoe industry with his machine to mass produce shoes. Granville T. Woods revolutionized the railroad industry with his Synchronous Multiplex Railway Telegraph. Norbert Rillieux revolutionized the sugar-refining industry in the United States, by inventing a vacuum evaporating pan which reduced the industry's dependence upon gang labor and produced a superior product.

Elijah McCoy revolutionized machines, period, by developing a process for automatic lubrication. Garrett Morgan invented both the gas mask and the traffic light. Andrew Beard invented a coupling device for railroad cars which prevented the maiming or death of countless railroad workers.

The list of black inventions is endless and includes such common household items as the dust pan, the pencil sharpener, the fountain pen and the paper bag. Just one more reminder that black is not only beautiful, but also creative and inventive and necessary for America's survival.

Long discriminated against, some women have launched a vigorous and now well-publicized campaign for equal treatment in the schools. The following article details some of the evidence for charges of sexism in schools. Does this essay, or the one by Levy and Stacey (p. 149) on sexist bias in elementary schools, convince you of a need for change? Can curricular reforms occur before a general shift in the whole society has happened?

THE FINAL REPORT CARD
Nancy Frazier
and Myra Sadker

In comments made by renowned educators, in goals and philosophies drawn up by various educational commissions, in lists of school objectives stored in forgotten corners of principals' files, a common theme reverberates—one of the most important purposes of education is to put all children in complete possession of their abilities and talents. It is reflected in goals that have been set forth by the Committee on Concepts and Values of the National Council of Social Studies: "Recognition of the dignity and worth of the individual" and "widening and deepening the ability to live more richly." There is an overwhelming verbal agreement that education is concerned with the sacredness of each individual and that one of its prime mandates is to encourage each child to grow and develop to his or her fullest potential.

In my personal experience as a university faculty member and as a supervisor of student teachers, I see examples of sexism daily at all ages and grade levels that belie these educational goals. This week I spent some time at an elementary school, at a junior high school, and at the university. I would like to relate some of the sexist practices I observed during these seven days, not because they are dramatic or outstanding, but simply because they provide an indicator of how casually and frequently sex bias occurs in schools.

In a fifth-grade classroom, a popular male teacher was about to collect money for a charitable cause. "Now what shall I collect the money in?" he mused half aloud. The students began calling out suggestions. "I've got it," he said. "Let's take this small pencil case and put the girls' money in it, and then we'll take this big, tall pencil case for the boy's money because the boys in this class are big and tall."

At a junior high school an enthusiastic student-teacher was working with a ninth-grade class, trying to illustrate the different kinds of conflict one might find in a novel: "You might read about a soldier who has a conflict with the enemy or about a boy whose dreams of becoming President are in conflict with his poverty and lack of education." Suddenly the teacher stopped short. "But I guess you girls wouldn't read those stories. What do you read? Love stories and books about *Marsha Blaine, Angel Nurse* and stuff like that?" Some of the girls looked down or twisted in their chairs with obvious discomfort. A few, more outspoken, shot back, "We do not. That's so dumb."

This week I had a conference with a university senior who was about to begin looking for a teaching job. Uneasy over the way the phrase teacher shortage was turning into teacher surplus, he said, "I went to an interview yesterday—an eighth-grade opening—and I think I stand a good chance to get it. The job description said 'male preferred' and in the interview they said they were really looking for a man."

Toward the end of the week I attended a dinner party with faculty members from various universities. At one point during the evening I became involved in a conversation with a professor who stated that he had never discriminated against a woman in his life. Later, when this professor became aware that I was carrying a full teaching load and had a baby, he reproached me for not remaining at home full time as my "biological responsibility dictates."

Most of these people are concerned—some even dedicated—educators. All would be appalled to think that they might be teaching inferiority to female students or limiting their potential in any way. In their practice of sex discrimination these educators are in no way atypical. When I now look back on my own career in public school teaching, I am uncomfortably conscious that I too was guilty of many of the sexist practices that I now watch others perform.

Keeping in mind the educational goal of each individual growing to his or her fullest potential, let us now complete in some detail the picture of what the female student is like after her trip through the educational process. To create this portrait, we will draw boundaries that are somewhat forced and artificial. Two areas to be looked at, cognitive development and emotional development, come directly within the purview of the school; the third area, that of developing occupational potential, is related to the school, but more indirectly. Some of the key studies will be drawn together in a list, meant to be representative rather than inclusive, to gain some sense of the growth that has been stunted and of the promise that has been denied.

Loss of Academic Potential

1. Intellectually, girls start off ahead of boys. They begin speaking, reading, and counting sooner; in the early grades they are even better in math. However, during the high school years, a different pattern emerges and girls' performance on ability tests begins to decline. Indeed, male students exhibit significantly more IQ gain from adolescence to adulthood than do their female counterparts.[1]
2. Although women make much better high school grades than do men, they are less likely to believe that they have the ability to do college work.[2]
3. Of the brightest high school graduates who do not go to college, 75–90 percent are women.[3]
4. In 1900, women earned 6 percent of all doctoral degrees, in 1920, 15 percent, and by 1968, only 13 percent. In short, the percentage of doctorates earned by women has actually decreased since the 1920's.[4]

Loss of Self-esteem

1. As boys and girls progress through school, their opinions of boys grow increasingly more positive and their opinions of girls increasingly more negative. Both sexes are learning that boys are worth more.[5]
2. Fewer high school women than men rated themselves above

1. Eleanor Maccoby, "Sex Differences in Intellectual Functioning," in Eleanor Maccoby, ed., *The Development of Sex Differences*, Stanford, Stanford University Press, 1966.
2. Patricia Cross, "College Women: A Research Description," *Journal of National Association of Women Deans and Counselors, 32*, no. 1 (Autumn 1968), 12–21.
3. *Facts About Women in Education*, prepared by the Women's Equity Action League. Can be obtained from WEAL, 1253 4th St., S.W., Washington, D.C.
4. Edith Painter, "Women: The Last of the Discriminated," *Journal of National Association of Women Deans and Counselors, 34*, no. 2 (Winter 1971), 59–62.
5. S. Smith, "Age and Sex Differences in Children's Opinions Concerning Sex Differences," *Journal of Genetic Psychology, 54*, no. 1 (March 1939), 17–25.

average on leadership, popularity in general, popularity with the opposite sex, and intellectual as well as social self-confidence.[6]

3. On the Bernreuter personality inventory, norms show that women are more neurotic and less self-sufficient, more introverted and less dominant than men.[7]

4. College women believe that men desire a woman who is extremely passive and who places wifely and familial duties above her own personal and professional development.[8]

5. College women respond negatively to women who have achieved high academic or vocational success, and at times display an actual desire to avoid success.[9]

6. Fifty-five percent of a group of women at Stanford and forty percent at Berkeley agreed with the following sentence: "There is a time when I wished I had been born a member of the opposite sex." Only one in seven male students would endorse such a statement.[10]

7. Both male and female college students feel the characteristics associated with masculinity are more valuable and more socially desirable than those associated with femininity.[11]

Loss of Occupational Potential[12]

1. By the time they are in the fourth grade, girls' visions of occupations open to them are limited to four: teacher, nurse, secretary, or mother. Boys of the same age do not view their occupational potential through such restricting glasses.[13]

6. Cross, *op. cit.*

7. R. G. Bernreuter, "The Theory and Construction of the Personality Inventory," *Journal of Social Psychology,* 4, no. 4 (November 1932), 387–405.

8. Anne Steinman, Joseph Levi, and David Fox, "Self Concept of College Women Compared with Their Concept of Ideal Women and Men's Ideal Woman," *Journal of Counseling Psychology,* 11, no. 4 (Winter 1964), 27–33.

9. Matina Horner, "Woman's Will to Fail," *Psychology Today,* 3, no. 6 (November 1969), 36–38. Reprinted from *Psychology Today.* Copyright © by Communications/Research/Machines, Inc.

10. Joseph Katz, *No Time For Youth,* San Francisco, Josey Bass, 1968.

11. John McKee and Alex Sheriffs, "The Differential Education of Males and Females," *Journal of Personality,* 35, no. 3 (September 1957), 356–371.

12. The attitude and competencies with which a young woman enters the labor market will become of increasing importance. It has been estimated that nine out of ten females will be working on a full-time basis at some point in their lives. Between 1968 and 1980, the Department of Labor estimates that the total number of women in the labor force will increase by 27 percent, whereas the total number of men will increase by only 20 percent. Jeanne Holm, "Employment and Women: Cinderella is Dead," *Journal of National Association of Women Deans and Counselors,* 34, no. 1 (Autumn 1970), 6–13.

13. Robert O'Hara, "The Roots of Careers," *Elementary School Journal,* 62, no. 5 (February 1962), 277–280.

2. By the ninth grade 25 percent of boys and only 3 percent of girls are considering careers in science or engineering.[14]
3. Decline in career commitment has been found in girls of high school age. This decline was related to their feelings that male classmates disapproved of a woman's using her intelligence.[15]
4. In a survey conducted in 1966 throughout the state of Washington, 66.7 percent of boys and 59 percent of girls stated that they wished to have a career in professional occupations. However, 57 percent of the boys and *only 31.9 percent of the girls stated that they actually expected to be working in such an occupation.*[16]
5. College women become increasingly interested in being housewives from their freshman to their senior year in college. This is at the expense of academic and vocational goals.[17]
6. In 1967, the median income for a white man was $7,396; for a nonwhite man $4,777; for a white woman $4,279, and for a nonwhite woman $3,194.[18]
7. The gap between men's and women's income is widening. In 1955, the median wage of women working full time was 64 percent of what men earned. In 1968 it had decreased to 58 percent.[19]
8. Fewer than 1 percent of working women earned more than $10,000. The proportion of men earning that much is 20 times higher.[20]

Behind these statistics and surveys and facts and figures are individuals who, during the school years, have suffered a devastating loss. This "report card" is a cynical testament to the failure of school to encourage, indeed, even to allow female students to achieve their full potential. And now with freshly awakened consciousnesses, concerned feminists are beginning to look at the school environment where their sons and daughters spend so much time. With increasing

14. Daryl Bem and Sandra Bem, "We're All Nonconscious Sexists," in Daryl J. Bem, *Beliefs, Attitudes, and Human Affairs,* Monterey, Calif., Brooks/Cole. Copyright 1970 by Wadsworth Publishing Co.
15. Peggy Hawley, "What Women Think Men Think," *Journal of Counseling Psychology, 18,* no. 3 (Autumn 1971), 193–194.
16. Walter Slocum and Roy Boles, "Attractiveness of Occupations to High School Students," *Personnel and Guidance Journal, 46,* no. 8 (April 1968), 754–761.
17. Linda Bruemmer, "The Condition of Women in Society Today: A Review—Part 1," *Journal of National Association of Women Deans and Counselors, 33,* no. 1 (Autumn 1969), 18–22.
18. U. S. Department of Labor Statistics, 1970, quoted in JoAnn Gardner, "Sexist Counseling Must STOP," *The Personnel and Guidance Journal, 49,* no. 9 (May 1971), 705–714.
19. *Ibid.*
20. *Ibid.*

awareness and anger they are learning to hold the magnifying glass up to school life in order to ferret out and to expose each sexist practice, and they are beginning to despair over the harmful lessons their daughters are learning there.

. . .

Obviously, it would be an exercise in senseless scapegoating to lay the full blame on the schools. Sexist attitudes are woven throughout the whole fabric of society: They are in the mass media bombardment that depicts enamored housewives extolling the hygenic cleanliness of their bathroom bowls; in religious institutions that allow only male spokesmen to lead congregations in prayer to a male God; in the more than one thousand state laws that restrict a married woman's property rights; in the marriage ceremony where the wife gives up her father's name only to assume that of her husband, never having a name to call her own; in the very nature of language where the universal pronoun is "he" and all humanity is subsumed in the word "mankind." No, the schools cannot be singled out when they are surrounded by mass societal participation operating to keep women in their place. However, our system of education, as perhaps the most organized and systematic agent of socialization, must assume a heavy share of the responsibility and of the blame.

Education does not have to be this way. Boys and girls do not have to be channeled into separate activities and courses and schools. There do not have to be discriminatory admissions policies and discriminatory hiring practices. There does not have to be a biased and prejudicial curriculum. Girls and young women do not have to learn in school to become less than their promise and their potential. There can and must be changes in staffing patterns, in curricular materials, in the way teachers are trained, in the very nature of instruction itself. Schooling must no longer be a sexist activity.

Since the 1954 Supreme Court decision that racially separate schools are illegal, there have been numerous approaches to "desegregate" or "integrate" schools. The following article analyzes the major approaches so far employed to end racially different treatment by schools.

When this article was written in 1972, it closed with the observation that it was still too early to judge the final success or failure of some remedies. Nevertheless, it was difficult not to be pessimistic about the results of many programs, based on current findings.

Evidence in the ensuing years has done little to change that mood. See, for example, the article by Gordon Foster, "Desegregating Urban Schools" (*Harvard Educational Review,* February 1973, pp. 5–36), or the studies cited by Harry Miller and Roger Woock in *Social Foundations of Urban Education* (Hinsdale, Ill.: Dryden Press, 1973, 2nd edition).

The reader may ask, after surveying the remedies: What ingredients must exist for a "successful" program? Why, after twenty years, has more not been accomplished?

James Coleman would remind us that we need to do more than look at the remedies. Not only are there disagreements about the most effective remedies, there are different interpretations about what constitutes equal educational opportunity. Is it integrated schools? Is it equal funds or resources for each school child? Is it achieved only when minority groups graduate significant percentages of students in various disciplines?

THE SEARCH FOR EQUAL EDUCATIONAL OPPORTUNITIES

Charles R. Kniker

On a spring day in 1954, the United States Supreme Court decreed that a Negro, Linda Brown of Topeka, Kansas, had the right to attend a white school. In its decision, based on psychological evidence as well as legal precedents, the Court insisted that a dual school system was inherently unequal. Writing for the Court, Chief Justice Earl Warren called on the states to provide equal educational opportunity for all students, "with all deliberate speed."

Since 1954, numerous plans have been proposed to alleviate the sufferings in racially imbalanced school districts. The claims at times have been grandiose and the evaluation of the remedies' effectiveness confusing. This article surveys some of the more publicized programs. Each remedy's assumptions and goals are discussed first, followed by one or more examples. A tentative assessment of each program's success concludes the description.

Four types of remedies have been advocated:

1. compensatory education plans;
2. school desegregation strategies;
3. teacher education programs;
4. the community control option.

This essay concentrates on the first two types of remedies. Most government programs and civil rights organizations have focused their attention on the first two strategies.[1] The third option, teacher training, is described briefly because of its relatively small size and recent beginning. Examples of some community control programs are described in Part Five of this text. More specific evaluation of many programs surveyed here can be found in Meyer Weinberg (ed.), *Desegregation Research: An Appraisal.*[2]

Although the four remedies are not given "equal time" (or space), it is important to ascertain some basic similarities and differences of the programs. The first three operate within current political structures. Only community control seeks extensive redistribution of power over school policies, most frequently from central school boards and administrators to local parent organizations. Compensatory education plans and school desegregation remedies are directly concerned with changing student attitudes and behavior. The former stresses changing student perceptions of himself; the latter concentrates on changes in school environment. Teacher preparation programs appear to be saying that changes in teacher selection and training may produce more dramatic changes in the school climate than programs that emphasize student changes.

1. U.S. Commission on Civil Rights, *Racial Isolation in the Public Schools,* Vol. I (Washington, D.C.: U.S. Government Printing Office, 1967), pp. 115–183. Much of the outline of this article comes from this source. The evidence presented in that major study has been condensed for student interest reasons.

2. Meyer Weinberg (ed.), *Desegregation Research: An Appraisal,* 2nd edition (Bloomington, Indiana: Phi Delta Kappa, 1970), 460 pp.

We cannot forget that most programs mentioned here are still adolescents. To predict their outcome is as difficult and meaningless as forecasting how our young nephews and nieces will turn out. Yet, one phenomenon has proved strikingly consistent about these programs. Most efforts show students improve markedly during their first years, only to "tail off" as they leave the program. Psychologists label this tendency the Hawthorne Effect. Experimental subjects overreact to their chosen status, and their "ego trips" distort the realistic aid the program may have given them. Longitudinal studies are needed to learn whether many of these remedies really do contribute to the search for more equal educational opportunity.

COMPENSATORY EDUCATION

Compensatory education plans begin by assuming the causes of racial isolation are deep-seated in America, and that integration is not likely to occur in the immediate future. Reminiscent of Booker T. Washington of Tuskegee Institute, proponents of compensatory education urge that academically successful blacks who gain responsible jobs will break down neighborhood segregation patterns more rapidly than national or state fair-housing laws will. Therefore, these plans tolerate segregation patterns.

Second, the compensatory plans concentrate upon individual student skills. Typically, they single out the child who has problems in reading, speech, and vision. Increasing efforts are being made to identify social skills the disadvantaged children may lack, as well as attitudes that may hinder their progress in school. Whatever the skill involved, the essential task is to select individuals with problems and provide them with intensive remedial help.

Finally, as Sloan Wayland of Columbia University Teachers College has noted, compensatory remedies are permeated with a quantitative air. "Start the child in school earlier, keep him in more and more months of the year; expect him to learn more and more in wider and wider areas of his experience, under a teacher who has had more and more training, who is assisted by more and more specialists."[3]

Examples of Compensatory Education Plans

1. *Remedial programs* are the most common form of compensatory education. As *Racial Isolation in the Public Schools* notes, this strategy incorporates such factors as the reduction of the number of

---

3. Sloan Wayland, "Old Problems, New Faces, and New Standards," in *Racial Isolation, op. cit.,* p. 115.

students per teacher, provision of extra help to students during and after school, counseling, and use of special teaching materials designed to improve basic skills.[4] Ninety percent of the counties in the United States qualified for remedial funds when Congress passed the Elementary and Secondary Education Act of 1965.

One highly controversial example of remedial instruction is found in the More Effective Schools program sponsored by the United Federation of Teachers in New York City. MES called for drastic reductions in class size and a vigorous pre-school program. There were only to be fifteen pupils in pre-kindergarten rooms, twenty in kindergarten, fifteen in first grade, and no more than twenty-two in grades 3–6. In their contract with the city, the union pressed for numerous staff specialists to complement the teachers' staff. Each MES location, for example, was to have four or five assistant principals, and a community relations teacher was to be responsible for teacher-parent problems and to follow up on cases of absence by students.[5]

Numerous studies were done on MES students. Columnist Joseph Alsop became an ardent supporter of the program. The Center for Urban Education, a regional U. S. Office of Education research bureau, conducted several studies which did support the conclusion that a more positive attitude toward schooling was the prime outcome of the MES program. On the other hand, critics noted that some studies indicated virtually no academic gains by participating students who reached fourth grade, compared with other fourth-graders who had not participated in MES.[6]

Under the Elementary and Secondary Education Act of 1965, the federal government has spent a billion dollars a year for remedial programs. Recently the U. S. Office of Education published a report of such efforts during the 1967–1968 school year. The USOE found that wealthier school districts were receiving higher amounts per pupil than the poorer school districts. The report said of Title I's compensatory reading program: "Pupils taking part in compensatory reading programs were not progressing fast enough to allow them to catch up to nonparticipating pupils."[7]

4. *Racial Isolation, op. cit.,* p. 116.

5. Anonymous, "The Controversy Over the More Effective Schools: A Special Supplement," *The Urban Review,* vol. 2, no. 6 (May 1968), pp. 15–34.

6. For a lively exchange between Alsop and MES critics, read Roger R. Woock (ed.), *Education and the Urban Crisis* (Scranton, Pennsylvania: International Textbook Company, 1970), pp. 216–234. See especially Robert Schwartz, Thomas Pettigrew, and Marshall Smith, "Fake Panaceas for Ghetto Education," pp. 216–222; and Joseph Alsop, "Ghetto Education," pp. 223–234.

7. U.S. Office of Education, *Education of the Disadvantaged: An Evaluative Report, Title I,*

2. Another avenue toward equal educational opportunity is the *cultural enrichment program*. Frequently found in the middle-class and affluent schools in the past, it has only recently been offered extensively to poor children. The pupils are taken to museums, theaters, other schools, and perhaps are entertained in their own school building by guest artists.

In 1956 the Higher Horizons program began in New York City, incorporating many of the facets suggested above, plus training teachers to have more positive attitudes toward student performance. Initial studies of the program suggested a major breakthrough had been made. However, a study completed five years after Higher Horizons had begun found no significant differences in school performance and educational goals between students who had and those who had not attended Horizon schools.[8]

3. A third compensatory remedy plan is the *curricular-extra-curricular* program. Some forms of this option focus on the student's self-image, and others seek to improve the parental attitude toward school. The central finding of the 1966 Coleman Report[9] supports this type of program. The study of 600,000 school children concluded that a student's self-esteem, built upon family and peer influence especially, had a strong correlation with success or failure in school.

Most typical of the curricular programs has been the black history movement. Some schools with large black populations have both required and elective black studies courses. Some have incorporated black studies in the social science area.[10] Another movement is instruction in the early grades in a language familiar to certain ethnic groups—American Indian and Puerto Rican children, for example.[11] Early evidence from studies done with Spanish-speaking children seems to indicate that beginning school in Spanish, their "home" language, enhances rather than retards school performance.[12] The black history program is so new that it is nearly impossible to evaluate its impact.

One of the most extensive extracurricular programs beamed at

Elementary and Secondary Education Act of 1965 (Washington, D.C.: U.S. Government Printing Office, 1970). Reaction was from Des Moines *Register,* September 7, 1970.

8. *Racial Isolation, op. cit.,* pp. 124–125.

9. U.S. Office of Education, *Equality of Educational Opportunity* (Washington, D.C.: U.S. Government Printing Office, 1966), 737 pp.

10. *U.S. News and World Report,* "Black History as Schools Teach It," November 4, 1968, pp. 68ff.

11. *The Center Forum,* vol. 4, no. 1 (September 1969). The whole issue is devoted to the subject of bilingualism.

12. *Ibid.*

parental involvement in school activities has been the Banneker Project in operation in St. Louis. The project started in 1957–1958 and by 1965–1966 involved twenty-three schools with black majority student populations. To build parental support of the schools, teachers made home visits and established programs and events at school sites. Like the Higher Horizons program, the students' initial reading scores indicated significant gains after the program was introduced. Evaluation of the program in 1966, however, suggested that the improvements were not permanent.[13]

More recently, parental involvement or extracurricular plans have attempted to employ parents in the schools, most commonly as teacher aides. In some cities, parents also serve on advisory boards. A program of this nature, now widely copied, was first tried in Tucson, Arizona. By having the parents in school to witness day-to-day routines and interact with teachers, it is hoped the parents can aid others in the community to build a more positive image of the school. In some cities, the teacher aides are assigned to Operation Headstart classes or classes made up of Headstart graduates. In Des Moines, Iowa, this plan is called Operation Follow Through.[14]

4. The last type of compensatory program is the *pre-school strategy*, which usually stresses verbal and social skills. Not unlike the remedial plans in most respects, it underscores the goal of building the student's self-esteem. Of course, its distinction is in its efforts toward preparing pre-schoolers to succeed once they begin in school.

The most prominent example of this program is Operation Headstart, first tried in Waukegan, Illinois. In some cities the program had to be administered through political channels, thus gaining some adverse publicity in its early stages. Under the motto, "Do Something Now," the program was expected to show immediate results. Studies done on the effectiveness of Headstart have not pleased some impatient observers. Generally, both critics and supporters note that disadvantaged children have gained verbal skills and appear near the national norms on school readiness tests for first grade.[15] The controversial Westinghouse study on "The Impact of Head Start" found, however, that the summer Headstart programs accomplished far too little to be worth the investment.[16] Most authorities con-

13. *Racial Isolation, op. cit.,* pp. 12–122.

14. Des Moines Public School System, *Annual Report 1969–70,* copyright September, 1970, by Des Moines, Iowa, Public Schools.

15. John F. Cawley, Will H. Burrow, and Henry A. Goodstein, "Performance of Head Start and Non-Head Start Participants at First Grade," *Journal of Negro Education,* vol. 39, no. 2 (Spring 1970), pp. 130–131.

16. Victor G. Cicirelli, *et al., The Impact of Head Start: An Evaluation of the Effects of Head Start on Children's Cognitive and Affective Development,* the report of a study

clude that the program appears to offer a great beginning, but it has not carried through sufficiently in later grades to hold gains made by students.

Conclusion

Compensatory plans, when used as a sole remedy to promote equal educational opportunity, seem ineffective. This is even more definite in areas of racial and socio-economic isolation. Dr. Thomas Pettigrew, professor of social psychology at Harvard University, summarized the position of many experts when he said, "All of the evidence we have available would strongly suggest that compensatory education in segregated both race and class wise situations, is in effect, wasted money."[17]

SCHOOL DESEGREGATION PLANS

Unlike compensatory education, school desegregation plans begin with the assumption that immediate efforts at racial mixing are essential for success in schooling. Advocates of this philosophy point to evidence in the *Racial Isolation* study and the Coleman Report for support. Some civil rights leaders have objected, since it implies blacks are less intelligent than whites and can only improve when mixed. In a provocative article, "Is Integration Necessary?" former CORE leader Floyd McKissick pointed out that blacks have never been in school systems they truly control, but if such a situation did exist, he felt academic advancements would compare with white student performance levels.[18]

Desegregation plans underscore group practices rather than individual programs. Virtually all remedies in this category are flooded with group terminology: moving this *class* of students, merging two *districts*, exchanging *groups* of grade levels.

Whereas compensatory plans concentrate on skills, this type of remedy usually implies that new facilities, improved curricula, and

undertaken by Westinghouse Learning Corporation and Ohio University under contract B89-4536 dated June 20, 1968, with the Office of Economic Opportunity (Washington, D.C.: Office of Economic Opportunity, June 12, 1969). The preliminary report was issued in April 1969.

17. Testimony of Dr. Thomas Pettigrew before the Select Committee on Equal Educational Opportunity of the U.S. Senate, May 13, 1970. His remarks appear on pp. 745–767 of the Committee report.

18. Floyd McKissick, "A Communication: Is Integration Necessary?" *The New Republic*, December 3, 1966, pp. 33–36.

experimental media equipment will more likely encourage improvement in learning.

While the compensatory remedies emphasized the quantitative "more," school desegregation plans stress movement. Many of the plans necessitate logistical planning, whether for busing or encouraging students to sign up for special electives at integrated schools.

Despite these differences, the two strategies have one significant bond. Both maintain the power decisions—hiring and firing of teachers and budgetary allotments—in the hands of a central school board. Whether Boston or New York City or Des Moines, most school boards and bureaucracies are dominated by white upper-middle class membership.[19]

Examples of School Desegregation Plans

1. Theoretically, the simplest and cheapest way to provide racially balanced schools is to redraw the boundary lines to counter population shifts or additions. Such an idea has not worked well in the largest urban centers. New York City, for example, made one hundred changes between 1959 and 1963 and was not able to keep abreast of the rapid white exodus and the influx of blacks and Puerto Ricans.[20] Also, some school districts such as South Holland, Illinois, were accused of racial gerrymandering when they realigned student populations.

2. Another plan which involves a minimum amount of travel for students would be a *site selection* concept. As the need for new buildings arises, could they not be placed at locations that would ensure maximum integration? Smaller cities have been more successful than large cities in doing this. Much depends upon the desires of the local school board, too. In Chicago, a new school was needed to meet the student enrollment increase of a black-white neighborhood. As Figure 1 indicates, the school actually built encouraged racial imbalance when it opened.[21]

3. One school desegregation option, *school pairing,* seems to work well in small cities. Frequently called the "Princeton Plan" because it was first tried in that New Jersey community, it merges two neighborhood schools into sister schools. Under this plan in some communities, one administrator is responsible for both build-

19. David Rogers, *110 Livingstone Street* (New York: Random House, 1968), describes the New York City system; and Peter Schrag, *Village School Downtown* (Boston: Beacon Press, 1967), details the Boston school system.
20. *Racial Isolation, op. cit.,* p. 150.
21. Figures 1–4 come from *Racial Isolation, op. cit.* This one is from p. 48.

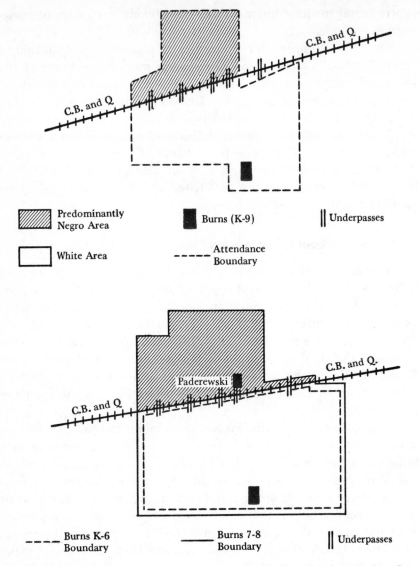

FIGURE 1. Burns Elementary School boundary before (top) and after (bottom) opening of Paderewski Elementary School in Chicago, Ill.

ings. The redistributing of the students is based on grade level rather than proximity to one school, as illustrated in Figure 2.[22]

4. *Open enrollment,* unlike the proposals just considered, involves much greater movement by students. Usually parents are given the choice of sending their children to any school in the system. For

22. *Ibid.,* p. 141.

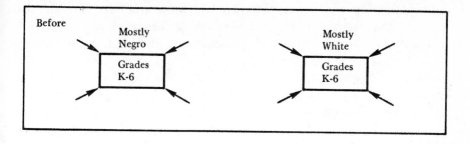

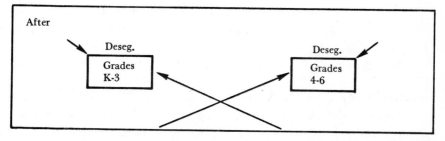

FIGURE 2. Pairing. Before pairing, students enroll according to each school's attendance area. After pairing, students of both attendance areas enroll in the two schools according to grade.

whites who believe in multiracial school environments and blacks who wish to escape decaying buildings, this plan provides hope. It also offers the possibility of relieving some overcrowded classrooms and filling underutilized buildings.

In practice, several problems have emerged. In 1965–1966 Boston adopted open enrollment. Despite the aid of a parents' organization and a plan called "Operation Exodus," the strategy failed, largely because parents had to bear the burden of transportation costs. New York City learned that such a plan increased segregation because open enrollment was frequently selected by the few white parents in some predominantly black areas.[23] Some school systems now correct this flaw by allowing transfers only if they improve the racial balance. For example, a white child in a 50 percent white school would not be allowed to go to a 75 percent white school. The most serious charge against the plan is that it rarely changes the situation of black majority schools in the inner city.

A variation of open enrollment is called "freedom of choice." Some Southern strategists believe that if they can convince the courts that each parent in their districts has the freedom to choose his child's school, the school system could not be found guilty of

23. *Ibid.*, pp. 147, 148.

discrimination and segregation. So far, the courts have consistently denied this argument. In Houston, Texas, for example, the school board advertised freedom of choice but added certain guidelines. Children were re-enrolled in the same school they attended before freedom of choice was declared in effect. The board declared that if a brother or sister of an applicant had previously attended a school, he would be admitted rather than an applicant who had no previous contact with the school.[24] Through such policies as these, the courts felt true freedom of choice was not guaranteed.

Open enrollment works best when school administrators actively publicize and fully finance the program. Rochester, New York, seems to have a successful program. In 1969 Waterloo, Iowa, initiated Project Bridgeway. It sought to create a two-way street by moving 200 black students from a 100 percent black elementary school and replace those students with white students. Via the media, the community was alerted to new programs to be instituted at Grant Elementary—team teaching, a nongraded curriculum, special resources, and such. Eventually, the goal of 200 students was obtained from twenty-seven other schools in the system and three parochial schools.[25]

5. A similar plan is called *school closing*. As is frequently the case, minority group members attend schools which are the oldest and in the worst state of repair.[26] By closing such a school and distributing the students to other schools, some measure of racial balance can be achieved. Figure 3 illustrates what occurred in Syracuse, New York. Englewood Cliffs, New Jersey, and Berkeley, California, as well as several cities in Florida, have tried this approach. Generally, the program appears to work.[27]

6. The school desegregation plan which has provoked the greatest discussion has been forced busing. One wonders why a mobile society can become so frightened by yellow vehicles that now bus half of the school children in the country every day. Obviously, most people grow upset when they envision their children in a strange neighborhood, or feel their children will be harmed academically by the addition of disadvantaged youngsters. Busing has usually been promoted on grounds that it relieves overcrowded schools and aids racial understanding. The evidence from several studies on the performance levels of both students who are bused and students at the

24. *Ibid.*, p. 66.
25. Interview with Dr. George W. Hohl, former Superintendent of Schools, Waterloo, Iowa.
26. Alvin Toffler (ed.), *The Schoolhouse in the City* (New York: Frederick A. Praeger, 1968), especially Ben E. Graves, "The Decaying Schoolhouse," pp. 61–66.
27. *Racial Isolation, op. cit.*, p. 144.

The program calls for each child to attend his neighborhood elementary school for four years. The second four years would be spent in a school drawing from several diverse neighborhoods. High school presumably would encompass more group representations. A feature of such a plan would be the pooling of teaching and administrative resources of the participating schools.[33]

If New York's "4—4—4" format is indicative of this program, the outlook is dim. A brand new intermediate school, I.S. 201, was erected in Harlem. It was supposed to attract white students from Queens. It never did. The demographic patterns in our large cities suggest that minority groups are effectively isolated for the pre-high school years.

9. The grandest (in scale anyway) school desegregation remedy is the *educational park,* or campus plan. In the late 1960's, some thirty communities considered erecting totally new campuses which would concentrate educational efforts at central locations. Some smaller communities were speaking about parks to accommodate 10,000 students. Larger systems speak of student populations from 15,000 to 25,000.

Such larger campuses would bring together children from many neighborhoods and presumably would break down racial walls as well as socioeconomic barriers. Some sites are as large as thirty acres. The projections include taking over land masses such as former military bases, or building over highways or filling in rivers next to cities. Sociologist Robert Havighurst of the University of Chicago has stated that the fallacy of many such plans is that they still do not include a broad enough spectrum of socioeconomic groups. For financial as well as social reasons, Havighurst advocates a new type of school district, one which would consolidate inner-city schools with suburban plants. Thus, a typical district would be pie-shaped, with its point in the city and its broad base in the affluent, suburban zone.[34]

Those opposing the park concept immediately suggested that the size would inhibit integration. They argue that most individuals and possibly even minority groups would not be blended together for meaningful relationships. Some also object to mixing pre-schoolers with high school students. To counter these arguments, most of the plans break down school units into grade-level areas. As Figure 4 indicates, several pods, each housing several hundred students, may be joined by a central-library-commons-auditorium. Perhaps one such unit would be pre-schoolers or grades 1—3.

33. *Racial Isolation, op. cit.,* pp. 166–167.
34. *Ibid.,* pp. 168ff.

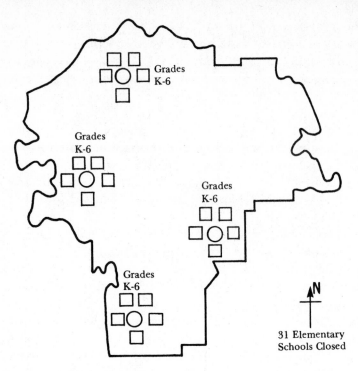

FIGURE 4. Syracuse campus plan.

East Orange, New Jersey, and Hartford, Connecticut, plan parks which would enroll all children at one site. Berkeley, New York City, and Pittsburgh envisioned several locations. Pittsburgh shelved their plans. Some cities had purchased land and were beginning construction. However, none is operative now. One serious problem, of course, is time. East Orange contemplated it would take twelve to fifteen years to finish their campus. In the current climate of financial conservatism about school expenditures, one wonders how many other plans will be halted.

Conclusion

Compared with compensatory programs, school desegregation remedies seem to have enjoyed more success since 1954. Small cities, as a rule, seem to have made more progress than large cities in overcoming the problems of racial isolation.

Yet no one can forget that today there is more segregation than in 1954. Although southern schools have responded to the challenge to integrate, *de facto* segregation in the North has offset gains made in the South.

Overall, results of both programs seem far from satisfactory. With many desegregation plans, the chief flaw appears to be that most schemes are brought into operation too late, or they involve far too few people.

TEACHER EDUCATION PROGRAMS

Teacher education programs turn the emphasis to the instructor instead of the student. Advocates say that having new equipment or placing students in new buildings will not solve what may be "communication" problems. To ensure that students may succeed in school, the school system must provide teachers that are sympathetic to the various cultural backgrounds of their charges.

In one 1965 survey of teacher education programs, less than 10 percent indicated they were attempting to provide special instruction for teachers who planned on going into urban education. It would be impossible to list programs that have come and gone for teacher preparation, but one may say it is doubtful that more than 20 percent of teacher preparation institutions have provided significant programs for urban teachers.

Examples of Teacher Education Programs

1. *Consortium* training appears to be a wave of the future. One such program is CUTE (Cooperative Urban Teacher Education), which began in Kansas City, Missouri, in 1966. Thirteen liberal arts colleges in Missouri and Kansas, together with representatives of the federal Mid-Continent Regional Educational Laboratory, developed guidelines for instructing student teachers in the Kansas City area. Students spend sixteen weeks at the Laboratory, and under the direction of experienced educational leaders and knowledgeable city experts, they learn about city life and conditions in their community and schools. Seminars are a frequent learning structure. One of the reservations about the program is that it still is small, with approximately twenty-five students per semester.[35]

2. *Residents in Training* programs are a second variety of teacher education. The idea is to encourage more people from ghetto areas to go into teaching. Some of these programs recognize that the talents of these individuals should not be shut off until they have completed

---

35. Mid-Continent Regional Educational Laboratory, "Innovation in the Inner City," a monograph published by McREL in January 1969.

college training, and so programs such as C.O.P. (Federal Career Opportunities Program) pay residents from inner-city locations to work in schools part-time and to go to school as students part-time. The academic goal would be a bachelor's degree in education.

Conclusion

Like the other programs, this appears far too small to make a major impact in the near future. Interviews with people in the programs reveal that many participants believe their training is valuable and will contribute to their success later on.

THE SEARCH GOES ON

The evidence presented here clearly indicates that America has not provided and does not now provide equal educational opportunity for all its students. Perhaps the negative cast placed on results of the programs described is due to the fact that we expected these proposals to deliver change in too short a time, and we have not provided participants with enough help.

Just as one is ready to give up, however, it appears that some programs do offer the possibility for nudging the nation closer to equal opportunity. At this point, however, no single remedy could be described as a major avenue for success.

Why have compensatory programs failed? To begin
with the obvious, Kniker noted that they were
given only meager funds and inadequate time and
yet were expected to produce radical changes.

Joan Smith underscores another reason. Failure
is ensured, she claims, when programs are built
upon faulty assumptions about students. Her article highlights research on self-concept and learning
capabilities of "disadvantaged" students.

Both articles do not discuss but nevertheless do
point to the question of succeeding articles: To
what degree does a political establishment deliberate allowing such doomed programs?

COMPENSATORY EDUCATION: GUARANTEEING FAILURE THE HELPFUL WAY

Joan K. Smith

Writing in the mid-sixties, Earl J. McGrath—head of the Institute of
Higher Education at Teacher's College, Columbia University, and
former U.S. Commissioner of Education—stated confidently that
"the decade of the sixties . . . will be most vividly signalized in the
United States by swift and lasting advances toward racial equality."[1]
With the onslaught of government spending for minority races
through the Elementary and Secondary Education Act of 1965, as
well as other federally sponsored programs, this prediction seemed
accurate. Both government agencies and educational institutions became actively involved in implementing remedial, college adaptor,
and cultural enrichment programs, and tutorial and other special
support services to help minority groups meet their goal of educational equality.

It was in this optimistic atmosphere that I accepted a job as
counselor in a midwestern city's New Careers program. The personnel were, in addition to me, a director, two work-site coordinators, a
secretary, and about 60 students. The program was for adults with

1. Earl J. McGrath, *The Predominantly Negro College and Universities in Transition* (New
York: Bureau of Publications, Teachers College, 1965), p. 1.

weak employment skills and poor academic records. Only five of the sixty had aptitude scores above the 15th percentile on the College Qualification Test. Every New Careerist had a $2.00 an hour "human service" job—teacher aide, day care assistant, hospital worker, drug counseling aid—in a non-profit organization. Ten hours per week were released from jobs during which New Careers people were to take courses at a nearby community college. Enrollment in college was mandatory for continuing in the program, but shorthand, typing, computer programing, TV repair, carpentry, or any other vocational or technical courses were not permissible. My responsibility as a counselor was to strongly discourage regular class participation, even in areas such as English, Biology or Sociology, in favor of non-credit remedial work or "sheltered" New Careers classes. No one ever defined the term "sheltered" but in actual practice it amounted to a specially created course, with a diluted content, imparted by an instructor who never gave F's if the person attended regularly. After three quarters of observing students in the sheltered classes and non-credit remedial work, I decided to let them enroll in regular academic classes if they wanted to. Seventeen students chose regular classes, thirty elected sheltered, and fifteen took non-credit remedial courses. Final grades for the sheltered and regular classes were in the B and C range, and for non-credit classes the range was B through D. Furthermore, teachers of regular classes, who did not know that any of their students were "special," never complained about New Careers students, but teachers of sheltered classes often made disparaging remarks. These results verified my growing conviction that if students were interested in schooling, they could survive well regardless of past academic records—especially if instructors did not know about these past records. During pre-registration for the next quarter, twenty-five people asked for regular classes; however, the director of New Careers effectively blocked regular class registration and the process ended with an enrollment of only five. The director herself was black, middle-aged and had strong aspirations to improve herself socially; but her skills and education were little different from the people she served, except perhaps in her own eyes. A short time after this incident, I discovered that she had written the counseling position out of the budget and I was no longer employed. As I looked back on the experience I couldn't forget what one of the community college instructors—a man who had previously taught New Careers classes in another state—had said: "These people are supposed to work hard and ensure their place on the bottom."

After having this experience, I wondered what effect other similar programs were having. Most of them, including New Careers, claimed successes, and an initial look at the U.S. Census reports

TABLE 1. Percent of 25–29-Year-Old Population with 4 or More Years of College.

	% of White 25–29 with 4 or More Years*	# of White 25–29-Year-old Population	# of White 25–29 with 4 or More Years*	% of Non-white 25–29 with 4 or More Years	# of Non-white 25–29-Year-old Population	# of Non-white 25–29 with 4 or More Years	Ratio of White to Non-white 25–29 with 4 or More Years
1940	6.4	9.904	.636	1.6	1.192	.019	30.1/1
1950	8.2	10.925	.896	2.7	1.313	.032	27.9/1
1960	11.9	9.556	1.137	5.4	1.313	.071	16.0/1
1970	17.8	11.812	2.099	7.3	1.665	.122	17.3/1
1971	18.2	12.467	2.270	6.4	1.560	.100	22.7/1
1972	20.1	13.024	2.625	8.2	1.454	.118	22.3/1

Numbers are in millions
*Inferred from the data given
Source: U.S. Bureau of the Census, Sixteenth Census of the United States: 1940. Vol. IV, Characteristics by Age, United States Summary, Pt. 1 (Washington: U.S. Government Printing Office, 1943), p. 8; Census of Population: 1950. Vol. II, Characteristics of the Population, United States Summary, Pt. 1 (Washington: U.S. Government Printing Office, 1953), pp. 1–165; Census of Population: 1960. Vol. I, Characteristics of the Population, United States Summary, Pt. 1 (Washington: U.S. Government Printing Office, 1964), pp. 1–153; Census of Population: 1970. General Population Characteristics, United States Summary (Washington: U.S. Government Printing Office, 1972), pp. 1–265; Statistical Abstract of the United States: 1969 (90th edition), p. 107; 1971 (92nd edition), p. 109; 1972 (93rd edition), p. 111; 1973 (94th edition), pp. 114, 116.

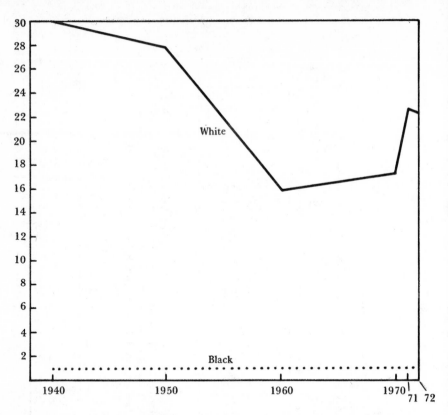

FIGURE 1. Ratio of White 25–29-Year-Olds to Non-White 25–29-Year-Olds with 4 or More Years of College: 1940–1972.

seemed to confirm this—larger numbers of minority students were entering and graduating from college during every decade from 1940 to 1970. In 1940 there were fewer than 20,000 "non-whites" in the 25 to 29 year-old-age group who had completed four or more years of college;[2] in 1950 there were 32,000; in 1960 the number had grown to 71,000 and by 1970 to nearly 122,000 (see Table 1). Moreover, the percentage of 25–29-year-old non-whites with four or more years of college increased during the same period—from 1.6% to 7.3%. But the numbers and percentages of white 25–29-year-olds with four or more years of college were also increasing, so the only realistic appraisal of whether or not minority groups were gaining

2. The terms "Negro and other minority races" and "nonwhite" are used more or less synonymously by the Census Bureau. Included in this group are: black, Puerto Rican, Mexican-American, Philippino, American Indian, Japanese- and Chinese-Americans. The category "four or more years of College" is not quite the same as a baccalaureate or higher degree, but it is the only category used by the Census Bureau which permits comparisons.

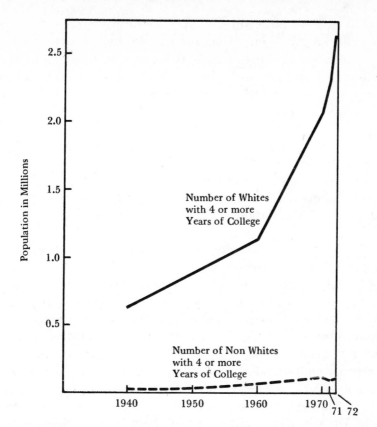

FIGURE 2. 25–29-Year-Old Population.

educationally was with reference to the rest of the population. By this criterion non-white Americans seem to have been gaining up until about 1960. In that year there were only twice as many white graduates as black, in proportion to their numbers in the whole population; but by 1971 there were three times as many white graduates as black, and in 1972 the figures were essentially unchanged.[3]

In view of this widening gap one is compelled to ask why the massive efforts contained in hundreds of programs across the country aren't resulting in more noticeable educational gains for "disadvantaged" students? One frequently given answer is that a lag exists between implementation and actual fulfillment—not enough time has passed to see the "true" results. This explanation assumes that the

3. There was one black person for every eight whites in the 25–29-year-old population; in 1960 there was one black graduate for every 16 white graduates; in 1971 there was one black graduate for every 23 white.

minority student possesses certain types of inadequacies or deficiencies which are "different" from the average student, but that through extensive remedial efforts these deficiencies can be overcome in time.

In a large portion of the recent literature, these inadequacies are mostly attributed to a lower class environment and can be categorized as follows:

1. low educational and occupational aspirations resulting in lack of motivation;
2. poor self-image and an insufficiently positive identity;
3. cultural deprivation and faulty socialization processes during the pre-school years culminating in impoverished educational skills.

Articles by Noble, Etzioni and Thinker, McClain, Boney, Bressler, Freedman and Myers, Rich and Spilerman support one or more of the above categories thereby effectively placing the blame on the minority person and his culture—or as William Ryan puts it, "blaming the victim."[4] After summer workshops in project Upward Bound, Don Boney clearly profiles the disadvantaged student as lacking curiosity, being too submissive and passive, deficient in conceptual understanding, and possessing too many feelings of debasement which interfere with full utilization of his academic resources. Through assessment of Cattell's Personality Questionnaire, Edwin McClain characterizes the southern Negro college student as lacking in masculine identity and ego strengths. He further states that the Negro's easy-going uninhibited and relaxed manner are qualities which can be associated with academic underachievement. Marvin Bressler also points the finger at the black and his culture by concluding that the Negro student is hard to educate because his social and travel experiences are restricted, because he has lower motivational levels, with impoverished language skills, and because he feels victimized by his substandard existence. Other writers such as Seymour Spilerman attribute the low achievement to inadequacies of early socialization and absence of language and sensory stimulation during pre-school years. Jeanne Noble correlates a positive personal identity with academic survival. Continuing with this premise she explores the history of the Negro's self-concept and his lack of and need for a positive identity. Being torn between two worlds he has suffered from the inner conflict of desiring the dominant groups' values but feeling more comfortable with his own reference group, while at the same time rejecting it because of the stigma of inferior-

4. William Ryan, *Blaming the Victim* (New York: Random House, Inc., 1972).

ity placed upon his race throughout American history. The black caught in this conflict has found himself suffering from a "self-hatred syndrome." Hence, the black student movement and push for black history is an attempt to recover a positive "surrendered identity," using the black community as its reference group. With the continuation of a strong black student movement on American campuses, Noble implies that a positive identity will result and academic success will follow.[5]

The current programs, virtually all of which were conceptualized in the sixties, are based on the assumption that the removal or mitigation of certain deficiencies associated with minority students and their culture will result in academic and social equality. Thus, today there are a series of programs which run the educational gamut: Project Headstart and Follow Through, Project Upward Bound, and various higher educational plans, such as SEEK and the College Discovery and Development program in New York City, plus New Careers, COPS, and other work-study and remedial programs.

If the assumption of lower class and minority group deficiencies is valid, educators are basically in a comfortable position. With curriculum changes, remedial work, and establishment of black cultural centers they are doing what they can to insure equal opportunity for even those with impoverished environments. Their only serious concern is to adequately staff and support existing programs. This makes the problem, if not simple, at least soluble through time and effort.

But a growing minority of the literature seriously raises doubts concerning the credibility of these assumptions. In a study of race and social class as related to both parents' and the child's own aspirations, Martin Deutsch found that young minority children were very alert, curious and highly motivated. Consequently, he concluded that something must happen in school to take this away. In assessing

5. Don Boney, "Some Dynamics of Disadvantaged Students in Learning Situations," *Journal of Negro Education,* XXXVI (Summer 1967), pp. 315–19; Edwin McClain, "Personality Characteristics of Negro College Students in the South: A Recent Appraisal," *Journal of Negro Education,* XXXVI (Summer 1967), pp. 320–25; Marvin Bressler, "White Colleges and Negro Higher Education," *Journal of Negro Education,* XXXVI (Summer 1967), pp. 258–65; Seymour Spilerman, "Raising Academic Motivation in Lower Class Adolescents: A Convergence of Two Research Traditions," *Sociology of Education,* XXXV (Winter 1971), pp. 103–18; Jeanne Noble, "The Black Student: A Search for Identity," *Journal of the National Association of Women Deans and Counselors,* XXXII (Winter 1969), pp. 49–54; Amatai Etzioni and Irene Tinker, "A Sociological Perspective on Black Students," *Educational Review,* XXIII (Winter 1971), pp. 65–76; Dorothy Rich, "Now: Infant Education," *Des Moines Register,* February 13, 1972, pp. A1, A6; Florence B. Freedman and Florence C. Meyers, "The College Discovery and Development Program: Disadvantaged Youth Prepare for College," *Journal of the National Association of Women Deans and Counselors,* XXXII (Winter 1969), pp. 90–95.

parental aspirations he discovered that Negro parents expressed higher educational and occupational goals for their children than their white counterparts.[6] In analyzing two of New York City's programs for black adults—SEEK and College Discovery Program— Solomon Resnik and Barbara Kaplan noted that what black adults lack in academic skills, they make up for in determination and drive, and that for these people there was no relationship between I.Q., grades, and ability to do college work. They go on to state that developmental reading courses are of little value, because they are conducted in a very boring and condescending manner relying on gimmicks that are easily forgotten.[7]

Several studies geared toward assessing self-image and identity dispute the premise that blacks are lacking in this area. To the contrary, most general conclusions revealed that Negroes had high self-esteem, high estimates of their ability and believed that they could achieve more in school than their white peers, even when achievement tests and report cards showed the opposite.[8]

Upon discovering that the "disadvantaged" held more positive self-perceptions than the "advantaged," Anthony R. Soares and Louise M. Soares explained this lack of congruence by stating that positive self-image is likely to be the product of a person's interaction with people like himself and most disadvantaged children are mainly exposed to other disadvantaged people.[9] Their explanation draws upon the work of James Coleman, who states that when Negro students become part of an integrated school system their self-concepts are likely to diminish.[10] However, the two following studies done in integrated school situations cast serious doubts on such a premise. Using the forty-two item Coppersmith Self-Esteem Inventory with 120 white, Negro and Puerto Rican students in fifth and sixth grades, Perry Zirkel and Gnanaraj Moses found that the Negroes' and whites' self-concepts were not significantly different.[11]

6. Martin Deutsch, Richard Bloom, and Martin Whiteman, "Race and Social Class as Separate Factors Related to Social Environment," *American Journal of Sociology*, LXX (January 1965), pp. 471–76.

7. Solomon Resnik and Barbara Kaplan, "College Programs for Black Adults," *Journal of Higher Education*, XLI (March 1971), pp. 202–18.

8. Marjorie Kirkland, "Effects of Tests on Students and Schools," *Review of Educational Research*, XL (October 1971), pp. 303–5.

9. Anthony R. Soares and Louise M. Soares, "Self-Perception of Culturally Disadvantaged Children," *American Educational Research Journal*, VI (January 1969), pp. 31–44.

10. James S. Coleman, *Equality of Educational Opportunity* (Washington, D.C.: U.S. Government Printing Office, 1966).

11. Perry A. Zirkel and Gnanaraj E. Moses, "Self Concept and Ethnic Group Membership Among Public School Students," *American Educational Research Journal*, VIII (March 1971), pp. 253–66.

Jerry Powers and others also found no significant differences in the self-perceptions of Jewish, non-Jewish and black tenth grade students in an integrated New York City high school. Administering the Soares and Soares Inventory to a school population that was 20% Negro, 55% Jewish and 25% non-Jewish, he found that the blacks' self-images were higher than the non-Jewish.[12]

If, then, there is any correlation at all between positive self-identity and educational success, perhaps it is a negative one—at least in lower class schools. Jerry Farber put it well when he stated that the educational process requires the student to play a subservient role to school authority figures. This process insists that in conflicting situations the student must appear to support a teacher's view over his own. Having too positive a self-image would make it more difficult to achieve this compromise.[13]

In the area of cultural deprivation growing out of an early and faulty socialization process, Rainwater has found some interesting evidence to support a very different set of conclusions from the traditional ones. After studying several culturally deprived families over a period of six years, Dr. Rainwater reports the following:

> Often in larger families quite a number of people attend to the baby's needs—older sisters, the mother, and sometimes the grandmother as well. In this situation the baby may be the subject of constant attention, being passed from hand to hand or later toddling from person to person and always receiving amused interest. Consequently, large babies and toddlers generally seem secure in their homes; they explore them freely and take gratification in the physical manipulation of objects and in interactions with the people there. . . . There is only mild pressure toward obedience through the toddler stage, and there is wide tolerance for messiness and "babyish" behavior.

Also, "The adults generally take a kind of amused pride in the apparent maturity of . . . [four and five-year-old] youngsters."[14] Textbooks in child development emphasize the need for children to have a permissive and accepting atmosphere in which to explore relaxed and protected. It seems that the above description closely fits a textbook ideal. Is it because it happens in a lower class atmosphere that it goes unnoticed?

The dissenting literature certainly casts a strong shadow on the traditional practice of assigning responsibility for educational failure

12. Jerry Powers *et al.*, "A Research Note on the Self-Perception of Youth," *American Educational Research Journal*, VIII (November 1971), pp. 665–69.

13. Jerry Farber, *The Student as Nigger* (New York: Pocketbooks, 1969). See especially the essay "The Student and Society," pp. 17–46.

14. Lee Rainwater, *Behind Ghetto Walls* (Chicago: Aldine, 1970), pp. 218–20.

to the minority person and his "substandard" culture. This research offers supporting groundwork for the kinds of assumptions made by educational critics such as John Holt, Jerry Farber and Jonathan Kozol. They advocate a position which places the blame on our social and educational system—an institutional process that has evolved to quite a complex and sophisticated level in a century's time—rather than on the people who are losing out educationally.

One of the most provocative exponents of the view that institutional racism may, in fact, exist on such a grand subconscious scale that it is actually invisible and continues virtually unquestioned is Annie Stein, who has had a long association as research analyst with the New York City public school system. In an article in the *Harvard Educational Review,* she mentions three different strategies used to insure minority race failure.[15] First, she asserts that school desegregation has not occurred. In 1955 New York had 52 segregated schools with 40% of the minority group attending them, and in 1965 there were 201 with over 50% of the minority group attending totally segregated schools. Community action has resulted in empty rhetoric and token gestures by those who control the schools. Secondly, she indicates that teacher training based on biased texts, which depict the minority student as coming from an impoverished sub-standard community, still supports erroneous assumptions about minority students. If anyone doubts this, note the following statement from a current text directed toward inner city teachers so they can "break their [students] chains of deprivation." Disadvantaged children cannot cope with change or success or waiting "and have a voracious desire for excitement. They are easily disconcerted and 'fly off the handle.' " One must be sure there are "no extra props that the children want to touch or throw." School must "assure them the stability they usually do not receive at home."[16] Stein points out that these attitudes prevent school success and asks: "How is it possible to fail to teach reading to the great majority of any population after eight years of trying?"[17] Taking this one step further, it is unlikely that the same teachers who have guaranteed failure heretofore are going to succeed in the remedial programs offered through

15. Annie Stein, "Strategies for Failure," *Harvard Education Review,* XLI (May 1971), pp. 158–204.

16. Quotes are from: Allan C. Ornstein, "Teaching the Disadvantaged," *Educational Forum,* XXXI (January 1967), pp. 215–23, and are quoted approvingly at greater length in Larry Cuban, *To Make a Difference: Teaching in the Inner City* (New York: The Free Press, 1970), pp. 164–67.

17. Stein, "Strategies for Failure," p. 159. In 1969, the average child in 85% of the black and Puerto Rican schools in New York City was functionally illiterate after eight years of schooling.

compensatory education at all levels, including higher education. Finally, she states that through devices such as tracking and diluted curricula the average minority student stays at the level of failure.

After reviewing the Census Bureau data, and after seeing that most of the research literature about minority group failure in school does blame the victim, I am convinced that my experience in one "compensatory" program was not unusual. The liberal argument that more time and more money and more helpful programs will remedy school failure has certainly not panned out so far. Indeed, after ten years of the most intensive activity of this kind in American history, minority groups seem to be worse off than before. If we as administrators and teachers seriously want to achieve greater equality of educational *results,* we must question existing modes of dealing with minority students at all levels of education. Especially we must question the implementation of more "learning disability" courses in teacher training and remedial programs in schools. If the fault does not lie with the minority student—if he is not essentially different from his white counterpart except in his academic record, and if indeed it's true that what some minority students lack in education, they make up for in drive—then change may occur when students are not automatically programmed into remedial work. School personnel should begin treating the student as an equal and not as a person whose past deprived condition generally needs to be remedied. Such an approach could hardly produce worse results than the "helpful" programs of the past decade.

The tension between the affluent and the poor in American schools is longstanding. In the 1870's a poor taxpayer in Kalamazoo, Michigan, sued the local school district for using his tax money to support high schools that were used by the middle class to the detriment of the poor. The taxpayer lost the case and, according to some, the poor have been losing ever since.

In 1971 the Supreme Court of California rendered a decision in *Serrano* v. *Priest* which is hailed in the following article as "an end to the school house scandal." The reader should be aware that the U.S. Supreme Court in March, 1973, in a similar case, *San Antonio Independent School District* v .*Rodriguez,* overturned a 1971 federal district court decision (*Rodriguez* v. *San Antonio,* 337 F. Supp. 280) which had held the Texas school finance system unconstitutional. This does not necessarily mean an end to all school finance reform, but it does mean that sweeping changes are unlikely. The *Serrano* decision is, therefore, probably less significant as an indicator of future reforms than as a specific example of the controversy.

EDUCATIONAL EQUALITY: AN END TO THE SCHOOL HOUSE SCANDAL

Victor H. Bernstein

In the winter of 1967–68, the principal of an elementary school in a Spanish-speaking section of Los Angeles called into his office the father of two small boys who had just been admitted to the school. "IQ tests show your sons to be exceptionally bright," the principal said. "If you want to give them a good education, get them out of here. Move your family into a neighborhood that can afford a better school."

In tossing off this candid piece of advice the principal could not know that he was helping to precipitate a crisis in the American system of public education—a crisis that in its ultimate ramifications is likely to overshadow the famous 1954 Supreme Court decision on school desegregation whose reverberations are still with us.

At the time, however, the father was no more aware of what the future would bring than was the principal. He simply took the friendly advice offered him and moved his family to Whittier, the middle-class Los Angeles suburb where Richard M. Nixon had attended college, and enrolled his sons in the local elementary school.

John Serrano, Sr., had performed his duty as a father. But perhaps because he was a social worker by profession he had an active social conscience, and the whole episode left him prey to a host of troubling questions.

Why, he wondered, should the children of a Los Angeles suburb have a better school to go to than the children of the Los Angeles inner city? Was it because their parents were wealthier? Come to think of it, was there any legitimate reason for *any* public school to be markedly better than another? All public schools by definition are government-supported, aren't they? Then by what right does government spend more money for education in one neighborhood or community than in another? Doesn't that constitute some kind of discrimination?

Soon after his move to Whittier, Mr. Serrano met two able and aggressive lawyers, and to them he posed some of the questions he had been asking himself. "Your questions are relevant and important," one of the lawyers said. "I think we ought to get some answers."

When lawyers want answers, they turn naturally to the courts. So the two attorneys, as a first step in building up a court case, began a systematic, state-wide probe of California's public-school system. And the deeper they probed, the clearer they saw that there were things about the system that were much worse than Mr. Serrano's worst suspicions. They found, in brief, that the poor, and quite often the middle class, not only were getting less out of the public schools than the well to do, *but also were paying more to get less.*

The investigation finished and briefs prepared, the lawyers went to court. The plaintiffs were the Serranos, father and sons, plus a score of children and parents from the Los Angeles school system. The defendants were certain appropriate state officials. And on August 30, 1971, the Supreme Court of California, having heard the case on appeal, ruled that the state's public-school system, as presently financed, was discriminatory and therefore unconstitutional and that the state's legislature had better get busy thinking up some more equitable system.

Meanwhile, what might be called the Serrano philosophy was spreading rapidly across a nation that in any case was growing increasingly unhappy about the skyrocketing costs of public education. Serrano-type challenges mushroomed, and within five months of the California decision state or Federal courts declared unconstitutional the school-financing systems of Minnesota, Texas and New Jersey. (As this is written, 40 additional challenges have been lodged against the school systems of some 30 other states and the Texas decision is in the hands of the United States Supreme Court on appeal.)

Defenders of the *status quo* in public education have good reason to wish that a Los Angeles school principal had kept his mouth shut five years ago.

Constitutionally, education is a function of the state. But because of the acknowledged intimate relationship between child education and family and community life, the states traditionally have turned control of the public schools over to the local authorities.

The local school board, then, administers the schools in its district as an agent of the state. It draws up the school budget, hires teachers, determines curriculums, approves textbooks and so forth, with the state's maintaining no more than an overseeing role.

The biggest proportion of the money needed to run the schools is raised locally. On a national average, 52 cents of every dollar spent on public education come mainly from local taxes, 41 cents from the state and seven cents from the Federal Government. But in many suburban and rural areas the local share of the school dollar may rise to 60 or 70 cents.

The crux of the Serrano complaint was the method used for raising the local share. In most of the 17,000 school districts in the country, the property tax provides up to 90 percent of the local share. A community of predominantly expensive homes of course will yield more revenue at the same property-tax rate than will a community consisting of moderate-priced homes. Indeed, it may yield more revenue at a *lower* tax rate.

And this is exactly what the courts have found. In the Serrano case in California, for instance, the court contrasted affluent Beverly Hills with the neighboring community of Baldwin Park, described as a "drab area" of homes valued at $15,000 and less. In 1969 Beverly Hills, with a property-tax rate of $2.38 per $100 of assessed valuation, raised enough revenue to spend an average of $1,231 on each of its public-school children; the same year Baldwin Hill, *with a tax rate more than twice as high,* raised only enough to spend $577 per pupil. Similarly, the New Jersey court contrasted the prosperous town of Millburn, which manages to spend more than $1,400 per pupil per year on a tax rate of $1.43 per $100, with the city of Newark, which, *with a tax rate four times higher,* could afford to spend only about $1,100 per pupil.

Such differences in per-pupil expenditures are to be found in every state in the country. "The greatest disparities are to be found in Texas and Wyoming," according to John Silard, a Washington attorney who has specialized in school-financing cases. "The highest-spending school district in Texas lays out $5,334 per pupil; the lowest-spending, exactly $234. In Wyoming, the extremes are $14,554 and $618. In other words, in both states there are children upon whose education there is lavished more than twenty times as much money per year as is provided for other children. I might add that in our eight largest states, which include nearly half the country's population, the disproportion between the high- and low-spending districts averages at least six to one. *And I am not talking about private schools; I am talking about tax-supported public schools.*"

Early in 1972 the Fleischmann Commission, an investigative body appointed by New York's Governor Nelson Rockefeller to look into the school-financing situation of that state, used eloquent language in reporting its findings: "It is repugnant to the idea of equal educational opportunity that the quality of a child's education . . . is determined by accidents of birth, wealth or geography. It is unconscionable that a poor man in a poor district must often pay local taxes at higher rates for the inferior education of his child. Yet, incredibly, that is the situation today in most of the 50 states. . . ."

What the commission found "repugnant" and "unconscionable," the courts—as has been indicated—have found illegal. All the decisions are based on what is known as the "equal protection" clause of the 14th Amendment to the Constitution. And with minor variations each of them echoes the words of the California Supreme Court in the Serrano case: "The [state] public-school-financing system makes the quality of a child's education depend upon the resources of his school district and ultimately upon the pocketbook of his parents, [and therefore] it denies to the plaintiffs and others similarly situated the equal protection of the laws."

With public education now challenged in more than half of our states there is no question that Mr. Serrano has helped to precipitate a major crisis. Does the crisis presage revolutionary reform? Are we on the threshold of a new era in education in which our children, no matter where they live or what the economic status of their family, will be assured equally excellent schooling, benefiting in equal measure from whatever revenues are devoted to public education?

I have talked about this to a number of educators, school administrators and lawyers involved in school-finance cases. All to whom I spoke approved wholeheartedly the courts' condemnation of the present system as blatantly discriminatory. But when it came to assessing the effect of the decisions in terms of revolutionary change, opinions were divided and generally cautious.

If to Sidney Marland, U.S. Commissioner of Education, the Serrano case represented a "fundamental breakthrough," to attorneys John E. Coons and John Silard the effects are more limited. "The courts forbid the old way," said Mr. Silard, "but they don't prescribe the new way. That is up to the legislatures." Said Mr. Coons: "The Serrano decision forbids the linking of affluence and spending, but that is all it does. It does not require the legislature to impose uniform spending state-wide." Or as Dr. R. L. Johns, of the University of Florida, project director of the National Finance Project, put it: "The courts are demanding equality in the *raising* of school revenues, not in how they must be *spent.*"

No equality in spending? From this interpretation one would think that the courts have been more concerned with the welfare of the taxpayers than of the children. Not so, say the educators. Dr. Johns was very firm on the subject: "A court decision directing us to spend exactly the same amount on every child in school would have wrecked everything we have been trying to build up in education." He was referring, of course, to the modern concept that schooling should be designed as far as possible to meet individual needs and that individual needs vary from child to child, family to family, neighborhood to neighborhood. To meet these needs requires variations in spending

But if inequalities in spending are inevitable and justifiable, why all the fuss? Why the Serrano case and all the other cases? The answer is easy. The inequalities that exist today are based not on the varying needs of children but simply on the varying ability of the parents to pay school taxes.

All the foregoing brings into focus the crucial issue: Is there in education a direct connection between expenditure and equality? Does spending more money on schools mean a more effective education for our children?

The experts to whom I talked all were convinced that more money, properly spent, would mean better schools. "Although there are schools with high costs and low quality," Dr. Johns told me, "it is difficult to find high quality at a low cost. Personally, I have never encountered a good cheap school."

Whatever may be the effect of money on education, the effect of a lack of money is likely to be less ambiguous. Judge Theodore Botter, of the New Jersey Superior Court, in his opinion declaring illegal that state's school-financing system, tells us something of New Jersey's elementary schools.

For example, in Paterson, New Jersey, a fourth of the schools are more than 80 years old; many fail to meet state lighting and safety standards; only two or three have libraries or librarians. A survey of Camden schools showed an almost total deficiency in such programs as art, music, science, home economics. In one Plainfield school, the sole history text was pre-World War II; in another, books could not be taken home because there was only one set for several classes.

Nor are deficiencies restricted to city schools. New Jersey's Pine Hill district, something between a suburban and a rural area, has 875 pupils in three schools. It is a poor district with a relatively high tax rate. There is no trained librarian in the district. The library of one school is housed in a closet. Some of the science textbooks go back to the 1940's; to the children who must rely on them, there is no such thing as an astronaut. Five of the teachers lack college degrees of any kind. Is it surprising that a large percentage of the pupils are below normal in reading and other basic skills?

Judge Botter summed up his findings this way: "In most cases, the rich districts spend more money per pupil than poor districts; rich districts spend more money for teacher salaries per pupil; rich districts have more teachers and more professional staff per pupil; and rich districts manage this with tax rates that are lower than in poor districts."

The courts tell us that a child's education must not depend upon the wealth of his parents or of his school district. But obviously it must depend upon *something*. Without public revenues there can be no public schooling. One way or another, the courts are saying, each state legislature must devise a plan guaranteeing that an equal amount of revenue will be available to every school district in the state, rich or poor—subject only to the varying needs of the children.

Many formulas have been proposed for achieving this objective, a number of them extremely complicated. But the general principle favored by most experts, including the Fleischmann Commission and the President's Commission on School Finance, is for the state to take over full responsibility for school financing. It is proposed that the state raise the necessary funds by increasing its sales, income or other existing taxes or by levying new ones.

Most experts dislike the property tax as a source of school revenue. "It is a regressive tax," a lawyer remarked. "Like the sales tax, it tends to hit hardest those least able to pay. It is particularly hard on old people with fixed incomes and on young couples whose housing costs are high relative to their beginners' incomes." There is nothing in the decisions rendered so far to ban the property tax, but it is clear that wherever the tax is retained, the rate must be made uniform throughout the state.

Formulas have also been developed for accommodating per-pupil expenditures to the children's varying needs. Different "weights" may be given to different categories of pupils. If the average child of middle- or upper-class background is given a weighting of 1, then the "slow learner," the physically handicapped or the child of deprived background might be given a weighting of 1.25 or 1.50 or even 2, depending upon the estimated special needs. School funds would then be distributed to the districts on this "weighted" per-capita basis. If the annual expenditure for a child with a weighting of 1 is $1,000, say, then the expenditure for the child with a 1.25 weighting would be $1,250 and so on.

The concept of full state funding of education has its critics. It runs counter, they point out, to the cry for decentralization that has swept so many of the country's big-city school systems. Many critics are appalled at the idea of teachers' bargaining over salaries with the state, opening the possibility of state-wide teacher strikes.

But proponents of state funding insist that local school boards still could retain control of curriculums, textbooks and teacher hiring. Indeed, they argue that under the present system, local control of schools in poor districts is an illusion anyway. Control means freedom to make choices, but what choices can be made when there is no money available to implement them?

At this writing, no states involved in the Serrano cases have as yet reacted legislatively to the court decisions; many observers think none is likely to do so formally until the Supreme Court gives its decision in the Texas case.

Assuming, as many observers do, that the Supreme Court will uphold the Serrano principle, what difference will it make to the children? To taxpayers? What will happen to our school system in the next ten years? I discussed these questions with Stephen Browning, of the Lawyers Committee on Civil Rights Under Law, a Washington, D.C., organization that has been functioning as a sort of clearinghouse for the Serrano cases.

"I foresee," said Mr. Browning, "a steady growth of the state's role in school financing. Some states will go all the way in state funding. Hawaii has done so from the beginning, and others will work out a system of supplementing local funds. In either case, present disparities between rich and poor districts will gradually lessen.

"Obviously, as the state increases its share of school funding, local school taxes will go down. Just as obviously, state taxes will rise, and perhaps Federal taxes too, for there is increasing pressure on Congress to raise the Federal contribution to education from its present seven percent level. Bills to do so have already been introduced."

On the whole, then, it appears that the Serrano decisions will not cut our education bill; indeed, if they are to serve their ultimate purpose, the bill will increase. But the burden of payment will be redistributed in such a way that the well to do will carry a fairer share of the load, with corresponding relief for the poor and lower-middle class.

School revenues not only will be raised more equitably; they will be *spent* more equitably too. The present astonishing disparities between poor and rich school districts gradually will disappear. But it is important to note at this point that the Serrano decisions deal with equality of schools *within each state;* nothing in them says that schools of one state must be equal to schools of another. That problem is left to later court challenges and later decisions.

To say that equality shall prevail within each state is certainly a contribution to democracy. Is it also a contribution to good education? Schools can be equally poor as well as equally excellent. How determined will state legislatures be to raise their poor districts to the level of their best? Perhaps if P.T.A.s start to affiliate on a state-wide basis, they might achieve, in co-operation with teachers' organizations, the political clout necessary to ensure that whatever changes come in our educational system will be for the better, not the worse.

In the following essay, Professor Christopher Lasch reviews four recent books in education, three of them historical essays and one a sociological monograph. All revolve about the debate over the extent to which schools have, are, or can play a role in promoting more equality—or in guaranteeing class stability. The books are: Christopher Jencks et al., *Inequality: A Reassessment of the Effect of Family and Schooling in America;* Michael B. Katz, *Class, Bureaucracy, and Schools: The Illusion of Educational Change in America;* Colin Greer, *The Great School Legend: A Revisionist Interpretation of American Public Education;* and Joel Spring, *Education and the Rise of the Corporate State.*

INEQUALITY
AND EDUCATION
Christopher Lasch

I

The most important finding of Christopher Jencks's much discussed study can be stated simply. There is little correlation between income and the quality of schooling, and school reform can no longer be regarded, therefore, as an effective means of equalizing income. To put the matter more broadly, equalizing opportunity will not guarantee equal results. If we wish to reduce inequality, we should adopt policies designed to equalize income instead of attempting to equalize opportunity in education, the goal of so much liberal reform in recent years.

Some of the widespread criticism of Jencks's book rests on misunderstanding. His findings became familiar long before his evidence was published, and they were presented in a way that made them seem to be part of a conservative reaction against the meliorism of the Sixties. It appeared that Jencks was saying that schools "are no longer important," in the words of one of his critics—an argument

Reprinted with permission from the *New York Review of Books,* May 17, 1973, pp. 19–25. Copyright © 1973 NY REV.

that would presumably contribute, whatever the author's intention, to a new social policy of benign neglect. Together with Edward Banfield, Daniel Moynihan, and Arthur Jensen, Jencks was seen as leading a "new assault on equality." Not only did he argue that schooling is unimportant, his study, it was said, gave support to the idea that IQ is largely hereditary. *Inequality* appeared also to stress the role of luck in economic success, thereby reviving the "Horatio Alger myth." The entire study, it appeared, was pervaded by an "air of resignation."[1]

By this time the misunderstandings surrounding the book—not noticeably dispelled by its publication—may be too widespread to be countered by further explanation. It is quite likely, moreover, that the real source of these misrepresentations is a determination to discredit the book by carrying its argument to absurd extremes. To many people—to professional educators in particular but also to many critics of the educational system—Jencks's findings are inherently unpalatable. Not only do they undermine the popular belief that schooling is an avenue of economic advancement, they also undermine the progressive version of this national mythology—namely that progressive educational policies can be used to promote social justice and a new set of social values: cooperation, spontaneity, and creativity.

Jencks's evidence strongly suggests that the school does not function in any direct and conscious way as the principal agency of indoctrination, discipline, or social control, and he therefore tends to challenge the progressive critique of the school that has recently reappeared in the form of demands for "open classrooms," "schools without walls," etc. The book thus offends both liberals and many radicals as well; while for conservatives, Jencks's advocacy of equal rights (as distinguished from equal opportunity) doubtless identifies him as a proponent of the "new equality."

As Irving Kristol has explained, the slogan of equality is used by alienated intellectuals and pseudo intellectuals as a battle cry in their struggle to seize power from the bourgeoisie (just as the bourgeoisie once used equality as a rallying-cry against the aristocracy). Fortunately the slogan does not have to be taken seriously, since "a society that does not have its best men at the head of its leading institutions," in the comforting words of Daniel Bell—comforting

1. For these criticisms see Maurice R. Berube's review in *Commonweal*, January 19, 1973, pp. 353–354, and the essay by Kenneth E. Clark and Lawrence Plotkin in *Christopher Jencks in Perspective*, a pamphlet published by the American Association of School Administrators (Arlington, Virginia, 1973), p. 35.

because they imply that this objective is well served by our present arrangements—"is a sociological and moral absurdity."[2]

Jencks's intentions are far more modest, and his conclusions stated more tentatively, than this angry debate might lead one to expect. In the first place, he does not argue that schools "are no longer important" or even that schooling is irrelevant to economic success. On the contrary, his study confirms the widespread impression that people with academic credentials get better jobs than people who lack these credentials. It adds two qualifications to this impression, however; here lies the book's importance.

It is the amount of schooling rather than the quality of schooling, according to Jencks, that explains why some people get better jobs than others. Even the amount of schooling, moreover, does not account for the great disparities of income within those occupations—disparities that are as important in explaining inequality as the disparities between different kinds of work. Educational credentials, in other words, do not fully explain why some people have much higher incomes than other people. Indeed they do not even account for all disparities in occupational status. Both these lines of argument need to be followed in some detail.

Jencks and his associates found that although the distribution of educational opportunity varies widely, these variations appear to have little influence either on occupational status or on income. In themselves neither intelligence, grades, nor the quality of schools people attend explain why some people end up as doctors and lawyers and others as janitors and mail carriers. Still less do they account for differences in income. What matters is the level of educational attainment—the achievement of academic credentials. What determines the distribution of these credentials?

2. Note the American conservative's penchant, illustrated again in these observations by Kristol, for a simplified pseudo-Marxism: equality is merely a slogan in the class warfare between the bourgeoisie and the "new class" of alienated intellectuals and half-intellectuals.

In the United States, where Marxism remains officially taboo and therefore unstudied, even conservatives draw freely on "Marxism"—probably because liberalism has become increasingly vacuous and remote from reality, absorbed as it is in purely technical approaches to the world; while conservatism itself is, obviously, unpopular, resting in religious assumptions that can be taken seriously only at the risk of ridicule.

Note also the familiar anti-intellectual gambit used by both sides in the current debate on equality. For Kristol, the new egalitarianism is a disease of the intellectuals. For Jencks's critics on the left, *Inequality* is a typical product of the academy. True, the book *seems* to have provoked disagreement in the academy, but this controversy itself is only a form of capitalist competition. "Just as capitalists compete in production, but unite to preserve the production system . . . so the presence of an 'intellectual class interest' is not contradicted by the presence of debate" (Stephan Michelson, "The Further Responsibility of Intellectuals," *Harvard Educational Review*, February, 1973, p. 94).

The answer, in so far as it can be inferred from statistical evidence, seems to be that some people find schooling less painful than others and/or have reconciled themselves to staying in school for a long time for the sake of the rewards to which it presumably leads. There is little correlation between the amount of schooling people end up with and the quality of the schooling to which they are subjected. Neither the great disparity in school expenditures among various districts, curriculum placement (tracking), racial segregation, nor the socio-economic composition of the school seems to have much to do with the level of education students finally attain.

Statistically the distribution of credentials is determined partly by the distribution of "cognitive skills"—ability to use language and make logical inferences, to use numbers easily, and to absorb and retain miscellaneous information—and partly by family background. Since family background influences cognitive skills, it is difficult to estimate their relative weight. Nor is it easy to distinguish between the influence of heredity and the influence of environment on the development of cognitive skills. "An individual's genes can and do influence his environment." A child who begins with a small genetic advantage may find it easier to attract the sympathetic attention of his parents and teachers. The important point is that schooling does almost nothing to equalize the distribution of cognitive skills. In general, "the character of a school's output depends largely on a single input, namely the characteristics of its entering children. Everything else—the school budget, its policies, the characteristics of the teachers—is either secondary or completely irrelevant."

This information points to the conclusion, in itself surprising perhaps only to professional educators, that the distribution of educational credentials is largely a function of class. Not that economic advantages are automatically transferred from parents to their children in the form of educational credentials. Only about "half the children born into the upper-middle class will end up with what we might call upper-middle class educational credentials," while "about half the children born into the lower class will end up with what we might call lower-class credentials."

The influence of family background depends only partly on socio-economic status. It also includes cultural influences that are by no means strictly dependent on socio-economic status. Jencks's data seems to show that "cultural attitudes, values, and taste for schooling play an even larger role than aptitude and money." If middle-class children are likely to "average four years more schooling than lower-class children," this outcome seems to derive largely from the fact that "even if a middle-class child does not enjoy school, he evidently assumes that he will have to stay in school for a long time."

This data helps to remind us that culture is an important component of class; that class, in other words, is much more than a matter of social and economic standing.[3] The middle class perpetuates itself not by handing down its economic advantages intact but by implanting in the young attitudes that help to keep them in school until they have acquired the credentials necessary for middle-class jobs (if not always for middle-class incomes).

Having established a connection between credentials and class, Jencks traces what happens to people who have acquired these credentials. Do people with college degrees end up with better jobs? Do they make more money than people without degrees? As we would expect, Jencks finds that although "there is a great deal of variation in the status of men with exactly the same amount of education," occupational status is "quite closely tied to . . . educational attainment."

On the other hand, his figures show little correlation between educational credentials and income. Intangibles, it appears, have more effect on income inequality than we had supposed—luck, differences of competence that can by no means be put down to education, and the cumulative effect of initial differences in competence, whereby those who have skills often get a chance to develop them more fully, while those who lack them are discouraged from aspiring to more interesting and rewarding work. "Once people enter a particular occupation, those with additional education do not make appreciably more money than others in the occupation." Of two men working in the same insurance firm, the more highly paid is by no means certain to be the one who went to the better school, got better grades, or even finished more years of schooling.

Even if it were possible to give everyone the same amount of

---

3. Accordingly terms like "upper middle class," "lower middle class," etc., are misleading. Such terms do not really refer to classes but simply to income groups. A superficial reading of Jencks's book might lead to the conclusion that the distribution of educational credentials has little to do with class, since it seems to be influenced by cultural considerations more than by socio-economic status. It is more accurate to conclude, however, that class is a cultural as well as socio-economic phenomenon, and that as such it has a great deal to do with the distribution of educational credentials.

The concept of class used by academic sociologists, which Jencks has unfortunately borrowed for the admittedly limited purposes of his analysis, is static, rigid, abstract, and hierarchical; whereas in reality classes are the product of a specific series of historical events, cultural and political as well as social and economic. The American middle classes, both the "old" middle class of propertied wealth and the "new" middle class of salaried employees, still shows many of the cultural characteristics of a class devoted to accumulation as opposed to leisure and display, including an emphasis on schooling as a means of getting ahead.

schooling, Jencks concludes, this would have little effect on the distribution of income. A direct political attack on inequality therefore makes more sense than an attempt to equalize educational opportunities. Jencks suggests that the government might provide incentives to employers to rotate jobs, giving employees the chance to develop a variety of skills. Again, it might legislate incomes directly. Whatever the particular measures, the point is "to establish political control over the economic institutions that shape our society," in short to adopt "what other countries usually call socialism."[4]

Some of Jencks's critics on the left, as noted, have accused him of reviving the myth that virtue is rewarded with economic success. "We are asked to believe in Lady Bountiful," writes Colin Greer; "we are asked to believe—strange as it sounds—in the rule of luck over the exploitative affairs of men, women, and children in this society."[5] But the Harvard study shows quite clearly that middle-class children start life with enormous advantages; that these advantages enable them to acquire college degrees; and that college degrees in turn have an important bearing on occupational status and even on income, at least to the extent that income is a function of occupational status.

The study also seems to indicate, however, that middle-class children are by no means assured of economic success simply by virtue of their socio-economic status. Jencks goes so far as to say that "there does not seem to be *any* mechanism available to most upper-middle class parents for maintaining their children's privileged economic position." Stephan Michelson has suggested that Jencks's strategy is to convince "higher status adults" that they have nothing to lose from an egalitarian income policy, since they cannot transfer their economic standing to their children. Whether or not this is Jencks's intention, his findings about mobility are quite consistent with his general purpose, to destroy the assumption that there is a

---

4. Stephan Michelson, whose radical gamesmanship I criticized in note 2, above, complains (*Harvard Educational Review*, February, 1973, p. 105) that Jencks trivializes the idea of socialism, which implies a change in the nature and relations of work and in the distribution of political power, by narrowing it to income equality. This time I think he is on firm ground. An egalitarian incomes policy is not necessarily "socialist" (although that is obviously no reason to reject it), and I do not see why Jencks unnecessarily alienates potential support for such a policy, and provides ammunition to its critics, by calling it socialist. One such critic complacently predicts that "his chief recommendation—that the country turn to a vast socialistic overhaul of its economic institutions as the only way to guarantee equality—will get little support" (Paul B. Salmon, foreword to *Christopher Jencks in Perspective*, p. v.).

5. Text of a radio broadcast by Greer, station WBAI, September 26, 1972.

close connection between opportunity and result, between the distribution of advantages and the distribution of income.

His study seems to show that there is a fair amount of social mobility in America, both upward and downward over small degrees of the social scale, but little equality. Some of the not-so-rich, it seems, get slightly poorer, while some of the not-so-poor get somewhat richer, but the gulf between wealth and poverty remains as wide as ever. Only by confusing equality with mobility, however, can we see these conclusions as reaffirming the "Horatio Alger myth."

In one respect, it must be said, Jencks's picture of American society is highly misleading. It omits the upper class, a class so tiny that it altogether escapes Jencks's statistical filter. Some people do pass on to their children all the perquisites of great wealth and power. They are not numerous, and their influence cannot easily be measured. A limitation of social science, as it has come to be defined, is that it simply ignores what it cannot measure. Another limitation is that it tends to confuse correlations with causes, or at least to encourage this confusion in the reader. One therefore has to insist that Jencks's study tells us nothing about the way class power is exercised in America, about the connections between money and power, about the underlying sources of inequality, or even about the role of the school system in perpetuating inequality. It merely examines a number of statistical correlations between income and schooling.

II

In order to understand how the school system really works, we have to examine its historical origins. There now exists a considerable body of historical writing on the development of the American public school, much of it prompted by recent criticism of the schools. Out of this writing—to which the recent books by Katz, Spring, and Greer are important contributions—it is possible to construct the following interpretation.[6]

The principle of universal compulsory education won general acceptance in the middle of the nineteenth century largely because reformers like Horace Mann and Henry Barnard convinced influential

---

6. The following account draws also on Michael B. Katz, *The Irony of Early Educational Reform* (1968); Lawrence A. Cremin, *The Transformation of the School* (1961); Raymond E. Callahan, *Education and the Cult of Efficiency* (1962); and Edward A. Krug, *The Shaping of the American High School* (1964).

portions of the public that the schools could perform tasks far more important than instruction in academic subjects. They insisted that the school could become an agent of social reformation and/or social discipline.

In soliciting public support, these reformers appealed to the belief that schools under proper professional leadership would facilitate social mobility and the gradual eradication of poverty or, alternately, to the hope that the system would promote order by discouraging ambitions incommensurate with the students' stations and prospects. The latter argument was probably more appealing to wealthy benefactors and public officials than the first. Both led to the same conclusions: that the best interests of society lay in a system of universal compulsory education which would isolate the student from other influences and subject him to a regular regimen, and that the system must be operated by a centralized professional bureaucracy.

The ideology of school reform contained a built-in, ready-made explanation of its own failures. Once the principle of the common school had been generally accepted and the memory of earlier modes of education had begun to fade, critics of the new system found it difficult to resist the logic of the position put forward by educators: that the admitted failures of the system could be attributed to lack of sustained and unequivocal public commitment, particularly in the matter of funds, and that the only remedy for these failures, therefore, lay in bigger and better schools, better professional training, more centralization, greater powers for the educational bureaucracy—in short, another dose of the same medicine.

Toward the end of the nineteenth century the school system came under heavy public criticism. The schools were inefficient and costly; monotonous classroom drill failed to engage the pupils' enthusiasm; too many of the pupils failed. This criticism, however, in no way questioned the underlying premises of universal compulsory education; its upshot was a concerted drive to make the schools more "efficient."

Joseph Mayer Rice, who had inaugurated the muckraking attack on the school system with a series of articles in the *Forum* in 1892, published in 1913 a tract called *Scientific Management in Education*. Here as in his earlier writings he stressed the need to remove education from political control. The application of this commonly held idea to education had the same consequences as its application to city government in the form of civil service reform, the city manager system, and other devices intended to end political influence and promote the introduction of "business methods." It encouraged the growth of an administrative bureaucracy not directly responsible to the public and contributed to the centralization of power.

The political machines which the new system displaced, whatever their obvious shortcomings, had roots in the neighborhoods and reflected—although with many distortions—the interests of their constituents. The new educational bureaucrats, on the other hand, responded only to generalized public demands for efficiency and for an educational policy that would "Americanize" the immigrant—demands the educators themselves helped to shape—and therefore tended to see their clients as so much raw material to be processed as expeditiously as possible.

In 1909, Ellwood P. Cubberley voiced a widespread concern when he referred to the new immigrants from southern and eastern Europe as "illiterate, docile, [and] lacking in self-reliance and initiative" and argued that the task of the public schools was "to assimilate and amalgamate these people as a part of our American race, and to implant in their children, so far as can be done, the Anglo-Saxon conception of righteousness, law and order, and popular government, and to awaken in them a reverence for our democratic institutions and for those things in our national life which we as a people hold to be of abiding worth." Charles William Eliot of Harvard, in a speech to the National Educational Association in which he urged fuller use of the "public school plant" as "the only true economy," insisted that educational reform "means a larger and better yield, physically, mentally, and morally, from the public schools."

The high rate of failure provoked the usual outcries of alarm. One of Colin Greer's sharpest ideas—an idea, incidentally, that is consistent with the drift of Jencks's study—is that the unacknowledged function of the common school system is to fail those whom the higher levels of the employment structure cannot absorb; whose class and ethnic origins, in other words, consign them to a marginal economic position. Failure in school thus reconciles a certain necessary part of the population to failure in life. (On this analysis, the current crisis in public education derives from the fact that failure is no longer functional. Since the number of unskilled jobs is rapidly diminishing, those who fail have no place to go and become permanent charges on the state. Many of them also become discontented and rebellious.)

The debates of the progressive period, beginning around the turn of the century, furnish support for Greer's interpretation. Critics of the schools attacked the high rate of failure while urging reforms that would inevitably perpetuate it. The continuing high rate of failure then served as the basis of renewed appeals to the public, both for money and for additional powers for the educational bureaucracy.

In response to the outcry about failure, systems of testing and tracking were now introduced into the schools, which had the effect of relegating academic "failures" to programs of manual and industrial training (where many of them continued to fail). Protests against genteel culture, overemphasis on academic subjects, "gentleman's education," and the "cultured ease in the classroom, of drawing room quiet and refinement," frequently coincided with an insistence that higher education and "culture" should not in any case be "desired by the mob."

The demand for "educational engineering" and the elimination of "useless motions" led to the adoption of an "index of efficiency" of the kind expounded in 1909 by Leonard Ayres in his *Laggards in Our Schools*, whereby a school's efficiency would be measured by the children's progress through the grades. "If we can find out how many children *begin* school each year we can compute how many remain to the final elementary grade. Such a factor would show the relation of the finished product to the raw material." Adoption of this principle reinforced the class bias of the educational system. Since children of immigrants and of rural migrants to the city commonly entered school at a later age, the number of "over-age" children did not necessarily reflect their failure to make satisfactory academic progress. Failure henceforth would be tied more firmly than ever to class and ethnic origin.

Even the more liberal ideas of the progressive educators were turned to the purposes of "efficiency"; when this proved impossible, they were ignored. John Dewey and his followers revolted against unimaginative classroom methods, against the authoritarianism that was built into the school system in so many ways, and against the school's inability to make modern life intelligible. Their ideas were worked out in such experiments as the Laboratory School in Chicago (1896–1914), the Gary Plan in Indiana (1908–1915), the Dalton Plan in Massachusetts (1919). Except in private schools for the very rich, their good intentions have left few imprints on the educational system. Instead the rhetoric and ideas of progressivism were appropriated by educational bureaucrats for their own purposes.

Ambiguities in progressivism itself facilitated this process. Like the advocates of efficiency, the progressives attacked impractical academic instruction, demanding what would be called today a more "relevant" education. They too exaggerated the influence of the school as an agent of social reform, seeing education as a panacea for all the evils of industrial society. Sharing with the advocates of efficiency a deep antipathy to genteel culture and perhaps to culture in general, the progressives had no secure philosophical basis from which to resist the perversion of their ideas in the practice of the public schools.

Progressivism in education helped to ease the transition from the backward and already outmoded version of the gospel of industrial efficiency promoted by F. W. Taylor and his disciples to the newer version, which stressed "cooperation" in the classroom as opposed to the factory-like drill. Joel Spring shows how many debates about education closely paralleled and were influenced by debates in corporate circles between Taylorites and advocates of "cooperation." The former wanted to speed up production by means of a crude system of incentives and rewards. The leaders of the "cooperative" movement, on the other hand—industrial innovators like John H. Patterson of the National Cash Register Company, the department store magnate E. A. Filene, and the managers of the H. J. Heinz Company—proposed to "humanize" the factory by introducing suggestion boxes, company newspapers, more "personal contact," pension programs and welfare plans, social activities, athletics, libraries, schools, training programs, and other integrative devices.

Part of the impetus for educational reform in the progressive period came from manufacturers who wished simply to shift the more costly of these programs, especially the training programs, to the schools. But the more imaginative educators saw that the school itself could become a miniature factory, a "workplace" in which the habits of cooperation could be "learned through doing." In addition they argued that the schools had to assume functions formerly performed by the extended family, now defunct.

Perhaps the most important effect of these reforms was that they gave rise to a pervasive belief that there is a close connection between education and industry and between schooling and status. Educators insisted that a highly rationalized society, in which arbitrary distinctions between persons were increasingly giving way to the more functional principle of merit, would depend more and more heavily on an efficiently organized system of compulsory education in order to select the right people for the right jobs.[7] Employers came to prefer educated workers because they assumed

7. This tenet of the professional educators' creed finds typical expression in a recent criticism of Jencks by the Nevada state commissioner of education, Kenneth H. Hansen. "The position taken by Jencks seems to divorce the schools from the needs of society,

that education instilled orderly habits and a "cooperative" disposition. Their hiring policies in turn appeared to give substance to a growing popular belief that economic advancement depends on aptitude for schooling.

Those who hoped to enter high-status occupations came to take it for granted that they had to submit to sixteen years of schooling and in many cases to extended professional training as well. Those who had no aptitude for school, who could not afford it, or who merely hated it, tailored their expectations accordingly. In this way the school system came to serve the function described by Jencks in one of the most arresting passages in his book, that of limiting the number of aspirants to high-status jobs—jobs that are widely believed (not without reason, but with less reason than is commonly supposed) to depend on schooling. Educational credentials came to serve as "a legitimate device for rationing privilege" in a society "that wants people sorted and graded but does not know precisely what standards it wants to use."

If there were general agreement on standards, a simpler system of certification could easily be devised—a system of examinations, for instance. In the absence of such agreement, schooling has the advantage not only that it is vague but that in some ways it replicates conditions on the job, providing employers, in Jencks's words, with something like "direct observation of an individual 'at work.'" The fact that a young person has attained a certain level of schooling, because it is believed to indicate submission to a discipline not unlike that of the job itself, matters more to prospective employers than the skills acquired along the way.

The American educational system, it would seem, rests on one of those illusions that acquire a certain validity simply because they are so widely shared—in this case, the illusion that schooling is an indispensable precondition of economic success. Because "the myth that schooling is synonymous with status [to quote Jencks again] is . . . even more widespread than the reality," the illusion is self-validating, like "confidence" in the stock market. So long as people believe in the myth and act accordingly, it has some semblance of

---

overlooking the seemingly inescapable relationship between changes in the social order and changes in education. In a society constantly demanding higher levels of skill to cope with new demands, in a society in which technological obsolescence makes career development and training a lifelong responsibility of the educational institutions, in a society where almost no one can satisfactorily perform any meaningful job (despite the income he might be awarded) without some mastery of the cognitive skills of reading, writing, calculating, and articulating, how can we possibly believe that the quality of schooling at the earliest levels doesn't make any significant difference?" (*Christopher Jencks in Perspective,* pp. 45–46.) Note the highly rhetorical, self-hypnotic effect of this characteristic bit of educationese.

reality. If events were to shatter the illusion—for instance, prolonged unemployment among a high proportion of college graduates and people with advanced degrees—the entire structure might gloriously collapse.

I have said that revisionist histories of education seem to suggest the foregoing interpretation. The authors themselves, however, would probably reject the two conclusions I draw from their work (as well as from Jencks's)—that inequality can be reduced only by economic and political action, not through educational reform, and that the merits of the present school system therefore have to be discussed without counting on the system's putative influence on economic success, social mobility, and the eradication of poverty. Educators themselves, these authors still retain a "fragile faith in the schools," as Herbert Gans puts it in a perceptive introduction to Greer's *The Great School Legend*.

Whereas Gans reads Greer's study as supporting the view that "an overall strategy" against poverty "must be mainly economic," Greer himself clings to the hope of school reform. Instead of changing the class structure, he proposes to change the school. He recognizes that "the actual educational power of public education" has been "vastly overestimated" and that in view of this fact, "we should really consider the school to be a symbolic mechanism that holds a diverse, highly competitive society together." Yet he cannot bring himself to relinquish the hope that under proper conditions "schools could be an agent for major change"—for example, by discouraging "hostile competitiveness." In his recent assault on Jencks, Greer retreats completely from his perception that education is a "symbolic mechanism" and insists that the content of schooling really matters—from which it follows that progressive educators, by changing this content, can change the direction in which society is moving.

Katz's book ends on a similarly indecisive note. On the one hand, Katz believes that radical critics of education "oversimplify" when they describe the school's function as the inculcation of "middle-class attitudes." Indeed he suggests that the newly fashionable educational radicalism, infatuated with creativity, spontaneity, and other neo-progressive slogans, "is itself a species of class activity," since it is only the affluent who can afford to worry about whether the school encourages children to "express themselves." The poor may well prefer a school system that teaches their children how to read and write, and Katz himself thinks that it might be a good idea "to take the schools out of the business of making attitudes."

At the same time, however, he describes the radical criticism of the schools as "profoundly true." Like Greer, Katz is unwilling to admit that recent educational radicalism is merely an updated version of progressivism. Yet this radicalism not only adds little to the progressive indictment of the schools, it reaffirms the very belief it claims to criticize, namely that schooling is a powerful instrument of social policy. Instead of disposing of the "great school legend" once and for all, it merely gives it a radical disguise.

The confusion surrounding the revisionist history of education is most clearly illustrated by Joel Spring's book on the progressive period. In many ways this is the best of the three historical accounts at hand. It both complements and corrects Raymond Callahan's earlier study, *Education and the Cult of Efficiency,* which identified the efficiency movement too narrowly with Taylorism and thereby missed the congruence between "efficiency" and progressivism.

Spring's analysis of the ideology of "cooperation" is shrewd and perceptive, not least because it exposes some of its inner inconsistencies. Thus the reformers of the progressive period introduced vocational guidance in order to channel people into careers appropriate to their "abilities," only to find that tracking systems divided the school along class lines, giving rise to tension and hostility instead of "cooperation." Another series of "reforms" then had to be introduced in order to overcome or to paper over these divisions, the same integrative devices previously tried out in the factory—clubs, extracurricular activities, homerooms and assembly, student government, "school spirit," and above all athletics.

Spring's study might have led him to conclude that educational reformers have never really succeeded in turning the school into a smoothly functioning machine that molds the human "raw material" into a single pattern. For one thing, this objective is inconsistent with the need to reinforce existing class distinctions. For another, the school has to compete with the family and the street, influences on the child which it has never managed to supersede. The intentions of educational reformers, therefore, have been consistently thwarted in practice; one cannot take their intentions as an accurate description of the system as it actually operates.

In his concluding chapter, however, Spring does just that, crediting the "cooperative" movement with having made the school into a controlled environment that destroys man's "ability to create his own social being." Like the reformers themselves, Spring forgets that the life of the child, indeed the social life of the school itself, is shaped only in part—often in very small part—by the school.

Quite apart from the family, we have to reckon with the influence of a youth culture that is at least partially self-created and autonomous, a culture created on the streets but having a large, perhaps decisive influence on the school. Judging the results of educational reform by its intentions, Spring assumes that the school has succeeded in its drive to produce well-adjusted individuals who fit smoothly "into the institutional organization." But if this is true, how can we account for the present chaos in the schools? Far from generating uniformity, the schools are plagued by boredom, disruption, violence, drugs, and gang warfare. The educational reforms of the progressive period may have subjected vast numbers of people to schooling, but this is not the same thing as bringing "a greater part of the population under institutional controls." It is precisely the collapse of those controls that those who live and work in the schools are now experiencing as a daily reality—the crumbling of authority and the replacement of authority with violence.

III

The great contribution of the Jencks study, it has been said, is that it forces us to consider proposals for educational reform on their merits, without regard to their economic effects.[8] The proper conclusion to be drawn from *Inequality* and from recent historical writing on the school is not that schools are "no longer important" but that they are important in their own right. Why have most of the contributors to the debate been so reluctant to draw this conclusion? The idea that education is valuable in itself makes educators uncomfortable because it forces them to struggle with questions they have spent most of their careers avoiding. Why *should* education be valued? What are the proper objectives of educational policy? Does the present system promote them?

The founders of this country, whose ideas about education are still worth at least a passing glance, believed that the most important objects of public education were to provide for intellectual leadership and to make people effective guardians of their own liberty, in Jefferson's phrase. Jefferson thought that the study of history, in particular, would teach the young to judge "the actions and designs

8. George Levine, "Inequality," *New York Times Book Review*, November 26, 1972.

of men ... to know ambition under every disguise it may assume; and knowing it, to defeat its views."[9]

The ideal citizen of Jefferson's republic was the man who cannot be fooled by demagogues or overawed by the learned obfuscations of professional wise men. Appeals to authority do not impress him. He is always on the alert for forgery, and he has the worldly wisdom of men's motives, enough understanding of the principles of critical reasoning, and sufficient skill in the use of language to detect intellectual fraud in whatever form it presents itself. In the political theory of early republicanism, the ideal of an enlightened electorate thus coincides with the goals of liberal education.

It is interesting to see how Jefferson proposed in practice "to diffuse knowledge more generally through the mass of the people." His bill establishing public education in Virginia (never enacted) entitled everyone to three years of free schooling (more if they wanted to pay) in reading, writing, and arithmetic. A handful of the most promising scholars were to be sent at public expense, along with the children of parents who could afford such schooling, to the grammar schools, where they would learn Greek, Latin, geography, and "the higher branches of numerical arithmetic." Half of the state-supported grammar school students would be discontinued at the end of six years (some of them becoming grammar-school teachers), while the rest would be sent to college for three years—once again, along with the children of the rich.

> The ultimate result of the whole scheme of education would be the teaching all the children of the state reading, writing, and common arithmetic; turning out ten annually, of superior genius, well taught in Greek, Latin, Geography, and the higher branches of arithmetic; turning out ten others annually, of still superior parts, who, to those branches of learning, shall have added such of the sciences as their genius shall have led them to; the furnishing of the wealthier part of the people convenient schools at which their children may be educated at their own expense. The general objects of this law are to provide an education adapted to the years, to the capacity, and the condition of every one, and directed to their freedom and happiness.

In the first stage of this program, Jefferson continued, "the principal foundations of future order will be laid." Here students will imbibe the first principles of morality, together with "the most useful facts from Grecian, Roman, European and American history."

9. *Notes on Virginia,* query XIV. All of the following quotations are taken from this chapter.

In the next stage—for children roughly between eight and fifteen, whose minds are "most susceptible and tenacious of impressions" but "not yet firm enough for laborious and close operations"— foreign languages are to be emphasized, a form of study that will contribute to the mastery of one's own language. The highest stage is to be devoted to "science," the special blend of liberal and professional training that Jefferson later tried to build into his plan for the University of Virginia.

Later generations would find these proposals curiously casual and offhand, indifferent to the "needs" of the young, insufferably elitist. The reformers of the mid-nineteenth century regarded the old-fashioned curriculum as much too restricted. Overly intellectual, it paid too little attention to the moral development of the child and to the possibility that a program of compulsory education could inculcate habits of industry, thrift, and obedience—qualities essential to the nation's economic development and to the maintenance of public order.

Educational theorists of the progressive period were even harsher in their condemnation of the Jeffersonian concept of education. Not only did it ignore the need to educate the "whole child," not only did it ignore the connection between "learning and life," but it left nothing to the initiative of the child, content merely to drum a dead culture into the young by means of memorization and drill.

In our own time, early republican ideas appear downright undemocratic. Jefferson's system assumes that education is largely a prerogative of wealth; nor are we reassured by his promise that "twenty of the best geniuses will be raked from the rubbish annually" and instructed at public expense. Yet in the light of what we have recently learned about our own educational system, these objections no longer carry quite the overwhelming force they might once have had. Our own system, it appears, also perpetuates existing class distinctions. It ensures that those who start life with the advantages of money and birth will go further than those who don't. But at the same time—here is the most important point of all—the prevailing system manages to make this education increasingly worthless. As job training, education is largely irrelevant to the skills actually required by most jobs.[10] As intellectual training, American education is half-baked at best.

10. Jencks's findings reinforce those of Ivar Berg's *Education and Jobs: The Great Training Robbery*. See also the recent study by Bennett Harrison, *Education, Training, and the Urban Ghetto* (Johns Hopkins, 1972), p. 30: " . . . even if minority (and particularly ghetto) education is inferior in quality to the schooling received by most urban whites, the

In short, our school system neither levels nor educates. We could more easily accept its intellectual failures, though we could not forgive them, if we knew that at least the system was an effective instrument of egalitarian social policy. Since it is not, the time has surely come to insist that the two objectives, egalitarianism and intellect, be separated, and that the schools be left free to address themselves to intellectual concerns while the state attacks inequality more directly and effectively through economic policies designed to equalize income.

I do not mean to argue that the entire drift of educational policy for the last 150 years has been an unqualified disaster. Whatever the merits of eighteenth-century educational ideas, they led in practice to a pedagogy that was often narrow and stifling. The best educators of the progressive period and their successors in recent years—Paul Goodman, Herbert Kohl, Colin Greer himself—revitalized classroom practice by appealing to the natural curiosity of the child instead of locking him into dogmatic formulas. Far from advocating a return to McGuffey, I wish to preserve and expand what is valuable in this pedagogy while stripping away the social ideology that has so often been attached to it—the ideology of school reform as the motor of social progress.

It is as a social theory of education that eighteenth-century ideas still have something to teach us. True, they assumed that a close connection between wealth, political leadership, and education was both inevitable and proper. Nevertheless they stated, with a clarity and candor subsequently lost, the two objectives a democratic system of education might reasonably expect to accomplish.

The first of these ends is to give everybody the intellectual resources—particularly the command of language—needed to distinguish truth from public lies and thus to defend themselves against tyrants and demagogues. Is it necessary to insist that this object is more urgent than ever?

The second purpose of education is to train scholars, intellectuals, and members of the learned professions. The eighteenth century saw no other reason for higher education. Neither do I. The dream of bringing culture to the masses, by making higher education

mechanism by which this contributes to nonwhite poverty and unemployment is not inadequate skills or low potential productivity, but rather the growing infatuation of private and public employers with educational credentials. The practice of 'credentialism'—the use of educational credentials as a quick and allegedly inexpensive device for screening out socially undesirable individuals—appears to be an increasingly important explanation of the correlation between completion of high school or college on the one hand, and income on the other."

widely available, has failed; mass higher education has only facilitated the spread of mass culture, impoverishing popular culture and higher culture alike. Higher education is necessarily "elitist" if it is to mean anything—an education for people with a pronounced taste for intellectual matters, who plan to spend their lives in intellectual pursuits; an education, it goes without saying, that should be made available to men and women of all classes, but only to those who are qualified for it and completely committed to it.

Because any higher education worth the name is unavoidably restrictive in this sense, it should be an object of policy to ensure that higher education is meagerly rewarded in worldly goods. Professionals should be underpaid; scholars should live on the edge of austerity. This will discourage people from seeking higher education because they see it as a means to wealth and power. A democratic society needs intellectual leadership as much as any other kind of society does, but it has a special stake in seeing that an intellectual elite does not become also a political elite, that it carries on its work in the critical spirit necessary to serious inquiry of any sort.

An egalitarian income policy is quite consistent with the type of educational reform that seeks to restore the intellectual value of education. Indeed these aims are mutually dependent. Equality of incomes would deprive education of its cash value (thereby completing a process that market conditions may already, inadvertently, have set in motion). If incomes were roughly equalized, the demand for extended education would diminish drastically; the overdeveloped educational bureaucracy would wither at its source. Is it possible to imagine a fairer prospect?

With the apparent failure of compensatory education and the probable end of serious finance reform, what is happening in other areas of school
reform? Other recent programs that have promised
to equalize school achievement are performance
contracting, vouchers, and alternative public
schools. The following essay examines these movements.

EDUCATIONAL INNOVATIONS
AND INSTITUTIONAL
BUREAUCRACY
Joan K. Smith

With President Johnson's War on Poverty, the Elementary and Secondary Education Act of 1965, and subsequent publication of the
Coleman Report, it became clear that American schools were neglect-
ing academically close to one-third of their students—from the lower
economic strata of society. Paralleling these activities in the mid-
sixties, the U.S. Office of Education developed an image of cham-
pioning educational and social reform in the schools. Commissioner
Harold Howe even told superintendents that racial imbalance was
going to be equalized and if school personnel couldn't take the heat,
they should get out of the kitchen. The Office of Economic Opportunity (OEO) was also established to correct these disparities. In
retrospect few if any of the federally funded programs have accomplished these reforms and neutralized performance differences among
social classes. Harold Howe has long since left the kitchen, OEO has
dissipated after a long siege with performance contracting and the
U.S. Office of Education is looking much less radical as it directs its
energies towards career education and other curricular innovations.

Why have there been so many failures when efforts were stren-
uously directed toward success? The answer may well be in what
Michael B. Katz calls "the illusion of educational change in
America." If one takes his premises that the educational institution

developed along bureaucratic lines with the Office of Education at the helm, and also that it has always maintained social class biases in its purposes and operations, then any type of educational innovation or reform that would minimize class bias or alter the bureaucratic structure of the schools would indeed have to be weakened, diluted or proved ineffectual, so that reform does not lead to revolution and power struggles. As Katz points out, bureaucracy resulted because men were confronted with "particular kinds of social problems with particular social purposes" that "reflected social class attitudes and interests." Therefore, the institutional form that is maintained "provides a segmented educational structure that legitimizes and perpetuates the separation of children along class lines and ensures easier access to higher-status jobs for children of the affluent."[1]

This does not mean that innovations cannot be incorporated into the structure, but they must be of such a nature that they do not fundamentally alter this configuration in any major way. For example, the introduction of kindergarten, guidance, testing, plus the current emphasis on values, career education, "open" classes, and even certain compensatory education programs (e.g., Headstart) have been or are now being successfully incorporated into the schools, because they do not threaten the vested bureaucratic, racial or class interests and biases. But three current innovations are encountering serious difficulty. Performance contracting was recently condemned as worthless by OEO and USOE; vouchers are undergoing a weak trial in a form which removes all the original potency they were to have had; and several experimental schools funded through ESEA are undergoing very careful scrutiny and being asked to present "hard data" to justify their continued existence. Taking Katz's premise as a guide, one can guess that these three approaches actually have possibilities for serious reform and must therefore be discredited, as has been done with performance contracting, or neutralized, as with vouchers and experimental schools. In any case, a closer look at the records of these three programs certainly weakens, even contradicts the conclusions drawn by establishment officials about their relative merits.

PERFORMANCE CONTRACTING

After Titles VII (billingual education) and VIII (drop out prevention) were added to the Elementary and Secondary Education Act in

1. Michael B. Katz, *Class, Bureaucracy, and Schools* (New York: Praeger Publishers, Inc., 1971), pp. xxiii, 122.

1968, the Boards of Texarkana, Arkansas and Liberty-Eylau, Texas selected Dorsett Educational Systems to operate six rapid learning centers (RLC's) on a guaranteed performance basis. The goal was to prevent drop outs by increasing the achievement levels of junior and senior high school students in reading and math. By November 1, 1969, four RLC's were in full operation and serving over 100 students. By March 2, 1970, over 300 students were enrolled in six RLC's for an average of two hours per day. All participants were diagnosed as potential drop outs who were performing two to three grade levels behind norms; most came from low income families with little education. Extrinsic rewards of transistor radios, games, puzzles, magazines, and green stamps were offered to students who successfully completed lessons or advanced one grade level in reading and/or math.[2] For these performances Dorsett was to be paid $80 for every pupil who improved one grade level in either skill area after 80 hours of instruction. Improvements were to be measured by standardized achievement tests administered by the school districts. If a child failed to advance after 168 hours, reimbursement dropped to zero.[3] On February 2, after completing 89 hours of instruction, 51 students were post tested with the Iowa Test of Educational Achievement (also used in Fall pretesting). Results indicated that the mean increase for each student was .99 grade levels in math and 1.50 grade levels in reading. A second post test involving 59 students was conducted March 2, after 120 hours of combined instruction in the two skill areas. Mean increases at this testing were 2.20 grade levels in reading and 1.40 grade levels in math. Vandalism was cut in half and drop out rates decreased significantly from 20 percent to 2 percent.[4] A third post testing of 106 students in May tended to support this trend and Dorsett was paid $20,000 for their results. Martin J. Filagamo, Project Director for the Title VIII RLC's, was optimistic about preliminary successes and pointed out that this program's success "could well lead the way to the direct involvement of private industry in the education of the nation's school children."[5] Plans were then made to include K-6 in Fall 1970.

The blow to Texarkana did not come until Epic Division Systems, Inc. conducted an audit of the project under a Department of Health, Education and Welfare grant. Epic learned of test contamina-

---

2. Stanley Elam, "The Age of Accountability Dawns in Texarkana," *Phi Delta Kappan*, LI, 10 (June, 1970), pp. 509–14.

3. Martin J. Filagamo, "New Angle on Accountability," *Today's Education*, LIX (May, 1970), p. 53.

4. "Texarkana Gets a Low Grade," *Nation's Schools*, LXXXVI, 4 (October, 1970), pp. 85–88.

5. Filagamo, "New Angle," p. 53.

tion (for the May post testing only) from two of the seven RLC managers who were hired by the school board to keep an eye on the project. Although the auditors did not check all instructional materials, they felt they had discovered sufficient contamination to discredit the project. Dorsett, on the other hand, after conducting its own check, announced that only three percent of the items on standardized tests were included in instruction programs with an additional eight percent being close or similar to those used in class. Superintendent Edward D. Trice agreed with Dorsett that the contamination was insignificant. Co-designer of the project Charles Blaschke objected to the weight given to standardized test results and the "teaching to the test" issue, since only one test in May was contaminated.[6] Nevertheless, the project was terminated and deemed a failure.

But was it really a failure? February and March results were never discredited, there were reductions in vandalism and drop out rates—originally considered legitimate goals of the program—and test contamination did seem minimal. Even if the latter occurred, one has only to remember that "teaching to the test" is a phenomenon that is allowed in middle class schools. As Herbert Kohl points out in *36 Children,* New York City school teachers spend weeks preparing middle class students to perform well on regency exams while ghetto school children, on the other hand, are not coached.[7] In most university student housing there are many test files and notes which help students do well in classes and on tests. At any rate, to discredit the whole program for this reason seems to indicate that there was an eagerness to get rid of it rather than find out if it really worked. If one were to prove the latter, class distinctions and bureaucratic structures might seriously be threatened.

During the summer of 1970 educational organizations continued to register heavy opposition to performance contracting. In July the NEA's Assistant Executive Secretary for Government Relationships and Citizenship appeared before the Senate appropriations subcommittee hearings on the OEO budget stating that NEA "deplores the OEO performance contracting program because we believe it can weaken the structure of the public school system and can discredit the schools in the eyes of the public."[8] Also, the executive secretary for the American Association of School Administrators stated that the AASA did not approve of performance contracting at that time.

6. "Texarkana Gets a Low Grade," pp. 85–88.
7. Herbert Kohl, *36 Children* (New York: Signet Books, 1968), pp. 176–177.
8. "Texarkana Gets a Low Grade," p. 87.

And finally AFT spokesmen cautioned against allowing big business to monopolize education and dehumanize the learning process. They even went so far as to demand their own monitors for all future performance contracting programs.[9]

Nevertheless, OEO turned a deaf ear to these criticisms and launched a nationwide experiment to test the relative merits of performance contracting. Six companies working with 28,000 students in 18 different school systems in towns throughout the country began their programs in the Fall of 1970.[10] To safeguard against Texarkana pitfalls, and to remove every possible advantage to the contractor and students, OEO announced that: (1) students would be selected on a random basis for one of three standardized tests chosen in turn from eight different types; (2) school personnel would not know which of the tests were to be used; (3) students' skills would have to improve an average of 1.6 grade levels, or four times the gain that they had been making in regular classes, before the company could be paid profitably; (4) control groups similar to experimental groups would be used for comparisons; (5) a disinterested and responsible corporation was to do the evaluating.[11]

Even so preliminary results again looked encouraging over the first year. As Charles Blaschke pointed out, average achievement rates were doubled for a cost slightly more than existing costs per student per year per subject, and attendance in experimental sites was better than in control sites. Even before final results were obtained from May tests, one-third of the systems planned to continue the programs for Fall 1971, one-third planned to adopt turnkey approaches (where projects are turned over to local boards from the private companies), and one-third remained undecided.[12]

The final independent evaluation was conducted by Battelle

9. Donald Levine and Bro Uttal, "Performance Contracting Policy," *Teachers College Record*, LXXIV, 3 (February, 1973), pp. 317–55.

10. Minnie Perrin Berson, "Information: Back to Gary," *Childhood Education*, XLVIII, 1 (October, 1971), pp. 51–55. School systems used were Anchorage, Alaska; Athens, Georgia; Dallas, Texas; Fresno, California; Grand Rapids, Michigan; Hammond, Indiana; Hartford, Connecticut; Jacksonville, Florida; Las Vegas, Nevada; McComb, Mississippi; Mesa, Arizona; New York City (Bronx); Philadelphia, Pennsylvania; Portland, Maine; Rockland, Maine; Seattle, Washington; Stockton, California; and Wichita, Kansas.

11. Jeffrey Schiller, "Performance Contracting: Some Questions and Answers," *American Education*, VII, 4 (May, 1971), pp. 3–5; and Gary Saretsky, "The OEO Performance Contracting Experiment and the John Henry Effect," *Phi Delta Kappan*, LIII, 9 (May, 1972), pp. 579–81.

12. Charles Blaschke, "From Gold Stars to Green Stamps" *Nation's Schools*, LXXXVIII, 3 (September, 1971), pp. 51–55 and John W. Porter, "Performance Accountability and the Michigan Education Program." Speech presented to Behavioral Research Laboratories Annual Seminar in Innovation in Education, June, 1972 (ERIC Microfiche ED#069-746), p. 16.

Memorial Institute and proved to be a shattering blow to the companies (three went bankrupt) and to OEO's experiment. Battelle concluded in the spring of 1972 that results were not reliable or generalizable due to inherent design flaws such as: (1) unequal control and experimental group matching—experimental students came from the lowest achieving schools and control from the next lowest, with students in 17 of the 18 control sites pretesting significantly higher than experimental; (2) lack of random selection or assignment of students to groups; (3) lack of control over what the "traditional" classroom instruction was to be in control groups; (4) evidence that control group students did significantly better than experimental students on pretests; (5) unavailability of criterion-referenced tests.[13] Battelle, however, ignored his own caution that no useful conclusions could be drawn from the study and generalized that there was little evidence to support the hypothesis that performance contracting as conducted in the 18 districts had any beneficial effect on reading and math achievement of its experimental students. Battelle justified this conclusion by the fact that most average experimental gains were below one year's growth in the 10 grade/ subject combinations used (grades 2, 3, 7, 8, 9); and in half of the 10 cases experimental and control gains were insignificantly different (although in four other cases differences were two-tenths grade in favor of experimental groups and the tenth case remained unmentioned). The Rand Corporation evaluated eight projects for USOE and similarly concluded that results were discouraging.[14]

Do these two reports also mean that performance contracting failed? Not if one remembers that average achievement gains for this group of students in past years of attending traditional classes were around four to five months.[15] But what the reports really indicate is that OEO, under intense political pressure—to the point of threatening its continued existence—realized that it was necessary to back off and quit bucking established educational and political bureaucracies.[16]

13. Saretsky, "OEO . . . and the John Henry Effect," pp. 51–55.

14. Office of Economic Opportunity, *An Experiment in Performance Contracting: Summary of Preliminary Results*, OEO Pamphlet 3400-5 (Washington, D.C.: U.S. Government Printing Office, February, 1972), p. 3; and Lawrence Feinberg, "Where Test Scores Mean Money," *Washington Post*, January 6, 1972. Reprinted in *The National Elementary Principal*, LI, 6 (April, 1972), pp. 82–83.

15. Bernard Asbell, "Should Private Enterprise Direct your Child's Education?" *Redbook*, CXXXVIII, 4 (February, 1972), pp. 56–63.

16. Not only did USOE and OEO back away, but also the highly publicized school district of Gary, Indiana, found encouraging results but ended up abandoning the program after state pressure from the board of education and local teacher strikes. See James A. Mechlenburger, "Epilogue: The Performance Contract in Gary," *Phi Delta Kappan*, LIV, 8 (April, 1973), pp. 562–63.

With performance contracting successfully discredited, USOE became more stringent in their evaluation requirements for all Title VII and VIII funding and announced that each director would be expected to prove his project's educational value with extensive facts and figures. The director of one of the evaluation programs said that in a sense Titles VII and VIII are to be considered performance contracts. Therefore, goals must be set and results measured against them. Also, evaluations should be made early by an independent educational auditor who has no connection with the project. Under Commissioner of Education Sidney Marland the Office started to take a harder line toward innovations that could challenge social and educational structures.[17]

EDUCATIONAL VOUCHERS

Part of Commissioner Marland's hard line was directed against the second of OEO's original two-pronged approach to school reform. This was the voucher plan, proposed in the early sixties by conservative economist Milton Friedman and elaborated by Harvard professor Christopher Jencks in the late sixties. The basic idea of vouchers was simple. Instead of parents sending their children to a tax-funded local school, dictated by their place of residence, credit would be given for each child in the amount that local school districts were spending per child. Parents would be free to buy schooling from public or private schools. Those schools which attracted the most students would flourish; those which attracted few students would improve or die. Public schools would then presumably be more careful to please their clientele—if children were not learning in one school, parents would look for a school where results were better.

Not surprisingly the teachers' unions were adamantly opposed and did not hesitate to say so. United Federation of Teachers president Albert Shanker predicted the complete demise of public schools, and the NEA published similar statements. AFT legislative director Carl Magel called vouchers "another safari into educational fairyland." The NAACP feared continued racial segregation and the American Jewish Congress thought religious segregation would result.[18]

Opposition was so strong that no voucher plans were inaugurated in 1970 or 1971, despite OEO announcements that one or more was

17. Patricia L. Cahn, "New Programs Face Stricter Evaluation," *American Education*, VI, 1 (January–February, 1970), p. 36.
18. Union-paid advertisement, *New York Times*, July 4, 1971, Sec. IV, p. 7, col. 6.

imminent.[19] In September, 1972, with performance contracting and other political realities fresh in mind, a much sobered OEO announced a two-year $1.8 million grant to Alum Rock Union School District in suburban San Jose, California. Alum Rock is mostly a lower income area of mixed racial composition: 50% Chicano, 40% anglo, 10% black. The plan which went into effect bore scant resemblance to Jencks' original proposal. It provided a green card for each child, theoretically worth $680 for each elementary pupil and $970 for seventh and eighth graders. The catch was that parents could redeem their cards at public schools only and at only six designated schools of the 24 in the district. Guidance counselors "advised" each parent on the best option for his or her child, but stress was on choosing from programs *within* a school rather than choosing between (or among) schools themselves. Only 3% of the 4,000 students went into different schools than they would have enrolled in anyway.[20] Was this because parents were happy with their schools or because they had no real choices?

During 1973–74 the number of schools was expanded to 13. The school board has allocated $5,000 for a feasibility study for an "alternative" school. The Rand Corporation has evaluated the program, but results have not yet been released. Informal sources indicate the report is likely to be positive. Whatever is finally reported is unlikely to make much difference for, in effect, the Alum Rock voucher system is really only a partial open enrollment system. No teachers or administrators will lose jobs if their programs are unpopular and no school will be closed; when a school is filled no more applicants can be taken. If voucher plans are operationally put into effect in this manner, they can scarcely become an ominous threat to the educational establishment, and it is highly unlikely that numerous academic successes will come from lower class echelons.

Another trial run for vouchers has been announced for fall, 1974 in New Hampshire. This time private schools as well as public are supposed to be eligible—but parochial schools will not be included. The New Hampshire Board of Education approved the plan with a narrow 4-3 vote in the first place. On the basis of what has happened so far with OEO's programs, it seems unlikely that New Hampshire will ever get off the ground with anything resembling Friedman's original proposal.[21]

19. Eric Wentworth, "Plan Test of Competition by Schools," *Washington Post,* December 16, 1970.
20. James A. Mecklenburger, "Vouchers at Alum Rock," *Phi Delta Kappan,* LIV, 1 (September, 1972), pp. 23–25; David Johnson, "Vouchers on Trial at Alum Rock," *Saturday Review of Education,* I, 1 (January 13, 1973), p. 52.
21. Evan Jenkins, "The Debate Intensifies: Stand by for Vouchers," *Compact* (November/

EXPERIMENTAL SCHOOLS

The third recent approach to school reform which is now losing ground is public funding of alternative schools. The USOE has controlled much of this activity through its experimental schools program (ESP). ESP started in the USOE as an attempt to provide voucherless alternatives committed to public education. It has recently been moved to the National Institute of Education—a newly created bureaucracy controlled by the DHEW which has taken over all of OEO's educational programs.

Alternative learning systems were the key in the three winning plans submitted by Minneapolis, Berkeley, and the Franklin Pierce District in the state of Washington. For example, Minneapolis offers five different options to its parents and children: First is a "contemporary school"—or the more typical graded school; second is the "continuous progress school" where elementary children will spend six to eight years in a non-graded situation; third is the "open school" for elementary students where the environment is more home-like and approaches the reformed British Infant Schools; fourth is the "school without walls" where secondary school students meet with advisors who help them plan their programs and are responsible for helping them evaluate their progress; fifth is a "free school" open to K-12 where students select from such options as personal tutoring, open labs, independent study, small and large group discussions and field trips. Minneapolis is responsible, as are the other two, for presenting hard data, including achievement figures, documenting the program's progress. At this point there appears to be little danger that any of these three programs will seriously threaten class lines or bureaucratic structure.[22]

In other situations where USOE has awarded grants to assess various alternative programs not funded by ESP, evaluation criteria have been set along traditional lines.[23] Generally, the purposes of these evaluations have been for self improvement, to establish public credibility, and to decide which alternatives can be successfully incorporated into public education.[24] But for the most part evalua-

December, 1973), pp. 7–9; "Experimental Schools Program," *Nation's Schools,* LXXXVIII, 3 (September, 1971), pp. 56–58.

22. Mike Heckey, "Evaluation Alternatives Schools," National Consortium on Educational Alternatives (ERIC Microfiche: ED#071-963), 1972, 18 pp.

23. Brian McCauley, Sanford Dornbusch, and W. Richard Scott, "Evaluation and Authority in Alternative Schools and Public Schools," Stanford Center for Research and Development (ERIC Microfiche: ED#064-787), June, 1972, 56 pp.

24. Richard A. Gibboney and Michael G. Langsdorf, "Final Evaluation Report for the Alternative Schools Project 71-72," ESEA Title III (ERIC Microfiche: ED#067-775), July, 1972, 80 pp.

tions have run into trouble because (1) achievement scores or "hard data" necessary for effective evaluations are not available, (2) evaluators cannot decide how to evaluate nontraditional programs, or (3) evaluations are poorly designed and incompetently executed. The USOE seems to have a penchant for awarding contracts to individuals or companies whose final reports will not bear close scrutiny. Many federally funded programs are not renewed on the basis of highly questionable analyses.

Philadelphia's "East and West School-within-a-school program" submitted to extensive scrutiny under a USOE grant after its first year of operation. Results indicated that while student and teacher morale was high, certain structures were missing for proper development of intellectual learning. Both schools were asked to provide data indicating that their students achieved *better* than students in traditional Philadelphia high schools. The evaluation committee felt that this criterion wasn't met. Although the two schools cooperated in the evaluation, the final report gratuitously cautioned innovators against closing doors to criticisms and experiences of others, for "in the final analysis few men are as reactionary as the dogmatic progressive."[25] Apparently, there was and perhaps still is some question that this program would effectively serve establishment interests.

Other alternatives, such as Chicago High School for Metropolitan Studies, have received the USOE's stamp of approval and, along with the Cleveland Urban Learning Community, have been accredited by the North Central Association. The famous Philadelphia Parkway project, on the other hand, has not met accreditation guidelines. Most of its funds, however, have come privately from the Ford Foundation. Another approach to alternatives is that taken by New York City, which has developed fourteen "minischools" within different high schools.[26] With such titles as Julia Richmond Minischool for Discipline Problems, John Brown Minischool for Disaffected and Low-achieving Students, and Evander Minischool for Learning Disabilities, there is little doubt that the minischools are destined to become dumping grounds for students who aren't successful in regular classrooms. UFT's president Albert Shanker alluded to this when he said that alternatives should be a supplement for those who don't make it in regular classes, rather than a replacement.[27]

It appears, therefore, that if experimental schools and other

25. *Ibid.*
26. Suzanne K. Stemnock, "Alternative High Schools: Some Pioneer Programs," ERS circular #4 (ERIC Microfiche: ED#066-812), June, 1972, 58 pp.
27. Douglas Watson, "Alternative Schools: Pioneering Districts Create Options for Students" Education U.S.A. Special Report, National Schools Public Relations Association (ERIC Microfiche: ED#071-150), 1972, 65 pp.

alternative measures do survive the very strict if somewhat ambiguous evaluations now being imposed through USOE and NIE grants, they will end up in the category of other innovations that supported existing social and political structures. If this is the case they will probably be incorporated into public education as were testing, guidance, kindergartens, etc.

Katz's bureaucratic model does indeed seem to help explain the outcomes of these three innovations. In the future any talk of developing new programs for accountability will have to take into account not just accountability of schools to the public, but also accountability to the bureaucratic structure of public education. When and if schools can wear both hats the stress on finding new and more successful programs will probably disappear. At this time, however, that possibility seems unlikely for two reasons: 1) they must still appear to promote equality while maintaining class lines; and 2) they must serve the public interest yet safeguard middle class attitudes that become the very power structure of the bureaucracy.

[Editorial postscript: By Winter, 1975, the future of the Alum Rock program was in doubt; New Hampshire had no voucher schools; and NIE was in serious trouble with Congress, partly over the voucher program inherited from OEO.]

The fact that schools are being charged with not doing enough to equalize people's life chances seems unwarranted to many educators, among them the distinguished author of the following essay. Schools should be the training grounds for community, says Professor Butts. Do you agree?

ASSAULTS ON A GREAT IDEA
R. Freeman Butts

The general quest for "alternatives" to the existing system [of public schools] is in part deliberately designed to weaken public education, in part unaware that it may have that effect. It is the convergence and mutual reinforcement of so many forces—political, social, eco-

Excerpted from *The Nation*, April 30, 1973, pp. 553–560. Reprinted by permission.

nomic, racial, religious, and intellectual—that makes the search for "alternatives" so beguiling. But if the American people should become disenchanted with the idea of the public school and turn in significant numbers to other means of education, they will weaken, perhaps beyond repair, a basic component of democratic American society. . . .

A public school serves a public purpose rather than a private one. It is not maintained for the personal advantage or private gain of the teacher, the proprietor, or the board of managers; nor does it exist simply for the enjoyment, happiness, or advancement of the individual student or his parents. It may, indeed it should, enhance the vocational competence, or upward social mobility, or personal development of individuals, but if that were all a school attempted, the job could be done as well by a private school catering to particular jobs, or careers, or leisure time enjoyment.

Rather, the prime purpose of the public school is to serve the general welfare of a democratic society, by assuring that the knowledge and understanding necessary to exercise the responsibilities of citizenship are not only made available but actively inculcated. "If," said Thomas Jefferson, "a nation expects to be ignorant and free, in a state of civilization, it expects what never was and never will be."

Achieving a sense of community is the essential purpose of public education. This work cannot be left to the vagaries of individual parents, or small groups of like-minded parents, or particular interest groups, or religious sects, or private enterprisers, or cultural specialists. Thus, when the population became ever more heterogeneous after the mid-nineteenth century, the need for compulsory education became increasingly apparent to the lawmakers of the states of the Union.

Today, however, this basic point is almost entirely overlooked in the furor over the studies of inequality in schools, stemming from the Coleman Report of 1966 and expanded upon since by the studies at Harvard of Daniel Patrick Moynihan, Christopher Jencks, and others. Their generalizations that public schools have not overcome economic inequality among races or social classes have led to a general impression that public schools do not make much difference and that the compensatory education advocated by reformers since the mid-1960's has generally failed. Economy-minded politicians pick up this theme with glee and racial minorities are discouraged that just as they are finally making some headway toward equal opportunity in the schools, the word comes down from the scholars, "Don't bother; the public schools don't really matter that much."

To make matters worse, Ivan Illich, Everett Reimer, and other radical critics preach that the schools are really instruments of oppression whereby the ruling class maintains itself in power and instills in the other classes attitudes of subservience designed to support the status quo. Illich and Reimer argue that, to effect genuine social change, the society must be "deschooled" and all kinds of informal and nonformal means of community education fostered instead. Compulsory attendance must be abolished, so that children, youths, and adults of the oppressed classes may be free to develop their distinctive talents and not be forced into a mold by a monolithic and oppressive public school system.

So the discussion has focused on the "economic" inequalities among classes and races and the inability of public schools to remedy what the entire society has wrought. However, there is still enormous disagreement about these generalizations. The historic and comparative evidence is overwhelming that American public schools have been one major factor in producing a higher per-capita economic level in America than in any other country, but that is not the critical point here. Even if Jencks should turn out to be right, that compensatory education for the disadvantaged in our society is unable to reduce the economic gap between the rich and the poor, the "economic" argument is not and never has been the fundamental reason for compensatory education. That reason is the public purpose of "justice." Our conception of a just society based upon principles of liberty and equality requires a public education available to all. . . .

If public schools also enable the disadvantaged to improve their economic position, as I believe in the long run they undoubtedly do, that is a social dividend, but the original purpose of public education in the early nineteenth century was not to provide vocational education or prepare people for jobs. That addendum came along in response to the industrialization and technological specialization of the economy in the later nineteenth and early twentieth centuries. To make the achievement of equal economic condition appear to be the "prime" purpose of public schools and to dismiss rather casually the school system as a "marginal institution" because it does not produce that equality (as Jencks does) is to ignore the fundamental "political" purpose of public education. In the words of Justice Frankfurter, "The school should be the training ground for habits of community." *That* is the ground on which the public schools should be criticized for failure, and where effort should be exerted for improvement. And that is the area in which there really is no genuine alternative to the public schools.

PART FOUR

TEACHERS AND THE LEARNING PROCESS

"No limit can be set to the power of a teacher, but this is equally true in the other direction: no career can so nearly approach zero in its effect."
—Jacques Barzun

"No boy genuinely loves and admires his teacher: the farthest he can go, assuming him to have all of his wits, is to tolerate her as he tolerates castor oil. She may be the loveliest flower in the whole pedagogical garden, but the most he can ever see in her is a jailer who might conceivably be worse."
—H. L. Mencken

Of all the functions that schools perform—custodial care, class reinforcement, socialization, entertainment, and others—there remains the inescapable fact that schools also exist to teach. We have already seen in the earlier readings that people do not agree about *what* schools should teach or *how* they should teach or about who should be the judge of whether or not an acceptable level of teaching and learning has occurred. People do seem to agree that there are effective and ineffective teachers, good and bad schools. But it is there that agreement usually stops. How to tell the difference between acceptable and unacceptable teachers is a serious problem for parents and administrators. How to be a good teacher is a serious concern for teachers and people who want to become teachers.

The readings in this section deal with who goes into teaching, what teachers are like, how they communicate, and the effect of teacher expectation on learners' performance; with how teachers are hired, how their work is assessed, and what some desirable characteristics for teachers are. Three of the articles are reports of particular teaching situations—how people responded and what happened. The last selection deals briefly with a few of the questions pertaining to a teacher's right to teach as she or he believes right and the extent to which there are legal guarantees of free speech in the classroom.

Every five years the Research Division of the National Education Association conducts a poll of its members to find out what some of the general characteristics of teachers are. The findings are useful, especially to show trends, but the reader needs to keep some cautions in mind. First, the poll is a sample of NEA members only. Several hundred thousand people who teach are not members of this organization. Second, the poll is done by a special interest group. The NEA is, quite naturally, interested in promoting the best salaries, fringe benefits, and working conditions for its members. The questions chosen, or omitted, reflect this interest. Third, comparisons of teachers with other occupational groups is usually not possible based on this information. It is not possible, for example, to say whether teachers see themselves as more or less conservative than attorneys because attorneys were not sampled. Finally, attempts to portray "the average teacher" on the basis of this information are very dangerous because there is no such person as *the* average teacher. Journalist Myron Brenton said in 1970 that "the contemporary American public school teacher is, on the average, about 36 years of age"—a statement which he based on the 1966 NEA survey's report of median age.[1] Another way of looking at the same information is that ninety-eight percent of the teachers in the country are *not* thirty-six years old, a fact which puts his "average" teacher in a very tiny minority.

"NEW PROFILE OF THE AMERICAN PUBLIC SCHOOL TEACHER"
NEA Research Division

Teachers are younger, better educated (but less experienced), and better paid than they were 10 years ago. They still work as many

1. Myron Brenton, *What's Happened To Teacher?* (New York: Coward-McCann, Inc., 1970).

Reprinted with permission of NEA Research from *Today's Education*, Vol. 61, No. 5, May, 1972, pp. 14–17.

hours a week both in and out of school as they used to and teach as many days of the year, but they spend fewer hours on unpaid work and have fewer extra nonteaching days of duty. They have slightly smaller classes, are less likely to be misassigned, and are more likely to have a duty-free lunch period than in the past. They are less likely to join organizations (although very likely to participate in political elections) and more likely to own or be buying their own homes and two cars.

These are some of the changes in the teaching profession during the 1960's that came to light in a recent study by the NEA Research Division. Every 5 years, the Division conducts a comprehensive survey of the American teaching profession by means of a questionnaire sent to a nationwide sample of teachers in public elementary and secondary schools. Topics covered range from details of the teacher's assignment to facts about his family and outside activities. The latest survey, made in spring 1971, received an 84 percent response from the teachers questioned. This article presents some of the major findings about what has happened to the teaching profession in the 1960's and where it stands at the beginning of the 1970's.

WHO ARE THE TEACHERS OF AMERICA?

The 1960's have seen some changes in the teaching population, including the following:

- The median age of teachers has dropped from 41 years in 1961 to 35 years in 1971. Men still have a median age of 33, but women have become progressively younger; their median age fell from 45½ to 40 between 1961 and 1966 and to 37 in the last 5 years.
- The percentage of men teachers in the profession has increased from 31 to 34 percent since 1966. More elementary teachers and more older teachers (age 50 or older) are now men.
- More teachers are married, an increase from 68 to 72 percent in 10 years. Four men out of 5 and 2 women out of 3 are married.
- The "old maid schoolteacher" was already a thing of the past in 1961, but single women in the profession have since decreased in percent from 17 to 14.
- The percentage of men with working wives has increased from 32 to 45 percent in the last 10 years, and the percentage of men with wives employed in full-time teaching has increased from 17 to 21 percent in the last 5 years.

- Women teachers tend to come from families of higher occupational and educational status than men. The percentage of women whose fathers were business or professional men has increased from 38 to 45 percent since 1961, compared with a constant 34 percent of men from such background. The mothers of 3 in 10 women, compared with 2 in 10 men, went to college.

Men and women teachers exhibit different and changing career patterns:

- The experience of men teachers has *increased* from a median of 7 years to a median of 8 years in the course of the 1960's, but the experience of women has *decreased* from 14 to 8 years in median terms since 1961.
- Two-thirds of all women teachers began teaching either within the past 5 years or more than 20 years ago. In contrast, 6 in 10 men began teaching within the last 10 years.
- The percentage of women teachers who have had a break in service has decreased from 53 to 40 percent since 1961, and the percentage of women with a break in service for marriage or homemaking has decreased from 17 to 10 percent since 1966. However, nearly 1 woman in 5 continues to report a break in service for maternity or child rearing, and 5 percent of women teaching in 1970–71 planned to drop out in 1971–72 for homemaking and/or child rearing.

Within the profession, positions held by teachers reflect traditional sex identification of occupational roles:

- Only 1 man in 4 teaches in elementary school and less than 1 percent of all men teach grade 3 or below. In contrast, two-thirds of all women are elementary teachers, and one-third teach grade 3 or below. Conversely, 42 percent of men, compared with 18 percent of women, are senior high teachers.
- In secondary schools, the largest percentage of women teach English, while greater percentages of men than women teach science and social studies.
- The principalship is a male preserve. Two-thirds of all teachers are female, but 89 percent of all teachers report to a male principal. In elementary schools, 84 percent of teachers are women, but 80 percent of elementary teachers have men for principals. In secondary schools, 99 percent of teachers indicate that their principals are men.

WHERE TEACHERS ARE

The nation's public school teachers are distributed among different types of communities:

- The largest proportion of teachers, 45 percent, are in school systems enrolling 3,000–24,999 pupils; 28 percent teach in large systems with 25,000 or more enrollment and 27 percent in small systems with less than 3,000 enrollment.
- More than one-third of all teachers teach in urban schools, more than half teach in suburban communities or small towns, and about 1 teacher in 8 is in a rural school. Two teachers in 10 are in large cities with a population of 250,000 or more, about half of them teaching in inner-city schools.
- Three teachers in 8 report that a majority of the pupils they teach come from the lower middle class; 2 in 8 report mainly pupils from the upper middle and upper classes; and 1 teacher in 6 indicates that a majority of his pupils are lower class in socioeconomic status. The rest report mixed economic classes among their pupils.
- Although 8 percent of teachers identify themselves as black and 6 percent report that they have a black principal, 12 percent report that half or more of the pupils they teach are black.
- In large systems, 29 percent of teachers teach in the inner city, 28 percent report that half or more of their pupils are black, and 29 percent that a majority of their pupils are lower class in socioeconomic status.
- Six teachers in 10 live within the boundaries of the school systems that employ them, but only 1 teacher in 3 lives within the attendance area of the school where he is teaching. In large systems, only 17 percent of teachers live within the attendance area of their schools, compared with 36 percent in medium-sized systems and 50 percent in small systems.

Teachers, like the rest of the population, are mobile:

- Only 29 percent of 1971 teachers were living in the communities where they had lived as children, a decrease from 33 percent in 1961. Recent newcomers to their communities increased from 11 to 15 percent in the same 10 years.
- About half of all teachers have taught in more than one school system. Three teachers in 8 have taught in a different system in

the same state where they currently teach, and 1 teacher in 5 has taught in another state.

- Five percent of those teaching in 1970–71 planned to teach in a different school system in 1971–72.

PROGRESS AND PROBLEMS IN TEACHING CONDITIONS

Improvement has occurred in a number of areas of teaching conditions, but evidence of continuing problems also exists:

- The percentage of teachers teaching at least part of the time in grades or subjects outside their major field of preparation has decreased from 31 to 23 percent since 1961. However, correction of misassignment has taken place where least needed: Fewer teachers are teaching some but less than half of their time out of field, but 1 teacher in 7 continues to be so seriously misassigned that he is teaching 50 percent or more of the time outside his field.

- The mean size of classes taught by elementary teachers has crept downward at a snail's pace from 29 pupils per class in 1961, to 28 in 1966, to 27 in 1971. Secondary teachers average 26 pupils per class, down from 27 in 1966 and 1961, but the mean number of pupils they teach per day is still over 130.

- Secondary teachers' unassigned periods have increased from a mean of 4 to a mean of 5 per week in the last five years, but 1 secondary teacher in 5, as in 1961, has no unassigned periods at all.

- Data on lunch periods show a victory for teachers in the second half of the 1960's. The percentage of teachers eating lunch with their pupils, which *increased* from 39 to 47 percent between 1961 and 1966, *decreased* to 31 percent in 1971. In 1966, fewer than 4 elementary teachers in 10 had a duty-free lunch period; in 1971, 6 in 10 had a duty-free lunch.

- The mean total working week for teachers is still 47 hours, as at the beginning of the 1960's. However, the mean number of hours spent by teachers on non-compensated school-related activities has decreased from 11 to 8 per week in the last 5 years.

- Teachers still teach a mean of 181 days a year, but their mean number of nonteaching days of contract has dropped from 5 to 4 since 1966.

TEACHERS' PROFESSIONAL QUALIFICATIONS

Academic preparation of teachers has improved greatly during the 1960's:

- Nondegree teachers have almost entirely disappeared from the profession. In 1961, 15 percent of teachers did not even have a bachelor's degree; now 97 percent have at least a bachelor's degree.
- The percentage of teachers with bachelor's degrees increased in the first half of the decade; the percentage with master's degrees, in the second half. Forty-two percent of men and 19 percent of women have a master's degree or 6 years of preparation.

Teachers also show a strong interest in continuing education and professional growth:

- In the last 3 years, 61 percent of teachers have earned a mean of 14 semester hours of college credit beyond the bachelor's degree.
- Six teachers in 10 have participated in workshops sponsored by their school systems during the last 3 years.
- Six percent of 1971 teachers had had sabbatical leave for study, travel, or other purposes at some time since fall 1968.

OUTSIDE ACTIVITIES

Teachers' participation in organizational activities has declined in the past decade, but they continue to show a high degree of interest in activities that have professional relevance:

- Percentages of teachers who are members of churches, political parties, youth-serving groups, fraternal organizations, women's groups, men's service clubs, and parent teacher associations have decreased during the 1960's, especially among younger teachers.
- The mean number of hours per week that teachers give to working for organizations during the school year has decreased from 2 to 1 in the past 5 years. The percentage of teachers who do not give time to working for organizations has increased from 33 to 41 percent in the past 10 years.
- A majority of teachers, however, are members of local, state, and national educational associations, and more than half of all secondary teachers are members of subject-matter or professional

special-interest associations. Despite the decrease since 1966, a majority of teachers also are still PTA members.

- Teachers are travelers. Apart from 4 percent who have traveled on sabbatical leave in the last 3 years, 26 percent have undertaken other educational travel in the last 3 years, and 35 percent traveled during the 1970 summer vacation.

Data on teachers and politics include the following:

- Formal membership in political party organizations dropped drastically from 31 to 13 percent between 1961 and 1971.
- However, 82 percent of teachers voted in the general election in 1970 and 75 percent voted in primary elections.
- By a ratio of 6 to 4, teachers who classify their political philosophy as conservative or tending to be conservative outnumber those who either are or tend to be liberal.
- Forty-three percent of teachers classify themselves as Democrats and 34 percent as Republicans, but 22 percent report that they are not affiliated with any political party. More than a third of teachers under age 30 have no party affiliation.

ECONOMIC STATUS

Teachers have to some extent participated in the rising affluence of the American middle class during the 1960's, but differences in salaries continue to leave a number of lower-paid teachers:

- The mean annual salary reported by teachers has increased from $5,264 in 1961 to $9,261 in 1971.
- Since 1966, teachers who own or are buying their own homes have increased from 62 to 67 percent, and teacher families with 2 or more cars have risen from 37 to 47 percent.
- Teachers in small school systems have a mean salary that is more than $1,000 lower than the mean salary of teachers in medium or large systems.
- The mean salary of Southeastern teachers is approximately $2,500 less than the mean salary of Northeastern teachers.
- Women continue to have lower salaries than men; however, a larger proportion of men have master's degrees. Although the percent of increase in the mean salary of men and women teachers has been similar over the past decade, the dollar amount of difference has increased.

- As in 1966, 1 out of every 6 teachers with a master's or higher degree has a lower salary than the mean salary of teachers with a bachelor's degree or less.

Few teachers rely entirely on their salaries as teachers to support themselves and their families:

- Teachers with income in addition to their teaching salary have increased in percent from 51 to 57 between 1961 and 1971. In 1971, 81 percent of men averaged about $1,900 in extra income, and 44 percent of women averaged just over $1,000. The percentage of women earning extra income during the summer or school year or both has doubled in the last 10 years.
- Although women have lower salaries than men and fewer of them have extra income, the combined total income of married women teachers and their husbands averaging $18,510, is higher than the $15,006 averaged by married men teachers and their wives.
- The teacher's salary represents an average of 52 percent of total household income for the families of married women and 72 percent of total income in the households of married men.

In 1964 John Holt wrote a book titled *How Children Fail,* based on his observations of "bright" children in a "good" school. He pointed out strategies used by students to "read" the teacher—to get the answer to a question from the teacher, without the teacher's awareness of the process. In other words, a lot of information was transmitted outside of direct verbal content, often without the *conscious* awareness of either student or teacher. The following brief report of research mentions some of the specific ways in which this information is transmitted.

BODY LANGUAGE

Several years ago a psychology professor at Stanford was teaching a graduate course in Skinnerian theory. His students secretly decided to try behavior modification on the professor himself. They wanted him to lecture as if he were Napoleon Bonaparte.

Whenever his right hand came near his torso, the students would lean forward, open their eyes wide, and start taking notes. Whenever he slumped or slurred or gestured with his right hand, they would look away, feign boredom, and talk to each other.

By the end of the semester, the professor was unknowingly lecturing in short, crisp sentences, standing stern and rigid, with his right hand inserted into his shirt over his stomach.

Body language is always present in the classroom, although not usually as an intentional device of the students. Yet most teachers are insensitive to facial or body cues inside their own classrooms. A study conducted by Nathan Maccoby at Stanford found that experienced teachers were little better than novices in judging whether children had understood their lessons.

Using hidden cameras, Maccoby filmed student behavior as the teachers conducted regular classes. Teachers were then shown the film and asked to predict how their students would fare in an objective test on the lesson's contents. Teachers were no better than other observers at perceiving nonverbal cues (amount of blinking, raising of eyebrows, hands on the face, etc.)

Reprinted with permission from *Saturday Review of Education,* I, 4 (April 14, 1973), p. 78.

"Educators," says Dr. Charles Galloway, a leading authority on body language in the classroom, "are multi-sensory organisms who only *occasionally* talk." Yet, he points out, little attention is paid to their nonverbal behavior. In a normal, nonprofessional conversation, the total message communicated is estimated at 55 percent facial, 38 percent vocal, but only 7 percent verbal. Here are some typical nonverbal cues found in most classrooms.

Eye contact. Sometimes a student will avoid eye contact when the teacher asks him a question. He may act very busy taking notes, rearranging his books and papers, dropping a pencil. Non-verbally he is saying to the teacher, "I don't know the answer; I don't want to be called on." Eye contact signals that the communication channel is open.

Arm extending. Have you ever seen a professor lecture all period without moving his hands at all? Galloway has shown that teachers who extend their arms toward the class have students who test better than teachers who keep their hands in their pockets. Arm movement can also communicate specific feelings. People more often stand with their hands on their hips when they are talking with people they dislike than with those they like. Arm folding is known to show disapproval and defensiveness.

Nodding. Teachers who nod affirmatively to their students encourage them to respond more and to respond better. Depending upon individual teacher, grade level, and class size, the optimum number of nods is usually one every 30 seconds. However, if the teacher consciously adopts the 30-second pattern, the kids pick it up, and it becomes ineffective.

Hand raising. In volunteering classroom information, a clever student knows how to make his raised arm look tired, as if he's been waiting interminably to be called on. He also knows how to raise his hand tentatively, as if he does *not* want to be called on. It seems that the hand-raising technique is not innate; students learn all these subtleties by around the fourth grade.

Territory. Teachers stand; students sit. The teacher puts himself at the front of the class, placing a buffer zone between himself and the first line of students. Standing higher and removing himself from the masses, the teacher nonverbally insists on his superiority in the classroom. "In the past," Galloway points out, "teachers moved around their desks as if they were isles of security. They rarely ventured into the territories of student residence unless they wished to check or monitor seatwork. To move forward or away from students signifies relationships. Distance establishes the status of interaction."

A professional educator, then, needs to move about the classroom, make repeated eye contact with his students, extend his arms, nod, smile, and encourage nonverbal responses from his students. A recent study made use of time-lapse photographs of a high school social studies class. The photographs candidly revealed changes in the students' posture as the class progressed. As the teacher droned on and boredom set in, students slumped lower and lower in their seats. At the final bell, some students could hardly be seen above their desk tops, but the teacher was oblivious to what was happening before him. It is essential not only that an educator be understood but also that he understand how he is being understood.

The work reported in the following article is similar to that reported in "Body Language." Taken in conjunction with the *Phi Delta Kappan* item titled "Discrimination Against Mexican-Americans" (pp. 193–195), it also helps explain minority student failure in school.

Psychology Today said of it:

> Almost five years ago, the author proposed that students live up, or down, to their teachers' expectations of them. He said teachers express their opinions consciously and unconsciously, in word, grimace and gesture, and that teachers who think their students are bright teach harder. The Pygmalion theory caused consternation and quarrels among teachers and researchers. Now comes the author again, with a larger sheaf of evidence to show that he was right.

THE PYGMALION EFFECT LIVES

Robert Rosenthal

Pygmalion created Galatea out of ivory and desire. In Ovid's account, Pygmalion fell in love with his own sculpture of the perfect woman, and Venus, who spent a lot of time granting requests in those days, gave life to Galatea. In George Bernard Shaw's version 19 centuries later, Henry Higgins turns a Cockney flower girl into an elegant lady, relying on language rather than love.

Most of us do not have Pygmalion's power to manufacture the ideal mate, nor do we all share Higgins' fondness for phonetics. But we may have an extraordinary influence, of which we are often oblivious, on others. Psychologists have not yet learned how to produce Galatea or her male equivalent in the laboratory, but they have demonstrated that the power of expectation alone can influence the behavior of others. The phenomenon has come to be called self-fulfilling prophecy: people sometimes become what we prophesy for them.

Reprinted from *Psychology Today* Magazine (September, 1973), pp. 56–63. Copyright © Ziff-Davis Publishing Company.

This point has long been argued on an intuitive basis. It is obvious, for example, that ghetto children, whose academic performance worsens the longer they remain in school, tend to have teachers who are convinced that the children cannot learn. However, one could argue that teachers expected little because the students behaved poorly, rather than the other way around. To see which comes first, the expectation or the performance, we turned to the laboratory.

In the first study of this problem, over a decade ago, Kermit Fode and I asked 10 students to be "experimenters." We gave each experimenter, in turn, about 20 subjects. The experimenter showed each of his subjects a series of faces, which the subject rated on "degree of success or failure" from +10 to −10. We had previously selected photos that most people consider quite neutral.

We gave our experimenters identical instructions on how to administer the test, with one exception. We told half of them that the "well-established" finding was that the subjects would rate the photos positively; we told the rest that subjects would probably rate the photos negatively.

EXPECTANT VOICES

In spite of the fact that all experimenters read the *same* instructions to their subjects, we found that they still managed to convey their expectations. Experimenters who anticipated positive photo ratings got them, while those who expected negative ratings got them too. How did the experimenters silently let their subjects know what they wanted? John Adair and Joyce Epstein repeated this experiment and tape-recorded the experimenters reading the instructions. They got the same results we did, and then repeated their experiment, this time using only the tape recordings of their experimenters to instruct their new sample of subjects. They found that subjects exposed only to these tape recordings were just as much influenced by their experimenter's expectations as were those subjects who had experienced "live" experimenters. Apparently, tone of voice alone did the trick.

Such results generated a spate of studies. Larry Larrabee and L. Dennis Kleinsasser found that experimenters could raise the IQ scores of children, especially on the verbal and information subtests, merely by expecting them to do well. Samuel Marwit found that patients will interpret Rorschach inkblots as animals or human beings, depending on what the examiner has been led to expect. And Ronald Johnson, in an ingenious and carefully controlled study, found that experimenters could improve their subjects' performance on a task requiring subjects to drop as many marbles as possible through one of several holes in the table top by expecting them to do well.

Self-fulfilling prophecies even work for animals. Bertrand Russell, who had something to say about nearly everything, noticed that rats display the "national characteristics of the observer. Animals studied by Americans rush about frantically, with an incredible display of hustle and pep, and at last achieve the desired result by chance. Animals observed by Germans sit still and think, and at last evolve the solution out of their inner consciousness."

FONDLING SMART RATS

Russell was not far off. Fode and I told a class of 12 students that one could produce a strain of intelligent rats by inbreeding them to increase their ability to run mazes quickly. To demonstrate, we gave each student five rats, which had to learn to run to the darker of two arms of a T-maze. We told half of our student-experimenters that they had the "maze-bright," intelligent rats; we told the rest that they had the stupid rats. Naturally, there was no real difference among any of the animals.

But they certainly differed in their performance. The rats believed to be bright improved daily in running the maze—they ran faster and more accurately—while the supposedly dull animals did poorly. The "dumb" rats refused to budge from the starting point 29 percent of the time, while the "smart" rats were recalcitrant only 11 percent of the time.

Then we asked our students to rate the rats and to describe their own attitudes toward them. Those who believed they were working with intelligent animals *liked* them better and found them more pleasant. Such students said they felt more relaxed with the animals; they treated them more gently and were more enthusiastic about the experiment than students who thought they had dull rats to work with. Curiously, the students with "bright" rats said that they handled them more but talked to them less. One wonders what students with "dull" rats were saying to those poor creatures.

If rats act smarter because their experimenters think they are smarter, we reasoned, perhaps the same phenomenon was at work in the classroom. So in the mid-1960's Lenore Jacobson and I launched what was to become a most controversial study.

INTELLECTUAL BLOOMERS

We selected an elementary school in a lower-class neighborhood and gave all the children a nonverbal IQ test at the beginning of the school year. We disguised the test as one that would predict "intellectual blooming." There were 18 classrooms in the school, three at each of the six grade levels. The three rooms for each grade consisted of children with above-average ability, average ability, and below-average ability.

After the test, we randomly chose 20 percent of the children in each room, and labeled them "intellectual bloomers." We then gave each teacher the names of these children, who, we explained, could be expected to show remarkable gains during the coming year on the basis of their test scores. In fact, the difference between these experimental children and the control group was solely in the teacher's mind.

Our IQ measure required no speaking, reading, or writing. One part of it, a picture vocabulary, did require a greater comprehension of English, so we call it the verbal subtest. The second part required less ability to understand language but more ability to reason abstractly, so we call it the reasoning subtest.

We retested all the children eight months later. For the school as a whole, we found that the experimental children, those whose teachers had been led to expect "blooming," showed an excess in overall IQ gain of four points over the IQ gain of the control children. Their excess in gain was smaller in verbal ability, two points only, but substantially greater in reasoning, where they gained seven points more than the controls. Moreover, it made no difference whether the child was in a high-ability or low-ability classroom. The teachers' expectations benefited children at all levels. The supposed bloomers blossomed, at least modestly.

This experiment, and the book we wrote based on it, met with vigorous criticism. Professor Arthur Jensen of UC, Berkeley, for example, offered three basic arguments.

First, said Jensen, we should have compared classrooms rather than individual children, and this would have produced only negligible IQ changes. But Jensen ignored the fact that we had done that analysis, and that it led to even larger effects than the per-child comparisons.

Second, Jensen objected to the fact that we used the same IQ test twice. The children were familiar with the test when they took it again, he said, so their scores might have improved for that reason. However, Jensen must then explain why the experimental children showed more of these "practice effects" than the control children, who also took the test twice.

Finally, Jensen did not think that the teachers themselves should have given the tests. However, we had already accounted for this problem by having people who knew nothing of the experiment retest the children. The effects of the teachers' expectations actually increased.

R. L. Thorndike added another objection, namely that our IQ test was an unreliable measure, especially for the youngest children, and that any inference based on such a test would be invalid. I do not think that our test was as worthless as Thorndike implies, but even if it was seriously unreliable we are still left with the basic question. Why did the experimental children improve significantly? An unreliable measure would make it *harder* to find differences between the two groups, not easier.

The most ambitious critique of our Pygmalion in the classroom work was a book by Janet Elashoff and Richard Snow, who completely reanalyzed our original data. They could not disprove the fact that the experimental children did gain more IQ points than control children, even though they transformed our original IQ measure into eight different forms, some of which were biased statistically to minimize any effects of teachers' expectations.

The debate continued, and so did the research. Others sought to discover the Pygmalion effect, and not everyone was successful, which contributed to the controversy. By now 242 studies have been done, with all sorts of subjects and situations. Of these, 84 found that prophecies, i.e., the experimenters' or teachers' expectations, made a significant difference.

But we must not reject the theory because "only" 84 studies support it; on the contrary. According to the rules of statistical significance, we could expect five percent of those 242 studies (about 12) to have come out as predicted just by chance. The fact that we have 84, seven times more than chance would dictate, means that the Pygmalion effect does exist in certain circumstances. Moreover, it is not limited to young children and rats; adolescents and adults are affected too.

OUTSIDE THE LAB

And the Pygmalion effect is as likely to occur in the real world as in the experimenter's tower. Of the 242 studies that have been done to date, 57 took place outside the laboratory—in a classroom, a factory, an office, and the like. The proportion of significant results is about the same for experiments conducted in the field as in the laboratory, some 37 percent for the field and 34 percent for the laboratory.

For example, Randy Burnham and Donald Hartsough found Pygmalion in the swimming pool. Their subjects were boys and girls, ages seven to 14, who were learning to swim at a summer camp. Half of the instructors were led to think that they were dealing with a "high-potential" group, and their students became better swimmers, by the end of their two-week camping period, than the regular group. And another team of researchers found that it took only two weeks for teen-age girls, who were institutionalized for various offenses, to show a marked improvement in their classroom behavior when they had been labeled "potential bloomers."

Even the United States Air Force Academy Preparatory School succumbed. W. R. Schrank randomly assigned 100 enlisted airmen to one of five math classes, and he told the teachers that each class contained students selected for different levels of ability. The boys in the supposed high-ability classes improved their math scores substantially.

J. Michael Palardy tested the popular assumption that boys have a tougher time learning to read than girls. First-grade teachers are well aware of this folk belief, and thus have clear expectations when they give reading lessons. Palardy surveyed 63 teachers and found five who believed that boys could learn to read as well as girls in the first grade. He matched these five on a number of factors—background, teaching methods, etc.—with five who believed in the stereotype. Indeed, teachers who expected to discover sex differences in reading ability found them. But the boys did just as well as the girls when their teachers thought they would. (As a footnote to this study, the "well-known" sex difference in learning to read also tends to disappear when the children learn from teaching machines rather than from teachers.)

Albert King moved the Pygmalion paradigm into the work world with an ingenious set of five experiments. King was interested in the effects of supervisor expectations on the job performance of disadvantaged workers (unemployed or underemployed, mostly black and members of other minorities). In three of his studies the workers were women in training to become nurses' aides, presser-machine operators, or assemblers of electronic equipment. In the other two studies, the workers were men who were learning to become auto mechanics or welders.

In each experiment, King randomly picked the names of some of the trainees, and told the supervisors that these workers showed a special potential for their particular job. King collected several measures of the workers' performances: objective tests, peer ratings, absences and so on. (King ignored the supervisors' ratings of trainees, since these might reflect only their perception and not actual changes in their performance.) The Pygmalion effect worked in four of the five experiments—for every group of trainees but the nurses' aides. Trainees whose supervisors had expected high job performance of them did much better than the control groups. However, the effect was especially marked among male workers, the welders and mechanics, and less so among female workers, the pressers and assemblers. Perhaps the supervisors found it harder to accept the idea that women could have "special potential" for their work.

TABLE 1. Average Performance Ranks (Lower Ranks Indicate Superior Performance):

Study	Control Group	Experimental Group
1 welders	9.9	3.6
2 mechanics	10.7	4.3
3 pressers	9.2	5.3
4 assemblers	11.3	7.8
5 nurses' aides	9.2	8.3

All of this research supported our feeling that self-fulfilling prophecy is a real phenomenon, that it occurs both in and out of the classroom and the laboratory. The next step was to figure out what subtle forces are going on in the exchange between teacher and learner. What makes average kids increase their IQ, neophytes swim better, and trainees learn faster? How does A *communicate* his or her expectations to B, especially when both A and B probably are unaware of the process?

EXPLAINING THE PYGMALION EFFECT

The current evidence leads me to propose a four-factor "theory" of the influences that produce the Pygmalion effect. People who have been led to expect good things from their students, children, clients, or what-have-you appear to:

—create a warmer social-emotional mood around their "special" students (*climate*);
—give more feedback to these students about their performance (*feedback*);

—teach more material and more difficult material to their special
students (*input*); and

—give their special students more opportunities to respond and
question (*output*).

There is nothing magical or definitive about the choice of these
four, and in fact, none of them is independent of the others. My
criterion for including each as a factor is that there be at least five
studies that support it and that no more than 20 percent of the
studies bearing on each factor contradict it.

The Climate Factor

"Climate" apparently has to do with warmth, attention, and emotional support. Fourteen studies have investigated this factor, 12 of
which came out as predicted. Not all of them dealt with the teacher-
student relationship; some took place in industrial and clinical con-
texts as well.

For example, Geri Alpert told a group of psychiatrists that some
of their patients had been specially selected for them on the basis of
"therapeutic compatibility." She gave them no expectations about
the rest of their patients. Later Alpert asked the patients to describe
their therapists and their sessions together. From a patient's-eye
view, psychiatrists behave more warmly toward people with whom
they expect to be compatible and who are likely to get well.

Alan Chaikin, Edward Sigler, and Valerian Derlega asked male
and female college undergraduates to teach a short unit on home and
family safety to a 12-year-old boy. One third of the "teachers"
thought that the boy had an IQ of 130 and did very well in school;
one third thought that the child had an IQ of 85 and did poorly in
school; and the last third had no information about the boy's IQ.
Then the experimenters videotaped the exchange between teachers
and student to see what nonverbal cues were going on.

Teachers who thought they were dealing with a bright student
were more likely to smile at the boy, nod their heads approvingly,
lean toward the boy, and look him in the eye for longer periods. A
variety of analogous studies have found that "special-potential"
subjects report their teachers or counselors as being more positive,
accepting, perceptive, friendly, fond of them, and supportive.

The Feedback Factor

The difference between this factor and the previous one (for both
involve warmth and attention) is that feedback depends on a re-

sponse from the student. A teacher can be generally warm, but still react critically or indifferently to a child's answers or comments. Feedback refers specifically to how much active teaching occurs: often the teacher rewards a desired response, corrects a wrong answer, asks for the student's further thoughts, and so on. Ten studies explored this factor, of which eight supported it.

Jere Brophy and Tom Good asked first-grade teachers to name their high and low achievers. The researchers then watched the teachers work with the children. The teachers ignored only three percent of the high achievers' answers but they ignored 15 percent of the low achievers' answers. The good students, then, get more feedback, whether their responses are right or wrong.

Teachers give more feedback to apt undergraduates as well as to apt first-graders. John Lanzetta and T. E. Hannah offered college students the chance to play teacher, and gave them the choice of five kinds of feedback for use in teaching a concept task: a strong electric shock, a mild shock, a neutral light, a small amount of money, and a larger amount of money. The "learner," who was a confederate of the experimenters, gave 36 correct and 84 incorrect answers in all cases.

When the student teachers thought the learner had a "high potential," they rewarded him with the larger sum of money when he was right, and shocked him more severely when he was wrong. When they thought that the learner had a "low learning potential," however, they gave him the lesser reward or punishment. In other words, teachers send clearer, stronger evaluations to students for whom they have greater expectations.

But another experiment found that children believed to be bright got more praise, but not more criticism; criticism was reserved for children believed to be dull. Yet a third study found that supposedly "gifted" children get more praise from their teachers, but found no difference between "gifted" and "regular" children in the criticism they got. The matter is complicated. Perhaps criticism for a wrong answer needs to be accompanied by enough praise and support on other occasions; otherwise the student may see the teacher as overly critical and cold. We can say with modest certainty that praise is a factor in achieving the Pygmalion effect, but the role of criticism is less clear.

The Input Factor

There are only five studies that directly deal with this factor, but all five find that teachers literally teach more to children of whom they expect more.

The most dramatic case in point is W. Victor Beez's work with 60 preschoolers and 60 teachers in a Headstart program. Beez told half of the teachers that they could expect poor performance from their supposedly "below-average" children; the rest expected exceptional performance from their "bright" children. Observers, who had not been told what the teachers' expectations were, noted the exchanges between teacher and child. The teachers worked much harder when they believed they had a bright child. In a unit on word learning, for example, 87 percent of the teachers of "bright" children taught eight or more words; but only 13 percent of the teachers of the "dull" children tried to teach them that many. Not surprisingly, 77 percent of the "bright" children learned five or more words, but only 13 percent of the "dull" children learned that many.

Such results tell us that a teacher's expectations about a student's performance are not simply transmitted in subtle voice nuances and a casual facial expression. The expectations may be translated into explicit, overt alterations in teaching style and substance.

TABLE 2.

Number of Words Taught:	Teachers' Expectation:	
	Dull Children	Bright Children
11 or more	0	14
9 or 10	1	10
7 or 8	7	3
5 or 6	15	1
4 or less	7	2
	30	30

The Output Factor

Eleven studies out of 12 done support this factor, indicating that teachers encourage greater responsiveness from students of whom they expect more. They call on such students more often, ask them harder questions, give them more time to answer, and prompt them toward the correct answer. Output is therefore closely related to feedback.

Mary Budd Rowe gives us a good example. She was interested in how long teachers wait for an answer to their question before going on to the next child. She found that many experienced teachers wait only one *second* before they ask the question again, often of someone else. However, Rowe found that teachers wait longer for the students whom they believe to be bright. When Rowe pointed this out to the teachers involved, they reacted with surprise and insight. "I guess we don't expect an answer [of the poor students]," said one, "so we go on to someone else." When these same teachers then deliberately increased their waiting time for their "slower" students, they got increased responsiveness.

Jeffrey Hersh's work illustrates another facet of the output factor. He asked graduate students to administer the Stanford-Binet IQ Test to children in a Headstart program. Examiners who had been told the children had high intellectual ability immediately began with more difficult questions. They demanded more of the children, and got more.

AN UNEXPECTED GALATEA

We knew from our original Pygmalion experiment in the classroom that favorable expectations could have a beneficial effect. At the end of the year the teachers had all sorts of good things to say about the "intellectual bloomers": they had a better chance of being successful in the future, said the teachers; they were more appealing, better adjusted, more affectionate and autonomous. So the teachers perceived them, in any case.

We thought that perhaps it was because the experimental children gained more in IQ that the teachers rated their behavior and aptitudes more highly. So we looked at the control-group children who had also gained in IQ that year, to see whether the teachers liked them as much as the bloomers. Such was not the case. To our astonishment, the more the control students increased in IQ, the *less* well adjusted, interesting and affectionate the teachers thought them.

It seems, then, that when a child who is not expected to do well does so, his teacher looks upon his behavior and personality as undesirable. This was especially true, we discovered, for children in low-ability classrooms. Teachers may have a difficult time thinking that a child who has a low-ability label can show an intellectual spurt. They may interpret this change as "maladjustment" or "trouble-making." Perhaps the child doesn't know his place. Several subsequent experiments confirmed this finding, so the hazards of unpredicted success are likely to be real rather than a freak of one study. Alfred Shore, for example, asked teachers to predict their students' intellectual achievement and to describe their students' classroom behavior. A month later, Shore gave the teachers the students' real

IQ scores and asked for a reappraisal. Again, teachers downgraded those students in personality and adjustment who had done "too well"—i.e., contrary to their expectations.

Eleanor Leacock studied four schools in four neighborhoods, two poor and two middle-income. Within each income level one school was essentially all black and the other essentially white. Leacock interviewed the fifth-grade teachers about their feelings for the children, and scored their comments for positive, neutral, or negative feelings and attitudes.

DOUBLE HANDICAP

Leacock found that the teachers were much less favorable to the lower-class children than they were to the middle-class children; 40 percent of their comments about the poorer children were negative, compared to 20 percent of their comments about the middle-class children. And the teachers were even more likely to talk negatively about black children than white children, 43 percent to 17 percent.

Leacock then went on to relate the children's IQ scores to the teachers' feelings toward them. IQ scores of the middle-income children, both black and white, were clearly related to the positive attitudes of their teachers. This relationship did *not* hold for the low-income children; in fact, it was reversed. That is, lower-income children who had *higher* IQs tended to have teachers who viewed them *negatively* and this was especially true for lower-income children who were black. The children who surpassed their teachers' expectations got resentment and complaints for their pains.

Thus children who are both black and lower-income have a double handicap. And this result cannot be attributed to white teachers' bias; both of the teachers of the black children were themselves black. The prejudice of stunted expectations knows no race barrier.

We still do not know exactly how the Pygmalion effect works. But we know that often it does work, and that it has powers that can hinder as well as help the development of others. Field and experimental studies are beginning to isolate the factors that will give some insight into the process. Such awareness may help some to create their Galateas, but it will also give the Galateas a chance to fight back.

> In case anyone believes that people do not take
> seriously what school authorities tell them is true
> about their own academic abilities, an educational
> measurements teacher tried an experiment on a
> group of people who were about to go out and
> teach. His findings certainly underscore the fact
> that few people can take a low I.Q. score report
> with equanimity. Is this perhaps further evidence
> for Rosenthal's theory?

TEACHERS DON'T WANT
TO BE LABELED
Harry W. Forgan

When teaching a course on tests and measurements at Kent State
University recently, I decided to administer an adult group intelligence test to the class. I wanted the students to "feel" what it was
like to take such a test and realize what items we use to measure
intelligence. I also thought they might be more aware of the short
time it takes to obtain a number which is regarded as very important
by many educators.

The students were told not to write their names on the test
papers, but rather to use a code such as their house number, physical
measurements, or any less obvious symbol. I explained that I really
didn't have faith in IQ scores; therefore, I didn't want to know their
IQs.

The administration of the test required only 50 minutes. The
students seemed to enjoy taking it and chuckled at some of the tasks
they were expected to perform. I had to laugh myself when I saw
some of them looking at their hands and feet when responding to
items concerning right and left.

Upon scoring the test I found that the lowest IQ was 87 and the
highest 143. The mean IQ for the 48 students was 117. I was not
astonished by the 87, even though all of the students had successfully completed the general education courses and student teaching
at Kent State and were ready to graduate by the end of the term.
After all, IQ tests have many limitations.

Reprinted by permission of the author and the *Phi Delta Kappan,* September, 1973.

Then I got an idea. I decided to prepare a report for each student, writing his code on the outside and "IQ 87" on the inside of each. I folded and stapled each paper—after all, an IQ is confidential information!

At the next class period I arranged all of the folded papers on a table at the front of the room. I wrote the range and the average IQ on the chalkboard. Many students snickered at the thought of somebody getting an 87. The students were eager and afraid as I began by explaining the procedures for picking up their papers. I made a point of telling them not to tell others their IQ score, because this would make the other person feel as if he too had to divulge his "total endowment." The students were then directed to come up to the table, row by row, to find their coded paper. I stood sheepishly—ready to laugh out loud as I watched the students carefully open their papers and see "IQ 87." Many opened their mouths with astonishment and then smiled at their friends to indicate they were extremely happy with their scores.

There was dead silence when I began to discuss the implications of the IQ scores. I explained that in some states a person who scores below 90 on an IQ test is classified as a slow learner. The fact that group intelligence tests should not be used to make such a classification was stressed. I also emphasized the fact that *someone* in this class could have been classified as a slow learner and placed in a special class on the basis of this test.

I told how many guidance counselors would discourage a child with an 87 IQ from attending college. Again I emphasized the fact that one person in this room was ready to graduate from college having passed several courses in history, biology, English, and many other areas.

I then went on to explain that the majority of elementary and secondary school teachers believe in ability grouping. This is usually done on the basis of intelligence tests, so I explained that I would like to try ability grouping with this class—again to see "how it feels." Some students objected right away, saying that "I did not want to know their IQ scores." I calmed them by saying it would be a worthwhile learning experience and assured them that I really didn't believe in IQ scores.

I told the students not to move at this time, but I would like all of those with an IQ below 90 to come to the front so they could sit nearer to me for individual help. I told the students who had an average IQ (between 90–109) to go to the back of the room and then take the seats in the middle of the class. The students with an above average IQ were asked to go to the side of the room and take the seats in the back because they really didn't need much extra help.

"O.K., all those who got an IQ below 90 can come to the front of the room." The students looked around to find those who scored below 90. I said that I knew there was an 87 and maybe a couple of 89's. Again, there was dead silence.

"O.K., all those students whose IQ is between 90–109 go to the back of the room." Immediately, to my amazement, 8 or 10 students picked up their books and headed for the back of the room. Before they could get there I said, "Wait a minute! Sit down! I don't want to embarrass you, but you would lie and cheat—the same way we make our students lie and cheat—because you don't want to be classified as 'slow.' I wrote 'IQ 87' on every paper!"

The class erupted. It was in an uproar for about five minutes. Some of the women cried. Some indicated that they needed to use the restroom. All agreed it was a horrifying and yet valuable experience.

I asked them to do one thing for me: Please don't label kids. Because we are all "gifted," "average," and "slow," depending on the task at hand. They promised.

Although there is some evidence to suggest that teacher performance correlates positively with teacher effectiveness, Dr. Naftulin and his associates raise at least an important caution in taking student assessments too literally. If it is true, as the "Body Language" (pp. 289–291) article indicates, that only seven percent of most communication is contained in the verbal content, then the findings of this article are not surprising. Does it follow that professional actors should be hired to give lectures? Is it possible to teach people how to separate the hidden part of the message from the verbal content?

THE DOCTOR FOX LECTURE:
A PARADIGM OF
EDUCATIONAL SEDUCTION

Donald H. Naftulin,
John E. Ware, Jr.,
and Frank A. Donnelly

Teaching effectiveness is difficult to study since so many variables must be considered in its evaluation. Among the obvious are the education, social background, knowledge of subject matter, experience, and personality of the educator. It would seem that an educator with the proper combination of these and other variables would be effective. However, such a combination may result in little more than the educator's ability to satisfy students, but not necessarily educate them.

Getzels and Jackson (1) have stated that the personality of the teacher might be the most significant variable in the evaluation of teaching effectiveness. Wallen and Travers (1) also supported this concept in stating that "we have tried to demonstrate that patterns

Reprinted by permission of the authors and publisher from *Journal of Medical Education,* July, 1973, pp. 631–635. This article is based on a paper presented at the 11th Annual Conference on Research in Medical Education at the 83rd Annual Meeting of the AAMC, Miami Beach, Florida, November 6, 1972.

of teacher behavior and the teaching methods they represent are mainly the products of forces which have little to do with scientific knowledge of learning."

Similarly, Goffman (2) viewed audience receptivity to a lecturer as highly influenced by the person introducing him as well as by the quality of the introduction. In addition, Goffman described an audience as influenced by the speaker's "involuntary expressive behavior" as much as by the expressed information he wished to convey. This is especially so if the audience has had little time to evaluate the information. Consequently, the learner's impression of the information conveyer becomes a decisive factor in how he responds to the information conveyed.

Rogers (3) stressed the importance of humanizing our educational institutions by bringing "together the cognitive and the affective-experiential" aspects of learning. He also discussed the significance of the educator's genuineness. He feels that the educator who does not present a facade is more likely to be effective. The educator, states Rogers, must have a "direct personal encounter with the learner."

In one study (4) in which student perceptions of educators in 1,427 seventh through 12th grade classes were factor analyzed, it was reported that the students regarded "teacher charisma or popularity" as the most important characteristic when rating teachers. The article further states that "students do not respond directly to specific questions regarding teacher effectiveness. Rather a kind of halo effect on teacher charisma or popularity determines to a large extent how students react to questions about their teacher."

If charisma or popularity have such an effect on the rating of teachers by junior high and high school students, the authors wondered whether the ratings of a highly trained group of professional educators in a learning situation might be similarly influenced. If that were the case, a demonstration of the personality factor in perceived learning might serve to arouse the group members' concern about the proper combination of style and substance in their own teaching.

METHOD

The hypothesis for this study was as follows. Given a sufficiently impressive lecture paradigm, an experienced group of educators participating in a new learning situation can feel satisfied that they have learned despite irrelevant, conflicting, and meaningless content conveyed by the lecturer.

To test the hypothesis, the authors selected a professional actor who looked distinguished and sounded authoritative; provided him with a sufficiently ambiguous title, Dr. Myron L. Fox, an authority on the application of mathematics to human behavior; dressed him up with a fictitious but impressive curriculum vitae, and presented him to a group of highly trained educators.

The lecture method was the teaching format selected since it is one used extensively in the professional educational setting. It has been described as the one teaching method during which most of the time the instructor talks to the students (1). Its acceptance as an effective teaching tool is attributable mainly to its time-testedness.

Dr. Fox's topic was to be "Mathematical Game Theory as Applied to Physician Education." His source material was derived from a complex but sufficiently understandable scientific article geared to lay readers (5). One of the authors, on two separate occasions, coached the lecturer to present his topic and conduct his question and answer period with an excessive use of double talk, neologisms, non sequiturs, and contradictory statements. All this was to be interspersed with parenthetical humor and meaningless references to unrelated topics.

Group I

Eleven psychiatrists, psychologists, and social-worker educators who were gathered for a teacher training conference in continuing education comprised the learner group. The purpose of the conference was to help this group be more effective educators of other health professionals by providing them various instructional goals, media, and experiences. Dr. Fox was introduced as "the real McCoy" to this unsuspecting group; and he presented his one-hour lecture in the manner described, followed by a half hour discussion period which was hardly more substantive.

At the end of his performance an authentic looking satisfaction questionnaire was distributed to which all 11 mental health educators were asked to respond anonymously (Table 1). The introduction of the lecturer as well as his lecture and discussion were videotaped for use with other groups.

Significantly, more favorable than unfavorable responses to the questionnaire were obtained (chi-square = 35.96, $p < .001$). The one item with most favorable responses was the first, "Did he dwell upon the obvious?" It was the feeling of half the group that he did. The remaining items received a majority of favorable responses. No re-

TABLE 1. Examples of Questions Used and Percentage of Responses* for Three Groups.

Questions	Group I		Group II		Group III	
	Yes	No	Yes	No	Yes	No
Did he dwell upon the obvious?	50	50	0	100	28	72
Did he seem interested in his subject?	100	0	91	9	97	3
Did he use enough examples to clarify his material?	90	10	64	36	91	9
Did he present his material in a well organized form?	90	10	82	18	70	30
Did he stimulate your thinking?	100	0	91	9	87	13
Did he put his material across in an interesting way?	90	10	82	18	81	19
Have you read any of this speaker's publications?	0	100	9	91	0	100
Specify any other important characteristics of his presentation.						

*"Yes" responses to all but item one are considered favorable.

spondent reported having read Dr. Fox's publications. Subjective responses included the following:

> Excellent presentation, enjoyed listening. Has warm manner. Good flow, seems enthusiastic. What about the two types of games, zero-sum and non-zero sum? Too intellectual a presentation. My orientation is more pragmatic.

Because the first group was few in number and quite select, the authors sought other subjects with similar experience and professional identity who might provide further data to test the hypothesis.

Group II

The second group consisted of 11 subjects who were psychiatrists, psychologists, and psychiatric social workers, all identified as mental health educators. A videotape of the previously described lecture and discussion period as well as the preparatory introduction was shown to the group. After the presentation group members responded to it using the same questionnaire as did the first group (Table 1). Favorable responses far outweighed unfavorable responses, and the difference between the two was (chi-square = 64.53, $p < .001$). All responded favorably to the first item, which means that they felt he did not "dwell upon the obvious." There were also significantly more favorable than unfavorable responses to the other items and one respondent reported having read the lecturer's publications. Some subjective statements were:

> Did not carry it far enough. Lack of visual materials to relate it to psychiatry. Too much gesturing. Left out relevant examples. He misses the last few phrases which I believe would have tied together his ideas for me.

Still more subjects were sought to further test the hypothesis.

Group III

The third group was different in that it consisted of 33 educators and administrators enrolled in a graduate level university educational philosophy course. Of the 33 subjects in this group, 21 held master's degrees, eight had bachelor's degrees, and four had other degrees which were not specified. Most of these educators were not specifically mental health professionals but had been identified as having counseling experience in their respective schools. The videotape of the lecture was again presented to this group, after which the educators responded to it by using the same questionnaire as the first two groups (Table 1).

Again the number of favorable responses was significantly greater than the number of unfavorable responses (chi-square = $102.83, p <$ .001). The majority of respondents from Group III also did not feel the lecturer dwelt upon the obvious, and they also responded favorably for the most part to the other items. Subjective responses, when given, were again interesting. Some were:

> Lively examples. His relaxed manner of presentation was a large factor in holding my interest. Extremely articulate. Interesting, wish he dwelled more on background. Good analysis of subject that has been personally studied before. Very dramatic presentation. He was certainly captivating. Somewhat disorganized. Frustratingly boring. Unorganized and ineffective. Articulate. Knowledgeable.

Given the responses of these three groups of educators to the lecture paradigm, the authors believe that the study hypothesis has been supported.

DISCUSSION

The notion that students, even if they are professional educators, can be effectively "seduced" into an illusion of having learned if the lecturer simulates a style of authority and wit is certainly not new. In a terse but appropriate statement on educators, Postman and Weingartner (6) emphasized that "it is the sign of a competent crap detector that he is not completely captivated by the arbitrary abstractions of the community in which he happened to grow up." The three groups of learners in this study, all of whom had grown up in the academic community and were experienced educators, obviously failed as "competent crap detectors" and were seduced by the style of Dr. Fox's presentation. Considering the educational sophistication of the subjects, it is striking that none of them detected the lecture for what it was.

In addition to testing the hypothesis, the paradigm was to provide these professional educators with an example of being educationally seduced and to demonstrate that there is much more to teaching than making students happy. A balanced combination of knowledge and personality are needed for effective teaching even if the student does not require the former to sustain the illusion that he has learned. It is hoped that this experience has helped respondents from these three groups to question their educational effectiveness more meaningfully.

To the authors' knowledge a simulated teaching paradigm such as this with student responses to subsequently perceived learning has not been reported. Despite the usual reservations about generalizing data from only 55 subjects, the results of the study raise some interesting questions. The first involves the content of the lecture. Does a topic seemingly short on content and long on ambiguity or abstraction lend itself more readily to such a lecture paradigm than a content-based factual presentation from a more concrete topic area? The answer is an equivocal "yes," as a subject in Group I noted after being told of the study's design. He said he felt that the lecturer might have had a tougher time talking nonsense about a more concrete topic but even under those circumstances a fake lecture could be "pulled off" with an unsuspecting group. This raises the next question.

If the group were more sophisticated about a more concrete aspect of the lecturer's subject matter, in this case mathematics, would he have been as successful in seducing the respondents into an illusion of having learned? Probably not. Or at least the lecturer would have to be extremely skillful to be successful. The study also raises the larger issue of what mix of style and substance in the lecture method is optimal for not just integrating information in a meaningful way but for providing learning motivation as well. Although the study was not specifically addressed to this question, the fact that no respondents saw through the hoax of the lecture, that all respondents had significantly more favorable than unfavorable responses, and that one even believed he read Dr. Fox's publications suggests that for these learners "style" was more influential than "content" in providing learner satisfaction.

A more ideal assessment of the relative value of content and style in determining learner-reporter satisfaction might consist of programming the same "lecturer" to systematically alter the content of his presentation before three equivalent groups of learners. Simultaneously, his "involuntary expressive behavior" would remain constant for each of the three groups; for example, Group A would receive sufficient content conveyed with sufficient "involuntary expressive behavior," Group B moderately insufficient content accompanied by the same "involuntary expressive behavior" as was displayed with Group A, and Group C totally inadequate content delivered in the same manner as to the first two groups; the three groups of learners could then be more systematically compared as to learner perceived satisfaction.

After the respondents in the actual study were informed of its purpose, numerous subjects from each group requested the article from which the lecturer was programmed. Reported intent of these requests ranged from curiosity to disbelief, but the authors were told by some respondents that Dr. Fox did stimulate interest in the subject area even after the respondents were told of the study's purpose. Despite having been misinformed, the motivation of some respondents to learn more about the subject matter persisted. Consequently, it is the authors' impression that the "arbitrary abstractions" suggested by Postman and Weingartner have some initial pump-priming effect on educational motivation.

The relationship of the illusion of having learned to motivation for learning more has not been fully addressed here, but should a positive relationship exist, this study supports the possibility of training actors to give legitimate lectures as an innovative educational approach toward student-perceived satisfaction with the learning process. The corollary would be to provide the scholar-educator with a more dramatic stage presence to enhance student satisfaction with the learning process. Either extreme has a soap-selling quality not likely to lather the enthusiasm of the pure scholar. However, this paper is not addressed to him but rather to student-perceived satisfaction with how well he has shared his information. More important, as has been noted, it suggests to the educator that the extent to which his students are satisfied with his teaching, and even the degree to which they feel they have learned, reflects little more than their illusions of having learned.

REFERENCES

1. Gage, N. L. (Ed.). *Handbook of Research on Teaching.* New York: Rand McNally, 1963, pp. 506, 464, and 481.
2. Goffman, E. *The Presentation of Self in Everyday Life.* New York: Doubleday, 1959.
3. Rogers, C. R. Bringing Together Ideas and Feelings in Learning. *Learning Today,* 5:32–43, Spring, 1972.
4. Coats, W. D., and Swierenga, L. Student Perceptions of Teachers. A Factor Analytic Study. *J. Educ. Res.,* 65:357–360, April, 1972.
5. Rapoport, A. The Use and Misuse of Game Theory. *Scientific American,* 207:108–114, December, 1962.
6. Postman, N., and Weingartner, C. *Teaching as a Subversive Activity.* New York: Delacorte Press, 1969, pp. 1–15.

Good teachers are really not very hard to tell from bad ones, according to Hamachek. The teacher's personality is vitally important and there are ten "behaviors" that help to separate the best from the worst teachers.

CHARACTERISTICS OF GOOD TEACHERS AND IMPLICATIONS FOR TEACHER EDUCATION
Don Hamachek

It is, I think, a sad commentary about our educational system that it keeps announcing both publicly and privately that "good" and "poor" teachers cannot be distinguished one from the other. Probably no issue in education has been so voluminously researched as has teacher effectiveness and considerations which enhance or restrict this effectiveness. Nonetheless, we still read that we cannot tell the good guys from the bad guys. For example, Biddle and Ellena[1] in their book, *Contemporary Research on Teacher Effectiveness,* begin by stating that "the problem of teacher effectiveness is so complex that no one today knows what *The Competent Teacher* is." I think we *do* know what the competent—or effective, or good, or whatever you care to call him—teacher is, and in the remainder of this paper I will be as specific as possible in citing *why* I think we know along with implications for our teacher-education programs.

WHAT THE RESEARCH SAYS

By and large, most research efforts aimed at investigating teacher effectiveness have attempted to prove one or more of the following dimensions of teacher personality and behavior: (1) personal characteristics, (2) instructional procedures and interaction styles, (3) perceptions of self, (4) perceptions of others. Because of space limits this is by no means an exhaustive review of the research related to the problem, but it is, I think, representative of the kind and variety of research findings linked to questions of teacher effectiveness.

Personal Characteristics of Good Versus Poor Teachers

We would probably agree that it is quite possible to have two teachers of equal intelligence, training, and grasp of subject matter who nevertheless differ considerably in the results they achieve with students. Part of the difference can be accounted for by the effect of a teacher's personality on the learners. What kinds of personality do students respond to?

Hart[2] conducted a study based upon the opinions of 3,725 high school seniors concerning best-liked and least-liked teachers and found a total of forty-three different reasons for "liking Teacher A best" and thirty different reasons for "liking Teacher Z least." Not surprisingly, over 51 percent of the students said that they liked best those teachers who were "helpful in school work, who explained lessons and assignments clearly, and who used examples in teaching."

1. B. J. Biddle and W. H. Ellena, *Contemporary Research on Teacher Effectiveness* (New York: Holt, Rinehart and Winston, 1964), p. 2.
2. W. F. Hart, *Teachers and Teaching* (New York: Macmillan, 1934), pp. 131–32.

Also, better than 40 percent responded favorably to teachers with a "sense of humor." Those teachers assessed most negatively were "unable to explain clearly, were partial to brighter students, and had superior, aloof, overbearing attitudes." In addition, over 50 percent of the respondents mentioned behaviors such as "too cross, crabby, grouchy, and sarcastic" as reasons for disliking many teachers. Interestingly enough, mastery of subject matter, which is vital but badly overemphasized by specialists, ranked sixteenth on both lists. Somehow students seem willing to take more or less for granted that a teacher "knows" his material. What seems to make a difference is the teacher's personal style in *communicating* what he knows. Studies by Witty[3] and Bousfield[4] tend to support these conclusions at both the high school *and* college level.

Having desirable personal qualities is one thing, but what are the results of rigorous tests of whether the teacher's having them makes any difference in the performance of students?

Cogan[5] found that warm, considerate teachers got an unusual amount of original poetry and art from their high school students. Reed[6] found that teachers higher in a capacity for warmth favorably affected their pupils' interests in science. Using scores from achievement tests as their criterion measure, Heil, Powell, and Feifer[7] compared various teacher-pupil personality combinations and found that the well-integrated (healthy, well-rounded, flexible) teachers were most effective with *all* types of students. Spaulding[8] found that the self-concepts of elementary school children were apt to be higher and more positive in classrooms in which the teacher was "socially integrative" and "learner supportive."

In essence, I think the evidence is quite clear when it comes to sorting out good or effective from bad or ineffective teachers on the basis of personal characteristics. Effective teachers appear to be those who are, shall we say, "human" in the fullest sense of the word.

3. P. Witty, "An Analysis of the Personality Traits of the Effective Teacher," *Journal of Educational Research*, May 1947, pp. 662–71.

4. W. A. Bousfield, "Student's Rating on Qualities Considered Desirable in College Professors," *School and Society*, February 24, 1940, pp. 253–56.

5. M. L. Cogan, "The Behavior of Teachers and the Productive Behavior of Their Pupils," *Journal of Experimental Education*, December 1958, pp. 89–124.

6. H. B. Reed, "Implications for Science Education of a Teacher Competence Research," *Science Education*, December 1962, pp. 473–86.

7. L. M. Heil, M. Powell, and I. Feifer, *Characteristics of Teacher Behavior Related to the Achievement of Children in Several Elementary Grades* (Washington, D.C.: Office of Education, Cooperative Research Branch, 1960).

8. R. Spaulding, "Achievement, Creativity, and Self-Concept Correlates of Teacher-Pupil Transactions in Elementary Schools" (University of Illinois, U.S. Office of Education Cooperative Research Project No. 1352, 1963).

They have a sense of humor, are fair, empathetic, more democratic than autocratic, and apparently are more able to relate easily and naturally to students on either a one-to-one or group basis. Their classrooms seem to reflect miniature enterprise operations in the sense that they are more open, spontaneous, and adaptable to change. Ineffective teachers apparently lack a sense of humor, grow impatient easily, use cutting, ego-reducing comments in class, are less well-integrated, are inclined to be somewhat authoritarian, and are generally less sensitive to the needs of their students. Indeed, research related to authoritarianism suggests that the bureaucratic conduct and rigid overtones of the ineffective teacher's classroom are desperate measures to support the weak pillars of his own personality structure.

Instructional Procedures and Interaction Styles of Good Versus Poor Teachers

If there really are polar extremes such as "good" or "poor" teachers, then we can reasonably assume that these teachers differ not only in personal characteristics but in the way they conduct themselves in the classroom.

Flanders[9] found that classrooms in which achievement and attitudes were superior were likely to be conducted by teachers who did not blindly pursue a single behavioral-instructional path to the exclusion of other possibilities. In other words, the more successful teachers were better able to range along a continuum of interaction styles which varied from fairly active, dominative support on the one hand to a more reflective, discriminating support on the other. Interestingly, those teachers who were *not* successful were the very ones who were inclined to use the same interaction styles in a more or less rigid fashion.

Barr[10] discovered that not only did poor teachers make more assignments than good teachers but, almost without exception, they made some sort of textbook assignment as part of their unyielding daily procedure. The majority of good teachers used more outside books and problem-project assignments. When the text was assigned they were more likely to supplement it with topics, questions, or other references.

9. N. A. Flanders, *Teacher Influence, Pupil Attitudes and Achievement: Studies in Interaction Analysis* (University of Minnesota, U. S. Office of Education Cooperative Research Project No. 397, 1960).
10. A. S. Barr, *Characteristic Differences in the Teaching Performance of Good and Poor Teachers of the Social Studies* (Bloomington: The Public School Publishing Co., 1929).

Research findings related to interaction styles variously called "learner-centered" or "teacher-centered" point to similar conclusions. In general, it appears that the amount of cognitive gain is largely unaffected by the autocratic or democratic tendencies of the instructor. However, when affective gains are considered, the results are somewhat different. For example, Stern[11] reviewed thirty-four studies comparing nondirective with directive instruction and concluded:

> Regardless of whether the investigator was concerned with attitudes toward the cultural out group, toward other participants in the class, or toward the self, the results generally have indicated that nondirective instruction facilitates a shift in a more favorable, acceptant direction.

When it comes to classroom behavior, interaction patterns, and teaching styles, good or effective teachers seem to reflect more of the following behaviors:

1. Willingness to be flexible, to be direct or indirect as the situation demands.
2. Ability to perceive the world from the student's point of view.
3. Ability to "personalize" their teaching.
4. Willingness to experiment, to try out new things.
5. Skill in asking questions (as opposed to seeing self as a kind of answering service).
6. Knowledge of subject matter and related areas.
7. Provision of well-established examination procedures.
8. Provision of definite study helps.
9. Reflection of an appreciative attitude (evidenced by nods, comments, smiles, etc.).
10. Use of conversational manner in teaching—informal, easy style.

Self-Perceptions of Good Versus Poor Teachers

We probably do not have to go any further than our own personal life experiences to know that the way we see, regard, and feel about ourselves has an enormous impact on both our private and public lives. How about good and poor teachers? How do they see themselves?

Ryans[12] found that there are, indeed, differences between the

11. G. C. Stern, "Measuring Non-Cognitive Variables in Research on Teaching," in N. L. Gage (ed.), *Handbook of Research on Teaching* (Chicago: Rand McNally, 1963), p. 427.
12. D. G. Ryans, "Prediction of Teacher Effectiveness," *Encyclopedia of Educational Research*, 3rd Edition (New York: Macmillan, 1960), pp. 1, 486–90.

self-related reports of teachers with high emotional stability and those with low emotional stability. For example, the more emotionally stable teachers (1) more frequently named self-confidence and cheerfulness as dominant traits in themselves, (2) said they liked active contact with other people, (3) expressed interests in hobbies and handicrafts, (4) reported their childhoods to be happy experiences.

On the other hand, teachers with lower emotional maturity scores (1) had unhappy memories of childhood, (2) seemed *not* to prefer contact with others, (3) were more directive and authoritarian, (4) expressed less self-confidence.

We can be even more specific. Combs,[13] in his book *The Professional Education of Teachers,* cites several studies which reached similar conclusions about the way good teachers typically see themselves, as follows:

1. Good teachers see themselves as identified with people rather than withdrawn, removed, apart from, or alienated from others.
2. Good teachers feel basically adequate rather than inadequate. They do not see themselves as generally unable to cope with problems.
3. Good teachers feel trustworthy rather than untrustworthy. They see themselves as reliable, dependable individuals with the potential for coping with events as they happen.
4. Good teachers see themselves as wanted rather than unwanted. They see themselves as likable and attractive (in a personal, not physical sense) as opposed to feeling ignored and rejected.
5. Good teachers see themselves as worthy rather than unworthy. They see themselves as people of consequence, dignity, and integrity as opposed to feeling they matter little, can be overlooked and discounted.

In the broadest sense of the word, good teachers are more likely to see themselves as good people. Their self-perceptions are, for the most part, positive, tinged with an air of optimism and colored with tones of healthy self-acceptance. I dare say that self-perceptions of good teachers are not unlike the self-perceptions of any basically healthy person, whether he be a good bricklayer, a good manager, a good doctor, a good lawyer, a good experimental psychologist, or you name it. Clinical evidence has told us time and again that *any* person is more apt to be

13. A. W. Combs, *The Professional Education of Teachers* (Boston: Allyn and Bacon, 1965), pp. 70–71.

happier, more productive, and more effective when he is able to see himself as fundamentally and basically "enough."

Perceptions of Others by Good Versus Poor Teachers

Research is showing us that not only do good and poor teachers view themselves differently, there are also some characteristic differences in the way they perceive others. For example, Ryans[14] reported several studies which have produced findings that are in agreement when it comes to sorting out the differences between how good and poor teachers view others. He found, among other things, that outstandingly "good" teachers rated significantly higher than notably "poor" teachers in at least five different ways with respect to how they viewed others. The good teachers had (1) more favorable opinions of students, (2) more favorable opinions of democratic classroom behavior, (3) more favorable opinions of administrators and colleagues, (4) a greater expressed liking for personal contacts with other people, (5) more favorable estimates of other people generally. That is, they expressed belief that very few students are difficult behavior problems, that very few people are influenced in their opinions and attitudes toward others by feelings of jealousy, and that most teachers are willing to assume their full share of extra duties outside of school.

Interestingly, the characteristics that distinguished the "lowly assessed" teacher group suggested that the relatively "ineffective" teacher is self-centered, anxious, restricted. One is left with the distinct impression that poor or ineffective teachers have more than the usual number of paranoid defenses.

It comes as no surprise that how we perceive others is highly dependent on how we perceive ourselves. If a potential teacher (or anyone else for that matter) likes himself, trusts himself, and has confidence in himself, he is likely to see others in somewhat this same light. Research is beginning to tell us what common sense has always told us; namely, people grow, flourish, and develop much more easily when in relationship with someone who projects an inherent trust and belief in their capacity to become what they have the potential to become.

It seems to me that we can sketch at least five interrelated generalizations from what research is telling us about how good teachers differ from poor teachers when it comes to how they perceive others.

14. Ryans, *op. cit.*

1. They seem to have generally more positive views of others—students, colleagues, and administrators.
2. They do not seem to be as prone to view others as critical, attacking people with ulterior motives; rather they are seen as potentially friendly and worthy in their own right.
3. They have a more favorable view of democratic classroom procedures.
4. They seem to have the ability and capacity to see things as they seem to others—i.e., the ability to see things from the other person's point of view.
5. They do not seem to see students as persons "you do things to" but rather as individuals capable of doing for themselves once they feel trusted, respected, and valued.

WHO, THEN, IS A GOOD TEACHER?

1. A good teacher is a good person. Simple and true. A good teacher rather likes life, is reasonably at peace with himself, has a sense of humor, and enjoys other people. If I interpret the research correctly, what it says is that there is no one best better-than-all-others type of teacher. Nonetheless there are clearly distinguishable "good" and "poor" teachers. Among other things, a good teacher is good because he does not seem to be dominated by a narcissistic self which demands a spotlight, or a neurotic need for power and authority, or a host of anxieties and tremblings which reduce him from the master of his class to its mechanic.
2. The good teacher is flexible. By far the single most repeated adjective used to describe good teachers is "flexibility." Either implicitly or explicitly (most often the latter), this characteristic emerges time and again over all others when good teaching is discussed in the research. In other words, the good teacher does not seem to be overwhelmed by a single point of view or approach to the point of intellectual myopia. A good teacher knows that he cannot be just one sort of person and use just one kind of approach if he intends to meet the demands of the moment. They seem able to move with the shifting tides of their own needs, the student's, and do what has to be done to handle the situation. A total teacher can be firm when necessary (say "No" and mean it) or permissive (say "Why not try it your way?" and mean that, too) when appropriate. It depends on many things, and good teachers seem to know the difference.

THE NEED FOR "TOTAL" TEACHERS

There probably is not an educational psychology course taught which does not, in some way, deal with the highly complex area of individual differences. Even the most unsophisticated undergraduate is aware that people differ in readiness and capacity to handle academic learning. For the most part our educational technology (audio-visual aids, programmed texts, teaching machines, etc.) is making significant advances designed to assist teachers in coping with intellectual differences among students. We have been making strides in the direction of offering flexible programs and curricula, but we are somewhat remiss when it comes to preparing flexible, "total" teachers. Just as there are intellectual differences among students, there are also personality and self-concept differences which can have just as much impact on achievement. If this is true, then perhaps we need to do more about preparing teachers who are sensitive to the nature of these differences and who are able to take them into account as they plan for their classes.

The point here is that what is important for one student is not important to another. This is one reason why cookbook formulas for good teachers are of so little value and why teaching is inevitably something of an art. The choice of instructional methods makes a big difference for certain kinds of pupils, and a search for the "best" way to teach can succeed only when learners' intellectual *and* personality differences are taken into account. Available evidence does not support the belief that successful teaching is possible only through the use of some specific methodology. A reasonable inference from existing data is that methods which provide for adaptation to individual and group differences, encourage student initiative, and stimulate individual differences, encourage student initiative, and stimulate individual and group participation are superior to methods which do not. In order for things of this sort to happen, perhaps what we need first of all are flexible, "total" teachers who are capable of planning around people as they are around ideas.

IMPLICATIONS FOR TEACHER EDUCATION

Research is teaching us many things about the differences between good and poor teachers, and I see at least four related implications for teacher education programs.

1. If it is true that good teachers are good because they view teaching as primarily a human process involving human relation-

ships and human meanings, then this may imply that we should spend at least as much time exposing and sensitizing teacher candidates to the subtle complexities of personality structure as we do to introducing them to the structure of knowledge itself. Does this mean personality development, group dynamics, basic counseling processes, sensitivity training, and techniques such as life-space interviewing and encounter grouping?

2. If it is true that good teachers have a positive view of themselves and others, then this may suggest that we provide more opportunities for teacher candidates to acquire more positive self-other perceptions. Self-concept research tells us that how one feels about himself is learned. If it is learned, it is teachable. Too often, those of us in teacher education are dominated by a concern for long-term goals, while the student is fundamentally motivated by short-term goals. Forecasting what a student will need to know six months or two years from now, we operate on the assumption that he, too, perceives such goals as meaningful. It seems logical enough, but unfortunately it doesn't work out too well in practice. Hence much of what we may do with our teacher candidates is non-self-related—that is, to the student it doesn't seem connected with his own life, time, and needs. Rather than talk about group processes in the abstract, why can't we first assist students to a deeper understanding of their own roles in groups in which they already participate? Rather than simply theorize and cite research evidence related to individual differences, why not also encourage students to analyze the individual differences which exist in *this* class at *this* time and then allow them to express and discuss what these differences mean at a more personal level? If one values the self-concept idea at all, then there are literally endless ways to encourage more positive self-other perceptions through teaching strategies aimed at personalizing what goes on in a classroom. Indeed, Jersild [15] has demonstrated that when "teachers face themselves," they feel more adequate as individuals and function more effectively as teachers.

3. If it is true that good teachers are well-informed, then it is clear that we must neither negate nor relax our efforts to provide them with as rich an intellectual background as is possible. Teachers are usually knowledgeable people, and knowledge inculcation is the aspect of preparation with which teacher education has traditionally been most successful. Nonetheless, teachers rarely

15. A. T. Jersild, *When Teachers Face Themselves* (New York: Bureau of Publications, Teachers College, Columbia University, 1955).

fail because of lack of knowledge. They fail more often because they are unable to communicate what they know so that it makes a difference to their students. Which brings us to our final implication for teacher-education programs.

4. If it is true that good teachers are able to communicate what they know in a manner that makes sense to their students, then we must assist our teacher candidates both through example and appropriate experiences to the most effective ways of doing this. Communication is not just a process of presenting information. It is also a function of discovery and the development of personal meanings. I wonder what would happen to our expectations of the teacher's role if we viewed him less as dispenser, answerer, coercer, and provoker and more as stimulator, questioner, challenger, and puzzler. With the former, the emphasis is on "giving to," while with the latter the focus is on "guiding to." In developing ability to hold and keep attention, not to mention techniques of encouraging people to adopt the reflective, thoughtful mood, I wonder what the departments of speech, theater, and drama on our college and university campuses could teach us? We expose our students to theories of learning and personality; perhaps what we need to do now is develop some "theories of presentation" with the help of those who know this field best.

This paper has attempted to point out that even though there is no single best or worst kind of teacher, there are clearly distinguishable characteristics associated with "good" and "bad" teachers. There is no one *best* kind of teaching because there is no *one kind* of student. Nonetheless, there seems to be enough evidence to suggest that whether the criteria for good teaching is on the basis of student and/or peer evaluations or in terms of student achievement gains, there are characteristics between both which consistently overlap. That is, the good teacher is able to influence both student feeling and achievement in positive ways.

Research is teaching us many things about the differences between good and bad teachers and there are many ways we can put these research findings into our teacher-education programs.

Good teachers do exist and can be identified. Perhaps the next most fruitful vineyard for research is in the classrooms of good teachers so we can determine, by whatever tools we have, just what makes them good in the first place.

That teaching is a relatively "high turnover" occupation is undeniable. One way to cut down on job
dissatisfaction is for teachers to make sure they are
taking "compatible" positions in the first place.
Olberg suggests eight questions the prospective
teacher should ask about any potential job.

TEACHER MISFITS
Robert T. Olberg

Within a few years after graduation from college approximately 50
percent of the graduates of teacher education programs have left the
profession. There are many reasons for this rapid attrition. The most
frequent reasons given include marriage, pregnancy and family obli-
gations, military service, further graduate study, and poor personal
adjustment on the job.

Beginning teachers more often are dismissed because of poor
personal adjustment than because of poor teaching techniques.
School principals frequently report that new teachers are released
because they can't "get along" with other faculty or with the
principal. They just don't seem to "fit in."

In these days of relative teacher surplus it is probably true that
many teachers accept positions in districts where they find they
don't "fit in." Prospective teachers should give careful attention to
the philosophy of education held by the principal and teachers at the
time of their initial interview. Below are several key questions each
beginning teacher should consider when assessing whether or not his
philosophy is in agreement with that of the interviewers and of the
school district.

1. Is the teacher's role as you perceive it similar to the roles which
   the teachers in this school are presently fulfilling? In addition to
   regular classroom teaching responsibilities some schools ask the
   teachers to supervise lunch rooms and playgrounds. Other
   schools have faculty teaching in teams or working with para-

From *Contemporary Education,* XLV, 1 (Fall, 1973), pp. 60–61. Copyright 1973 by the
School of Education, Indiana State University, Terre Haute, Indiana. Reprinted by permission of the author and Indiana State University.

professional employees. Still others ask teachers not to get involved with the student's home problems but to stick to the "3 R's."

2. How does the classroom atmosphere in the school compare to the atmosphere which you consider most conducive to learning? For a beginning teacher, nothing is more devastating than to be told by his principal or colleagues that his class is entirely too noisy, when, in fact, he perceived the atmosphere as being a good learning climate. On the other hand, if you will be expected to teach in an unstructured classroom and this makes you uncomfortable, it would be wise to give serious consideration to this conflict.

3. What help or supervision does this school provide for beginning teachers? Some schools employ experienced teachers solely to help neophytes plan, execute, and assess their teaching. Other districts offer no supervision to new teachers. Since the first year of teaching is very often a traumatic year, it is helpful for a beginning teacher to have a mentor, guide, or just a professional friend to whom he can turn if needed.

4. What decisions are left to the teachers? Such decisions might include selection of textbooks, attitudes toward and selection of content to be taught; availability of funds for enrichment activities, and amount of teacher freedom in deciding how to spend these funds. It is important for candidates to know what major decisions teachers make.

5. What is the role of the principal as he perceives it? Principals fulfill various roles such as curriculum innovator, educational leader, evaluator of teachers, disciplinarian, spokesman for the school, and long-range planner. Where does the interviewing principal place his main emphasis? If he doesn't measure up to what you would like in a principal, it is likely to be a point of friction if you teach under his supervision.

6. In what way does the school system encourage professional advancement and growth? Do you have aspirations of administrative or middle echelon teaching positions such as curriculum director or classroom consultant? Some school officials seek qualified persons from among teachers within the school system to fill these positions. Other officials tend to hire new people from outside the system. Are you planning to pursue an advanced educational degree? Some school systems will pay for part or all of the cost incurred while others make no provision for this.

7. What is the socio-economic background of most of the children in the school? Teaching in communities of higher or lower socio-economic backgrounds than your own probably will present additional problems for you. However, you may find this to be a most rewarding experience.
8. What is the relationship between the community and the school? In many communities the school is open to the parents at all times and for any purpose and communication between home and school is openly solicited. In other communities the school communicates with the parents only for the purpose of reporting the progress of the students.

Perhaps you have never been faced with the question—What is your philosophy of education? Your responses to the questions above will at least indicate your general philosophy of education. Matching your philosophy of education with that of a school system cannot guarantee success, but it will certainly remove hurdles which trip many beginning teachers.

Olberg's advice that teachers should locate themselves in congenial situations is good in theory, but
difficult to follow in practice, as Pat Michaels'
experiences show. Actually, her article touches on
social class issues, too: "The student body was split
between the working-class 'greasers' and the middle-class 'scholars' or honors students."

Many questions arise out of this article. After
Michaels realized "that the school was designed to
teach the majority of students to adjust to the lives
already laid out for them after high school," did
she have a right (or even an obligation) not to go
along with this assumption? Are teachers, as William Jennings Bryan said, like house painters—
obligated to do only what those who pay them
require? Or should they be autonomous professionals doing what their own best judgment dictates? Should Michaels have "cooled it" in order to
keep the job? How free should teachers be?

TEACHING AND REBELLION
AT UNION SPRINGS
Patricia Michaels

In 1967 I got a job teaching high school in a small industrial
community in upstate New York. I didn't think the job would have
political significance for me. I had been involved in civil rights
demonstrations and anti-Vietnam marches and in general I identified
with the movement. I had also taught in an urban ghetto school. No
liberal or left activity existed in Union Springs, so I saw my job there
as a retreat from politics and as an opportunity to teach without the
pressures of the ghetto. But, in fact, teaching in Union Springs
turned out to be a profoundly political experience. I learned there
that decent human relations and meaningful work and education are
impossible in this country even in those little red schoolhouses that
seemed impervious to the crisis affecting the rest of society.

Patricia Michaels, "Teaching and Rebellion at Union Springs," *No More Teachers' Dirty
Looks,* vol. 52, no. 5 (January 1971), pp. 262–266. Reprinted by permission.

One of my first discoveries was that most of my students, who looked like Wonder Bread children, were non-college bound and hostile to school. I asked them why they hadn't quit when they were 16. Most replied, like a chorus, "Because to get a good job you have to go to school." They understood that the boredom and discipline were preparation for the future. One boy parroted an administrator on the subject of keeping his shirttails in: "When you work in a factory you're going to have to follow rules you don't like, so you'd better get used to them now."

After a few weeks of teaching, I began to discover that the school was designed to teach the majority of students to adjust to the lives already laid out for them after high school. It reinforced what they had learned at home and in grade school: to blunt feelings, distrust feelings you do have, accept boredom and meaningless discipline as the very nature of things. The faculty and the administration saw themselves as socializers in this process. This point was brought home to me at one faculty meeting following an assembly. In an effort to bring culture to Union Springs, the school sponsored a cello concert, one of several longhair events. The students, tired of having their "horizons broadened," hooted and howled throughout the concert. The cellist was almost as indignant as the teachers and administration. The teachers expressed the sentiment that somehow they had failed to do their job; to train kids to accept things they did not like. Teacher after teacher admitted that while the assembly may have been boring, so were many things in life. *They* had made it; so could the kids. "Culture isn't supposed to be fun," said the principal, "but if you get something out of it, that's all that counts. For most of our kids this is the only time they'll ever get to hear a cellist and their lives will be richer for it."

The school was also designed to promote a definition of work that excluded emotional satisfaction. To the degree that the kids accepted this definition, they distrusted the very classes they enjoyed. Students would often tell me, "This isn't English, it's too much fun," or "School is where you learn—not have a good time." Enjoyment was drinking, speeding cars, minor lawbreaking activities that involved little creativity or effort. Having defined school (i.e., work) as joyless, joy, they thought, must be effortless.

They didn't connect their feelings of depression and anger with the socialization they were undergoing. While putting themselves down as failures, they would tell me everything that was wrong with the school. The petty vandalism, the screaming in the halls, the "cutting up" in class were their means of psychological survival.

They didn't see this behavior as an attack on the school system. They were certain, too, that if they didn't shape up, they would pay a terrible price.

Their response to the first novel we read in class, Warren Miller's *The Cool World*, reflected their sense of futility. They admired Duke, the gang-leader hero, and thought he was "cool" because he said what he felt and did what he wanted. At the same time, he was "stupid" because his actions could only lead to poverty, violence, and death. They were infuriated at the ending of the novel when Duke "gets rehabilitated." In the endings that they wrote as an exercise, they had Duke killed or imprisoned. As one boy wrote, "This was the only honest ending because the price you pay for doing what you want is defeat in one form or another."

Resigned to the "realities" of life, they had difficulty accepting praise. They had been taught that they were unworthy and to distrust anyone who thought they were not. Praise challenged their self-image. John B., for example, was a senior who planned to pump gas after he got out of the army. He also wrote poetry. He alternated between being proud of his work and telling me that it was "bullshit." He was threatened by his creativity. The school had "tracked" him into a "low achiever" class since grade one, and after 18 years he wasn't about to challenge that authoritative definition. The only other job he considered was as a state policeman. "At least you'd have some power," he told me.

The student body was split between the working-class "greasers" and the middle-class "scholars" or honors students. The students from working-class homes saw the honors kids as sellouts, phonies, and undeservedly privileged. The honors kids, for example, had a lounge. The rest of the student body congregated in the bathrooms.

The honors students were more ambivalent in their attitudes toward the greasers. Their own school experience was a grind, and they both resented and envied the relative casualness of the other students.

A few college-bound kids protested against my lenience in grades and the lack of discipline in my classes. They demanded that I lower the grades of the "less gifted" and enforce school rules. Some honors students admitted that behind their demands was a conception of learning as drudgery. Success, in turn, meant the failure of others. But this, they added, was the way things are. Society, they were convinced, owed them nothing. Reality was the status quo, and people should be judged by how well they coped with that reality.

The "scholars'" game in school consisted of conning the teachers. Establish your reputation and slide through. At times, they acknowledged the hypocrisy of the game, but rarely acted on it. While the "scholars" had nothing but contempt for the administration and most of the faculty, they couldn't get close to the other kids because of their unwillingness to give up the privileges that came with being honors students.

The student body was also divided along sexual lines. Men at Union Springs were more individually rebellious; they expressed their hatred of the school in ways that were considered "manly": haphazard disobedience, drinking before coming to school, vandalism. The women, however, were passive about school on a daily basis, since their major concern was the prestige that came from having a boyfriend and their status among the men.

One day I assigned my senior class an article about a girl who had been thrown out of college for living with her boyfriend. The boys in the class acknowledged that while they wouldn't marry a girl who did "that," they didn't think it was the school's right to punish her. The girls said nothing. In their compositions they expressed anger at the injustice of punishing the girl and not the boy. One girl wrote: "It's always the girl who suffers in this situation; nothing ever happens to the boy."

The following day I spoke with the girls (the boys were out of the room) and asked why they hadn't said in class what they had written on their papers. They said that they were afraid. One girl told me that the only time she would talk freely in a class was if no boys whom she liked romantically were present.

On another occasion a boy criticized my assigning a novel that contained obscene language, because, he said, it embarrassed him to read those words in front of girls. At the end of the class, a few girls told me that while people should be free to read and write what they wanted, they were glad at least one boy respected them enough to watch his language.

In spite of these divisions among the students, the oppressiveness of the school sometimes brought them together in action. Smoking in the bathrooms was the most controversial issue in the school. Breaking the smoking rules enraged the teachers. Several of them spent their free time catching the smokers, bringing them into the office, and getting them suspended for three days. The administration, in an act of desperation (20 cigarette butts had been found on the floor in one day), removed the entrance doors to the bathrooms. After unsuccessfully petitioning the principal, 25 students lined up in front of the men's room and refused to proceed to their first-period class. The principal threatened to call the police if they wouldn't obey his order to move.

Inside the faculty room, some teachers said they wanted to bust heads and hoped that the administration would allow it. Others joked about how our students were trying to imitate the college kids.

In an assembly later that afternoon, the principal announced that he was replacing the bathroom doors, but only because of the responsible behavior of the majority of students. "All over the country," he said, "bearded rebels are tearing up the schools and causing trouble, and now we have their younger versions at Union Springs. We know," he added, "that while the troublemakers demonstrate, the cream of the crop is dying in Vietnam. These are the true heroes. The boys who stood in front of the men's room this morning are the riffraff."

The students had not thought of the demonstrators as riffraff. They were among the most popular kids in school. But neither had they seen them as part of a national movement. By making that association, the principal had helped to break down some of the students' antagonisms toward the left. Later, when SDS people tried to link up with students at Union Springs, some of the groundwork had already been laid by the principal.

By my second year at Union Springs, I was intensely sensitive to the repressiveness of the school system and my own role in it. My way of dealing with that was to make my classes more relevant to students' lives. I told them to write about about what they felt in the language with which they were most comfortable. The first papers I received were filled with obscenity, and I criticized them on stylistic rather than moral grounds. In the second papers, the students' efforts to shock me changed into honest attempts at good writing. I told one class of seniors who were working on short stories that I would mimeograph and distribute some of their work. The most popular story was a satire concerning soldiers in Vietnam; it was sprinkled with obscenity. I said that I would reprint the story as promised, but I wanted the class to be aware of the risk. They all agreed that the author had written what he felt and that there was nothing objectionable about the piece.

A few weeks later the principal told me that I would have to "cease and desist" from accepting students' work that made use of "poor" language. The principal also criticized me for playing rock music in my classes. "You're allowing too much freedom in your classes." He told me that while these methods were all right for "Negro kids," since "that's the kind of life they're used to," or for very responsible college-bound students, they were not all right for youngsters whose future success in the army or on their jobs depended on their following rules.

As a result of my classes, he said, students were becoming defiant and teachers and parents were complaining. He said that I was doing a disservice to students in allowing them a freedom that they were not going to have later on.

Up to that point I had not thought of my work as political. In fact, I had berated myself because I hadn't spent more time talking about the war, blacks, tracking, and so on. Movement friends I had spoken with warned me that far from "radicalizing" my students, I was providing them with a "groovy classroom," making school more palatable and adjustment to a corrupt system easier for them. After speaking with the principal, however, I concluded that my classroom methods were political. In order for the students to fit into the society, they had to believe certain things about themselves, about their teachers, and about their work. By permitting my students to use their own language in the classroom and to wander the halls without passes, by helping them to discover that schoolwork could be creative, I was challenging the values of the school and, therefore, those of society. That was the beginning for the students of understanding the relation between their lives and the movement.

I told the principal that I could not comply with his order but would discuss the issue with my class. He warned me that I was close to losing my job and that he couldn't figure out why I wanted to be a martyr for the students.

The next day I told my class what had happened. They agreed that we should continue to do what we were doing, although a few students argued that I was teaching revolution and disrespect for authority. One boy told me that his father said that if I were teaching in Russia I would have been jailed long ago. Other students defended our classroom activities, saying that this was the first time they'd been able to express themselves in school. "Everybody in town is calling Mrs. Michaels a Communist," one girl said. "Everything they don't like around here they call Communist. We've done nothing wrong and neither has she. Those who don't like it here should transfer to another class, and not ruin it for the rest of us."

Although the students expressed concern about my losing my job, they knew that the issue was them, as well as myself. It wasn't *my* class that was on the line, but *our* class. Crucial to their understanding of the issue as it deepened was my continuing to inform them of developments. By breaking down the traditional teacher-student relationship, I could speak with them not only about their own oppression but mine as well. In that process, the students had begun to listen to me when I raised questions about the war, the draft, and the tracking system, although they weren't ready yet to ask those questions for themselves.

In January of my second year, a local SDS chapter sponsored a festival and several workshops for high school students. I announced the events to my students and urged them to go. In spite of warnings from administrators, teachers, and parents, a number of students attended. Several teachers showed up to "learn about SDS," but the students knew that they were spies.

The SDS organizer asked the students if they wanted the teachers to stay. "They are part of the reason we're here," one boy said. "We can never talk honestly in their presence and we can't now. They have to leave." When the teachers refused to go, the students walked out of the room and set up another workshop—a liberating experience, defiance without punishment, a taste of collective power.

The festival changed the students' attitude toward the left. Their disdain for the "peace freaks" was based on a stereotype of the cowardly college student. Their brothers were fighting in Vietnam and if the leftists took their beliefs seriously, they "would be fighting too." One boy told me that the only time he took college demonstrators seriously was when he saw them on TV at the Chicago convention. The students at Union Springs disliked the college protestors because they saw them as a privileged group and they couldn't figure out why they were rebelling.

Students at Union Springs felt ambivalent about leftist culture. Although they talked about "filthy hippies," they listened to the Doors and the Rolling Stones. Rock music was vital to their lives. To hate hippies was difficult for them because Mick Jagger was one, too. The longhaired radicals who spoke to them at the SDS festival acted tough, brave, and "tuned" into the kids' experiences. That the principal and teachers defined these people as outlaws only made them more attractive.

The festival and the presence of high school students at an SDS function frightened the community. The newspapers were filled with letters for the next few weeks condemning the SDS and the students who attended. Kids brought the newspapers to school and we discussed reasons for the community's and administration's terror at SDS presence. Gradually the kids began to connect the local issue with the anti-Communist, pro-war rhetoric they had heard all their lives. They had begun to identify their own rebellion with the rebellion of the people they had earlier called "rioters," "peace creeps," and "commies."

Earlier that year I had talked with some students about Cuba. They had insisted that Castro was a dictator who filled the prisons with anyone who disagreed with him, and that the United States ought to invade the island. When I questioned the reliability of media reporting, they didn't respond. Only after they read the distortions about themselves in the local newspaper stories did my argument have some meaning for them. When they were not involved in their own struggle, they accepted what the TV and the newspapers told them. They had even resented my raising questions about Cuba, Vietnam, or blacks. As one student told me after I talked with him about the war, "Our government couldn't be doing all of those terrible things." What made those "terrible things" believable to him was his new-found consciousness of what the school had been doing to him every day and how the principal and teachers responded when he began to act.

In the months that followed the SDS conference, I talked with students in class, during free periods, and in my home, where many of them became frequent visitors, about everything from Vietnam to dating problems. In April of that year, some of them joined an SDS demonstration against Westmoreland.

As the opportunity to rebel began to develop at Union Springs High, many of the women held back. They didn't see the relevance of the rebellion to their own lives, and some even discouraged the boys from participating since it disrupted the normal social life of the school. The girls who did participate, however, were the most militant and committed of the rebels. Some were girls whose dating unpopularity had made high school hell for them and who identified with me because in my classroom they could assert themselves in ways that won them respect. Others were girls who were more assured of their popularity and, because they were not hung up in the individualism of the boys, could act together more easily.

The male students, on the other hand, were beginning to challenge the traditional values of individualism and competitiveness that had made it difficult for them to rebel together. Previously much of their prestige had depended upon *individual* defiance. As one boy told me earlier that year: "I talk back to teachers, but when everybody starts doing it, it doesn't mean anything anymore."

About two weeks after the Westmoreland demonstration, seven students decided that they were going to boycott an honors assembly and asked if they could use my room. The assembly was an annual ritual to humiliate the majority of students and to honor the handful who had "achieved." The students felt that their refusal to participate was justified, but were uncomfortable about the action. One boy said, "Listen, I don't like this: 'Cutting up' in class is fun, but this is different. It's too serious. I'm not scared or anything, but everybody's acting like it's such a big deal." The boy may have expected punishment for his action, but he felt threatened because he had involved himself with six others in a collective decision to defy the school system. If they escaped without punishment, he would be only one among seven heroes. If they got into trouble, his act couldn't be dismissed as a prank. Another boy replied, "This is different from setting a cherry bomb off in the halls and running away. We're identifying ourselves and we're trying to figure out why we're doing it. If you don't see that, you'd better leave."

In early May, I was fired. Many students prepared to sit in. They made signs, held meetings, and argued with their parents, who urged them not to get involved. The administration responded with threats of police, suspensions, and warnings to seniors who "might not graduate" if they participated. Administrators phoned the parents of the student leaders and urged them to keep their kids at home. Police watched the entrance of my house. On the morning of the sit-in, teachers in the halls urged the students to hurry to class. Many students did stay home. Others were confused and stood around the halls. About 50 sat in. Six students were suspended for five days, and one boy was beaten by the vice-principal when he refused to move on to class.

The next morning the principal met with the students and tried to calm them. There wasn't anything they or he could do to get me back in school, he said. But he would listen to their grievances about the school. After a few days of restlessness and more meetings with students, Union Springs High had ostensibly returned to normal.

But many students had changed during my two years there. When I first met them, they had been resigned to the limited world that the school had defined for them. They didn't believe that they were capable of creating anything larger. Experiences in my classes and their struggle opened the possibility of new definitions of work, of teachers, and of themselves. When they had to defend those discoveries to parents, contemporaries, and school personnel, the students learned how to work together.

I did not come to Union Springs to be a political organizer. I came to teach. But I refused to be the teacher that both the administration and the students expected me to be. I had rejected the role of cop and socializer not out of any revolutionary commitment, but out of my need to relate to my students. This same need made me reject the labels "lower track," "non-college bound," and "slow learner" that were placed on my students. My refusal to play the traditional teacher role was linked to my refusal to accept them as inferior because they had been treated as such. By breaking down their stereotypes of themselves and of me, I also helped them break down their self-confining images of the world around them.

One letter I received from a female student indicated the achievement as well as the limitations of my work at Union Springs: "Up until you came to us, I'm sure no student knew where he or she stood in the school. They didn't know the powers they had. Now we know them and are trying to use them as best we can. It's going to take time to get organized, but the way things are going now, I'm sure the time will come. I remember the time I was accused of smoking. The principal told me that I had no alternative but to admit I was smoking. I told him that I wasn't and that he could get the Supreme Court on it if he wanted to, but he couldn't prove it. That was the first time I really used the power I had and I won. It didn't seem like much power when it was all over, but I can still remember looking at his face and noticing that his smirk was gone and that he really looked afraid of me. I don't know if you realize it or not, but that small power has affected almost every kid in school and I think that's why you were fired."

Energy had been released at Union Springs, but where will students go with this energy, what will they do with it in that same school this year, in the army, in the factories, and in their marriages? The students were ready to join a movement. Right now there is no movement for them to join. Those who are still in school write me that Union Springs is quiet again. Those who are out say pretty much the same thing. The movement that speaks to the needs they experienced and acted on at Union Springs is yet to be created.

Ghetto schools, nearly everyone says, are the worst kind to teach in. Sociologist Gerald Levy spent a year teaching with and watching thirty-five new teachers at "Midway." Twenty-one of them, he reports, were destroyed. Most of the new teachers, apparently, saw only two choices open to them: either (1) to be a "nice guy" and try to bargain with the students to get them to do what the teacher wanted, or (2) to be tough and repressive like the established (chronic) teachers they deplored. The reader may well ask whether there are other possibilities.

ACUTE TEACHERS
Gerald E. Levy

About half of Midway's staff are acute teachers, most of whom are products of an emergency summer program of college-level courses designed to alleviate the acute shortage of teachers in ghetto schools. Open to anyone with a college degree, the emergency program is paid for by the city and guarantees the untrained recruit a job in the fall. In exchange, the acute recruit has to sign a statement pledging to teach for a year.

The "open recruitment" of teachers attracts a mixed bag of applicants whose motives, interests, and ages are determined by a variety of factors not necessarily directly related to teaching.

Among the recruits who finally received positions at Midway, ten can be described as wishing to pursue a teaching career. Eight of them are women who have just graduated from college. Two are mothers in their forties whose children have grown up and who wish to begin or return to a teaching career. Some of these more career-minded teachers actually want to teach in a ghetto school.

The rest of the acute teachers are primarily motivated by their desire not to be drafted. They enrolled in the emergency summer program because it offered them the opportunity to avoid the war in Vietnam. Several afternoon sessions of the training program were

From *Ghetto School* by Gerald E. Levy, Copyright © 1970 by Western Publishing Company, Inc., reprinted by permission of The Bobbs-Merrill Company, Inc.

devoted entirely to convincing the 1000 or more draft-age men that their draft deferments would be forthcoming upon completion of their training and assignment to a school.

The vast majority of acute teachers are just out of college, graduate schools, and previous jobs which did not offer them protection from the war. Thus, young aspiring lawyers, accountants, businessmen, and graduate students in psychology, sociology, political science, and history comprise a major block of teachers at Midway. After being in the school for a short time, these teachers come to feel that they are doing a form of alternate service not too different from their fantasies about Vietnam. They often joke about the advantages and disadvantages of the two alternatives. In view of their experience with the children, the war imagery can take on a reality which an outsider could not imagine to be appropriate to a school. After particularly bad days in the classroom, these acute teachers congregate and compare their difficulties with the children. The teacher having the most difficulty with his class is soothed with the comment, "At least it's not as bad as Vietnam."

In spite of their questionable motives for coming to Midway and the forced or tentative nature of their commitment, many acute teachers would like to do a good job. In their own and others' eyes, they would like to be successful. Many want good references for future jobs. Almost all would like to feel that they were earning their pay.

THE AMELIORATIVE IMPULSE

Acute teachers initially express no public disdain for Black or Puerto Rican children. Indeed, many acute teachers pride themselves on their liberal and progressive politics, their opposition to the war in Vietnam, and their support of the War on Poverty and other ameliorative programs. Some of the graduate students see themselves as budding college professors, intellectuals, and social critics. A few have read Paul Goodman and would like to change the school system. Several have been active in the civil rights movement and would like to continue their civil rights activities as teachers. A few have had jobs in welfare, social work, and poverty programs. These latter are less optimistic about achieving their political goals in the school.

When the acute teachers arrive at Midway, their basic sympathies are with the children and the parents. They would like to "reach out to" or "make it" with the children whom they view as "disadvantaged" individuals to be "helped" through "sensitive and creative teaching." But these humanistic intentions and sympathies are not, in most instances, based on personal experience with ghetto inhabitants. Acute teachers have learned about the ghetto from newspapers, magazines, TV, movies, and books. Their sympathies have been cultivated in suburbs and universities which are totally divorced from the objects of the sympathy. They assume they can successfully apply their suburban and academic morality to Midway School.

THE RHETORIC OF ORIENTATION

Before being assigned to a school, these good-intentioned acute teachers are given a brief orientation in the district office by the district superintendent:

> We have called this meeting to accomplish three goals. We would like to tell you what our district is like. We would like to assign you to a school which is closest to your home. And we want to personally welcome you to the district. District 7 has eighteen elementary schools, four junior high schools and two high schools. It encompasses the Rogers Park and Randolph Park areas. In this district we have a very active community and school board which is interested in only one thing—good schools and good teachers. We have in District 7 the support of the community. Now the principals in District 7 do not think that they are God's answer to education. They are down to earth, accessible, and want to do everything in their power to help you new teachers to have a satisfying and successful experience.
>
> Now we do have problems in our schools. However you will be happy to teach in this district. You will not be afraid to come to any school in this district. There has not been any picketing. We are happy that the community is behind us. So now that we have cleared up any misconceptions you might have about the district, we can turn to more technical matters.
>
> First of all, I have to tell you something that may disturb many of you. Those of you who are from the high school part of the emergency summer training program, I have to tell you that you will be teaching elementary school. There are just no vacancies in the secondary schools and we only have vacancies in the elementary schools. Now if you can get some secondary school outside the district to request you I will release you. But if for any other reason you wish to change to another district I will not release you. Now I know that many of our high school people who are young men will take the assignment because of the draft. I will not go further into this.

The superintendent conveys to the acute teachers that problems which occur in the district are not occurring, and reminds them of the consequences of refusing the assignment.

Upon being assigned to Midway, acute teachers are informed by chronic teachers that almost everything they were told by Superintendent Stratton and his assistant Golden is the opposite of what actually exists in the school. Chronic teachers say that "the school is in a state of complete chaos," that "Dobson doesn't do anything but sit in his office," that "all Morton and Ryley do is tell the teachers to meet deadlines and send them notes when they don't," and that "Mrs. Jackson wants to fire all of the white Jewish teachers" and "take over the school":

> The administration will attempt to hide and gloss over a lot of problems in the school, but you will find out soon enough how difficult the children will be and what you will have to do to survive.

Interspersed between these conversations with chronic teachers are formal orientation conferences with the administration:

> *Morton:* Now I'm just going to say a few important things until the principal comes in. School will be on three different sessions because the new wing is not completed. Now one of the most important things in getting started is the establishment of routines for the children and for yourself. Now you're going to have problem children—children who will give you trouble. The minute you have a problem you can't expect us to immediately do something about it. But you can keep a file on him, an anecdotal record, and if patterns emerge, we'll eventually take care of it. Now of course the instructors in the universities say "be creative with the children," "work with them," "love them." But this cannot be accomplished without routines and we expect you to concentrate on this aspect.

(Dobson is introduced)

> *Dobson:* You constitute almost half of our present staff and we have the job of making you into teachers. It takes anywhere from three to five years to become a teacher. Some make it in less. Your first year of teaching will be the most difficult job you will have in your life. Plan books are to be submitted every two weeks. Sometimes they will have comments on them. Sometimes they will have few or none. We will read them carefully or casually, depending on the individual involved or the situation. The purpose of the plan book is to see that you have a plan and cover the curriculum so that you know what you are doing. The children will do everything in their power to confuse you, take advantage of you, obstruct your teaching until you are firm with them—until you let them know that you know what you are doing. We have one guidance counselor and referral is made to her through the supervisors. But remember you are responsible for classroom discipline. The more you have to call a supervisor for help, the less efficient you are in classroom control. You are to use anything and everything to maintain classroom control except physical violence. First of all, it's against the law. Also, parents are sensitive to any physical violence and children will sometimes tell their parents. No matter what a parent tells you, even if she says, "Give him a good beating," never lay a hand on a

child in anger because there can be repercussions. It's all right to put your arm around a child if you have established rapport with him or if it is an appropriate situation for touching him—putting your arm around him in a friendly way.

Even stronger is the chronic teacher's stress on the overriding necessity for control.

A lot of new teachers, well, they want to be very idealistic—want to be a buddy to the kids—have a nice relaxed atmosphere in the classroom. Well, if you do that the kids will destroy you. You've got to be firm at the beginning, keep them busy, organize the routines. Don't take any nonsense. Then, after a while you can accomplish something and let up later. But if you start off on the wrong track, it will take you maybe a whole year to control the class. The first few weeks, if you accomplish nothing but control, you are doing a job.

Thus, the acute teacher is advised that his inability to control the children will be taken as evidence of his inadequacy as a teacher. The teacher who loses control becomes dependent on other teachers and administrators to regain it. But other teachers resent having to "stop whatever they are doing" to help a teacher "break up a fight," "remove a child from a classroom," "take a disruptive child to the office," or "quiet down a class." The teacher who relies heavily on other teachers and administrators for the solution of his problems with children gets a reputation for incompetence. He is thought to be "not doing a job." All his humanitarian dreams, liberal ideas, and sympathetic inclinations are redefined as the basis of failure. His commitment to becoming competent, to being self-sufficient in his work, to working for his pay, and to his self-image as a white-collar professional is threatened by the prospect that those teaching methods demanded of him will be inconsistent with his personal morality.

The practical education of the acute teacher begins when he observes at first hand how children are treated at Midway. He sees them being marched around the hallways. In a *controlled* classroom, they sit in their seats with their hands folded, go to the blackboard, clean up the floor, get their coats, put them away, clean the erasers, sharpen pencils, line up straight, two by two. The typical teacher gives commands in a stentorian voice. Often he shouts them. The volume of the commands increases in relation to the degree that they are not being followed. When commands and shouts do not work, he uses the hand or the stick. He "knocks heads." To the acute teacher it looks like what he had imagined boot camp might be like.

The military techniques and the methods of violence that he observes conflict with the moral codes of his own academic and suburban past. He views them as ethically and aesthetically repugnant. The acute teacher finds himself in the position of being expected to participate in activities for which he would immediately condemn himself as well as others. Nevertheless he must face the practical problem of teaching the children. The children severely test his ability to hold to his previous values.

THE EFFORT TO BARGAIN WITH THE CHILDREN

In spite of the warning and example of administrators and chronic teachers, an acute teacher is likely to attempt a soft line with the children. He may greet his class informally, not demand that they keep a perfectly straight line to the classroom, and not try immediately to establish rigid routines. He allows the children drinks of water and trips to the bathroom. He does not immediately clamp down when the children attempt to talk to each other, leave their seats, or leave the classroom. He may even look the other way when he observes children eating in class. He initiates a policy in keeping with his liberal ideology that enables him to sustain his feelings of moral superiority over the chronic teachers.

He may assume that if given a certain amount of leeway, the children will recognize his partiality toward them. He hopes that the children will reciprocate by appreciating his humanitarian efforts. The teacher's easy-going approach is an indirect plea to the children for exemption from the battle over control.

THE ACUTE TEACHER IS DESTROYED

The children do not take up the bargain on his terms. Seeing that the teacher is not concerned with a straight line, the children dispense with the line. If he fails to clamp down on talking, eating, and moving around, the children talk, eat, move, and leave the classroom as much as possible. Children see the liberal policy not as an invitation to participate in a well-mannered civilized classroom, but as an opportunity to realize objectives of their own. The acute teacher is at first not aware that the children may have their own objectives.

Still the acute teacher's liberalism is conditional on the children's empathy toward his problem. He expects the children to be as sensitive to his problem as he feels he is to their problem. He reacts angrily to their lack of appreciation and unwillingness to uphold their end of the bargain. He feels personally betrayed and begins to shout at the children, demanding that they keep quiet, stay in their seats, and stop eating. The demands are ineffective, for he had granted these freedoms previously. So the teacher must begin to threaten. He threatens to send a child to the principal's office, write a letter home to his mother, or have him suspended. He may chase a child around the room, pound his fist on the table or threaten to hit him. With each betrayal of the teacher's sense of decency and fairness, he depends more and more on the very "indecent" techniques he previously condemned.

But the shouting and threatening fail to pacify the children. For they are cognizant of the teacher's inexperience. They are furthermore aware that his permissive policy has been an experiment. The children distinguish between acute and chronic teachers' use of techniques. The shouts and threats are not part of a disciplinary plan but merely an emotional response to the situation. Thus, the children regard attempts at control as a loss of control. They experience the loss of control as a higher form of victory than the freedom to eat, talk, or move around. The more the teacher screams at the children, pounds his fist on the table, and chases them around the room, the greater their delight in the victory.

The children are delighted because they are invulnerable. The teacher is making all sorts of threats he has no intention of carrying out. They are extremely sensitive to the discrepancy between threats and action. The discrepancy is established by calling a series of bluffs. The rebel leader tests the teacher to see how far he can go without being punished. If the teacher backs down the rebel leader ups the ante. The called bluff and the upped ante define for the less courageous children the level on which they can safely pursue their disobedience. If the rebel leader screams at the teacher and gets away with it, the other children feel they can talk to each other without consequence. If he runs around the room, they get out of their seats and walk around. If he starts a fight, they run around the room. Soon all the children, even those who are usually obedient, start leaving their seats, getting drinks, talking, screaming, fighting, eating—anything that is at least one degree less extreme than the rebel leader's activity.

Finally, all commands are useless. The teacher gives orders knowing they are not going to be obeyed. The children know that he acknowledges his impotence. Each escalation in shouting, stamping, and pounding is seen by the children as a further admission of impotence. It takes ever more extreme measures to get a response from them because they immediately become accustomed to the current level of escalation as the norm. The more the teacher escalates, the more he establishes his impotence.

The teacher's awareness of his impotence finally precipitates a desperate act. After shouting at the children with no apparent results or just staring at them for a few minutes, he suddenly grabs a child and makes an example of him in front of the class by dragging him across the room, twisting his arm, grabbing him on the back of the neck, or hitting him on the shoulder or face. He may even drag him out of the room to an administrator's office and deposit him there.

Control in the classrooms of some acute teachers breaks down to the point where the teacher feels like a cop in a ghetto riot. Fights break out. Books, spitballs, thumbtacks, paper airplanes, paper clips, food, and chairs fly across the room. Occasionally, children consciously caricature a riot. They stage elaborate fights, organize group chanting, and sing dirty songs for the teachers' benefit. Regardless of the intensity of the disruption, the children never lose sight of the teacher's response. Their delight in their activity is directly proportional to his desperation.

In the process of losing control, frenzied teachers lose all perspective. Their faces get red and puffed. Their clothing is rumpled and covered with chalk dust. At times, classes and teachers become completely hysterical. In the midst of the hysteria, a teacher may beg the children for a few minutes of peace. Another may try a number of things in rapid succession, hoping that one of them will work. First he screams at the children. Then he makes a joke. Then he appeals to their guilt. Then he begs again. Some are driven to tears. Finally he makes an example of someone. The more hysterical the teacher becomes the more desperately random his behavior.

The children's energy and staying power is limitless. With each hysterical outburst the children appear more confident in their disobedience and intent on their rebellion. Very rapidly the acute teacher is physically and emotionally exhausted.

The acute teacher responds to his loss of control with feelings of personal inadequacy and unworthiness. Among men, these feelings border on anxiety about their masculinity. They begin to compare themselves unfavorably to the chronic male teachers who strut around the school. Among certain teachers the initial experience with the children is destructive to the point where previous successes, financial, academic, occupational, and erotic, temporarily lose their salience. They talk about their inability to sleep nights worrying about what the children are going to do to them the following day. Their experience in Midway School causes deep personal fear, even terror.

The sense of being destroyed is accompanied by an awareness that they are reneging on their intentions to be human with the children and their desire to be a respectable professional. The anger felt toward the children for not allowing them to live out their liberal ideas and be a good teacher is complicated by an awareness of using "chronic techniques." At different points for different teachers a sharp battle line is eventually drawn between themselves and the children.

For the teacher, the crucial issue is then defined as who is going to be destroyed. One put it tightly, "It's them or us." Reluctantly, the teacher then must admit that he is beginning to brutalize the children. If brutalization of the children (and himself) is seen as the only basis for survival and guilt is the only possible response to his brutalizing, the acute teacher is destroyed.

In actual fact twenty-one of the thirty-five acute teachers were "destroyed." In educational circles outside of Midway School the term "being destroyed" is defined as "failure" because the teacher becomes "personally involved" and is unable to control his class. The phrase "being destroyed" conforms to usage at Midway School where everyone knows personally many examples of teachers who were driven to the verge of madness before they began to give up the teaching methods which they hoped would be consistent with their ethical and moral standards. Under ordinary circumstances some of these teachers would have quit their jobs and left Midway. But as devastating as their experience is, Midway as a way of life is thought to be a better alternative than Vietnam. They wish to avoid Vietnam for the same ideological reasons that they hope to avoid the methods of the chronic teachers. Thus when their own teaching methods don't work, and they feel destroyed, the acute teachers react as if they had been sent to Vietnam and look for any means to survive.

CLOSING RANKS WITH THE CHRONIC TEACHERS

Previous to their initial encounter with the children, chronic teachers were objects of moral indignation for acute teachers. Initial observations of chronic teachers at work confirmed their preconceptions about the quality of teachers in ghetto schools. But now, contact with the children has made it difficult for acute teachers to sustain an unambivalently critical attitude toward those teachers whose advice and warnings about their relationships to the children have turned out to be so accurate.

Teachers who, a few days earlier, criticized and condemned the "immoral" activity of the chronic teachers, actively seek their advice. Desperate acute teachers buttonhole well-known chronic teachers in the teachers' lunchroom, the halls, and the general office, to seek information as to how they can gain control and prevent their own destruction. Chronic teachers are generous and explicit with their advice. They view the interest in their techniques as a further indication of their competence, and a vindication of their position toward the children.

Acute teachers seek the ear of other acute teachers who they hope will not moralize about their behavior with the children. To his relief the acute teacher discovers that many others are having similar problems. Whenever the opportunity arises, acute teachers congregate in the lunchroom, the office, the halls, and outside their classrooms to relieve each other of their burdens.

The mutual confessions often become contests. The object is to determine who is having the greatest difficulty with the children. Teachers claim that they have been more totally destroyed and have taken more drastic counter-measures than any other teacher. Through competitive confessions the acute teachers exempt each other from any moral accountability for their actions with the children. Add to this the advice-seeking from chronic teachers, and the acute teacher has taken the first hesitant steps toward a redefinition of his *modus operandi* in the school.

Once the acute teacher realizes the impracticality and self-destructive effects of his ethical standards, the emphasis of his activity rapidly shifts from attempting to maintain the standards to developing a method by which he can survive. Only when experience forces the acute teacher to loosen the moral inhibitions of his past can he hope to attain the "experience" necessary to becoming a "competent" teacher. Having learned that control is synonymous with education and now being willing to try anything to establish control, he has adopted the very moral psychology he would have needed to survive in Vietnam.

Nearly all teachers want to feel successful. Yet
many people find themselves in school rooms
where things do not seem to be going very well.
Kim Marshall was, by his own declaration, in just
such a pinch when he decided to try "learning
stations." They worked for him. Perhaps the moral
of his experience is not that everyone else should
try learning stations, but that if one way of approaching a teaching situation does not work, it
may be time to try something else.

THE LEARNING STATION WAY
Kim Marshall

After an almost totally disastrous first year at the King School in
Boston, I discovered learning stations in summer school and decided
to try them in my sixth grade class in the fall of 1970. So I took a
deep breath, pushed the desks into groups, each one for a different
subject, and wrote worksheets for each station—math, English, social
studies, spelling, creative writing, general and reading. On the first
day, the kids came in and found seven worksheets tucked into
"pockets" taped to the side of a desk at each station. That arrangement led them to circulate around the room musical-chairs fashion,
stopping at each station to do the worksheets.

The system, such as it was, had an immediate and dramatic effect
on my teaching. I found myself spending most of my time actually
teaching and talking to kids individually or in small groups, and the
struggle for control was superseded by a beehive of academic activities, conversations and flirtations, all going on at the same time, all
legal. Yet the place didn't fall apart; and in retrospect, I think the
most important thing holding it together was that I insisted that each
student hand in seven finished worksheets by the end of the day. At
first it seemed like a lot of work to some of the kids, but they soon
realized that there would never be more than seven sheets, that the
material was tailored to their interests and abilities, and was quite

Reprinted by special permission from *Learning,* The Magazine for Creative Teaching, 1973.
© 1973 by Education Today Company, 530 University Avenue, Palo Alto, California
94301.

often fun to do. So they cheerfully accepted hard work in return for freedom, and I had very little trouble convincing them to get through their stations.

So things went well for a few weeks. Kids circulated happily from one station to another, and there was a kind of treasure-hunt quality to moving around the room. The worksheets at each station were always fresh and often contained incidents and names from the class or stories of recent events in the news (Arab hijackings and Angela Davis were big that September). Very quickly I began to feel like a good teacher and spent almost no time bellowing to the whole class or dealing with "discipline" problems.

I found it necessary to address the class as a group less and less; I did so only if there was something I wanted to discuss or go over, or if things got too noisy or hectic. Even though there were seven different pieces of work being done simultaneously in the room, most of it was self-explanatory to most of the kids, and the remaining problems I could solve if I moved fast and succeeded in juggling jealous personalities. In the early weeks, the work time filled almost the entire day and kept the place surprisingly stable, to the point where there could be a small riot out in the corridor and the kids in my room wouldn't even notice it.

What kind of class was this I was running? There was a lot of freedom and movement and a constant hum of noise, which I suppressed only if it got too loud; there was a lot of work being done and a lot of nonacademic activities and conversations as well; and some of the work at the social studies and general and reading stations was quite unconventional. But while many people in the school regarded this kind of classroom as nothing less than revolutionary and subversive, it was hardly an open classroom.

The only real choice the kids were making was the *order* in which they did the seven worksheets. They still had to finish all the papers or I would keep them after school. The kids couldn't do other work or projects instead of a worksheet because they never asked and I never suggested any. They couldn't leave the room without a pass. They couldn't play cards or other games. There were no books or magazines in the room. And the worksheets in the four primary subjects were quite narrowly focused, the essential objective being to prepare them for very conventional tests on Friday. Their grades on these tests went onto progress charts on the wall—full boxes for A's, half boxes for B's and C's, a diagonal line for a failing grade. (I did allow students to retake the tests and change their standing on the charts.) In each of the 36 weeks of the year, we covered a new skill in math and English, a new topic in social studies and a new list of 20 spelling words, most of which I gleaned from "official" sixth grade curricula.

A pretty uptight regime, no? Not a classroom that John Holt would think was groovy, nor one that would escape the charge of radical educators that it was mere sugar-coating on the poisoned apple of conventional education. Yet in September of 1970, nobody could have convinced me that I hadn't made a real breakthrough in classroom techniques and successfully neutralized the pressures on the classroom from uptight parents, administrators, colleagues and kids who had a deeply ingrained notion of the way the class was "spozed to be."

I was wildly excited because I felt I had a system that satisfied the most conservative pressures (stiff work requirements, conventional curriculum, progress charts), yet gave the kids freedom to interact naturally, make some choices, do creative writing and topical reading and get truly individualized attention from me. I felt the system also liberated my own teaching talents by allowing me to write my own curriculum and teach kids in manageable groups or all alone. And last, it seemed to have ended the constant battle for order in the classroom by decentralizing activity and setting up the place so that it virtually ran itself. Learning stations also opened the door to one of the most delightful sets of personal relationships I have ever had, thus creating an atmosphere in which both the kids and I grew enormously.

I have used the learning-station system for three years now, but it hasn't stayed the same for more than a month at a time.

The first change came when the kids decided they didn't want to keep moving around the room to all those seven stations. What if you felt like doing creative writing and all the seats at that station were full? What if your friend was just finishing the one station you had left to visit and you couldn't sit with him? What if you were tired and just didn't feel like moving around? Moreover, why go all the way to the math station when all that was there was a jive worksheet that could be done at the North Pole as well as the math station? So the kids quickly modified my system by making a quick trip around the room to collect the seven papers, then staying put at one station with their friends.

At first I saw this as a grave threat and fought it. But one night I asked myself, why not? What intrinsic value was there in having them move around the room, unless I was going to put a great many props at the different stations—math games and puzzles at the math station, maps and globes and artifacts at the social studies station, dictionaries and word games at the spelling station—and wrote the worksheets so that they led the kids to use these materials?

I didn't feel able to write that kind of worksheet and couldn't afford all that stuff, so the value of moving around the room was simply social, giving kids a chance to meet each other and make friends. Now that friendships had more or less formed for the rest of the year, I allowed the children to sit in groups all day, and began putting the worksheet pockets on the walls. It turned out not to be the end of the system—just an admission that it wasn't a learning-station system per se. (I admit that it's a misnomer, but I have continued to use it for sentimental reasons.)

The next crisis came when a lot of the kids got too fast and began finishing all the worksheets by lunch. Later, some of them were finishing by morning recess. This presented me with the problem of kids rattling around an otherwise empty room all afternoon with an "I've-done-my-work-so-why-should-I-do-anything?" attitude. It also tested my belief in the system I was using. I knew that seven worksheets were more than an honest day's work for sixth graders and certainly more than many conventional classes in the same school were plodding through in lock step in two days. So why did I have to put up with these noisy, empty afternoons? What was I doing wrong?

The problem was that I wasn't playing the game of stretching work throughout the day and chewing up spare time with little five- or ten-minute breaks, meaningless busywork and housekeeping activities. I wasn't controlling the pace at which the kids were doing their work, and I was giving them enough help both in person and in the content of the worksheets to enable them to zip through the day's labors quickly. The system also encouraged the kids to work very hard for two or three hours because there was a finite amount of work to do and a definite reward at the end. The freedom at the end of the work struck most kids as a fine deal, so they threw themselves into the work with real gusto, certain that I wasn't going to trick them by heaping more work on them as soon as they finished.

So I convinced myself that I wasn't doing anything wrong, that my class should simply be allowed to go home two hours before the rest of the school. When this proved impractical, I had to face increasingly ugly discipline problems and loud, obnoxious behavior in the second half of each day. My own sense of humor and ability to see crazy situations as funny tended to evaporate at around 1 p.m., and that only fed the flames.

My first counterstrategy was to try stalling at the start of the day, instigating discussions and going over papers from the day before and thus keeping from putting out the station worksheets until around 10 o'clock. The kids promptly complained that I was holding them back and spoiling their free time and retaliated by doing the work even faster or finding where I had hidden the worksheets and doing them secretly while I stalled. I tried making the worksheets longer and meatier, and I started typing them, which allowed me to squeeze more time-consuming material onto each page. This was fine but caused the kids to heave even noisier sighs of relief when they finished plowing through the work.

Not only did I lack a plan for the latter part of the day, but both the kids and I lacked the will to make proper use of that time because we thought we had already done a fine day's work. I prayed for a schedule that sent them out to their art, science, music, gym and shop classes in the last two periods of the day knowing full well as I did so that every other teacher in the school was praying for the same thing.

Eventually a number of obvious solutions emerged. I played songs on a tape recorder and had the kids read along with the lyrics. We played charades and other guessing games. We read plays. We occasionally had discussions, despite the fact I am the world's worst leader of discussions.

Slowly, as my pay increased and I got my personal spending under control, I bought some old typewriters, games, more and more paperback books and a rug for one corner. And the loose time began to take care of itself.

During the 1972–73 school year, I got together in a two-room team-teaching arrangement with a guy who had the energy and imagination to bring in decent art projects and movies on a regular basis. We also instituted a quiet reading time in the last 50 minutes of every day when kids would have to choose a book or magazine and read it in tomblike silence. This was a great success, providing welcome relief from a rising noise level and for frayed nerves in the last part of the afternoon. Moreover, it proved an excellent strategy for getting kids immersed in books. Our original hope was that just by having groovy books around we would get kids to read, but that proved somewhat naive. Nor had forcing students to do book reports accomplished anything, because the reports were easily faked by those who didn't want to read. The quiet reading time thus became the solution for two problems.

For my own part, I have found writing the worksheets one of the most stimulating parts of the whole system. At first it was time-consuming, but after a couple of months I developed a knack and cut the writing time for the seven worksheets down to about an hour and a half. Last year, I shared the writing with my colleague, Paul Casilli. That cut the work load even more and increased the input of different ideas because we constantly discussed the worksheets and compared notes on how they went over with our kids.

I still haven't reached what I think may be the ideal system—five or six teachers sitting down after school during free periods and tossing around ideas, then delegating the job of writing the sheets to various members of the group and sharing the output among the classes.

Paul Casilli and I learned that one problem with a sequential, unit-a-week approach to math, English and social studies is that kids forget what they learned a few weeks ago and usually don't get a chance to review it. So we got rid of the creative-writing station, incorporating it in the general station two days a week, and substituted a review station, which every day relentlessly harped on old skills. This was a real success in helping kids retain basic skills. The review station also provided a way of teaching kids things they missed the first time around.

Another problem I ran into with my learning-station system back in 1970 was that there was an awful lot of correcting to do; with 25 kids, I had around 175 papers to do four days a week. At first I plowed through all these to the tune of about one and a half hours a day, the theory being that this kept me in touch with how the worksheets were being received. But as I got better at writing the worksheets and assessing the kids' abilities, I began to wonder whether that one and a half hours was really worth it—a doubt that was reinforced every time I saw a kid take his carefully corrected work and tear it to shreds without even looking at it.

Slowly I slid into less arduous ways, telling myself that if I circulated effectively during the day, I would catch the people who were really having trouble and praise the people who were doing well. Besides, the sheets tended to be self-correcting and self-reinforcing since they led people through the steps so carefully. Still, many kids demanded grades and red marks all over their papers, and I felt under some obligation to give them what they wanted. After all, if I didn't correct papers, someone would realize after a couple of weeks that they were doing work just for the satisfaction and fun of doing it, not for grades, and then where would we be?

Last year, I sought a compromise by recruiting Dolores Jackson, a community aide, who corrected most of the papers, leaving two or three for me. But this tied her down with paper work and limited the time she could spend helping kids. When she had to leave us briefly for a family emergency, we developed what seems the best method yet of dealing with all that correcting. During the quiet reading time, Paul and I both sat down and corrected like mad. We found that in 45 minutes we could get through most of the work, leaving only about 15 to 20 minutes of correcting for after school. Then the next morning we tried to go over the previous day's papers with each student.

The summer before we began our team-teaching project, Paul and I spent a lot of time planning how we would use our adjoining rooms to best effect. We came up with what seemed to be a logical scheme. One room would be the "quiet room," with the seven learning-station worksheets and all the books; the other would be the "open room," with science experiments, games, animals, art projects and several typewriters. The kids would split the day between the two, my class having the quiet room for three hours and then trading places with Paul's class in the open room.

We abandoned this plan within a week, when Dolores pointed out that (1) three hours wasn't enough time for both finishing the worksheets and reading, and that (2) the kids who were assigned to the quiet room in the afternoon were in no mood to work at that point in the day—the first three hours of the day were the prime time for academic work. So we put seven pockets for station worksheets in both rooms and had the kids stay in their "home" room until about 12:30 doing the worksheets. Then we opened the door and allowed a free flow between the rooms and a free choice between books, games, typewriters and other attractions. Both rooms ended up having the same noise level at this stage, but we got our quiet in the reading time at the end of the day.

The biggest advantage of the two-room format is the escape from isolation within one classroom that we had both felt in previous years; it is a real delight to be able to chat with another adult during the day. Other benefits include exposure to a greater number and variety of kids, the happy discovery that we can survive on one engine (when one of us is sick, the other stuffs all the kids into one room), and the greater range of choices provided for the kids, since the two rooms have developed quite different personalities. Thus the kids can always leave one when they're sick of it rather than raising hell or going out into the corridors.

But perhaps the best thing we gained with the two-room arrangement was the recognition of how convenient it was to take field trips around the city during the school day. (Previously I had taken them only on Saturday afternoons.) Almost every Tuesday afternoon I took about nine kids field-tripping in a friend's minibus while Paul and Dolores held down both rooms—with dire threats that the kids who didn't behave wouldn't go on a trip when their turn came. Then on Thursday Paul took a trip while I held the fort. By the end of the year, most members of both classes had taken about ten field trips around the area.

During my first two years with learning stations, my classes were in the middle of the tracking spectrum, 6-G and 6-D (the range is from 6-A to 6-K). The 6-G class had only two or three kids with severe reading problems, and even they could read at about third grade level and do the worksheets with a certain amount of help from other kids and me during the day. The 6-D class was an academic section—part of the elite; the kids could read quite well. Consequently, the station worksheets I wrote for 6-D were considerably more meaty and difficult than those of the previous year.

Last year, Paul and I requested and were given 6-K and 6-J, the rock bottom of the sixth grade, the dumping ground for its academic and emotional problems. This both changed the way the learning-station system worked and hardened our attitudes toward the tracking system. The two classes had a number of repeaters, some of whom, purely for disciplinary reasons, were in the sixth grade for the third time. The average reading level in November was around third grade, with fully half the two classes reading below that level and seven or eight youngsters being virtual nonreaders. During the year, several more kids with severe emotional and academic problems were thrown into the rooms, complicating an already difficult academic situation.

The only solution we could see was to give the nonreaders almost all our teaching time and encourage brighter kids to help them, too. Our morale was often low; we were giving so much and seemingly getting back very little from the kids. Most of them were absorbed in their own problems and rivalries and seemed to take a lot of what we did, including spectacular improvements in the physical layout of the rooms, for granted. At the same time, some of the brighter kids lowered their standards and clamored for help they didn't need because we weren't paying enough attention to them.

What really got us through this difficult period was the fact that Paul and I shared the same problems and could talk about them and thus shore up each other's morale. The first encouraging signs came after the Christmas break. Several of the original group of nonreaders broke through enough so that they could do most of the work on their own. Our numbers remained small, around 19 in each class, and the concentrated attention and help we had been delivering day after day began to pay off. Before spring had arrived, and with a lot of help from some of the brighter kids, we were able to get everyone through all the work. And a few of the "problem" kids began to warm up to us and give us the much-needed feeling that we were good people and good teachers.

Out of the experience came a deepening anger over the tracking systems that create the 6-K's and 6-J's of the world, an anger made deeper by the really brilliant kids we saw buried in the self-hate of these classes. We explained to the kids during the year why we refused to refer to the class by these labels. Then they would go to other classrooms in the school and be called just that by insensitive teachers. Outraged by this situation, I waxed demagogic one day: "Are we the dumb class?" I asked. "No," came back weakly, uncertainly. "Are we the dumb class?" I asked again. "No," a little stronger. "Are we the dumb class?" I asked once again. "*No!*" shaking the walls. This attitude and the hard, grade-level work and constant attention and praise we gave them increased their self-respect enormously. We got real rewards out of watching several cowering, uncertain kids blossom during the early months. But clearly our efforts were small and didn't attack the beast itself—the tracking system.

This year, I hope to have a genuinely heterogeneous class. Ideally, it will have only two or three nonreaders, a lot of kids in the middle, and three or four really bright ones. In a class like this, I could return to the more active and mobile role I had my first two years, giving attention more equally around the room; kids might be able to get more help from each other; and the nonreaders would be swept along by the momentum of the class rather than pulling their more literate peers down. My own ideal is to be able to spend at least 15 minutes each day alone with pairs of kids, listening to them read and talking to them, and thus giving everyone in the class a modicum of close personal attention and help on specific problems.

A really heterogeneous class in which most kids are self-sufficient would also allow me to handle more children. I concluded after dealing with last year's small class that open classrooms don't generate enough interaction and bustle with fewer than 20 kids. A perfect number would be 24 or 25, assuming that among them there were not more than three nonreaders.

This leads to a question that I have been asked frequently by other teachers: How can you teach kids of widely varying abilities with only one level of worksheets? How can you cater to individual differences when everyone in the class is doing the same seven worksheets? What about enrichment activities for the brighter kids, remediation for the slow kids?

My answer is that a choice can be made between having a multilevel curriculum that caters to every different ability level and allows the teacher to give similar amounts of time to each student, and a single-level curriculum in which the teacher gives widely different amounts and kinds of attention to students according to their individual needs. The crucial element in either approach is being able to recognize exactly where the kid is and taking him from there to where he can go. So far I haven't found any published books or materials that can communicate with my kids at several different levels. So my system has been to write a common set of materials geared to the general tone and interests of the class, then zero in on the individual differences in my conferences with kids. I have found that hard work and a willingness to devote large amounts of time to a few kids will make a single-level curriculum work, even with an ability range from nonreaders to grade-level students.

There are other reasons this is so. First, kids can derive different academic benefits from the same worksheet. An advanced student who does an entire reading worksheet by himself and gives sophisticated, original answers to the open-ended questions gets more out of it than a student who must read it with the teacher and then copy answers from the text. A spelling worksheet that asks kids to use words in sentences is a flexible tool because each kid will produce sentences at his or her own level of skill and originality. The same is true of creative writing and many of the social studies sheets. It is only the cut-and-dried worksheets that may be too easy for the bright students. But even then, many bright kids enjoy doing work at different levels and may gain additional confidence from exercises below their top potential.

Second, the same well-written worksheet serves different levels of competence if the teacher is sensitive and selective in the amounts of help he gives around the room. A reading worksheet written for a sixth grade level becomes manageable and instructive for a kid reading at the third grade level if the teacher reads along with the student, explaining hard words and encouraging him. Conversely, many kids on the lower rungs of the tracking system are very sensitive about doing separate, special work and insist on trying to do what the rest of the class is doing, even if it is too hard for them.

Third, it is the brighter students who finish early and have more time to use the books, games and typewriters in the room, all of which are in themselves an enrichment program. I think these kids get a good feeling from knowing that they have finished the day's work by lunch and can then structure their own program and not be harassed by a teacher anxiously trying to keep them out of trouble with busywork. Sure, they waste some time, but the activities they ultimately get involved in are freely chosen and therefore more meaningful to them.

Fourth, the brighter kids sometimes help explain worksheets to friends who are having trouble, and in teaching others they gain a deeper understanding of the material themselves. Besides, it is good for advanced kids to understand through experience the differences between other kids and themselves, and perhaps in the process see areas in which they are not the bees' knees.

So let's sum it up: The main advantage of the learning-station system is that it enables a class to plow through a good deal of academic work, trains kids in basic skills and reading, and defines a very concentrated, self-disciplined work period and a very free activity and reading period. The system has the additional advantage of presenting a regular, predictable and finite amount of work in a do-able and familiar format, and of giving equal weight to relevance and fun and basic skills.

The main disadvantage is the sometimes lethargic and uninvolved feeling kids have after they have finished the worksheets, which might prevent some of the creative departures found in a less structured class from occurring. There is also an insufficient allowance for individual differences, which puts the burden of individualizing the program on the shoulders of the teacher. I am happy to assume that burden; perhaps others aren't.

But then the stations system is not one you have to take or leave—rather it is my own personal compromise between freedom and structure. There must be lots of changes and improvements that others would want to make for themselves. The thing is to begin.

The issue of censorship has already been treated in Part II and the question of teachers' rights to free speech arose indirectly in Michaels' experiences. Additional aspects of this question are discussed by Schimmel, though the reader must remember that local school systems do not necessarily follow court decisions rendered in other areas or states.

TO RISK ON THE SIDE OF FREEDOM

David Schimmel

Robert Keefe taught high school English in Ipswich, Massachusetts. He was a creative teacher who wanted to do more than the curriculum required. He wanted to expose his students to relevant and provocative contemporary writing. Therefore, on the first day of school in September, 1969, he gave each member of his class the current issue of the *Atlantic Monthly* and assigned the lead article. Entitled "The Young and the Old," the article dealt with dissent, protest, radicalism, and revolt. It contained the word "motherfucker" and repeated it several times. Keefe explained the article and the "vulgar" term, its origin and context.[1] And he told the class that any student who felt the assignment distasteful could have an alternative one.

Reprinted by permission of the author and the *Phi Delta Kappan*, April, 1973, pp. 542–545.
1. The following excerpts illustrate the language, tone, and style of the article: "The Columbia rebellion is illuminating. What it lacked in graffiti, it more than made up for in its already classic slogan, 'Up against the wall, motherfucker!' I make no claim to full understanding of the complete psychological and cultural journey this phrase has undergone. But let me at least sketch in a few steps along the way:

> 1. The emergence of the word 'motherfucker' to designate a form of extreme transgression. . . .
> 2. The use of the word in contemptuous command by white policemen when ordering black (and perhaps other) suspects to take their place in the police lineup, thereby creating the full phrase, 'Up against the wall, motherfucker!' . . .
> 3. Finally, Lionel Trilling's pun, in characterizing the striking students (not without affection) as 'Alma-Mater-fuckers'. . . .

From "The Young and the Old: Notes on a New History," Part I, Robert Jay Lifton, *Atlantic Monthly*, September, 1969, p. 47.

Although there was no evidence of negative student reaction to the article, a number of parents found the "dirty" word highly offensive and protested to the school committee. Members of the committee asked Keefe if he would agree not to use the word again in class. The teacher replied that he could not in good conscience agree. After a meeting of the school committee Keefe was suspended and proceedings were initiated to dismiss him. Keefe, however, believed that this action violated his civil rights. He went to court to stop his dismissal.

The case raises a number of questions regarding controversial speech in a high school classroom. Here are the answers given by one federal appeals court:[2]

Isn't an article that repeatedly uses a vulgar and offensive term pornographic and improper?

It depends on the article. In this case the judge read the article and found it "scholarly, thoughtful, and thought-provoking." The court said it was not possible to read this particular article as "an incitement to libidinous conduct." If it raised the concept of incest, wrote Judge Aldrich, "it was not to suggest it but to condemn it"; for the word was used "as a superlative of opprobrium."

Assuming the article had merit, couldn't the teacher have discussed the article without considering the controversial word?

Not in this case. The offending word was not artificially introduced but was important to the development of the thesis and conclusions of the author. Therefore, no proper study of the article could avoid considerations of the offensive word.

Can't a school committee protect students from language that some parents find genuinely offensive?

This would depend on the specific situation—the age of the students, the words used, and the purpose of their use. In this instance the word was used for educational purposes. Most high school seniors knew the word, and it was used nationally by young radicals and protesters. The judge questioned whether quoting a "dirty" word in current use would be a shock too great for high school seniors to stand. "If the answer were that the students must be protected from such exposure," wrote the judge, "we would fear for their future." Thus he concluded that the sensibilities of offended parents "are not the full measure of what is proper in education."

Does this mean that a teacher may assign any book that is legally

---

2. *Keefe* v. *Geanakos,* 418 F 2d 359 (1st Cir. 1969). Unless otherwise indicated, quotations in this article are from the opinion of the court in the case being discussed.

published? Are obscenity standards the same for students as for adults?

No. The court does not go that far. The issue is one of degree. Whether the use of offensive language is proper depends on all of the circumstances. In fact, Judge Aldrich acknowledged that "some measure of public regulation of classroom speech is inherent in every provision of public education." But the judge concluded that the application of such a regulation in the Keefe case "demeans any proper concept of education."[3]

Concern for the protection of academic freedom goes beyond the selective protection of offensive language, of course. It is based on a historic commitment to free speech, on the importance of academic inquiry to social progress, and on the necessity for both teachers and students to operate in an atmosphere which allows established concepts to be freely challenged.

The *Keefe* case indicates that teachers cannot be fired simply because they assign articles that contain vulgar language offensive to parents. Whether the language used can be considered protected by academic freedom depends upon the circumstances of the case: the intention of the teacher, the opinion of educators in the field, the age of the students, and the effect on the students. The problem is, How can a teacher know *before* he assigns an article or uses controversial language whether he will be fired or protected? In the *Mailloux* case, Judge Charles Wyzanski tried to answer this question.

Roger Mailloux was an eleventh-grade English teacher in a co-ed high school in Lawrence, Massachusetts. In the fall of 1970 the class was discussing a novel about a young teacher in rural Kentucky and his encounter with conservative local practices such as seating boys and girls on opposite sides of the classroom. During the discussion some students commented that the practice of seating boys and girls separately was ridiculous. Mailloux said that other things today were just as ridiculous. As an example, he introduced the subject of taboo words and wrote the word "fuck" on the blackboard. He then

> . . . in accordance with his customary teaching method of calling for volunteers to respond to a question, asked the class in general for an explanation. After a couple of minutes, a boy volunteered the word meant "sexual intercourse." Plaintiff [Mailloux], without using the word orally, said: "We have two words, 'sexual intercourse,' and this

3. As the U.S. Supreme Court has pointed out, unwarranted inhibition of the free speech of teachers affects not only the teachers who are restricted but has an "unmistakable tendency to chill that free play of spirit which *all* teachers ought especially to cultivate and practice." J. Frankfurter, concurring in *Wieman* v. *Updegraff.* 344 U.S. 183, 194 (1952).

word on the board; one is accepted by society, the other is not accepted. It is a taboo word." After a few minutes of discussion of other aspects of taboo, plaintiff went to other matters.[4]

On the next day the parent of a girl in the class complained to the principal. After an investigation by the head of the English Department and a hearing before the school committee, Mailloux was dismissed for "conduct unbecoming a teacher." He went to court to seek reinstatement on the grounds that the school committee deprived him of his rights under the First and Fourteenth Amendments.

After evidence was presented in court, Judge Wyzanski found that: 1) The topic of taboo words was relevant to the teaching of eleventh-grade English. 2) The word "fuck" is relevant to a discussion of taboo words. "Its impact," commented the judge, "effectively illustrates how taboo words function." 3) Boys and girls in the eleventh grade are sophisticated enough to treat the word from a serious educational viewpoint. 4) Mailloux's writing the word did not have a disturbing effect on the class. 5) In the opinion of some educational experts, the way Mailloux used the word "fuck" was appropriate under the circumstances and served a serious educational purpose.

On the other hand, the judge also found that: 1) Other qualified educators testified that Mailloux's use of the word was not reasonable or appropriate. 2) The teaching methods used by Mailloux "were obviously not 'necessary' to the proper teaching of the subject and students, in the sense that a reference to Darwinian evolution might be thought necessary to the teaching of biology." For Mailloux certainly could have used other methods to explain the concept of taboo words. Thus the case illustrates "the use of teaching methods which divide professional opinion."

Should the ruling of the *Keefe* case apply to Mailloux? The *Keefe* case, wrote Judge Wyzanski, "indicated that the use in the classroom of the word 'fuck' is not impermissible under all circumstances—as, for example, when it appears in a book properly assigned for student reading." But where a secondary teacher chooses a teaching method that is not necessary, that is not generally regarded by his profession as permissible, it is undecided "whether the Constitution gives him any right to use the method or leaves the issue to the school authorities."

4. *Mailloux* v. *Kiley*, 323 F Supp. 1387, 1388 (1971). "At all times in the discussion," added Judge Wyzanski, Mailloux "was in good faith pursuing what he regarded as an educational goal. He was not attempting to probe the private feelings or attitudes or experiences of his students, or to embarrass them."

After acknowledging a national tradition of academic freedom, Judge Wyzanski explained why he believed the secondary school situation should be distinguished from higher levels of education. This controversial explanation set the stage for his ruling which limits academic freedom in secondary schools.

> The secondary school more clearly than the college or university acts *in loco parentis* with respect to minors. It is closely governed by a school board selected by a local community. The faculty does not have the independent traditions, the broad discretion as to teaching methods, nor usually the intellectual qualifications, of university professors. Among secondary school teachers there are often many persons with little experience. Some teachers and most students have limited intellectual and emotional maturity. Most parents, students, school boards, and members of the community usually expect the secondary school to concentrate on transmitting basic information, teaching "the best that is known and thought in the world," training by established techniques, and, to some extent at least, indoctrinating in the mores of the surrounding society. While secondary schools are not rigid disciplinary institutions, neither are they open forums in which mature adults, already habituated to social restraints, exchange ideas on a level of parity. Moreover, it cannot be accepted as a premise that the student is voluntarily in the classroom and willing to be exposed to a teaching method which, though reasonable, is not approved by the school authorities, or by the weight of professional opinion. A secondary school student, unlike most college students, is usually required to attend school classes and may have no choice as to his teacher.[5]

Bearing this in mind, Judge Wyzanski ruled that for a controversial teaching method to be constitutionally protected, it is not enough for a secondary teacher to prove the method was used in good faith, is relevant to his students, and is regarded by some experts as serving a serious educational purpose. He must also show that the teaching method "has the support of the preponderant opinion of the teaching profession or of the part of it to which he belongs." If this is not shown, "the state may suspend or discharge a teacher for using that method, but it may not resort to such drastic sanctions unless the state proves he was put on notice, either by a regulation or otherwise, that he should not use that method." This procedural protection is afforded a teacher because he is engaged in the exercise of "vital First Amendment rights." In his teaching capacity, he should not be required to "guess what conduct or utterance may lose him his position."

Since at the time Mailloux acted he did not know that his conduct was prohibited by any regulation or understanding among teachers, Judge Wyzanski ruled that it was a violation of due process

5. Id. at 1392.

for the school committee to discharge him. The court therefore compensated Mailloux for lost salary and reinstated him as a teacher.[6]

The Lawrence School Board appealed Judge Wyzanski's decision to the U.S. Court of Appeals. In September, 1971, the appeals court agreed with the trial court's ruling that Mailloux had not received adequate notice informing him that the techniques he used would be considered improper. However, the court rejected the guidelines Judge Wyzanski devised, believing that "they would introduce more problems than they would resolve." Instead, the court preferred the "balancing test," which requires that the judge consider each case individually and balance all of the circumstances to determine whether a school board's interest in reasonable discipline is "demonstrably sufficient" to restrict a teacher's right to free speech.[7]

In the spring of 1970 Marilyn Parducci assigned her eleventh-grade class a comic satire by Kurt Vonnegut, Jr., entitled *Welcome to the Monkey House.* The following day Parducci's principal and the associate superintendent of the Montgomery, Alabama, schools expressed their displeasure with the story she had assigned. They described the content of the satire as "literary garbage," and they construed the "philosophy" of the story as "condoning, if not encouraging, 'the killing off of elderly people and free sex.' "[8] They were also concerned that three students had asked to be excused from the assignment and that several parents had called the school to complain. And they advised Parducci not to teach the story in any of her classes.

Parducci was bewildered by their interpretation. She considered the short story to be a good literary work and, while not meaning to cause trouble, she felt she had a professional obligation to teach it. As a result of the subsequent hearing before the school board, Parducci was dismissed for assigning materials which had a "disruptive" effect on the school and for refusing "the counseling and advice of the school principal." Parducci felt that her dismissal violated her First Amendment right to academic freedom and went to court to seek reinstatement.

6. Despite this ruling, notes the judge, school authorities are free "after they have learned that the teacher is using a teaching method of which they disapprove, and which is not necessary to the proper teaching of the subject, to suspend him until he agrees to cease using this method." Id. at 1393.

7. *Mailloux* v. *Kiley,* 448 F. 2d 1242 (1971).

8. *Parducci* v. *Rutland,* 316 F. Supp. 352, 353–4 (1970).

In considering this case Judge Johnson first summarized the basic constitutional principles involved:

> Although academic freedom is not one of the enumerated rights of the First Amendment, the Supreme Court has on numerous occasions emphasized that the right to teach, to inquire, to evaluate, and to study is fundamental to a democratic society.... The right to academic freedom, however, like all other constitutional rights, is not absolute, and must be balanced against the competing interests of society.... While the balancing of these interests will necessarily depend on the particular facts before the court, certain guidelines in this area were provided by the Supreme Court, ... [which] observed that, in order for the state to restrict the First Amendment right of a student, it must first demonstrate that "the forbidden conduct would *materially* and *substantially* interfere with the requirements of appropriate discipline in the operation of the school. ...."[9]

The first question considered by the court was whether *Welcome to the Monkey House* was appropriate reading for high school juniors. While the story contains several vulgar terms and a reference to an involuntary act of sexual intercourse, the court, "having read the story very carefully," found "nothing that would render it obscene."

The court's finding that the story was appropriate for high school students was confirmed by the reaction of the students themselves. Rather than there being a threatened or actual disruption of the educational process, evidence indicated that the assigning of the story "was greeted with apathy by most of the students." The court, therefore, found that the conduct for which Parducci was dismissed was not such that "would materially and substantially interfere with reasonable requirements of school discipline."

Since the school board "failed to show either that the assignment was inappropriate reading for high school juniors or that it created a significant disruption to the educational processes," the court concluded that Parducci's dismissal "constituted an unwarranted invasion of her First Amendment right to academic freedom."[10]

In sum, each of these decisions acknowledged that academic freedom—the right to teach, to inquire, and to evaluate—is fundamental to a democratic society. Judicial protection of academic freedom is based on the First Amendment, on the importance of academic inquiry to social progress, and on the belief that teachers

9. Id. at 356.

10. The court noted that one of the recommended novels on the reading list for juniors is *Catcher in the Rye*, "which contains far more offensive and descriptive language" than that found in the story Parducci assigned.

and students should be free to question and challenge established concepts. Like other constitutional rights, however, academic freedom is not absolute; it must be balanced against the competing interests of society.

The *Keefe* case held that a teacher cannot be fired simply because he assigns a controversial book or article or uses, in a classroom, vulgar language that offends some parents. Whether such language is protected by the First Amendment depends on the circumstances of the specific case. The circumstances a court would consider include the relevance of the controversial language or publication to the subject matter of the class, the teacher's method and purpose, the age and maturity of the students, the quality of the book or article used, and the effects on the students.

According to the *Mailloux* case, if a teacher uses vulgar language (or assigns a controversial book or article) which is not necessary to the teaching of the subject and is not generally regarded as appropriate by professionals in the field, constitutional protection is uncertain. In order to be protected by the First Amendment, Judge Wyzanski ruled that a public school teacher must prove that his use of a controversial method or material has the "preponderant" support of the teaching profession or the part to which he belongs. If, however, there is a difference of opinion among educators, school boards have the right to prohibit controversial publications and language and discharge teachers who violate these prohibitions— provided the teachers have clear notice of what is prohibited. While Judge Wyzanski's rule may be used as a practical guideline by some administrators, it has not been accepted by the courts.

The *Parducci* case applied a different test. According to this decision, a school board cannot restrict the First Amendment rights of a teacher unless it demonstrates that the teacher's conduct would "materially and substantially interfere with reasonable requirements of school discipline." As the *Parducci* opinion pointed out: "When a teacher is forced to speculate" as to what speech is permissible and what is prohibited, he is "apt to be overly cautious" in the classroom. A fear to experiment with new and controversial ideas is contrary to the concept of academic freedom.

Therefore, the courts in the *Parducci* and *Mailloux* cases provided certain tests or guidelines which could be used to determine what classroom speech was protected by the Constitution.

The *Mailloux* ruling, allowing school boards to prohibit methods or materials which are not supported by a wide majority of the teaching profession, has advantages and disadvantages. It has the advantage of letting teachers know in advance the probable consequences of their action. On the other hand, it can be used to inhibit innovation and narrow the academic freedom of public school teachers. In addition, this test has not gained judicial acceptance.

Thus we are left with the "balancing test" that is used in the *Keefe* case and by most federal courts—a case-by-case inquiry that balances the teacher's right of academic freedom against the competing interests of society in maintaining reasonable school discipline. In most instances this means that a teacher's use of controversial material or language will be protected by the First Amendment unless a school board can demonstrate that: 1) It is not relevant to the subject being taught, 2) it is not appropriate to the age and maturity of the students, or 3) it disrupts school discipline.

Have courts gone far enough in protecting the academic freedom of teachers? Some say they have gone too far. They argue that the rights of parents to influence the education of their children and the responsibilities of administrators to maintain school discipline have been eroded by a permissive judiciary.

In contrast, others say the courts have not gone far enough. These critics resent Judge Wyzanski's distinction between high school and college teachers and the second-class academic freedom that such distinctions imply. They also object to the subjective and ambiguous nature of the "balancing test" which allows teachers' rights to be "balanced away" by parental pressure and cautious administrators. And they argue that any parent or student who objects to a teacher's exercise of academic freedom can cause a disruption and thereby remove the protection of the Constitution. This argument, however, seems exaggerated. For, as the *Keefe* case pointed out, the sensibilities of offended parents "are not the full measure of what is proper in education." And as the *Parducci* decision held, a teacher cannot be discharged for conduct protected by the First Amendment unless it "materially and substantially" disrupts the educational process.

There are no easy legal answers to questions that split public opinion. Judicial "solutions" usually involve a balancing of competing rights and risks. The case of academic freedom in public schools is no exception. Thus we cannot affirm the rights of teachers without also recognizing the rights of parents and the responsibilities of administrators. In the area of free speech, however, the First Amendment represents a national commitment to risk on the side of freedom. It is a commitment that Keefe, Mailloux, and Parducci took seriously, and one that requires continuing support.

PART FIVE

DIRECTIONS
SCHOOLS EXPLORE

"Free public schools are the cornerstone of our social, economic, and political structure and are of utmost significance in development of our moral, ethical, spiritual, and cultural values. . . . The public school system is not expendable. Any movement that would diminish this vital asset will be opposed by the Association."
—National Education Association Resolution, 1969

"What is the realistic meaning of alternatives 'within the system,' if the system is the primary vehicle of state control? . . . School cannot at once both socialize to the values of the oppressor and toil for the liberation and the potency of the oppressed. If the innovation is profound, it is subversive. If it is subversive, it is incompatible with the prime responsibility of the public school."
—Jonathan Kozol

Following the Revolutionary War, American nationalists liked to call the fledgling country the "Great Experiment." The title seemed to fit the democratic social system and the restless spirit of its settlers. Experimentation was also a mark of the nation's efforts at schooling.

Throughout the country's development, there have been many individuals and groups who chose to explore alternative paths to educate their children. It is ironic today that public education is so often assumed to be the American way, for as Part One intimated, the near monopoly of public schooling is a recent phenomenon.

On every major rung of the educational ladder, private instructional models preceded public forms. The Congregational Church instituted Harvard, the first college. Before the first public high school in Boston in 1821, private academies for boys and seminaries for girls had operated for years. Before elementary school patterns crystallized, young children had been exposed to dame schools in New England, Sunday schools in the Midwest, and charity schools in the Middle Atlantic states.

Historians of education have minimized the growth of non-public schools. Their accounts applauded the growth of and the improvement in public schools following the Civil War. To bolster their case that the American mainstream supported universal education, historians mustered a variety of examples: the courts' approval of community tax support (Kalamazoo, Michigan, 1874), improved teacher training and certification programs (such as the Normal school movement), development of textbooks to replace such haphazard teaching tools as the Montgomery Ward catalog, and more orderly administration of school programs (the introduction of the Carnegie unit, to measure a student's exposure to a subject area).

But while public schools were becoming the dominant pattern for the majority of American youth, the non-public school has also grown rapidly. It was during the 1880's and 1890's that Roman Catholics and German Lutherans began parochial systems of instruction. Private "progressive" nurseries grew alongside the kindergartens. Adult study clubs, such as the Chautauqua Literary and Scientific Circle, enrolled millions. In 1890 approximately 40 percent of the high school students in the country were in non-public schools.

Also, non-public schools have grown steadily since World War I. Ninety-five percent of all Jewish day schools now in existence were founded after 1930. More than 80 percent of today's Baptist, Presbyterian, and Episcopal schools originated during that same period. Although Roman Catholic school enrollments are declining dramatically, some new forms of schooling being tried may offset the loss. Currently about 12 percent of the nation's students in elementary and secondary schools are not attending a public school.

Further, the Roman Catholic decline will be partially offset by schooling efforts of "new" groups. For a variety of reasons—belief that the public school curriculum is too secular, desire for racial isolation, support of a more humanistic pedagogical approach—non-public schools are springing up in every part of America. The sponsors of such schools include Episcopalians, Southern Presbyterians, Jewish synagogues, fundamentalist sects, Black Panthers, White Citizens' Councils, and Summerhill-type groups.

The story of America's educational experiments may be viewed as a profile of changing national values. Frequently the school has been modeled after another institution in the culture. In colonial times school was usually patterned after a church fellowship. Early twentieth-century educators liked to think of the school as a factory. More recently, schools have been likened to motels or franchise outlets, providing a standardized diet for a mobile nation. We may ask now: What are schools modeled after today? What should be the model for tomorrow?

The reader will note that the chapter title omits the words "new" and "alternatives." The omissions are deliberate. These historical notes may aid the reader in posing another basic question: Are the directions taken significantly different from experiments in the past?

The order of the readings should invite another type of question. It is obvious that the directions being explored vary considerably. Have the major goals of schooling been altered? Have new power alignments behind school policy been changed?

Part Five raises questions about the emerging shapes of schooling, and asks the reader to examine their advantages and disadvantages.

The opening article represents the struggles faced by those parents who have given serious thought to what constitutes the best education for their children. As Ms. Hentoff concludes, there is no easy answer.

The school that symbolizes, in fact as well as in theory, the most radical departure from conventional American schools is Summerhill. Some of the people who deplore American schooling today ask for alternatives like Summerhill. For others, the free school movement has not delivered all that it hoped, as the Fremon essay shows.

The next group of articles explain some school programs that have recast some segment of the school system, such as a building design, the curriculum and media aids, and computer instruction. In light of Summerhill, one may ask if these changes in schooling are as significant as they first appear? Still other articles in this group describe changes in where schooling occurs, who controls policy, and how schools can be financed. Again, are these changes critical ones?

The book ends with two selections that encourage the reader to examine broader educational questions for the future.

Margot Hentoff's reflections may mirror the concerns of many parents, who have worried about the value of their children's schooling. Not always able to pinpoint our discontent, how many of us have concluded, as she does, "I knew more of what I didn't want than what I did"? She recalls her own education, both its strengths and weaknesses. She goes on to state her reservations about schooling today, including the free schools her husband favors.

Questions she faced that readers may also find pertinent are: What do I want in a school? How can I determine what a school is really like? Would I probably force my values upon my children through my selection of their school?

THE SCHOOLS WE WANT*
Margot Hentoff

> There is a profession in Latin America which is the training
> of young colts. The man who does this is called a domador.
> The horses are often very expensive, highly treasured by
> their owner who has a very precise idea of what he wants
> those horses to be. . . . The domador is always a mental
> wreck, because what the horse is and what the owner
> wanted it to be are completely different.
> —Philip Hazelton, This
> Magazine Is About Schools.

Before I was twenty, I was an educational philosopher—a Summerhillian beyond argument. Myself a product of so many and such inferior schools in which I had idled at my desk during math, science, geography, and languages that, by the end of high school, I knew no French or Latin, although I had been taught them for years; no

Reprinted with permission from *Saturday Review of Education,* September 19, 1970, pp. 75–76.

* Nat Hentoff, who teaches at the Graduate School of Education of New York University, wrote the first section of this article, which we have omitted. Calling for more humane schools, he also cautioned readers to avoid concluding that all "free schools" would liberate, and that all public schools would depersonalize.

algebra nor where Ohio was; nothing, in fact, but what I had read in books I found in bookstores and on the family library's shelves.

But read I did—Freud at ten when I bought *The Interpretation of Dreams,* assuming it was a Gypsy dream book; Swedenborg because he was mystical; Robinson Jeffers' poetry because there was sex in it, *Forever Amber* for the same reason; the Harvard Classics because they were in the bookcase, along with Edward Bellamy, Jacob Riis, T. S. Eliot, and old law books. Also old medical books so I could know which disease I was most likely to die of imminently.

My grades in school were dreadful, and I got into college only because I had landed in an entirely corrupt, small New York private school where the headmistress kited my transcript grades to a minimally acceptable average. At college, the same perverse business went on. If we studied Freud, I read Reich or Jung. Taking geology, I discovered biology, and when I finally talked my way into an experimental creative writing major, I suffered a massive writer's block and got a D- on a paper on Norman Mailer.

For me, the classroom was a hopelessly dreary place where it was always 4 in the afternoon on a winter day with someone droning on under a glaring fluorescent light. Teachers were, for the most part, witless, and courses that looked great in the catalogue were dull in the realization. Once or twice in an entire school career, a good teacher might direct you to something you might not have found otherwise. But, on the whole, intelligent friends were more reliable.

I suppose the reason I could manage to be both totally turned off by school and still not be turned off intellectually was because my parents made no fuss whatever about academic achievement or grades as long as I appeared to be intelligent and stayed in school and off the streets.

When my two older children were ready, I looked for a school with the same attitude as my parents had. As an autodidact, I believed that, in the absence of requirements, a child would be unerringly drawn to those areas of knowledge I felt were valuable. It is an index of my shortsightedness that it never occurred to me that children, left alone, might find other areas of interest entirely; ones that did not fit at all within my value system.

I chose a place that gave no tests or grades, and that allowed free movement and conversation and a wide choice of activity. It was a school manned by extremely dedicated teachers who created their own teaching materials, totally eschewing the use of workbooks and textbooks; a school that acted on the premise that learning is an organic process during which a child learns only when he can see the direct connection between knowledge and action. There, intellectual achievement was not valued above other kinds of achievement, and the sense of accomplishment a child got from what work he did was not diminished by the superimposition of conventional academic demands.

By the time they were nine, my children wrote delightful and original poems and essays, misspelled and unpunctuated, handed in to appreciative teachers on scraps of crumpled paper. The trouble was that at thirteen they were still doing the same thing and, by this time, kids from other schools who had mastered some technique and who had some fundamental background knowledge were beginning to write better poems and essays than my children. Also, it turned out, my children were not readers. Not that they couldn't read—they didn't read. Since the school was rooted in the group-as-an-experience-in-community theory in which each child was supposed to excel at something in which he was naturally best, my daughters discovered they were best at being popular, forming cliques, gossiping, and running races in the yard. One of them was also good at making copies of ancient Greek pots. Somehow, they never connected with any real intellectual interest. I might have thought they were just an odd pair of kids if I had not seen the same syndrome in many of their classmates. Further, when my elder son began to behave in the same way in the same school it occurred to me that perhaps the school was not so much helping the child to find out who he was as it was assisting him to discover that he was inadequate.

In any case, when we began looking for new schools for our two boys this past year, I knew more of what I didn't want than what I did. I no longer wholly subscribed to what has been called the romantic theory of education. For some children, it seemed to me, the traditional quiet classrooms with a great deal of structured activity might be exactly the atmosphere that would allow them to concentrate on the work at hand for a sustained period of time. In the third grade at his old school, one son, whose teacher had told me he got math to do whenever he wanted it, seemed to have wanted it about five times during the entire year. He thought his handwriting looked terrible; so he didn't write. And it was true: His handwriting looked terrible because no one ever insisted that he practice it. No one insisted, because it was felt he didn't write well. The whole school began to strike me as Red Queen territory: *"Here,* you see, it takes all the running you can do to keep in the same place."

In making a change, I specifically did not want one of the new free schools, the growth of which so heartens my husband but which seem to me uncomfortably like the old permissive schools with a few technical innovations tacked on. There are many teachers with whom

I do not *want* my children to have an intimate relationship: those teachers who imagine themselves therapists; those who, having entered the teaching profession as social crusaders, politically indoctrinate children in the manner of the old church schools; and those who do not understand that in order for healthy growth to take place there *must* be a distinction between adult and child, something real for kids to test themselves against rather than that confectionery mist surrounding those who are always "on the side of the child."

I also had never seriously considered the public schools, less because they might not be "good" than from a fundamental aversion to committing my children to the hands of the state. If they are to be miseducated, I prefer that it be my mistake rather than the state's. This is one reason why I am so much in favor of public independent education and the educational voucher system.

Having the option, I didn't want a traditional school either—although some of our best people have come out of them. They are too arbitrary, too stifling, and too rigidly demanding within such a narrow scope that only the most competent students feel a sense of personal worth. In other words, not enough children win.

What I do want is an experimental school that is willing to try anything promising without succumbing to the current anti-intellectual mode; one that sets intellectual standards. My husband complains of his term of servitude at stuffy Boston Latin School, but I have noted over the years that he has the kind of puritan self-discipline that keeps him working whether or not he is having a particularly rich experience with the job at hand. Also he has a nice grasp of basic areas of knowledge and does not have to ask me questions about Roman history.

I have discovered it is not enough to act on the premise that if you merely expose a child to enough of those areas that make up our culture, he will make good use of the exposure. There is such a strong drift away from the passing-on of the traditional culture that it is quite easy for a child to avoid absorbing even the best of it, and I find it patronizing for an educator to assume that children should be "reached" largely through material relevant to the present, and through the kid culture of rock music and slogan politics.

I like the idea of a school that groups students according to their achievement level in each area of classroom work so that a child is always being taught with others of the same degree of expertise; neither left behind in a bewildered fog, nor bored and squirming because he has gone past the work being done. Not only does this permit the natural competitive drive of the child to exert itself within areas of possible gratification, but it also gets rid of that pernicious example of misdirected benevolence: automatic promotion, no matter what.

Finally, I have got straight in my own head what the real rules of the game are, rhetoric notwithstanding. I want my children to have a solid body of knowledge and, hopefully, to be intellectuals as well. And this means that, sooner or later, they should be able to enter reasonably good colleges—all of which require a background of solid accomplishment. Even those colleges, such as Sarah Lawrence, Bennington, and Reed, that are properly scornful of test scores, grades, and other paraphernalia of evaluation seem to use them when it comes to selecting their students. It is still kids who have been taught to achieve who are admitted to those schools and all the other good ones. It may well be that my children will have something quite else in mind for their lives, but as long as I am responsible for their education, I think I should see to it that they have the choice.

In September, 1973, Alexander Sutherland Neill died quietly a few days short of his ninetieth birthday. Although he had been in the United States only once (in 1968 for a brief appearance with Orson Bean on the *Tonight* show), he was among the best known educational figures of the mid-twentieth century, not only in America, but also in West Germany, Japan, Scandinavia, Canada, New Zealand, and Australia, where his book *Summerhill: A Radical Approach to Child Rearing* (New York: Hart Publishing Company, Inc., 1960) has attracted much attention. The book was based on many years of experience in operating a "free school."

Neill founded New School in 1921 in Dresden, Germany. Two years later he moved his school to Sonntagberg, Austria, and a short time later to Lyme Regis, England, where he adopted the name Summerhill. In 1926 he located in Leiston, England, where the school has remained, except for a few years during World War II when he moved to Scotland. The school is in many ways a reflection of Neill's unhappy childhood, which grew out of Scottish Calvinism, a stern schoolmaster father, and a somewhat indulgent but socially upward-mobile mother. Neill did not do well in school himself, finding it impossible to study effectively those subjects which did not interest him. He did, however, graduate from the University of Edinburgh (though he did not enter until he was twenty-five after he tired of being a low-level primary school teacher).

In founding Summerhill, Neill intended to minimize the negative influence he had felt as a child. To do this, he tried to avoid external authority and morality as much as possible by allowing each child to form his own judgments in matters which affected only him, and having the whole group rather than the headmaster or faculty make policy and arbitrate disputes for the community. This was accomplished in weekly parliamentary meetings. The school has consisted at any one time of twenty-five to seventy-five pupils, aged five to sixteen, and usually under ten staff members. Neill admitted his direct democracy would not work without a good proportion of older pupils. Classes consist of the usual school subjects, including arts and crafts, but class attendance has always been left to individual choice. No pupil need ever to go to class unless he wants to. Swearing and masturbation are not frowned upon—a fact which has led some critics to classify the school as one of the "goddamn and fornication at five" variety—but sexual intercourse, while approved of in theory, has been discouraged in practice for fear the school would be closed.

For many years Summerhill attracted mostly "problem" children, and Neill spent a great deal of time giving private lessons (P. L.'s)—psychoanalytic sessions—to liars, bedwetters, thieves, and pyromaniacs, and children suffering from rejection and repression. He himself underwent analysis for many years, first with Homer Lane and Wilhelm Stekel and finally with Wilhelm Reich, so that much of what he has written deals with personality difficulties and especially with sexual repression. After the popularity of the book *Summerhill*, the school has had a waiting list of children so that the student population no longer consists overwhelmingly of children with difficulties. They do, however, still come almost exclusively from middle-class families, because of the relatively high tuition cost.

Since Neill's death the school has been run by his wife, Ena. Visitors are no longer accepted—there had been anywhere from a few to several dozen visitors every Saturday for a decade up to 1973—and the future of the Summerhill venture is not clear. Whatever happens, the impact of Summerhill as a symbol would be difficult to overestimate. The following interview took place shortly before Neill died.[1]

1. Readers who are especially interested in Summerhill may wish to consult, in addition to *Summerhill* itself, Neill's autobiography: *Neill! Neill! Orange Peel!* (New York: Hart Publishing Company, Inc., 1972), and W. A. C. Stewart, "A. S. Neill and Summerhill," Chap. 15 in *The Educational Innovators*, Vol. II: *Progressive Schools, 1881–1967* (London: Macmillan & Co., Ltd., 1968), and Robert Skidelsky, *English Progressive Schools* (Baltimore: Penguin Books, 1969).

FORWARD FROM THE SUMMERHILL EXPERIMENT

Mark Vaughan

"I'm just afraid," said Neill, "that when I die—which cannot be long now, I'm 89—that the Ministry will step in and say we've tolerated this bloody school for all these years, and now the old man's dead we've got to make statutes to enforce lessons. . . . I'm almost sure they'll say that. . . .

"I don't think I'm afraid of death because I think death's an extinction. I don't believe in an after life. There's no other living thing gets an after life, so why should we. But what annoys me is never to know what's happened. That's what I hate about dying. Never to know what's happened to freedom for kids. To make it local, never to see my granddaughter grow.

"I wish you could come back every 20 years for a week to earth off some unknown planet and see what was happening; I think after a day you'd want to go back again. I'd like to know what's going to happen to humanity. Damn it all, I've fought for years for kids to be free and I'd like to see what effect it's going to have, not only my fight for freedom but other people's, to see if kids will ever get away from this indoctrinated establishment they live in."

What did he think had inspired the free school movement which has grown in various parts of the country during the past 18 months or two years?

"I don't know. I think it's the spirit of the time. I wouldn't say that anybody special has inspired it . . . it is a new stimulus, and an excellent one, but it's no good trying to trace origins, because one cannot tell.

"People say to me that Summerhill has had a big effect on the modern free primary school, but how the hell can you know? It's an intangible thing and, anyhow, it doesn't matter who has influenced them, it's what they're doing that matters."

For those thinking of starting free schools because they want to get away from the state system, Neill had this advice:

"First they should have teachers who have no authority, who have no fear, who give no fear, who have no dignity and then, as soon as you can, try a self-government of some kind."

Reprinted with permission from *London Times Educational Supplement*, February 9, 1973, p. 10.

"This is not possible with very young children. All our children come to the general meeting, and some of them never listen at all at six or seven. But as they grow older they begin to take part. I couldn't have self-government if all my kids were nine and under.

"We don't decide on the age of nine, but although every kid comes to the meetings, the six and seven-year-olds will speak about things like . . . 'so and so kicked me . . . so and so bullied me,' and that's their line. They are not old enough to make constructive ideas about bigger things concerning themselves, bed time, for example. They don't know enough at that age."

A free school was impossible unless started with free teachers. Summerhill has had its difficulties in finding the right teachers. "Quite a few like their jobs ostensibly because they want freedom for children, but you soon discover that they want freedom for themselves. I think America is having the same problems with starry-eyed people who are only there for their own freedom. The main thing is to have people who believe in what they are doing, and not using the school as a means of enhancing their own ego."

In Summerhill no child goes to lessons if he or she does not want to, but the teachers are there giving lessons all the time for those who decide they like what is being given. There is no corporal punishment. The school is run by the school community which meets regularly to decide on issues that come up, on complaints and on policy decisions. Everyone in the school, the 64 pupils and the eight teachers, has one vote.

Neill believes that the free school movement in any country has to spring from the middle classes, and even of most of those benefiting from the more recently established schools are working-class children—many of them truants and non-learners, from deprived backgrounds—it is always going to be the middle-classes who bring in innovation.

"That is always bound to happen I think. The middle-class after all are more conscious, I wouldn't say better educated, but they are more conscious than the sort of football crowd, the proletariat.

"It's a difficult question to answer, but so far, all reforms, so to speak, have come from middle-class people like John Dewey, Homer Lane and myself—we're all middle-class people. Wilhelm Reich found that in the Communist Party in Berlin. . . . After all the middle-class read Freud and the working-class don't."

Did he think then that fee-paying schools had social drawbacks?

"Oh absolutely! Summerhill, unfortunately has had to be middle-class because it has lived (or not lived) on its fees and I cannot take proletarian children, which is a tragedy."

Ray Hemmings's book, *Fifty Years of Summerhill*, contained a survey of head teachers which said that Neill's greatest influence on the English state system of education had been on pupil-teacher relationships and pupil participation in school affairs. Would Neill have liked it to have been something else, or something more?

"No. That's quite enough for me. Seeing children getting more part in the say in what they are doing is excellent. I feel rather annoyed at the slowness of the breaking down of the teacher, the dignified teacher relationships."

Mr. Hemmings's survey said he had noticeable influence on moral and sex education, but little on curriculum and on the way teachers actually teach, but Neill seems unworried.

So far as he can tell, his ideas and Summerhill during its 50 years' existence had had the greatest effect at primary level although he still believes that the state system "is all wrong." The largest ingredients in state schools are fear and discipline, and he criticizes the fact that children are "sitting on their backsides" for six hours a day.

Neill's fear about the future of the school, which curiously enough is more secure under a Conservative than a Labour government (it was Mr. Edward Short, the then Minister of Education, who thought seriously about closing the school in 1968), is based on visits by the school inspectors over the years.

"I know they do not approve, they do not like it here. We are not doing what they want . . . 'Why cannot this boy read?' . . . 'Why is this room untidy?' and this sort of thing."

"I said to John Blackie, who was the best inspector of the lot who came: 'Look here, Blackie, you can inspect the teaching of English or French or history, but you cannot inspect sincerity, freedom, charity or happiness.'"

How did he feel state schools would evolve?

"The next step is to bring the same atmosphere into a comprehensive or other secondary school that you have in the junior school, the freedom of choice and freedom to move about."

As the following article indicates, some of the bright hopes about free schools, such as Summerhill, have faded. That is not to say that free schools are a now-declining fad. There is conflicting evidence now about the growth or decline of such schools.

Does this selection, in its criticisms of free schools, also give clues about the ingredients that make for a "successful" school? What prediction would you make for the future of Summerhill-type schools in the United States?

WHY FREE SCHOOLS FAIL
Suzanne S. Fremon

In this country the term "free school" has come to mean many things to many people. The term "free" does not mean without cost, but free of conventional curriculum and discipline. At the extreme, a free school rests on the ideas that human beings are basically good, the aim of life is happiness, and development of the heart should take precedence over development of the brain.

According to this conception, British Infant Schools, Montessori Schools, Open Corridor classrooms, multi-age classes, and the mini-schools beginning to burgeon within the public school systems are not free schools. Nor are the storefront academies in the inner cities. Like free schools, these are also responses to the rigidity, narrowness, and failure of our public schools, but they differ from free schools in one crucial respect. They all accept the idea of school as a place where children come to learn specific things—reading, writing, math, science, social studies, languages, manual skills. A free school, on the other hand, embraces first and foremost the idea of the free individual, his relationship with other individuals, and his happiness. As for academic learning or vocational training, according to free school supporters, a student should and will acquire these on his own initiative as he needs them. His school must provide materials to learn with, but the timetable and development of his learning is up to him. It must never be imposed from without.

Reprinted with permission from *Parents' Magazine*, September 1972, pp. 50–1, 96, 98.

It is abundantly clear by now that our traditional system of schooling is not working well today. Among its failures are the large numbers of young adults who cannot read well enough to cope with contemporary life, and the alienated young people—drug users, dropouts, and criminals—who offer highly visible proof of the shortcomings of our educational process.

There are a great number of parents across the country to whom the public schools have proven so unsatisfactory—and to whom the idea of the free school is so appealing—that they are willing to work hard and spend large sums of money to provide this alternative form of schooling for their children. At one point last winter, the New Schools Exchange—clearinghouse for many free schools—listed more than 400. Many more are never listed in any directory.

We can no longer afford to turn our backs on the free school philosophy, dismissing it as the notion of impractical idealists. It is the serious response of serious people who are rightly concerned with the inadequacies of education, and it needs to be considered on its merits as an alternative to traditional schooling.

The sad fact is, however, that nine months is the average life of a free school. When one considers the enormous amount of thought, debate, money, energy, and time that are required to establish a school, nine months seems a pathetically short life span.

Why, if free schools are such fine places—at least in the early and middle grades, do they close almost as regularly as new ones open? Partly because many of them, however high their ideals, are unable to put these into practice. Something obviously comes between the vision and the accomplishment.

MONEY PROBLEMS

The first and most obvious "something" is lack of money. Most free schools are supported by tuition from parents, usually scaled to income, and contributions. Another barrier is the failure to manage the school properly. A school must take in money and pay it out. It must have permits from governmental agencies. It keeps books and must monitor its own finances. At least it should do all these things. Often, however, the people involved in running a given school are not competent at these tasks and, worse, not willing to be responsible for them This is a pity, since a promising school can be forced to close down simply because the adults in control lack sound business sense.

TEACHING PROBLEMS

On the other hand, lack of money is often given as the reason for failure when other factors have been more crucial. Of these, the most important is probably the quality of the teaching. Most educators and parents agree that the individual teacher's personal and professional qualities determine more than anything else whether or not— and what—children will learn in the school setting.

Unfortunately, good teachers are rare. Because we need so many teachers, we must use some who are not, by any stretch of the imagination, good teachers, even in public schools. Free schools share this problem. The young people who set out to run free schools are, by and large, not yet good teachers. Most of them are untrained and inexperienced. And many have abandoned their own educations prematurely. In many instances their visions are bold and beautiful, but admirable as their idealism may be, it does not automatically make them good teachers.

The inadequacies of free school teachers also stem from other sources. They are seeking for themselves—not just for the children they teach—an atmosphere of freedom and love. But unfortunately the person concerned primarily with his own problems is hampered in his efforts to help others develop. Even with the best of intentions, he is likely to project his own feelings onto the lives and relationships of the youngsters he works with. Any teacher in any kind of school may do this, but the openness of the free school style as well as the youth of the men and women who mainly make up their staffs seem to increase the chances of its happening there.

OTHER PROBLEMS

A consequent and correlated problem is that many free school teachers seem unwilling to assert themselves as strong and stable forces in the lives of the children in their charge. This may well be the major educational and psychological weakness of free schools. For example, a teacher may refuse to acknowledge that as an adult he knows more than a seven-year-old student. There is, in the free school, a general willingness to allow students to abandon projects when they become difficult, without helping them overcome the difficulties. The instructors pride themselves in not imposing their values on children—a consequence of the misguided belief that a teacher shouldn't "teach" but should exist solely as a "resource person," available for help when a child decides he wants to learn something.

These attitudes are understandable, even, in isolated cases, commendable. They come from a deep and valid suspicion of rigidity, intolerance, and dishonesty that the organizers of free schools see as the major problems of traditional education and the society which supports it.

Unfortunately, however, in the determination of free school teachers not to oppress and rubber-stamp their students, they are often guilty of other faults. Even their most sympathetic champions recognize that they have swung too far away from the dominant teacher figure of traditional education. In their fear of imposing meaningless values, they decline to express even their own, leaving a vacuum that children are not able to fill. And some free school teachers are confused in even their definition of "values." One instructor, for example, declined to teach her students how to spell, on the grounds that this would be "imposing values" on them.

Most important, in their horror of misusing power, free school teachers often decline to use their own legitimate control. In abdicating the natural authority an adult has in a group of children, or that held by any person who knows something other people want to know, a teacher fails to give his students an adult model to observe and learn from. He gives them instead a model of an ineffectual, insipid adult, whose words and deeds lack conviction.

In failing to use their teacher power more forcefully, free schools are missing a vital lesson from their own model, A. S. Neill, who has always been the unquestioned center of power at England's Summerhill, the original, purest, and longest-lived example of the free school. Several experienced observers of free schools have suggested that perhaps a strong, dynamic leader is the key to survival of any free school. In their fear of the misuse of power, the founders and teachers in many free schools may be condemning their institutions to an early death.

There is, however, one plus that keeps coming up when free schools are discussed—the fact that with all their problems and inadequacies, free schools do provide a warm and nurturing atmosphere for students.

There are always some children who need a sheltered environment and loving relationships with other people more than anything else. And there may be more of these children than any of us suspect. It seems likely that many of the older students in a free school would be lost if forced into the uncongenial atmosphere of a large, impersonal, public high school. What such children need is not so much a school as a loving family, and for many children, that is what a free school is.

This may, indeed, be one of the primary reasons that free schools do not appeal strongly to most parents. Free schools are not really schools at all. They are at one end of the educational spectrum, authoritarian schools at the other. Most parents and teachers would agree that free schools are not *the* answer to the nation's educational problems. But the free school movement has let in light and air on an educational system too long suffering from rigid adherence to an often arbitrarily chosen curriculum and a gross disregard for the human rights of children. And for that welcome light—which will, we hope, be shed on all schools—we should be grateful.

When one looks for changes in schools, it can be seen most easily in building designs and in the instructional materials used. It is understandable, then, why Apollo school has drawn so much attention.

How do you rate the changes made from the former school system? Is the learning climate significantly better? Have the roles of teachers/learners been altered dramatically? Would Margot Hentoff send her children here? Would you send your children to a school like this?

LOUISIANA'S HIGH FLYING APOLLO SCHOOL

Margaret Martin
and Charlotte Burrows

It is almost paradoxical that in an area of the old South where tradition is revered and change comes slowly a public school system should pioneer two of education's sharper breaks with the past: the

Reprinted by permission from *American Education,* March, 1973, pp. 5–9.

open space school building and continuous progress learning. Yet down in Bossier Parish, Louisiana, the high-flying Apollo Elementary School, which is the pilot for these innovations in that State, has had such rewarding results that it has become the model for districts up and down and across the entire country that want to introduce similar changes in their own schools.

The Apollo School sprawls in the middle of Red River cotton fields, where plantations still largely dominate the economy of rural Northwest Louisiana, but close by is Barksdale Air Force Base and the roar of jet airplanes, a reminder that this is the 20th century. The Air Force people have without question contributed much of the progressive community spirit which brought about Apollo, and their presence is seen in the name of the school and in the makeup of its student body, giving it an oddly cosmopolitan complexion in its rural setting. Students might include the sharecropper's daughter and the general's son—for anyone living within the school district is routed to Apollo. With its air-conditioning, wall-to-wall carpeting, closed circuit television, and futuristic teaching equipment and methods, the $750,000 building is a far cry from the little one-room schoolhouses cherished in legend. The one-room concept is nevertheless reflected at Apollo, side by side with an array of modern educational techniques and innovations aimed at educating the whole child while at the same time giving maximum time to the individual.

Roy Breznik, director of the Bossier Parish Educational Resource Center, calls Apollo "the school without failures." It is a place, he says, where the child is never tagged as inferior, where report cards have no grades, where the children want to learn, and where they learn to learn. The zesty and yet relaxed atmosphere of the operation is symbolized by a building with few walls and dividing partitions and by a daily regimen marked by only two bells—one signifying the opening of school in the morning and the other the end of school in the afternoon.

Children are grouped homogeneously on levels for skill subjects rather than in grades, and they progress at their own speed. The number of youngsters in each group ranges from 12 to 27, though an effort is made to keep the maximum at 20. The students may work at one level in language arts and another in math, and they are grouped and regrouped as they progress at their own speed. Although an individual boy or girl occasionally needs prodding, as in a conventional classroom, at Apollo there is no insistence that a student finish a book at a certain set time. There are no deadlines.

This lack of pressure and the absence of grades on report cards is not to imply that less is expected of students at Apollo than at other schools or that parents are not informed about their children's standing. By the end of their six years of elementary education the youngsters are still expected to achieve a level of learning at least equal to that of children in conventional schools, and their report cards reflect their rate of progress. But the slow starter is not branded in the beginning with the stigma of a "D" or an "F." The rapid learner is not confined with youngsters who cannot keep pace with him, and there is a built-in flexibility in the plan for grouping and regrouping that provides for transfers if it becomes apparent that a student is outdistancing or falling behind the others in his group.

The theory is that, freed of undue pressures, the students will in due course work their way through all levels. The principal, Don Truly, acknowledges that inescapably there will be some students who cannot keep pace, and so there is provision for holdovers for a seventh year. But significantly, a seventh-year child at Apollo is not considered a failure—it just takes him longer to get where he is going. No child is detained beyond the seventh year.

Standardized textbooks are used, but teachers are at liberty to introduce various aids and enrichment materials of their own choosing. They follow a specially prepared curriculum guide which carefully lays out the levels in the program, subject by subject, and there is a detailed testing system for a continuous check on the grouping.

Truly uses the show-and-tell method for the frequent tours he conducts for visitors—as many as 200 in a week sometimes—who come to see the school from throughout the Nation. He has learned that most people have to see for themselves that 700 children can study and learn in one room without mass confusion. The fact is that, even when the children change classes, there is order and little noise, and it is a source of pride for Truly that discipline problems are rare. He had just made this latter point to a visitor when one little boy had to be isolated in the school foyer. Truly grinned and noted that "rare" is not the same as "never."

Most Apollo classes consist of small groupings of desks located in various parts of the large, green-carpeted room that is the principal element of the school plant. Though there are no windows, the absence of interior walls and the bright and cheerful decor provide a light and airy atmosphere. Colorful cutouts and displays decorate shelf ends, and here and there are various exhibits attuned to particular lesson themes. The central portion of the building is given over to a 7,200-square-foot resource center, the core of the overall operation. The center is, among other things, Apollo's version of the school library—containing not only books and other printed materials but tapes, reading labs, games, kits, models, film loops, filmstrips, and transparencies—as well as the focal point for most learning activities. This is where everyone comes together—an arrangement that seems to be enjoyed by faculty and students alike and which teachers are convinced benefits all of them. Everybody is tuned in to everybody else at Apollo.

"This way if someone does something great, we all know about it," says Jackie Sidaris, a faculty member who was a member of the planning committee for the school. She talks with enthusiasm that has not dwindled in the three years since Apollo first opened its doors, although she does not think the system is perfect—not yet. Like other members of the staff, she is particularly struck by two propositions: the ability of the children to study despite distractions, and the self-reliance that the system seems to promote. So accustomed have the children become to the openness of the school that visitors walk around at will without disturbing classwork, and the building custodian and maid hardly get a glance as they pass, dragging equipment behind them.

However, there is an elevated observation room with closed-circuit television that affords parents and instructors an opportunity to focus on a particular class or child. Sound comes from small microphones mounted in the ceiling tiles, with special filters largely eliminating such distracting sounds as the noise of air-conditioners and the rattle of paper.

On a recent Friday morning, visitors "tuned in" on John Castore, a teacher originally from New York City who came to Apollo via military service at Barksdale. He was teaching his fourth-level boys and girls a language arts lesson, and in general format it could have been a spelling drill and word study in any school. However, the impact of homogeneous grouping was apparent in the responsiveness of the students: All were usually attentive, few got off on tangents, everyone seemed eager to participate. Even when they were subsequently working alone, most of Castore's students pushed steadily forward on their own initiative, supplying their own stimulation.

There were, of course, exceptions. At one point, while giving instructions, exasperation penetrated Castore's voice. "We did this last week and the week before," he said. "You really ought to know what we are doing by now." And subsequently during the study session, a little blond girl bobbed up and down in her chair for a few minutes, shook her long curls, fidgeted with her pencil, and said a few words to another little girl across the aisle. With that brief break, however, they then both went back to work without a word of reprimand from their teacher, and no one seemed disturbed by the incident.

Elsewhere, large groups of children were studying science, physical education, music, and art. Such large heterogeneous groupings for these subjects and social studies are necessary to free a certain number of teachers to preside over small groups for the skill subjects—math and language arts. Shelves and storage bins sometimes serve as partitions between adjacent groups, thus reducing distractions without producing the closed-off formality of walls. For certain activities, of course—physical education and music classes, for example, and special seminars—the one-room, no-walls concept is not practical, and a few separate rooms have been established for these purposes.

An interest in innovative teaching methods is evident even in physical education. Thus Diane Collier dragged numerous thick cane poles from a local college fraternity garbage can (they had been discarded after a dance) so she could teach the Philippine dance known as "tinikling." "It's particularly useful and a good sport for coordination, balance, and flexibility," she says. Old familiar games and calisthenics are also included in her curriculum, but she frequently introduces new exercises that she makes up.

When it was opened in 1969, Apollo was considered downright revolutionary by many people in that section of the South, but in fact many of the concepts involved had been tested and tried in various other areas of the United States. The Bossier school is specifically based for the most part on Matzke School in the Cypress Fairbanks Independent School District near Houston, Texas. Bossier school officials, headed by former School Superintendent Emmett Cope, studied Matzke closely and devised a program they believed would incorporate its best features and at the same time improve them. Subsequently other schools have taken Apollo and improved on *it*.

Matzke did not have an observatorium as Apollo does. On the other hand, Harper Elementary School, which was modeled on Apollo in nearby Webster Parish, not only built more glassed-in areas for large groups but drew on the Bossier school's experience to do a more effective job of dealing with noise problems.

Apollo itself was launched with a $119,000 planning grant from Title III of the Elementary and Secondary Education Act. As a first step the Bossier School Board appointed a 55-member committee— composed of teachers, administrators, and specialists from cooperating universities—to study the educational needs of the parish and to develop alternative approaches to meeting those needs. As the occasion arose, consultants were brought in to provide advice in special fields. Then building on the year-long work of the committee, five teachers were put on leave to devote their full time to curriculum development.

Development of the curriculum was no simple matter. Mrs. Sidaris recalled that the five teachers were "put in a huge room with nothing but five old desks plopped in it. We stayed there one month and read everything we could get our hands on about nongraded programs," she says. Before they were through they had made contact with every State department of education in the Nation and received more than 500 pieces of material.

Cope's orders were to design a curriculum that put the child and his or her needs first, and to come up with material that would involve the senses. In hammering away on the "senses" theme he stressed the need to enable Bossier children to see and hear and feel the educational experience. He had a compelling conviction, he said, that the schools could not succeed in getting their message across unless they engaged the whole child. Thus the extensive use of teaching tools that utilize sight and sound in instruction.

The nongraded—or continuous progress—program which was approved uses levels of attainment and checklists for placement and evaluation of progress. Children are placed at particular levels through evaluation tests, ratings of past performance, and teacher judgment. A child must accomplish at least 80 percent of the progress expected at one level before he can move on to the next. Children coming from conventional schools are administered evaluation tests, and recommendations for levels (or grades) are rendered for children leaving Apollo for another system. Instead of six grades, there are 14 small steps in reading and 13 small steps in mathematics.

According to Breznik, the library stocks over 1,000 tapes that can be used for reading lessons. Children are given a prescription form and sent to the resource center with a "captain," a youngster who knows how to work the equipment. The center is used for remedial work or for makeup purposes. A child who has been absent can go there and get his instructions independently without the teacher having to go through it again and boring the other children. The center may be used for enrichment work, when, for instance, a child gets through with his work early and would otherwise be at loose ends.

Jan Scott, resource center director, notes that the procedures there are part of a plan to develop self-reliance by letting the students do as much as possible for themselves. "The basic thought," she explains, "is to start where the child is and take him as far as he can go, rather than set him in a mold and follow the mold."

In planning the curriculum, Bossier officials made their own reading materials or repackaged existing materials to meet Apollo's approach. Each tape was color-coded, with a blue dot for math and red dot for reading. But by and large the learning process is pretty much in the hands of the students themselves. On a typical day a group of children may come to the resource center and get Mrs. Scott's help in setting up a tape to work on spelling, but from that point on they handle the lesson themselves. Elsewhere in the center other children are sitting in carrels writing stories incorporating certain assigned words.

"The children check one another's work as soon as they are finished," Mrs. Scott says. "They don't have to wait for the teacher to grade it. They are going to have to take on more and more responsibility as they get older, and they won't be led by the hand. We help them learn to work by themselves."

Both Cope and Truly emphasize that there is nothing new in the academic concepts of the school. "They are all tried and true," Cope says. "The changes we have undertaken lie in such things as the organizational patterns and teaching techniques and, of course, the emphasis on trying to engage all the senses. There are no walls, but that doesn't mean that the teachers are of some special breed or that they are not on top of the situation." The teachers were not hand-picked, and they range in experience from beginning teachers to people who have been in the system for 25 years.

One aspect of the operation in which Bossier school officials take particular satisfaction is the furniture, which was designed and built by the school and, Breznik says, "saved us a lot of money." Cost of the carrels, shelves, and cabinets for the resource center and the teacher area was $17,000. The nearest commercial bid was $30,000. The furniture has since been copied by Webster Parish for use in the open space school there; Breznik adds, "We have given the plans to lots of other people as well."

Everyone at Apollo seems to like the no-wall concept, but it does exact penalties. Where do you put a bulletin board or hang examples of the students' work? and What do the youngsters do with their coats? Solution: specially designed and fabricated units constructed of tubular steel and equipped with corkboards, a magnetic chalk-board, a pull-down projection screen, and storage space for coats and books and other materials—all this mounted on coasters to provide mobility. Hinged drop leaves at each end serve as a teacher's temporary desk, and each teacher also has a carrel and filing drawers in a space adjoining the teachers' lounge.

Other Apollo-made carts—these with wooden panels on the ends and plastic laminate on the tops—take the place of traditional library bookshelves, which the planners felt would detract from the feeling of openness. Much of the other equipment is also on wheels, and most of it is child-sized.

"A good deal of planning went into all this," Breznik says, "and I think we did a good job, thanks in part to the fact that we could learn from the mistakes of other continuous learning schools." Equally important, he adds, the end result is not the product of one person, a flaw that was fatal in some cases elsewhere. The program is not a single individual's inspiration but a team-developed system. The principal became a member of this team only in the last stages of the project, and the team itself was broken up a year after the school opened, with only two of its members remaining at Apollo. Moreover, "Everything has been put down on paper. Everything is in the curriculum guide."

Why do Bossier educators feel that Apollo is successful? There are three reasons:

☐ Apollo is many innovations combined into a whole, an integrated entity whose parts include the building, the staff, the approach to teaching, the curriculum, and the coordinated application of technology.
☐ The community was brought into the planning early in the game, through presentations at Parent-Teacher Association sessions, service club meetings, and the like, and through such printed materials as pamphlets and even sample report cards.
☐ There is built-in accountability in the curriculum design.

As for the latter, Breznik notes that there are "literally thousands of tiny measurable skills that are divided into small packages that enable the individual child to work at the speed most suited to his or her ability. At each pre-established plateau, a child at Apollo is tested to determine his mastery of the skills expected at that level. Thus there is a direct reflection back to the teacher if groups of children consistently fail to master the skills for which that teacher is responsible."

No one at Apollo regards the system as perfect, and though no major mistakes have as yet surfaced, Truly acknowledges that "it's not the answer to all problems."

Perhaps the biggest disappointment is the $30,000 television unit, the problem being that the TV planning and production processes require people with experience and backgrounds that Apollo has not yet been able to develop. Thus use of the closed-circuit television apparatus is limited to observation.

As for other imperfections, Mrs. Sidaris feels that there is need to re-examine the curriculum. "We need to go back and look at the content of the various levels," she says, "particularly in terms of eliminating inessential details and broadening the concepts involved." Some of the others think that the noise level is at times a serious distraction, even though it is muffled considerably by the carpeting and the low ceilings. Some teachers and students as well have reservations about being constantly "on stage," and not everyone likes the endless togetherness. Nonetheless, a faculty group agreed over coffee in the lounge that the advantages of the system outweigh the disadvantages. The fact that they were able to break away for a few minutes during midmorning classes demonstrated, they said, the effectiveness of the system in developing self-reliance among the students.

The crucial question and the one that remains unanswered is how Apollo students stack up against their counterparts elsewhere. Everybody involved "feels" that the system is working—really believes it—and reports filtering back from transfers to other systems seem to bear that feeling out. Still, the administration cannot be positive that Apollo students are learning as much in six years as are children in other schools because so far there has been no testing program that could be used as a yardstick.

The Bossier School Board is so convinced of the success of the project that two years ago it extended the continuous learning approach to all of the elementary schools in the parish. But Breznik points out that no arrangements were made to set up a "control" school, and thus there is no way of documenting the effectiveness of one system as compared with another.

This is not a matter of Apollo teaching staff trends to fret about. The children are demonstrably interested in learning, they say, prominently including children who failed to respond to traditional classrooms either because the classes moved too rapidly for them or because they felt they were being held back.

Reflecting on her experiences before Apollo, Mrs. Sidaris recalled a youngster who occupied himself in a reading class by digging a fair-sized hole all the way through the back of a desk. "He managed to do that with a pair of scissors," she says with a shake of her head. "Plain old scissors." She doesn't expect anything like that to happen at Apollo, because no one there is bored.

The foremost symbol of modern technology is the computer. Schools have been criticized for not making enough use of the computer. The following article reviews how computers are being used in classrooms today.

Lendt's article details some of the developments in the PLATO system. You may find yourself surprised by the capabilities of this system, and by its low cost (now nearing fifty cents per student hour). You may conclude, nevertheless, that computers still do not fundamentally improve education.

PLATO, FAMOUS TEACHER, TAKES UP RESIDENCE AT ISU

David Lendt

Plato is alive and living in Room 206B in Curtiss Hall on the Iowa State University campus. I'm no name-dropper, but I met him recently.

That's Plato IV (Programmed Logic for Automatic Teaching Operations, Fourth Generation), not exactly a direct descendant of the Greek philosopher but a sophisticated piece of hardware whose umbilical cord reaches to the University of Illinois.

It is a keyboard-and-display panel monitor with which Iowa State researchers can experiment with new methods of computer assisted instruction (CAI). Proponents of CAI tout it as the "coming thing" and one of the few avenues available to schools for increasing the quality of teaching while reducing instructional costs.

Whether CAI is all its allies claim remains to be seen. The National Science Foundation has allotted $5 million to an extended test of the Plato system and the legislature of Illinois has provided another $5 million to check out the brainchild born on the Urbana campus.

The topics available through the Plato keyboard are wide-ranging. They include such programs as an animated lunar landing and an

Reprinted by permission of the author from *News of Iowa State*, July–August, 1973, p. 7.

experiment in social behavior, testing the territorial limits of animated birds on a telephone wire.

The machine can be utilized in either an "author's mode" or a "student mode." The former allows an instructor to put his CAI lesson into the computer at the University of Illinois. That requires more sophistication and, in some respects, more skill, than the "student mode." In the latter, the "student" may select from a sheet listing the various lessons and learning games those he or she prefers.

Plato is important to researchers in the College of Education, whether they are analyzing lessons already in Plato's transistorized portfolio or are experimenting with programming lessons of their own into his inventory of subjects and classes.

Virgil Lagomarcino, Dean of the College of Education, believes the console is an important addition which will benefit teachers, students and researchers in the College. "The practice of using the computer as a learning aid will probably be with us for a long time to come," he says. "Any experience we can derive from this experimental arrangement is bound to be helpful to our students and teachers-researchers."

Plato, in the short time since he occupied his office, has become a popular teacher. Seems everyone wants to visit with him and one secretary in Curtiss Hall keeps his busy appointment calendar as one of her several duties. The tireless fellow generally has visitors from early in the day until well into the night, including weekends.

Except for his tendency to stare, Plato is easy enough to be around. In addition to being an electrophysical wonder, he is an entertaining fellow. Rex Thomas, assistant professor of education and computer science, introduced us and I initiated our chat (Plato never starts a conversation) by pressing several appropriate buttons—codes which allowed me to communicate with "control central" in Illinois. Plato spewed some data upon his plasma television-like display panel, including an invitation to press more buttons until I got what I wanted.

I eventually requested, and received, a biology-genetics experiment—the simulated reproduction of fruit flies. I began with a male and female fruit fly, placed on the screen by Plato. I mated them by pushing a button and, in response, Plato threw a "hatch" of 18 (any number could have been requested) fruit flies on the screen, numbered 1 through 18. From among them, I could choose any two and mate them and get another hatch. The possibilities were virtually endless but the point was made clear that certain dominant and recessive traits appeared, disappeared and reappeared with various parental combinations.

In essence, Plato, with his super speed, could show me instantly what fruit flies in a laboratory might take days or weeks to reveal. In 20 minutes, I could examine as many generations as in a quarter-long laboratory experiment with real flies.

One of the pleasantries of conversing with Plato is that he won't embarrass you unless you ask for it. Once the lesson becomes too complicated (trying to follow a given trait of fruit flies through 10 inbred generations, for example) you can simply press the "Back" button on the console and Plato will clear his screen and ask you to choose any programmed lesson you wish.

I chose "Happy Addition." Plato flashed various addition problems (on the order of 8 + 3) on the viewing screen. The problems appeared in the mouth of a familiar "Happy Face" and I was asked to tap out the answers on the number keyboard. When I pressed the correct answer, the "Happy Face" mouth filled with teeth and the smile turned up even more. When I pressed an incorrect answer (nobody's perfect) the "Happy Face" suddenly frowned. Frantically, I tried again. Wrong again. And the Unhappy Face became even unhappier and tears began to fall from one of its eyes. It was depressing.

I pressed the "Back" button.

Next, I selected "Guess the Number." Plato stated on his screen that he had a number "in mind" and asked me to type in questions with which I might be able to tell what the number was. The more inquiries I made, the higher my score and a high score in "Guess the Number," as in golf, isn't the sort of thing you tell your friends about.

My lightning mind suggested, "Is the number more than 50?" Plato said, "Yes." I asked, "Is the number more than 10,000?" "No," he answered. Quick as that, I had the number narrowed down to something between 50 and 10,000!

"Is the number more than 5,000?" was my next probing inquiry. "No." Already I had the number "bracketed" between 50 and 5,000.

Rex observed that my score was rising rapidly. "Why not ask if the number is divisible by another number?" he suggested.

"Is the number divisible by 5?" I asked. "No. When divided by 5, there is a remainder of 2." Now I knew that it was a number between 50 and 5,000 and that it ended with a 7 or 2. With the help of a pencil and scratch paper, I determined that I had the number suddenly reduced to about 990 possibilities! "Is it divisible by 7?" I asked. "No. When divided by 7, there is a remainder of 3."

(Plato, surprisingly, understood my questions regardless of how I phrased them and generated appropriate responses to them. He also "scored" me on a rising scale for ineffective questions and penalized me less for more incisive inquiries. The exercise encourages the student to discover the properties and relationships of numbers and to apply those discoveries through a well-constructed questioning scheme. An electrical engineer, given the information I had generated, devised a single additional question which would reveal the number!)

I pressed the "Back" button.

Next, I selected one of several "Phys-games" which Plato provides for his guests' frustration. Each is an experiment, concerning principles of physics. He allows you to vary certain inputs, keeps a record of what you've done and plots a chart of various results. It's all very scientific. I tried an experimental lunar landing. I controlled the expenditure of fuel and Plato kept track of time, height of lunar landing craft, velocity and fuel consumption.

I'd watched, with millions of fellow Americans, when our astronauts landed on the moon. And I knew enough physics to figure that the closer you get to the surface of the moon, the more power you give the landing craft so that it doesn't land too hard, right?

I carefully watched the data appear on the charts as I varied the fuel consumption. The craft descended on an irregular curve. Closer to the surface, I poured more fuel to the roaring engines. Everything was "A-OK" as we say at NASA. The craft finally touched the moon—and exploded. I checked the columnar data. It had made contact at a velocity of 23 feet per second, or about 15 miles per hour. That could be a jolt.

I pressed the "Back" button. . .

To many students, the exotic changes in building design or the introduction of computers will not be as significant as reform in the grading system.

Current terminology, such as non-graded, pass-fail, credit-non-credit, and the contract approach, suggests that beleaguered students and harried professors may be in for an easier time when evaluation periods roll around. Alan Small, however, reminds us of some previous attempts at revamping the marking system that did not succeed. He also infers some of the required ingredients needed to lessen the role that grades now play.

MARKING PRACTICES IN HISTORICAL PERSPECTIVE
Alan A. Small

One of the liveliest issues on the educational circuit these days centers on the question of whether our marking (grading) practices urgently need reform. Already many colleges and secondary schools, under pressure from faculty, students, and community are experimenting with a wide variety of alternative systems, the reported results of which have been, predictably, ambiguous, conflicting, and altogether inconclusive.[1] This article, in examining our present dilemma from the historical perspective, will not solve the problems facing educators, but it may engender a better understanding of the sources of our discontent.

HISTORICAL CONSIDERATIONS IN REPORTING STUDENT PROGRESS

The issue of marking reform has been one of long standing—so long, in fact, that we have forgotten that the "innovative" reforms of the present, such as pass-fail options and criterion-based systems, have

From *Educational Studies,* 1973, 4, 4, pp. 189–197. Reprinted with permission of the Editor, *Educational Studies.*

1. See, for example, Jonathan B. Warren, *College Grading Practices: An Overview,* Research Bulletin RB 71–12 (Princeton, N.J.: Educational Testing Service, March, 1971).

flourished previously. It appears as if all conceivable "systems" have been tried before and will be tried again by each generation in the seemingly endless quest for a solution to the problem of evaluating and reporting student achievement. Considering the central role that "marks" play in the academic and adult life of the student, and in the professional career of the teacher, one can but wonder why there has been so little progress made in arriving at a few fundamental principles and practices which would have the general consent of the teaching profession.

The evolution of marking systems will be considered from three points of view: one, how marks have been reported (i.e., in what form); two, what criteria have been used to arrive at the distribution; three, who has the responsibility for appraising student achievement. Each of these topics is inextricably involved in our current efforts to find a solution to the dilemma of "grades."

REPORTING STUDENT PROGRESS: THE FORM

It should be noted at the outset that reporting on student progress in some differential manner has been characteristic of our schools from the beginning. The earliest form of such reports was *verbal* in nature. For instance, from the *Literary Diary of Ezra Stiles,* the president of Yale, we learn that 58 students in the year 1785 were classified as follows: "twenty *Optimi,* sixteen second *Optimi,* 12 *Inferiores* (*Boni*), ten *Pejores.*"[2] Another example of the verbal style, taken from an 1817 report from William and Mary, appraised the student's progress thus: "No. 1—The first in their respective classes, orderly and attentive and have made flattering improvement. No. 2—Orderly, correct and attentive and their improvement has been respectable. No. 3—They have made very little improvement and as we apprehend from want of Diligence. No. 4—They have learnt little or nothing and we believe on account of escapaid and Idleness."[3]

The appearance of *numerical scales* dates from the beginning of the nineteenth century. Unlike verbal reports, numerical scales allowed the reporting of student progress in terms of "averages." In addition, when the scale was based on 100, it carried with it the suggestion of preciseness—that there was something significant between a difference of one percentage point. The earliest report of the use of a numerical scale is found in the 1813 Yale *Book of Averages.*

2. Mary Lovett Smallwood, *An Historical Study of Examinations and Grading Systems in Early American Universities* (Cambridge, Mass.: Harvard University Press, 1935), p. 42.
3. *Ibid.,* p. 44.

It was the duty of each senior tutor to enter into his book the average attainment of each of his students. The marking scale was 4 and for that year the lowest average was 1.3 and the highest was 3.7.[4]

In 1825, under the presidency of Josiah Quincey, Harvard instituted its infamous Scale of Merit. A student's mark or grade was based on a blend of his academic achievement and his citizenship. The initial scale was based on 8; by 1830, it had been changed to 20; and by 1837, marking on the basis of 100 was implemented. According to Morison, the Scale of Merit, because it sought to combine in a single mark two distinct criteria—the academic and the ethical—served to undermine student-teacher relations: "Almost every graduate of the period 1825–1860 has left on record his detestation of the system of instruction at Harvard; and . . . that the root of the evil was the marking system."[5]

The numerical scale, especially the percentage-based system, dominated the reporting of student progress in the latter half of the nineteenth century and the first quarter of the twentieth. But it was not without its critics. Even before the pioneer work of F. W. Johnson in 1911 and Starch and Elliott in 1912, which showed that a difference of between 5 to 7 percent in measured achievement was the smallest that could be reliably estimated, faculty had become concerned over the illusion of precision fostered by the percentile system and were alarmed over the growing phenomenon of students working only for the grade. Efforts to ameliorate both these problems took two directions: one direction aimed to eliminate the race for grades by removing them, so far as was possible; the other direction, by far the more common, was to rank students according to five broad categories.

The "removal" of grades approach found some institutions experimenting with varieties of the "pass-fail" concept. Perhaps the first institution to abandon conventional marking practice was the University of Michigan. In 1851, it adopted a strict "pass-fail" system which by 1864 had been modified to three categories based on a scale of 100: "passed," "conditioned," and "must review."[6] By 1895, the University of Michigan's grading system had been modified into five categories: "passed," "incomplete," "conditioned," "not passed," "absent."[7] For a short time at the end of the nineteenth

4. *Ibid.*, p. 43.
5. Samuel Eliot Morison, *Harvard College in the 17th Century* (Cambridge, Mass.: Harvard University Press, 1936), p. 260.
6. Smallwood, *An Historical Study*, p. 49.
7. *Ibid.*, p. 52.

century, Harvard had a three category system: "passed," "failed," and "passed with distinction."

More popular and more enduring than the pass-fail concept, however, was the practice of differentiating among levels of student achievement on the basis of broad categories signified by a letter. Letter-based systems began in the last quarter of the nineteenth century, but it has been in the twentieth century that most colleges and secondary schools have accepted the letter as the most meaningful reporting device for any classification system.[8] W. R. Thayer, in his historical sketch of Harvard, described the letter system adopted in 1890: "In each of their courses students are now divided into five groups, called A, B, C, D, E. . . . To graduate, a student must have passed in all his courses, and have stood above the group D in at least one-fourth of his college work."[9]

REPORTING STUDENT PROGRESS: THE CRITERIA

On what basis should student achievement be differentiated? Interestingly during the entire history of American education there have been but two fundamentally contrasting principles employed: one is the principle of "absolute" achievement or performance; the other is a variation of the normal distribution principle. Of these two systems the one with the longest tradition (which today is experiencing a resurgence under such labels as "criterion-referenced" or "performance-based") is that which forces the student to demonstrate his proficiency against some "fixed" or "absolute" standard. The Egyptian scribe, the Greek grammaticus, and the Roman rhetor all used models of excellence which their pupils were required to emulate. Students were taught to be "letter perfect" by having them conform to the contours in a wax tablet with a stylus. The student of the medieval and Renaissance periods was likewise evaluated on the basis of demonstrated *mastery* of the particular skill or subject, and advanced study was withheld from those who failed.[10] Moreover, students were grouped on the basis of profiency rather than by their ages.[11] At the medieval university we know that degree examinations were public affairs and the fate of the disputant did not lie with

8. Arthur E. Traxler, *Techniques of Guidance* (New York: Harper, 1957), p. 38; R. M. Roelfs, "Trends in Junior High School Reporting," *Journal of Educational Research* 49 (1955): 241–249.
9. Smallwood, *An Historical Study*, p. 53.
10. Philippe Aries, *Centuries of Childhood* (New York: Vintage Books, 1962), p. 147.
11. *Ibid.*, p. 153.

grade-point averages, but with his ability to demonstrate his proficiency and gain the favorable consensus of his masters.

Thus, throughout the ancient and medieval world a crude but effective pass-fail system of education prevailed. This system of demonstrated performance against a fixed norm continued to be the accepted means of measuring student attainment into modern times, and in the United States at least, was used throughout most of the nineteenth century where it was combined with various *forms* of reporting as previously described.

First-hand accounts of American schoolmastering in the first half of the nineteenth century tell us of the crucial importance of the annual examination day at the end of the winter term. It was a combination social-academic occasion when the families would assemble to observe their children being "examined" by the appointed examining committee. Each student would be examined *orally* in each subject he had studied that term (spelling, arithmetic, reading, grammar), and each notebook would be inspected for thoroughness, accuracy, and neatness. The committee's judgment was based on true "performance criteria"—there could be no cheating or bluffing: the pupil either knew the rule of 3, how to spell "Connecticut," the location of Albany, N.Y., or he didn't.

That a pupil might fail was a real possibility. In his recollections *The School District As It Was* (1833), Warren Burton remarks that, "If the school had been under the care of a good instructor, all was well of course; if a poor one, it was too late to help."[12] A good description of the graded performance scale for reading is provided by Burton: first, the "abecedarian stage" wherein the child must memorize the alphabet; second, the child passed on to the study of syllables such as "ab," "ib," "ub," etc.; if he accomplished this he was allowed to advance to the study of whole, one-syllable words; then, multi-syllabic words; and finally on to simple sentences, and so on.

Another example of the use of explicit performance criteria comes from this sample of the standards for admission to the eighth grade in a Boston grammar school in 1847: the student "ought to be able to write sentences and parse, showing the relation of all parts of speech; to write all the parts of Speech; to write all the words in his reading lessons; to read distinctly and fluently any piece of narrative or didactic prose or verse in his reader and give the meaning of any of the words which occur therein; to give the boundaries of all the States and to draw them readily from memory upon the slate or

12. Warren Burton, *The District School As It Was,* ed. Clifton Johnson (New York: Crowell, 1928).

black board; and to enumerate the principal productions, natural and artificial, of the different countries, and the principal rivers, mountains, lakes, and towns of each."[13]

While the evidence for the prevalence of performance-based criteria cited here has come from the lower schools, the same criteria can be said to have been employed by the institutions of higher education. For example, the 1646 entrance requirements to Harvard College specified that "when any Schollar is able to Read Tully or such like classicall Latine Authour ex tempore, & make and speake true Latin in verse and prose suo (ut aiunt) Marte, and decline perfectly the paradigmes of Nounes and verbes in ye Greeke toungue, then may hee bee admitted into ye Colledge, nor shall any claime admission before such qualifications."[14]

However, by the latter half of the nineteenth century a search for a more "scientific" means of appraising the distribution of academic talent was underway. The search for such a method resulted in the ultimate and widespread acceptance of the principle of the normal probability curve coupled with a scale of five divisions. In the early decades of the twentieth century such advocates of this principle as Cattell, Meyer, Dearborn, and Finkelstein were convinced that student ability and accomplishment conformed to the principle of normal biological distribution and that, therefore, it constituted the only sound and consistent basis for classifying scholastic performance.[15] The University of Missouri pioneered in the use of the normal probability curve, and the "Missouri System" soon became in the twentieth century the nearest thing to a standard grading system this country has ever had. The most popular variation of this principle was that which held that student accomplishment will most likely fall in a distribution that is skewed to the right and that the most accepted measures of student achievement should approximate the following percentages: 3 percent, Excellent; 21 percent, Superior; 45 percent, Average; 19 percent, Poor; 12 percent, Unsatisfactory to Failure.[16]

13. Otis W. Caldwell and Stuart A. Courtis, *Then and Now in Education (1845–1923)* (New York: World Book Co., 1924), p. 125.

14. John Hardin Best, ed., *The American Legacy of Learning: Readings in the History of Education* (Philadelphia: J. B. Lippincott, 1967), p. 35.

15. J. McK. Cattell, "Examinations, Grades and Credits," *Popular Science Monthly* 66 (1905): 376–378; Max F. Meyer, "An Experiment with the Grading System of the University of Missouri," *Science* (New Series) 33 (April, 1911): 661–667; W. F. Dearborn, "School and University Grades," *University of Wisconsin Bulletin*, No. 368 (1910); I. E. Finkelstein, "The Marking System in Theory and Practice," *Educational Psychology Monographs*, No. 10 (Baltimore: Warwick and York, 1913).

16. W. T. Foster, "Scientific vs Personal Distribution of College Credit," *Popular Science Monthly* 78 (April, 1911): 388–408; Finkelstein, *op. cit.*

In principle and practice the normal curve continues to have its adherents today, but it is being challenged by a resurgence of interest in fixed, performance-type tasks. Over the past two decades the assumptions about the applicability of the normal curve principle to a teacher's class have come under heavy criticism: one, that the normal curve only works when applied to large, randomly selected numbers, not classroom size student bodies; two, that the principle, literally applied, arbitrarily and automatically demands that a certain percentage of students will "pass" and "fail" regardless of their actual achievement; three, that when one bases his standards on the curve, he is allowing the talent of the learners to determine the criteria for academic excellence.

The renewed interest in the value of "absolute" standards is today most commonly referred to under the label of "criterion-referenced system." It utilizes performance-based objectives worded in terms of what the learner is to be able to do at the conclusion of the learning, rather than in terms of vague and ambiguous teacher expectations.[17] The chief advantages of this system are said to be: 1) with the quantity and quality of what the student is to learn explicitly spelled out to him *in advance*, both teacher and student will know precisely what is to be expected and given emphasis; 2) with the criteria for noting student progress lying solely between the individual student and the clearly prescribed tasks to be accomplished, the idea of "grading on the curve" is abandoned altogether; 3) with the learning tasks clearly in view, more efficient teaching and learning will take place (students will no longer have to "guess" what will be on the test); 4) improved student-teacher relations will come about as a result of the more open atmosphere and objective criteria by which the student will be marked; 5) academic standards will be less affected by group performance, as under the "curve" system, thereby protecting the principle of educational quality.

Behind the development of criterion-referenced systems is the growing awareness that the persistent confusion over grading is but a symptom of a deeper confusion over educational objectives. The fact that marking practices are integral to the total educational situation in any school was the central point brought out in Wrinkle's study, the most comprehensive analysis of the marking issue ever made in this country.[18] Reporting on the ten-year study at Colorado State

17. Robert Glaser, "Ten Untenable Assumptions of College Instruction," *The Educational Record* 49 (Spring, 1968): 154–159.
18. William L. Wrinkle, *Improving Marking and Reporting Practices in Elementary and Secondary Schools* (New York: Rinehart and Co., 1947).

College (1929–1939), Wrinkle concluded that the problem of marking was dependent upon the clarification of the learning objectives of
the institution and of each individual department and teacher within
the institution. The report advocated a thorough study of one's
institutional philosophy, the participation of each segment of the
academic community (including especially the students), and the
formation of learning tasks in explicit performance terms. Wrinkle's
conclusions are supported in Smith and Dobbin's 1957 review of
marking systems: "no commonly accepted [marking] system has
emerged from half a century of inquiry. Perhaps the development of
such a system awaits wider agreement on the goals of instruction and
the purposes of marking."[19] Whether criterion-referenced systems
will eventually gain this "wider agreement" is, as yet, uncertain.

REPORTING STUDENT PROGRESS: WHO SHOULD BE RESPONSIBLE?

One of the most interesting questions to ask about reporting student
progress is, "Who should be responsible for examining and reporting
on student achievement?" The American practice in this regard has
been to rest this responsibility upon the classroom teacher. This
tradition is well over a century old, and we have forgotten that it was
not always so. Until, roughly, the middle of the last century the two
functions of teaching, on the one hand, and examining-reporting, on
the other hand, were kept quite distinct. "Teaching" at all school
levels was considered a full role in itself, and "examining" was left to
special "examining committees" appointed by the president of the
college, or, in the case of the lower schools, by the school board.
    Under this system of external appraisal, a teacher's competency
was judged as well as that of his students. The schoolmaster and the
college professor functioned as a coach—he listened to each student's
recitations and he drilled them in the arts of the particular subjects
involved. He drove them with various motivational techniques ranging from benevolent kindness to the use of the rod. In the end,
however, the teacher depended upon the judgment of the examining
committee, not on any test he, himself, might devise. It was the duty
of the teacher to prepare his students against the time when they
would be called upon to demonstrate their proficiency "before all
Commers" as is suggested by these regulations concerning final

19. A. Smith and J. Dobbins, "Marks and Marking Systems," *The Encyclopedia of Educational Research,* ed. C. W. Harris (New York: Macmillan, 1960), pp. 783–791.

examinations at Harvard College adopted May 6, 1650: "To the Intent that no schollar may mispend his time, to the dishonour of God and the society or the grief and disappointment of his friends, but that the yearly progresse and sufficiency of Scollars may be manifest: Its therefore order'd: that hence forth there shall bee three weeks of visitation yearly foresignifyed publikely by the Praesident of the Colledge . . . wherein . . . all scholars two years standing and upward shall sit in the Hall to bee examined by all Commers in the Latine, Greek and Hebrew tongues and in Rhetoricke, Logike and Physicks . . . and in Case any . . . faill in the premises required at their hands according to their standings respectively or bee found insufficient for their time and standing in the Judgement of any three of the visitors being overseers of the Colledge they shall bee deferred to the following Year but they that are approoved sufficient for their degrees shall proceed."[20]

The critical importance of these annual final examinations may be difficult for us to grasp. Promotion from class to class and all degrees depended entirely upon the student's performance during the weeks set aside to public examination. There was nothing like the averaging of marks over a semester's time as is commonplace today. There was no graduated scale of merit. There were no written exercises. The practice of maintaining a strict separation of the teaching and examining functions continued at many institutions until the middle of the nineteenth century as witnessed by the report on the examination of students shortly after the founding of the University of Michigan in 1842: "Some of the Visitors have attended the examinations of the students at the conclusion of the last two terms of the University, and had a full opportunity to judge of the improvement of the scholars, the mode of instruction, and the competency of the Professors. In each of these particulars, the Visitors were fully satisfied."[21]

Evidence exists that this tradition of separation had begun to disappear as early as the last quarter of the eighteenth century. The *Faculty Records* of William and Mary College for the year 1770 tell us that by that time the "academic officers"—the masters and the president—had replaced the outside examining committee.[22] William and Mary's 1851 catalogue tells us that "each class shall be examined . . . by a committee of the Faculty consisting of two Professors."[23] Another early instance of the use of faculty to examine the

20. Morison, *Harvard College in the 17th Century*, p. 67.
21. Smallwood, *An Historical Study*, p. 20.
22. *Ibid.*, p. 18.
23. *Ibid.*, p. 21.

students is found in an 1827 *Report to the Overseers at Harvard,* in which it is stated that "on Thursday April 3rd they attended an Examination of several members of the Sophomore Class in French, Spanish and Italian. The examination was conducted on the part of the Immediate Government by Professors X. C. and T. Every exertion was made on the part of those Gentlemen to render the examination as thorough and accurate as possible."[24]

The investing of professors and schoolmasters with both the teaching and examining functions was due to a number of factors operating throughout the first half of the nineteenth century. With increasing student enrollment, increasing subject matter complexity, the addition of new subjects such as modern foreign languages and the sciences, and the experiments in "volunteer studies" (electives) at some institutions, it was becoming increasingly difficult to find outsiders as competent as the teaching faculty to judge student proficiency. Another contributing factor was the introduction of written examinations. Inevitably, the evaluation of these papers fell increasingly on single members of the faculty.

Smallwood supplies evidence of the first use of written examinations at Harvard in the 1833 Report to the Overseers. At this time it was apparently experimental and used in combination with oral examinations. While written questions made it possible to "standardize" the examination by asking large numbers of students the same questions, it had the disadvantage of removing from the student the benefit of several judges. In addition, the impersonal written examination allowed no opportunity for spontaneous communication between the mind of the examiner and the examined. Also, with the growing spirit of professionalism, the college professor was no longer content with the role of coach or tutor, but rather viewed himself as an expert in his "discipline." In the lower schools a more humanitarian motive was at work serving to change the image of the "schoolmaster" into that of the "educator." No longer was he a mere coach, a young man in his late teens or early twenties with but a common-school education himself who seldom viewed schoolmastering as a lifetime career. He was now a graduate of an academy or one of the new normal schools, and he was beginning to consider himself an instrument for molding a better society on earth. He believed this if he listened to the prophets of education like Horace Mann, James G. Carter, and Henry Barnard. A final contributing factor was the "class system." By 1850, most city schools had adopted the class system perfected by the Prussians. The typical sub-secondary school

24. *Ibid.,* p. 19.

of this period was of two stories with four rooms to each floor, and each room had its own class and its own teacher. Within this school were children ranging in age from 5 to 7 (primary), 7 to 10 (intermediate), and 10 to 14 (grammar). The age of specialization, standardization, and homogeneous grouping (by age) was dawning. The promotion of pupils on the basis of individual proficiency was being replaced by the lock-step practice of grouping and promoting chiefly on the basis of age coupled with standards designed to reflect "average" attainment for each age group. In his new status position, it was left to the discrimination of each teacher to set his own standards of promotion or failure. The tradition of outside examination had passed.

The fact that by the middle of the nineteenth century teachers no longer had to suffer independent appraisal was not an unmixed blessing. An external examining committee may have been an annoyance, but it did provide a measure of "objectivity." With each teacher his own authority, there was no longer any common standard for appraising student achievement. Writing in the *Public School Journal* in 1886 one schoolman observed: "There is nothing definite about them. No two teachers would mark the same paper alike; and I have sometimes wondered how much a night's rest or a breakfast has had to do with papers marked 98 or 99 on the one hand, and 15 and 0 on the other."[25]

The significance of having an educational system which operated without a distinct examining body was not lost on Charles W. Eliot, president of Harvard, who in his 1869 inaugural address observed that "it would be a great gain if all subsequent college examinations could be as impartially conducted by competent examiners brought from without the college and paid for their services. When the teacher examines his class, there is no effective examination of the teacher. If the examinations for the scientific, theological, medical, and dental degrees were conducted by independent boards of examiners, appointed by professional bodies of dignity and influence, the significance of these degrees would be greatly enhanced. . . . The American practice of allowing the teaching body to examine for degrees has been partly dictated by the scarcity of men outside the faculties who are at once thoroughly acquainted with the subjects of examinations, and sufficiently versed in teaching to know what may fairly be expected of both students and instructors."[26]

25. James Mulhern, *A History of Secondary Education in Pennsylvania* (Philadelphia, 1933), p. 593.
26. Smallwood, *An Historical Study*, p. 22.

The American practice of the teacher also serving as the evaluator deprived the student of impartial multiple evaluation and made it impossible for there to be any objective criteria by which to evaluate the teacher. Yet another consequence of the assumption of the examining function by the teacher was that it brought with it the responsibilities and problems of marking papers, preparing and grading tests, and deciding on final marks. It should not be too much to say that the loss of the distinction between teaching and examining constitutes one of the major pedagogical developments of the nineteenth century.

CONCLUDING COMMENTS

Some of the main criticisms of grading being raised today are: 1) that the responsibility of marking is one of the principal bugbears of the teacher; 2) that teacher marks are a major cause of poor student-teacher relations; 3) that marks serve to motivate the student to get the mark rather than the material to be learned; 4) that marks foster a ruthless competition turning academic study into something like an athletic contest; 5) that overattention to academic talent can give a distorted view of a student's full potential; and 6) that identification with the grade may serve to distort the student's self-estimate.

As the preceding section of this article has shown, the responsibility for examining students for the purpose of recommending them for promotion, degrees, and scholarships has not always rested with the instructor. From the colonial period to the mid-nineteenth century the teaching function and the examining-grading function were kept quite distinct: the teachers "taught"; a separate body of examiners "examined." However, as the teachers assumed the dual role, they could no longer honestly side with the student in order to prepare him against examination day. The assumption of the examining-grading function inevitably placed the instructor in an adversary position vis-à-vis the student. From this time to ours the teacher has been living with his greatest dilemma: that of trying to reconcile these two distinct functions. It is doubtful if this can ever be satisfactorily done. Closer student-teacher relations may require the removal of the onus of examination from the back of the teacher.

Since the teacher did not prepare students for his own examination, the maintenance of scholastic standards was in the hands of an independent body. The advantages of this situation were many. The time-consuming responsibility for preparing and grading tests was removed from the individual instructor. Also, the problems attendant to the variability of teacher marks did not exist. Hence, with standards independently set, students, as they do today, did not spend their time comparing and complaining about the grading philosophies of their professors. A corollary of this was that with independently run examinations, some objective means for evaluating teacher effectiveness existed. The professor whose students consistently outperformed the others on independently prepared examinations would have good reason to be commended. And finally, not only did students not have to face examinations made up by their own teachers, but the evaluation of their performance was made by the examining committee—a group, not a single individual. Thus, his fate was decided by consensus, not by a single opinion. The remnants of this rich democratic tradition survive mainly at the graduate level today.

With reference to marking systems, we find today in the writings of the critics a call to minimize the "making the grade" syndrome. As has been shown, present pass-fail systems had their nineteenth-century counterparts and constituted the policy used by our colonial predecessors. Too, the current attention being given to developing "performance objectives" is but a return to the earlier and perhaps more modest concept of "schooling" as opposed to the more ambitious concept, "education."

Nevertheless, earlier practice failed to distinguish between individual achievement: the pass-fail philosophy is based on *minimum* standards only; it ignores both maximum performance and the varying degrees in between. Not only does a simple pass-fail system ignore individual differences, but, more importantly, it ignores the concept of relative standards, or degrees of excellence. Would we accept a pass-fail philosophy toward the grading of agricultural produce or meat? Would we accept it for field and track competition? The answer should be obvious. Already schools experimenting with pass-fail systems report that they fear students are working only hard enough to "pass"; there may be little incentive to excel in pass-fail courses.[27]

If schools are to expect high-level performance, they will probably have to modify or abandon the simple pass-fail philosophy. Some system which recognizes varying degrees of attainment seems both desirable and inevitable. However, the chief problem of marking is

---

27. J. H. Blackhurst, "Do We Measure in Education?" *Journal of Educational Research* 27 (December, 1933): 273; John S. Brubacher, "Axiological Aspects of Method," *Modern Philosophies of Education* (4th ed.; New York: McGraw-Hill, 1969), pp. 268–274; J. O. Urmson, "On Grading," *Mind* 59 (April, 1950): 145–169; John M. Rich, "A Philosophical Analysis of Educational Standards," *Educational Theory* 17 (April, 1967): 160–166.

not marking per se, but with the question of who prepares and marks the examinations. When these duties rest with each single teacher, as they have for the past 125 years, it necessarily creates the kind of problems we have today both in how the teacher spends his time and in regard to student-teacher relations.

There is no reason why academic standards could not be maintained as well or better by an independent examining-marking process. Independent examining committees need not be made up of "outsiders," but might be composed of department members who would be charged with the responsibility of drawing up the course objectives and syllabus as well as conducting the examinations and reporting marks. They might, if they chose, also employ standardized examinations.

Lessening the importance which students give to grades could be accomplished by the simple expedient of making academic performance only a part of, and not the whole of, the transcript. One's future should not be predicated on academic measures alone. It has been noted that academic talent, as such, may have but limited value and may not be an especially useful attribute in the world at large. [28] It may be time to give careful consideration to the insight expressed by the Harvard Overseers in 1886: "It is well that young men in college should become used to the standards which prevail in the world outside, where a man's rank among his fellows is determined by many different considerations."[29]

28. See J. L. Holland and J. M. Richards, Jr., "Academic and Non-academic Accomplishment: Correlated or Uncorrelated?" *Journal of Educational Psychology* 56 (August, 1965): 165; John Holt, "I Oppose Testing, Marking, and Grading," *Today's Education* 60 (March, 1971); F. R. Kappell, *From the World of College to the World of Work* (New York: American Telephone and Telegraph Co., 1962); P. B. Prince et. al., "Measurement of Physician Performance," *Journal of Medical Education* 39 (1964).
29. Smallwood, *An Historical Study*, p. 84.

The schooling innovations described so far have in fact been located, for the most part, within classrooms. Philadelphia's Parkway school, and similar schools in other cities, have "broken down the walls" and use museums, businesses, and parks as classrooms.

Some observers claim that Parkway's use of paraprofessionals is a significant departure from the more traditional school. But there are questions that need to be considered: Are "schools without walls" a good model for change, or do they merely offer an escape for a handful of students? Can any city accommodate tens of thousands of students roaming the streets? To what extent can society "tolerate" noncertified teachers?

A SCHOOL WITHOUT WALLS
DRPA Staff Member

It's the only high school in the country that has a biology department with a collection of two million insects from all parts of the world, an art museum containing 100,000 master works ranging from medieval to modern, a library that houses nearly a million volumes.

The school is Philadelphia's Parkway Program, an experimental attempt by educators to bring the community and students together to breathe new life into a suffocating urban educational system. It is called "a school without walls" because it has no building that can be identified as the traditional schoolhouse.

Parkway's classrooms surround the two-mile length of the 12-lane, tree-shaded Benjamin Franklin Parkway. Soon they are expected to dot other parts of the city. One area under consideration is the historic Independence Hall section overlooking the waterfront.

Anchoring the western end of the Parkway, is the impressive Museum of Art. On the banks of the Schuylkill River, the museum's U-shaped building of Greco-Roman architecture covers 10 acres of ground. Within its walls, students can absorb the styles of Van Eyck,

"A School Without Walls," *Delaware River Port Authority Magazine* (*DRPA LOG*), pp. 14–19. Copyright 1969 by The Delaware River Port Authority. Reprinted by permission.

Cezanne, Picasso, Rubens and Renoir. And a short distance away is the Rodin Museum.

At the other end of the Parkway lies the heart of center city Philadelphia. It is here that Parkway students have been able to see the operations of government and business first hand. "The city is learning from our kids," says Cy Swartz, a Parkway teacher in evaluating the success of the school since it began operation in February. "Many of them have made positive impressions on the people they've come in contact with. A significant part of the program is to help society understand our adolescents—these youngsters feel so cut off in so many ways."

The city itself offers a classroom filled with sights and sounds no four walls could contain. "We've gone to Penn Fruit, the Greyhound Bus Terminal and City Hall for some of our subjects," said a young art teacher. And one sunny morning she took her students over to Rittenhouse Square, where the annual flower show was in full bloom. The young artists busily began working to capture the colorful swirl of babies, balloons and blossoms.

Between the art museum and city hall are a number of the school's other classrooms: the library, the county court house, the Academy of Natural Sciences, the Franklin Institute and the Moore College of Art.

Aside from the fact that these places contain facilities that no other school could afford to match, there is another practical reason for operating this kind of setup: The taxpayers did not have to spend $15 million on a new school building. "We're a bargain!" chuckles John Bremer, the director of Parkway School. But he sees Parkway as more than a way to save dollars. "I just don't think what we have been offering in our schools meets the needs of a sizable percentage of students."

Bremer's office, as well as the school headquarters, is at 1801 Market Street. The second floor quarters provide space for administrative offices and room for students to store their books and papers in da-glo decorated lockers.

The walls of the community room are festooned with the eclectic selection of prints from Rembrandt to Picasso. Movement up and down the narrow stairs is constant and the noise level fluctuates from a low buzz of conversation to loud punctuations of students and teachers greeting each other.

Casual. On the surface that's the word to describe Parkway. Dress ranges from conventional to mod for both teachers and pupils. Students may address teachers by their given names. "I had to get used to hearing myself called by my first name for the first couple of class meetings," recalls Jay Galambos, an Insurance Company of North America training specialist who teaches basic insurance to Parkway students.

Galambos is one of several specialists on the faculty who have been donated by their companies. He taught for several years in a suburban school district before joining INA. "Having lived and worked in that kind of situation, I had never been exposed to the nitty-gritty of urban life. These are sophisticated kids and every time they hear talk, they want the truth."

Open. That's another word to describe Parkway. Students are able to attend the school's free-wheeling Friday faculty meetings. They take place around a long table in the school's headquarters and are attended by the "regular" teachers on the faculty. The staff numbers nine full-time, fully certified teachers and 13 university interns who work along with the instructors in class and tutorial programs. The teachers like Galambos, contributed by business and institutions, help reduce the student-teacher ratio to two to one.

Although there is the air of casualness surrounding Parkway, Bremer insists that it is a tightly structured program. "The structure is just different from the type of school we're used to. Our students spend more time studying than their counterparts in regular high schools." The school day lasts from nine to five for many Parkway youngsters. And a special class on television techniques held with an instructor from Channel 29 takes place on Saturday morning.

In order for Parkway to offer courses in such things as television and insurance, it depends upon the business community of Philadelphia. "We now have more offers of help (from business) than we can use," says Bremer. "And I think all educators should welcome the chance of help from business."

Smith, Kline & French Laboratories is another of the companies that is helping Parkway. In a bright, walnut-paneled room at the company offices on Spring Garden Street, a psychology class discussed drug abuse. Al Strack of SK&F's research and development department parried some of the verbal thrusts made by the group:

"Eighty percent of the kids taking drugs really dig it," one commented. "Kids know what they're getting into."

"Every heroin user says he can handle it," Strack replied. "Ask the kids at Synanon. People who use drugs are people in trouble."

The discussion spilled into overtime as several students continued the conversation with Strack after the class was dismissed.

Students studying law enforcement have the benefit of Harvey Steinberg's experience as an assistant district attorney. A law graduate of the University of Pennsylvania, he too is a former teacher.

One of his class sessions was held in a courtroom at the city juvenile court. First they heard the case of a youthful runaway and another about a gang incident. After the hearings ended, the group stayed in the courtroom to talk about the cases and about law in general. The next session was to meet in City Hall, where they would hold their own mock trial, a case of aggravated assault upon a police officer. "I thought it was going to be a murder case," said one disappointed member of the class.

Budding engineers and scientists are able to take classes at the Franklin Institute. The Institute itself is a pioneer in public education. After it was founded in 1824, it provided free education to the young men of Philadelphia. This led to the establishment of the city's first public high school.

As one group toured a section of the Institute, they learned the principles of electricity. As one girl shyly laid her hand on a shiny metal sphere her hair literally stood on end. This group will be qualified ham radio operators by the time they finish their course.

Other courses offer the students unique experience that they would never find in the traditional classroom. A Spanish class is held in the home of a Philadelphia Spanish-speaking family. The film-making group assembles twice a week in the Board of Education's film media center in South Philadelphia. The anthropology class meets at the Philadelphia Zoo. All in all, there are more than 90 specialized courses offered.

The student body at Parkway School is probably the most heterogeneous collection of personality types and IQs to invade any school, according to one faculty member. One reason is that they come from all parts of the city—and a few from the suburbs. More than 2000 applied for the 120 places available to city students. Selection was made by dividing the applicants into eight districts and drawing 15 names from each area out of a hat. The remaining 20 were chosen from a special lottery involving the suburbs.

The students come from academically tough schools such as Central and Girls High, from large ethnically mixed metropolitan junior and senior high schools, from the white, middle class neighborhoods in Northeast Philadelphia, the Negro neighborhoods of North Philadelphia and from the Italian and Irish sections of South Philadelphia.

Most, like the student from a large city high school, are pleased with the program. "The school I came from was just too crowded. When we took tests or handed in homework, we put a number after our name. At Parkway, I know just about everybody and they know me."

A fellow student agrees. "At the junior high school I used to go to I was in ninth grade. Here, I'm a student."

The teachers share the students' enthusiasm. One commented: "When a parent notices a dramatic improvement in a child's personality in just three months, that's fantastic! Something must be happening." Not only are the students being affected, but the teachers are too: "I'm certainly not the same person I was six months ago," stated another young teacher.

Parkway's ungraded classes combine youngsters in all four high school levels. Pennsylvania state law requires courses in mathematics and English but most offerings selected by the students are the ones they want to take—and this cuts across all grade lines.

The students not only came to Parkway from different cultural backgrounds, their academic records are equally mixed. Some were "A" students under the old system; some were barely surviving. "But I don't care either way," says Bremer. "Whatever their record was, we can provide them with a better framework in which to learn." An informal (what other kind) survey of Parkway students indicates that roughly one-third would have dropped out of school eventually.

The tutorial program provides students who are scattered throughout the city with an identifiable group and regular contact with the school. During sessions, which number 15 students, teachers can determine if a child needs special help in areas like math and language skills.

Bremer and the other teachers are optimistic about the potential growth of Parkway. He hopes to have other units set up throughout the city. He says that half of the present students want to continue with courses during the summer and he expects enrollment to reach 700 by the end of the upcoming academic year. This means that expansion will be necessary.

Two sites are under definite consideration. One is near the Philadelphia College of Art on Broad Street, five blocks south of City Hall. And the other is in the historic area along the Delaware River near Independence Hall.

The program has been funded by a $100,000 grant from the Ford Foundation and Bremer's salary is paid by federal money. But, the Parkway School will be included in the Board of Education's capital budget for next year. "All we're asking for is the $680 per student that is now being spent by the Board. We're still going to have to depend on Philadelphia's businesses and institutions because if they withdrew their support, we couldn't operate. As long as we can show them that they get some profit from the program—and some fun out of it—that support will continue."

It's not unusual that Philadelphia should be the place where one of the most innovative experiments in education is taking place. For it is here that one of the first organized programs for public education in the U.S. was put into practice, in 1818.

Many articles on alternative schools, here and elsewhere, have implied that the dominant thrust in such schools is toward a freer, Summerhillian atmosphere. There is growing evidence to suggest that a counter current is gaining momentum. As Ringle's article documents, some schools are stressing stricter discipline, a return to a more traditional curriculum, and a general moral education.

D.C. SUBURBAN SCHOOL SYSTEMS ARE SWEPT BY CHANGES— 'CHRISTIAN SCHOOLS"

Ken Ringle

A search for "basic American" values in a shaken society is creating in the Washington suburbs a rival to a basic American institution, the public school.

A strata of society that once considered private schools the preserve of the prosperous is now scrimping to send its children to a new class of "Christian schools," Protestant, usually nondenominational, educationally basic and intentionally lacking the "frills" of public schools in Washington's wealthy suburbs.

This new variety of private school caters generally to the new type of suburbanite whose annual income lies in the $12,000 to $15,000 range and for whom the cost of a private education is usually a major sacrifice.

Reprinted with permission from *The Washington Post*, Metro, December 31, 1973.

This suburbanite is attracted to the Christian schools because he wants a school that will help instill academic and social values in his children—values he feels modern public education has somehow mislaid in its march to sophistication and diversity.

In the Washington metropolitan area at least nine such Christian schools are now operating, educating an estimated 6,000 pupils, with more added every year.

In the nation as a whole, some 600 such schools have grown up in the past few years. They range in style and ambition from the all-white "segregation academies" of the Deep South where the primary emphasis is on patriotism and Bible, to schools like Virginia Christian Academy in Dale City, which has a 10 percent black enrollment and first graders learning German.

Ronald Brouillette, a 30-year-old career enlisted man in the Navy whose wife works as a secretary in Woodbridge, sends his two children to Virginia Christian Academy because, he says, "when you get down to basics (in education) the only thing that really matters is the relationship between the teacher and the pupil.

"The public schools don't spend enough time on that relationship. They spend more time on recreation and outings and PTA meetings than they do on education," he says. Robert L. Thoburn, director of the Fairfax Christian School, says that the basic educational techniques used in the Christian schools are things as memorization, rote learning, phonics. But what underlies that is the belief in the traditional American values of hard work, discipline, thrift and basic no-frills education.

For many parents, such an approach is appealing because it promises to recognize and develop whatever basic ability their children have. Many of the parents believe that public schools did not do that for them, and they want to assist their children in obtaining that opportunity.

Perhaps surprisingly, the religious training at Christian schools is frequently low-key, and officials say few parents enroll their children because of prayer bans in the public schools.

"We study Bible stories as a basis for knowing right and wrong," says Dr. Thoburn, an ordained Presbyterian minister himself. "But the real Christian significance of our school is that it's God-centered: the children learn that there is a God above themselves.

"I believe that education and religion are necessarily inseparable. The public schools of today are religious schools, but their religion is humanism."

Dr. John Hurley, director of research and testing for the Fairfax public school system, says of the comparison between public schools and Christian schools: "It's a trade-off. We in the public schools are paying at least lip service these days to the concept of individualized instruction. How well we're doing in this I suppose is a value judgment."

He points out that Fairfax schools offer hundreds of "enrichment programs" ranging from planetarium visits to French class trips to Paris. "In Fairfax County," he says, "public interest has encouraged us to go in this direction.

"Now maybe we produce a child that reads better than 70 percent of the school kids in the country in his grade and, say, the Christian schools, which can't furnish these enrichment programs, focus most of their effort on how much are enrichment programs worth? These are value judgments.

"If we start producing poor readers we might have to rethink the system, but so far this isn't happening," said Hurley.

But for Brouillette, who repairs dental equipment for the U. S. Navy in Washington, the $120 a month—12 percent of the Brouillette income—they spend on top of regular school taxes to send their children to Virginia Christian "is well worth it." His elder daughter Monelle, now 7, "was in that school (in first grade) less than two months and she could read. Now she's in the second grade and she's doing research work—using a dictionary and an encyclopedia. That would never happen in the public school."

The Christian schools around Washington claim their successes with reading as one of their major accomplishments.

As opposed to the "look-say" word-recognition method popularized by the Dick and Jane readers still used by many public schools, the Christian schools use phonics almost exclusively, teaching the child to spell out each syllable and how to read long words even when he can't understand them.

At Fairfax Christian School, director Thoburn says "we give 'em phonics till it's coming out of their ears," even in kindergarten.

Phonics is not exactly revolutionary: that was how you learned to read in the 1800's. But Thoburn, who draws from an eclectic grab-bag of new and traditional curriculum approaches and teaching methods, believes it's still the best method. He even uses the same McGuffey Reader popular in the early 1900's.

For parents like Marjorie Jones, 31, of Woodbridge, those techniques offer an educational shortcut for the children to the American dream they themselves never quite reached.

Mrs. Jones describes herself as a coal miner's daughter married to a Navy chief petty officer. They live in Woodbridge and scrimp to keep four children in Virginia Christian Academy.

"My parents had to work so hard just to keep meat on the table," she says, "that there was just never any question of me going to college. The subject was never even raised. Later I found out that I had ability, but it was never uncovered by the public schools, and that's what I'm trying to do for my children. Whatever they achieve in their life or don't achieve, at least they will know they had every opportunity."

She and other parents of children in Christian schools speak of private schools achieving a "teacher-child" relationship compared to a "teacher-pupil" relationship in the public schools.

They are convinced that children get more individual attention in the Christian schools and are more encouraged to realize their full educational potential.

She and some other parents and Christian school officials talk about a lower ratio of students to teachers in the Christian schools, but Dr. Thoburn of Fairfax Christian says that's ridiculous.

He says what makes his school good is its efficiency: the fact that it's a tax-paying private institution that must provide the best service at the lowest cost in order to make a very necessary profit.

"If one teacher can't educate 30 children well in her class then we aren't doing our job," he says.

Thoburn's school is the oldest in the Washington area, begun 13 years ago. It has expanded to more than 600 pupils ranging from kindergartners to a couple of students in a first-year college course.

Nearly one-third of the students at Fairfax Christian, however, are kindergartners. At that level, Thoburn says: "If the body's warm and the check is good we take 'em." Later on, he says, Fairfax Christian becomes more selective and he—like directors of other Christian schools—shuns problem children from the public schools.

"There are some schools who specialize in that and do a great service," he says. "But it's not worth it for us.

"We like to have children who have been with us in the beginning, whose parents take an active part in their children's education. And believe me when they are paying extra, they care. And because the children know they care, we very seldom have any disciplinary problems in this school."

Nonperformers are not re-enrolled. Spankings, though rare, are permitted. ("Only when a child has intentionally hurt another," says Dr. Robert Copeland of Manassas Christian School.)

And at Fairfax Christian School a child who wastes a piece of paper must pay 50 cents of his own money into a charity fund.

"That helps us avoid waste," says Thoburn, "and it teaches them respect for property." He also believes it encourages pupils to respect themselves by banning blue jeans, discouraging really short mini-skirts and very long hair on boys and requiring that girls wear dresses.

The situation at Manassas Christian School is much the same.

"How can they enforce any kind of rule in public school?" Dr. Copeland says. "They let them walk around looking like a bunch of bums."

Some school directors, like Dr. Copeland, credit part of their school's success to its involvement of the parent and its freedom from the political encumbrances of local and state school boards.

Thoburn, however, says he is convinced many of the methods proven at Fairfax Christian could be transferable to the public school environment, even to such troubled inner-city systems as those in the District of Columbia.

"Those children, like all children, need guidance and discipline," he says. "It's fashionable to talk against such things as rote learning and memorization, but a certain amount of this is very, very valuable to the individual child. It teaches him the rewards of a challenge mastered, and in the hands of the right teacher it can be made very interesting."

Public school officials generally shy away from any firm evaluation of the Christian schools' effectiveness, saying they attempt no analysis of where each child comes from or how strong his educational background is.

Both they and the Christian school officials note that most Christian school alumni tend to end up in public high schools because of the increased space, fees and facilities required by secondary school curriculums.

Because the Christian schools concentrate almost exclusively on the primary and junior high grades, they say, they may indeed achieve better results in some areas than the public schools.

The public schools, says Hurley of the Fairfax public schools, don't normally compare their test scores with those of private schools in their own area.

Interest in Christian schools, however, keeps growing.

Thoburn has taken to the lecture circuit and has had so many inquiries about the structure and administration of Fairfax Christian he has written a how-to-do-it book on setting up a private school. He sells it for $100 a copy.

"I think eventually if the schools keep growing and people keep making the kinds of sacrifices they're making to send their children here, we're going to influence the public schools," he says.

"They're going to have to take a look at what we're doing and I think that, in the end, will make them better."

In Part One, historian Lawrence Cremin spoke of the impact that *Sesame Street* has had on our educational system. He has since suggested that the most important educational battle today may not be in classrooms, or in the formal school structure, but in the area of cable television. With its many options, including open channels for general public usage, the potential good or harm of this medium is staggering.

Welby Smith gives us a summary of the educational and ethical questions that need to be examined in the coming years.

YOU, ME AND CABLE TV
Welby Smith .

No doubt you've heard of Cable Television (CATV). Who hasn't? It's the latest technological marvel—guaranteed to furnish all the wonderful benefits that previous technological marvels didn't provide. Isn't it amazing? Just about the time we begin to wonder what happened to all the bright promises of last year's "Major New Innovation," along comes an even newer one, with even brighter promises, to lure us back into the comforting Nirvana of *future* (choose one) *competence, creativity, excellence, innovation, diversity, etc.* But, always in the Future, Never in the Now.

Comes now Cable Television, offering a cornucopia of mediated delights, limited only by the imagination of whoever happens to be writing the article. Scholars will have access to vast stores of computerized data, instantly retrievable in facsimile printout at their living room terminals! Welfare mothers will learn about cheap, balanced diets for their offspring! Educators can interconnect schools and maximize the impact of master teachers, bringing their excellence to bear on multitudes of students! Citizens, at long last, can "talk back to their TV sets" via public access channels, ending their dependence on the uncertain intermediation of "newsmen," "commentators," and assorted other pundits!

All these things *can* happen—if they are *allowed* to happen. But they have not happened, are not happening, and will not happen

Reprinted from *Media and Methods*, February, 1973, pp. 16–20. Used with permission.

automatically. And our talking about them as though they were realities already, as we are wont to do with all new technological innovations (e.g. Helical Scan Videotape Recording, Videocassettes, Pre-recorded Videotapes, etc.), simply fuzzes over the gap between possibilities and realities. Just because a thing is possible, there's no guarantee it will happen. In fact, I strongly suspect that overexposure of a particular innovation, prior to its practical incorporation in a working system, may very well militate against its eventual acceptance, since its performance is bound to fall short of the adman's hyperbole. The pathetically low utilization rate of videotape recording equipment in schools, businesses and Government agencies seems to substantiate this hypothesis. Everyone expected the VTR to turn out broadcast quality programs at the press of a button. That's what the ads and the salesmen promised! When that didn't happen, and when it became painfully apparent that helical scan videotape recording systems, like other forms of communication, required knowledge, experience, planning and operational competence to produce useful programs, back they went into the closet.

I reiterate the educational establishment's unfortunate experience with helical scan VTR because I sense that the same thing is happening with Cable TV. NEA, among others, has gone on record in favor of school systems grabbing as many CATV channels as they can get from cable franchise winners. Educational magazines are rife with articles on the promise of CATV. Public access to Cable television is very big in non-profit/Government/foundation circles. Even the giant holding companies that already control so much of CATV are paying lip service to educational/public access applications. And didn't the Federal Communications Commission (FCC) rule that all cable operations with a subscribership of 3500 or more *must* provide one channel to the schools, one channel to the local government, and one channel for public access? So what's the problem?

In one word—programming. What kind? Produced by whom? Produced for whom? Produced where? Controlled by whom? Paid for by whom? Watched by whom?

In its concern for the acquisition of channels, the educational establishment is accurately reflecting our society's characteristic attention to means, almost to the exclusion of ends. "Never mind what we'll *do* with the channels, just grab them before somebody else does!"

However, in Cable Television, perhaps more than in any other potential educational medium, programming *is* what matters. Grabbing channels with little planning and even less capacity for using them may be positively counterproductive of the well-intentioned aims of the educational community. In order to really appreciate the logic behind this premise, we need to look more closely at the nature of the medium, and at those people and institutions involved in it. At the risk of offending cable cognescenti, let's begin with a brief description of Cable Television.

In the early days of broadcast TV, before coaxial cables linked the land together, broadcast television signals (which are straight-line, or line-of-sight), tended to have problems with natural obstacles like mountains. The prevailing myth has it that an enterprising entrepreneur named Tarleton, a seller of TV sets in a small town in Pennsylvania, realized one day that his market would increase as the quality of television reception improved. Consequently, he erected a tall antenna on a nearby mountain, trapped the signals from a neighboring big city broadcast TV station, amplified them to near their original quality, and piped them down the hill and into the homes of people who bought his TV sets. Thus was Cable Television born. It is crucial to remember the original reason for Cable TV—*To Improve The Reception Quality of Broadcast TV Signals.* Mr. Tarleton charged the users of his system a modest monthly sum, and this concept of subscription forms the basis of the income potential of Cable Television today.

All a cable operator needs for the services described above is an antenna, an amplifying system, and a distribution cable system. He doesn't need a studio, a camera, or even much of a crew. While his initial investment may be quite high (particularly if local ordinances require laying the cable underground), his operating cost is very low. Thus, the original concept of cable television as a supplementary distribution medium for broadcast TV could become very profitable in areas where broadcast television signals were either non-existent or of poor quality. Obviously, people were unlikely to be willing to pay for a cable system of this type in areas where normal, off-the-air broadcast television reception was quite good, as in most urban areas where most of the broadcast TV stations are located. Thus, at the outset, Cable Television tended to develop in relatively rural or small city areas, away from the urban environment.

Before long, however, the entrepreneurial instincts of the early CATV pioneers, and the medium's capacity for multiple transmissions through a single cable, combined to dramatically change both the nature and the *raison d'être* of Cable Television. Originally a slavish, supplementary distribution system, Cable Television became a sort of all-purpose White Knight. It could crowd more than 40 channels of programming into one cable, offering escape from the dull, repetitive inanity of network broadcast fare. Its ability to accept programming from relatively cheap, half-inch and one-inch VTR systems offered individual citizens and groups an opportunity to compete on an equal basis with giant corporations and Government agencies in getting their messages to the public. Its capacity for two-way communication promised interactive applications ranging from cooking schools to computer-human interfaces. Diversity, here we come! In print, that is. And in newspapers, magazines, and books. But in fact, Cable Television, with a few notable exceptions, has remained more or less what it was—a means of improving the reception quality of broadcast TV signals.

The reason for this unhappy state of affairs is fairly obvious. CATV is not going to offer significant competition even to the mediocrity of broadcast TV by showing its current staples: old training films, pictures of the AP ticker printing out the news, and local weather reports. But innovative, imaginative programming doesn't grow on trees! It's got to be learned, planned, and properly executed. It costs money, time and people, and these are precisely the scarcest items around most Cable TV operations. Why? Because Cable TV operators are usually mortgaged to the hilt to the company that sold them their equipment, and to the people who installed it (frequently one and the same). The amount of money necessary for the installation of a major (3500 or more subscribers) CATV system can run into millions of dollars. With capital equipment and installation running at this level, the CATV operator is obviously going to be chary of running his own inherently expensive in-house production operation. As for outside production, the National Cable Television Association says that people who want to produce for CATV operations had better be able to make money by selling their programs for *$300 per hour, maximum.* That's $5 per minute. One look at the production-cost rule-of-thumb for a 16mm scripted color film ($1500–$2000 per minute), or even a "cheapie" commercially-produced black-and-white one-inch videotape ($50–$100 per minute), makes it obvious that there aren't going to be many commercial competitors for this market; that the quality of productions which do compete for it will probably be relatively low; and that the Cable TV operator should welcome with open arms any source of reasonably good programming that has the additional advantage of being free.

Does this mean that you, as a producer of pre-recorded video-tapes of reasonable quality, have it made? Is this the long dreamed-of opportunity for total community education? Don't bet on it. There are at least three problems standing directly in the path of progress.

First, there's the equipment problem. The major manufacturers of broadcast television equipment are not going to stand by and see themselves put out of business—not on your high-band machine! They are already agitating in the high echelons of the Federal Government and in the regulatory agencies of state and local governments for a freeze-out of half-inch (and even one-inch) videotape recording equipment in CATV systems. They plead "technical quality," and shed crocodile tears of concern for a public subjected to the "low quality" of the helical scan television image. What they are really afraid of isn't the helical scan VTR's low quality, but its low cost—approximately one-tenth to one one-hundredth that of the lowest-priced broadcast equipment. Furthermore, it has been convincingly demonstrated time and time again that one-inch and half-inch videotape recorders can be used successfully to originate Cable TV programming. It's done every day. And, though the broadcast industry doesn't like to admit it, one-inch and half-inch helical scan videotape recorders can also be used to originate *broadcast television programming*—and is—when the content is important enough. A large portion of the NET-televised documentary report of the commission on the riots at Attica prison in New York State was taken directly from half-inch Sony videotape shot by state police. It was the only material available, so they used it. Segments from a CBS News "60 Minutes" show on the *French Connection* were also taped with half-inch VTR equipment.

Are these demonstrations enough? Will the truth make us free? Not without a fight. Those educators who have broadcast studios will have to band together with the ones who don't to defeat this transparent attempt to force onto cable television the same constricting and innovation-destroying technical requirements that sterilized the broadcast medium. It is about time we begin to give content at least the same amount of concern that these special pleaders demand for "technical quality."

This brings us to the second major problem. Even if we manage to keep the vested interests from closing off CATV to half-inch and one-inch origination, how can we convince CATV operators and others that educators can and will produce programs which offer a relevant, viable alternative to the reprocessed broadcast fare that they must compete with on other cable channels? Certainly an appeal to past achievements in helical scan educational programming will be of no avail. One could scarcely imagine a less convincing argument. Nothing less than a new commitment to the realities of the medium will suffice. Educators must open up access to the medium *within the educational establishment.* This means basic training in helical scan VTR systems for every teacher who is interested. For much too long, access to videotape recording equipment has been available only to so-called "specialists"; or, if to teachers, on a basis so haphazard and ill-planned as to constitute an insult to their intelligence. Steps must be taken to *demystify* media! Teachers must realize that a videotape recording system is no more complex a concept than an electric typewriter (and a good deal simpler to learn to use). And, as is the case with a typewriter, learning to use a VTR system isn't an end in itself—you also need something to say! This is, in fact, the primary fallacy involved in so much of educational media production. If the enormously expensive media complements purchased by schools over the last decade are ever to become cost-effective, we need to train *teachers* in their operation and application. And we need to stop differentiating endless strings of sub-specialities which, in the long run, only provide people with excuses for not doing what needs to be done. If educators can open up access to media within the educational milieu, and can extend this access to students as well as teachers (as has been done in a few outstanding cases—but all too few); if they can free themselves of the artificial distinctions of rank and function beloved of all petty bureaucrats, then we may expect some relevant and viable and truly "educational" programming for Cable Television. If things are not going to change *within* the educational hierarchy, then grabbing channels from now until next Christmas isn't going to do any good. You'll just lose them, like the AM band educational radio stations and the VHF educational TV stations of yesteryear. If you have nothing new to say, it's hard to justify the demand for channels on which to say it.

The third problem is competition. But, you thought I said that the Cable TV operator was wildly searching for programming, right? What's all this about competition? Remember what we said about program costs—that most Cable TV operations could only afford about $300 per hour maximum? It hardly makes sense to try to produce quality programs for that price unless you're not dependent upon them for revenue (as is the case in educational programming), *or* unless somebody else is footing the bill—as in the case of national advertisers, large scale local advertisers, or others with lots of money and a vested interest of some kind. Already, plans are afoot to distribute, for free, syndicated programming to CATV stations nation-wide who will run the programming *and the ads it contains.* These programs will be "broadcast quality"—with all that this phrase implies, both good and bad. You have only two ways of competing with them. First, you are on your own turf. *Localize.* In those very few instances where Cable TV operators have made a real commitment to local programming, audience response has been very positive. Second, *Be Original.* Originality combined with localization is hard to beat—and hard to come by. But it can be done.

This brings up something I mentioned earlier—a very hazy but vitally important concept called public or community access. Public access isn't new. In theory, we all have equal access to newspapers, radio and television stations; and now to Cable TV. In practice, as we know, our access to newspapers, radio and television is so limited and random as to be almost meaningless. But Cable will be different—so they say. The FCC has required Cable TV operators with 3500 or more subscribers to make available to the public one channel. Access to this channel will be free, for the first five minutes at least, and will be open on a first come, first served basis. These are the basic guidelines. Local political jurisdictions can add to these guidelines at will within the intent of the concept of freedom of access. Thus, the local franchise agreement will determine whether the Cable TV operator can get by with an "open camera, open mike" operation (which is liable to turn into a gripe channel that people watch only as comic relief), or if he is required to provide (or contribute to) an independent production facility, with the kind of training available for citizens which will allow them to produce their own programs, independent of technical assistance from the CATV operator. School systems, particularly those with reasonably sophisticated production facilities, could go a long way toward providing early training and assistance to the public in this area. I realize that it's easy to say, "That's not what we were funded for" and slip the responsibility. Frankly, that's what I expect most educational technologists will do. That's the kind of behavior that's been reinforced by the system. But a few may take the plunge and develop a viable partnership with the public that can assist in easing some of the very painful transitions that educationalists will be facing in the near future.

In summary, it appears to me that there are at least eight areas of concern for educators looking into Cable Television:

1. If at all possible, the school system should be involved in the *franchise award* process from the beginning. Remember, letting the franchise to a profit-making entrepreneur isn't the only course. Local non-profit groups, institutions, or the county or city itself could put in and run the system. Why not have the school system's local political jurisdiction purchase the system, and the media center operate it? This would provide the jurisdiction with a source of revenue (from subscriptions and adver-

tising), and constitute a valuable career education experience for media-minded youngsters. A lot of the "educational" programs produced by the media center could also do double-duty on the cable.

2. Don't be greedy when it comes to channels. Justify your requests for channels with hard-nosed program planning. The CATV operator who'll promise you the moon *before* the franchise is granted will be just as quick to demand return of unused channel capacity once he's in the driver's seat. If you can't fill those channels, he can. And, unlike broadcast TV, the Cable TV operator can tell who is watching what. He'll probably give you more channels if your programs warrant them.

3. Don't let the Cable Operators, Broadcast Industry or anyone else close out half-inch and one-inch VTR origination. These constitute the only means that the public, and most teachers, will ever have of developing and producing programs. Broadcast studios require a degree of specialization and structural rigidity that is positively inimical to the kind of generalized, broad-gauged thinking so necessary to the origination of innovative programs. If you don't believe that, turn on your TV.

4. Free up access to program origination equipment within your own system. Teach your teachers to *use* the equipment, not to fear it. Furnish high-quality, one-inch editing to polish up their half-inch origination. Set up training programs for teachers interested in learning more about the medium. Arrange with a local college or university for course credit for teachers who take your training courses.

5. Form a partnership with the public. Provide training, access, advice. Don't shut out anybody, or allow anybody to be shut out, by appeals to your philosophy, vanity or expertise. You may be next.

6. Once you get your channel(s), make sure you also have control of the production process. Input, even content control, is not enough. You need nothing less than the capability to develop and produce your entire program, down to a final edited tape playable on or transferable to the CATV operator's distribution VTR. This isn't as difficult as it may sound, provided you aren't trying to produce "Studio One" with a half-inch, single camera VTR system. Fit your programming dreams into a cold, hard appraisal of your production complement's potential. No matter how nice he is, don't depend on the CATV operator for production equipment or advice. There are some things you just have to do for yourself. This is another good argument for keeping access open

to half-inch VTR—the only production system that many people have the time and inclination to learn to operate effectively.

7. Explore the concept of a "Media Ombudsman"; someone independent of the CATV operator who can furnish necessary technical and production assistance for systems that don't have in-house resources. He could be paid by the local political jurisdiction, but should be as independent of political muscle as possible. Sooner or later, he'll need that independence if he's doing his job.

8. Fight for maximum freedom of expression in both educational and public access programming. Cable TV is a medium of choice, not one broadcast to be picked up willy-nilly by everyone. People can exercise an effective choice to watch, or not to watch, any program or any channel. The CATV operator must be absolved of any legal responsibility for educational or public access programs. It's high time the educators and the public began to take responsibility for themselves.

Is it foolish to speculate about the future of education and schooling? Previous selections have cautioned us about being too optimistic about how
rapidly schools change. Yet Alvin Toffler's thesis in
his famous *Future Shock* tells us that we invite
disaster if we do not constructively attempt to deal
with the changes that he sees crashing around us.
His analysis of schooling in the future poses several
pertinent questions for all who are keenly interested in the shape of education: Must we make the
supreme effort of divesting ourselves of the traditional image of a school? What kind of person will
be the best "teacher" of tomorrow? Has Toffler
succumbed to several myths himself, especially the
myth of progress?

A CONVERSATION
WITH ALVIN TOFFLER
James J. Morisseau

Alvin Toffler is a journalist, an author, and, above all, a futurist.
Unlike some of his fellow forecasters of the future, he sees the world
of tomorrow not simply as an oversized, overblown extension of the
present, but as a world that will be dramatically, even radically
different. He sees a world characterized by rapid and accelerating
change, not only in our technology but in our values, in our sexual
attitudes, in our relationships with family, friends, and organizations,
and in the way we structure government, politics, business . . . and
education. And he questions whether the human being is prepared to
experience—and survive—the traumatic changes that lie ahead.

"I think," he says, "that we are in the process of a tremendous
human revolution that will dwarf the industrial revolution and all the
political revolutions, from the Russian to the French to the American, and make them look small by comparison."

The new revolution, he feels, will produce—indeed already is
rapidly generating—a new, "superindustrial" society, one that will be

From *The National Elementary Principal,* Vol. LII, No. 4, January, 1973, pp. 8–18.
Copyright 1973, National Association of Elementary School Principals. All rights reserved.

"fast paced, highly diverse, nonuniform, filled with intergroup variety and conflict, nonbureaucratically organized."

This vision of the future, he adds, is "180 degrees the opposite of the vision of the future as presented in *Brave New World, 1984,* and much of science fiction, all of which, despite their brilliance, picture a uniform future and a homogenized, regimented form of society."

The future as seen by Huxley, Orwell, and others is not impossible as Toffler sees it. But he believes that "there are powerful pressures leading toward diversity, variety, and heterogeneity rather than uniformity. Indeed, some of the real dangers may eventually come from a society so fragmented that its members no longer can communicate."

Alvin Toffler's ideas, set forth in *Future Shock,* already have had a powerful, worldwide impact. That impact can be measured by the fact that *Future Shock* has been published in fifteen countries, already has sold more than four million copies, and in 1972 was honored as the best foreign book published in France.

Future Shock includes a chapter on education that should be must reading for anyone involved in the public schools or interested in their future. Meanwhile, the editors of *The National Elementary Principal* asked me to interview Toffler and to obtain a more detailed view of the implications of the future shock syndrome for the schools and for public education.

Morisseau: Educators will be concerned at the outset with a crucial question: Can the individual and, in particular, the individual child, adapt to the rapid, traumatic changes you envision?

Toffler: In order to understand the adaptive abilities and limitations of the individual you must first ask: "What does this revolutionary upheaval do to the individual?" It does a number of things that ought to be of extreme concern, especially to educators. One is that it creates a world of temporary relationships. The individual no longer can surround himself with objects, people, organizations, and other environmental components that are permanent. Take friends, for example. When I was a child, a best friend was one who lasted all of one's childhood and indeed right on through adolescence. . . .

Morisseau: And sometimes through adulthood. . . .

Toffler: And sometimes throughout life. But that's rarely the case in our society. More and more you can visit schools, even elementary schools, in this country and ask the children: "How many of you have lost a best friend in the last year because that best friend moved away?" The hands go up in very large numbers. That fact begins to condition the child to believe that temporariness is the essential characteristic of human relationships.

The same thing is true of the relationship with things—the toys the child plays with, the building he lives in or sees every day, the classroom he works in. More and more we find ourselves moving toward throwaway toys, throwaway classrooms, and portable playgrounds. We begin to create a temporary physical environment as well as a temporary social environment around the child.

We do the same thing with respect to the informational environment. We used to teach that there were certain eternal verities, not only moral verities but factual, empirical verities. Now, we know that the latest verity is likely to be found untrue next week. Information becomes a perishable product; the individual's image of the world is forced to undergo continual revision.

Even the individual's relationship with his own images becomes temporary. Instead of having a permanent relationship between himself and his or her image of the reality, the relationship becomes telescoped, temporary, impermanent.

Morisseau: But is the human animal psychologically capable of handling such impermanence? Are we talking about a massive explosion in mental illness?

Toffler: I'm not sure that I would use those terms, but I would put it this way: When you accelerate the rate of change and create a milieu based primarily on temporary relationships, you increase the rate at which the individual is called on to make adaptive decisions. You're asking individuals to make more coping decisions in shorter intervals of time.

But you ask whether people can handle this. If all we do is ask the individual to decide faster, I suppose he could handle it. But we are also changing the nature of the decisions, making them more complex. When you introduce change into a social order, you introduce new things—surprises, unpredictable situations, new circumstances, bizarre or unusual conditions, crises, and opportunities. This means that the individual is less and less able to deal with reality through pre-programed decisions, through habitual responses, and through routines. He is forced into more creative decision making, which relies on inventing a response rather than repeating one. The faster the rate of change, the more nonroutine the responses.

I believe all this creates a fundamental cultural conflict that has very painful effects for the individual. But I also believe that individuals have a much greater potential for adapting to change than most of us realize. I think we can vastly enhance the individual's ability to cope, particularly if we pay attention to these questions in our dealings with children.

Morisseau: Doesn't the phenomenon you described earlier—children losing their friends at an early age—help in that process?

Toffler: That's part of it. They are being conditioned to change. On the other hand, there are certain very expensive costs involved. If you live in a world of temporary friends, there usually appears to be a decline in emotional involvement, in committedness, and in warmth. We're moving from a society that is based essentially on hot emotional relationships to one that is based on cool emotional relationships punctuated by explosions of heat and violence.

Morisseau: There's a potential for trauma?

Toffler: There's a potential for trauma, and I'd like to argue that the human potential is not, as most liberal educators like to believe, infinite. I know it's a controversial position, but I believe that we are biologically limited, that the rate at which we can accept information and make decisions is bound by certain biological limitations. Short of some biological mutation (or tremendously dangerous experimentation with genetic engineering), we must operate with the biological equipment we have. That imposes certain limits. I do not think we're near those limits; I think that if we were smart about education, we could do wonders. But I think it is a mistake to simply assume, in blind faith, that human beings are going to be able to adapt smoothly to this revolutionary upheaval without some kind of difficulty, pain, and, in some cases, traumatic upheaval within the individual.

Morisseau: You said that, if we were smart about education, we could develop a lot of untapped potential in the human animal. What do you mean by being smart about education?

Toffler: I think, first, we must recognize that we're dealing with a revolutionary situation. That means that the changes in education must be directed to the *goals* of education, not just to its methods and techniques.

But how does one design goals for an educational system, particularly when you are talking about a system that involves some fifty million human beings in the United States alone? How do you begin to think rationally about goals or objectives for education unless you first think sensibly about the future?

Now, it's easy to know what the future is going to look like if you live in a static society, because you know that the future is going to look like the past and like the present. But in a society of high speed change, such as ours, you can no longer make the assumption that the future is going to resemble the present. The question then becomes, "Can we in any way anticipate the outlines of that new world, and, from our assumptions about the future, can we work back to some sort of rational curriculum?"

Morisseau: And, in your view, we can?

Toffler: We can, if we recognize that it is extremely difficult to *know* anything about the future, to make any precise, hard, fast, accurate statements about the future—and impossible if we are looking for scientific certainty. On the other hand, it must be recognized that, even today, we base our curriculum on assumptions about the future. The fact, for example, that we teach children to read is based on our assumption that reading is going to be a required skill. The only difference between what I am proposing and what is currently done is that we be explicit about the dilemma of the future and thoughtful about it, rather than making implicit, unexamined assumptions.

Morisseau: Explicit about it?

Toffler: I mean that right now we make assumptions about the world without ever stopping to think about them. We make the linear assumption that the world is going to be the same basically, but in large outline. To me, that's a highly simple-minded form of forecasting, a dangerous one for a world caught up in profound upheaval. It leads to a curriculum that conditions children, that sets them up to be candidates for future shock. It means that when big changes do come, children are going to be bowled over by them.

Let me give you an example. Some time ago, I asked a high school class to write down seven events that were going to happen in the future. These students, being very sophisticated, came up with a phenomenal list—advanced computers in 1977, a Soviet-Red China rapprochement by 1993, food supplies from the oceans, manned stations on the planets. But, on examination, virtually all of the forecasts had to do with "the world out there" and not with the future of the individual.

I then asked them to predict seven things they thought would happen to them, personally, in the future. For the most part, their responses indicated an unchanged way of life. There was an absolute gulf between their perception of rapid change in the environment and their lack of understanding that the changes would have an effect on their personal lives. It was as though they were describing themselves living in yesterday and the world living in tomorrow.

Morisseau: Does that represent a commentary on education?

Toffler: It suggests to me that the educational system—and in that I would be forced to include the mass media and all of the influences that bear on the education of young people—has done a very poor job of integrating a knowledge or picture of the future and of preparing young people in any way for the jolt or jolts that face them. Basically, what today's system does is to say to youngsters that the world of the future is going to be more of the same, only bigger and more bureaucratized.

But if I am correct, the future is not going to be more of the same. We need another set of assumptions about what it is going to be like. I believe that, if we are in fact moving toward more and more temporary relationships, there will be increasing pressure on young people to know how to relate to other human beings in that kind of world. It seems to me that one of the tasks education must concern itself with is the task of relationships. If we are moving into a world of increasing variety and heterogeneity, that by definition means a world of greater individual choice.

Morisseau: But is that the sort of thing that can be taught?

Toffler: Yes, I think it is possible to design experiences within the framework of education that at least give people a taste of what they might later experience. As an example, let me return to the point that we are moving toward a world of more fluid relationships—not only with things, with people, and with information, but with organizations. Individuals no longer work with the same company all their lives, or belong to the same church, the same PTA, or the same political organization.

We are moving away from the bureaucratic form of organization, based on permanence, toward a structure honeycombed with temporary organizations, ad hoc committees, task forces, problem-solving teams, or the Nader style protest movement that disappears and then springs up someplace else. The implication is that, in the course of a lifetime, an individual will have to deal with many different kinds and sizes of organizations, many different styles of organizational behavior, and many different levels of complexity.

But how do we teach children about organization? We put them in a class of twenty-five or thirty with a single teacher. Then, year after year, we move them through an organization that resembles the first organization we ever had anything to do with. At the end of the line, out comes a teenager, almost an adult, who has experience with being, in effect, a subordinate in a group dominated by a single person. But he has no experience with other organizational designs.

Morisseau: But what you're describing is no longer universal.

Toffler: I know that. I'm describing the typical, industrial style school system. I'm well aware that it's beginning to break down, that there is a lot of experimentation, and that's a good adaptation of the system. But I'm willing to bet that most children still go through the standard organizational training.

If you believe that you're moving into a world of temporary and complex organizations, you want to design into the educational process experiences that give children a taste or smell of different kinds of organizational life.

Similarly, if you're going to be dealing with high diversity in the society—a plethora of different consumer products, conflicting subcultural values, a kaleidoscopic value system—then it becomes a world of very difficult choices. This suggests that the schools must give students some experience not only with organizational styles but with the definition and clarification of their own value systems. To me, one of the crucial things the schools must focus on is the issue of values, but not in the traditional sense of inculcating a set of fixed, permanent values. Rather, the schools need to deal with the question of better values, to accept the value of value clarification.

Schools should create conditions in which students are encouraged to ask, debate, and discuss; to explore such topics as sex, politics, religion, and drugs; to discuss the morality of different kinds of work. I certainly don't think we should aim toward uniformity in the values of our children; we would fail if we tried. The nature of the new society itself demands variety, creativity, and individuality. We should be careful not to try to impose a homogenized, uniform value system, but that does not mean ducking the issue of values.

Morisseau: You've said that the schools should pay more attention to interpersonal relationships, expose students to organizational variety, and deal more effectively with the issue of values. What other changes would you propose?

Toffler: I would add two more suggestions. One is more attention to what happens outside the classroom. I believe much of what now happens in the classroom ought to be moved out into the community. We have experiments with this under way around the country, and I think they are on the whole very healthy.

Unlike previous societies, we live in a world that, through the interminable prolongation of adolescence, robs children and young people of the sense of being needed. In our well-intentioned hurry to spare children the misery of child labor, we have taken away the sense of being needed and replaced it with a lot of rhetoric about love and a lot of rhetoric that says, "You are going to be the leaders of the future."

In reality, the message to the child from most families and most schools is: "You are not needed." This is the most debilitating, crippling, painful message any human being can receive. We need to create a system that does not look on students as parasites—as they are frequently regarded by conservatives—or as investments—as they are viewed by liberals and the majority of educators. I prefer to look on students as neither parasites nor investments but as resources for the community.

Morisseau: What sort of resources?

Toffler: We have enormous problems in every community that are not being met by government or by the private sector. Whenever we ask why a problem—air pollution, noise, traffic congestion, or crime—is not being resolved, we are usually told we don't have the budget or the resources to solve it. And yet there are more than fifty million young people in our society, representing an enormous pool of imaginative, energetic, enthusiastic, but as yet relatively unskilled resources for helping us deal with some of these problems. I would like to move much of education into the community, with teams of young people working with community adults, as well as with faculty, on the whole range of neighborhood problems that are presently neglected due to "lack of resources."

And I would extend this idea to the elementary schools by selecting small tasks. We did this in a rudimentary way when we gave a handful of children Sam Browne belts and sent them out to direct traffic on school crosswalks. That was a very small start, but if we were imaginative about it, we could develop enormously enriching activities for elementary school children.

Morisseau: What about education itself? Why not use students as teachers?

Toffler: Absolutely—each one, teach one. Ironically, this is done both in Red China and in the U.S. military academies. It seems to me that the schools have missed a fantastic opportunity here.

Morisseau: Yes, and I think it comes to grips with another problem. In the low income communities of this country, there is no visible career ladder, no organized way for the deprived to take the first steps toward a paraprofessional or professional career. Why not, then, let youngsters at age six start on their way toward a teaching career?

Toffler: That makes so much sense. Simultaneously, it seems to me that the schools—and here I must be critical of the NEA and the teacher unions—through an overemphasis on professionalism, have been backward in taking advantage of community resources, adults who know things that children ought to know.

It seems to me that we could create a system of mentorships for any number of occupations—accounting, carpentry, or photography, to name a few—and recruit a list of community people in these occupations who are willing to sit down periodically with one child and demonstrate and discuss what they do. The value of this lies in the fact that inevitably they are not only going to talk about the occupation, but also about the world. It would serve as a great improvement in intergenerational communication, a "generational bridge," instead of the breakdown in communication we are now experiencing.

Morisseau: From your vantage point, is the schoolhouse as we now know it going to survive? Is it going to be effective in housing the new education?

Toffler: Most schools are built, physically, in a way that parallels the way they are organized. Both their physical shape and their organizational structure are essentially modeled after the factory. They are built for mass production in education. I believe the superindustrial revolution is going to change most of our assumptions about the way society ought to be organized. It is going to force a reevaluation of the notion that mass production equals economy. This is already having an impact on education; we are already beginning to move toward more individualization of instruction. We're experimenting with efforts, such as the voucher system, to break the lockstep of big city school systems. We are having struggles over community control, which is part of the battle to overthrow standardization.

I think all of this is eventually going to be reflected in new conceptions of architectural designs for schools. If we are not running groups of students through a mechanical process but, instead, paying attention to individual needs and individual schedules and teaching different things to different people, we obviously need a different kind of physical structure. Moreover, if we recognize that a great deal of learning can go on outside the classroom, perhaps we will realize that we need less in the way of physical structure—fewer seats and fewer "classrooms," if indeed that is what we will call them.

Now, I wouldn't go so far as to say that we will no longer have lectures or seminars, or that we will have no more need for classrooms. But the idea that the classroom is the heartland of education, that it is where education takes place, is absurd, and it's going to fall by the wayside. The day of the massive, factory style school is at its end. But it is hard to say what exactly will replace it.

We are not moving from one uniform system to another uniform system, but from a uniform system to a heterogeneous system. Therefore, there is no single answer to what the school of the future ought to look like. Maybe it ought to look like a local office, a local store, a world's fair, an automated factory, or a sports arena. There are different purposes to be served, and therefore different environments required for learning to take place.

Morisseau: We have a prototype in Philadelphia, the Parkway School, where an insurance company, governmental offices, the courts, the museums, and the scientific institutions all serve as the "schoolhouse."

Toffler: I would add one dimension to that. The idea of moving the school into the community and its existing institutions is an enormous forward step. It's probably administratively and architecturally inconvenient, but it is educationally highly sensible. The only cavil I have is that, while it is a very good way for students to learn about their present environment, it is still focused on the present society. I would like to see an emphasis on possible futures built into such a program.

Morisseau: But doesn't that relate to the curriculum rather than the physical environment?

Toffler: Yes, it certainly ought to be in the curriculum. But a student working in a government office and learning about governmental procedure, for example, ought to be exposed to a discussion of governmental operations of the future. And that discussion might include questions about the architectural requirements of future governmental operations. While it is difficult for us to actually create the physical environment of the future, we can imagine it and we can simulate some of it. We can represent it in physical form, through scale models and drawings. Indeed, through the use of sophisticated audiovisuals, we can even simulate the feeling of what it might be like to be in such a place.

At any rate, I think the schoolhouse is the last place in the world in which education is likely to be focused in the future.

Morisseau: Are you saying that for all age levels?

Toffler: Obviously there are differences in age level. There is one function the school provides that is difficult, if not impossible, for even the wealthiest family to replace. I often thought during the years my daughter was going through her elementary school education that I could do a better job than the school in teaching her the basic subjects. But the one thing I couldn't do was provide a social setting for her. I could not provide other students, other children of her own age. Consequently the school has a very important social function, and that may well be one of the residual functions of the schoolhouse. I suggested before that we need to send students into the community to establish generational bridging by working with different age groups. That, to me, is terribly important because our system has denied them that opportunity. However, we should not, by the same token, deny them the opportunity to interact with groups of their own age.

Morisseau: With their peers?

Toffler: Yes, although I wouldn't slice it as fine as one year. But there well may be certain peer functions in which the schoolhouse continues to play a role.

Morisseau: The schoolhouse becomes more of a neighborhood social club. . . .

Toffler: The school becomes more of a neighborhood resource and social center than what it is now—the Fort Knox of knowledge, surrounded by barbed wire fences.

Morisseau: What happens to the people who now manage and operate the educational enterprise—the teacher and the administrator? What does the future hold for them?

Toffler: Everybody's always attacking the poor teacher and the school administrator. It's easy for people like me to criticize. I don't have to face the daily difficulties of running a school and dealing with large numbers of children. This is particularly true in a society that is in many ways fundamentally hostile to the process that is supposed to be going on in the school. As a critic of education, I am not making the assumption that the required changes are going to be easy ones or that I, put in the shoes of a classroom teacher, could make those changes with any less pain.

But it's quite clear that if the schools are going to help smooth the path for young people as we make the transition into the new superindustrial society, there will have to be fundamental changes. Teachers, for example, are going to have to do something that will be very difficult—forget most of what they have been taught about professionalism in the past half century. As part of the process of gaining decent salaries and working conditions, teachers have been taught that they are professionals and the community has been taught that education is the business of professionals and not non-professionals. The consequences of this have been disastrous.

I think that teachers will suddenly have to reverse roles. The best teachers are going to discover that there are many educational games going on and that they are going to have to be participants in those games—learning at the same time that they are teaching. To the degree that the educational focus shifts to the future, teachers will no longer be the transmitters of inherited and verified "facts." They will become leaders, but participants nevertheless, in the process of the redefinition and rediscovery of the facts.

In this situation, it seems to me that the classroom authority that went with the professional status and with age and on which many teachers relied to protect themselves, is going to be less useful to them. Students are less and less willing to accept authority blindly, and they should be. They are less and less willing to listen to a teacher who doesn't listen to them. Again, this is easy for me to say. I don't go into a school and face twenty to forty kids who don't want to be there in the first place but who are compelled to be there by our presumably humane compulsory education laws.

Morisseau: Are you advocating repeal of compulsory education laws?

Toffler: I see them being gradually reduced rather than extended. And I am opposed to two things: I am opposed to compulsory public education starting at age four or even three, and I am equally opposed to the extension of the age at which children leave school. It seems to me that it is a mistake to continue to prolong the period of formal, inschool education. We would do better to reduce the age at which young people can leave school but provide options for them to return by their own choice later on.

Morisseau: Under current economic and social conditions, it is difficult to employ young people, even at age sixteen, which is the legal school-leaving age now in New York. What do you propose to do with the even younger dropouts that would result from your proposals?

Toffler: There are two answers to that: First, we must admit that the schools are custodial agencies in which we freeze our young people and keep them off the job market; and second, we must recognize that employment is not and must not be the prime consideration. The custodial function may be convenient for the rest of society so long as young people don't rebel against it, as they are now doing, and properly so.

We must not fall into the trap of assuming that, just because there may not be jobs available for young people, the only alternative is today's school in which students are incarcerated against their will. The question of what we do with them is a tough one. The economic structure of the society is such that we cannot absorb more student-age youngsters into the economy; nor should we necessarily. It seems to me that there is a way of reconceptualizing the relationship between young people and the economy. And that, as I suggested earlier, is to begin regarding students as assets—rather than as "parasites" or "investments"—and to begin to employ them to help resolve the myriad unresolved problems of our society.

I would like to see more programs designed for young people in which they have action and service learning and are paid at least enough to subsist on their own, to move out of a parasitical relationship to their families at an earlier age. This would permit them to experience at an earlier age a sense of social and community responsibility, through providing services that the rest of the society values and respects. And all of this could be done, not in place of an education, but as a central part of the educational process itself.

Morisseau: In this pattern the teacher becomes much less the purveyor of knowledge.

Toffler: I'm not arguing that a teacher does not have to have a command of information and facts, though perhaps they ought to be relabeled as "temporary facts." I'm not arguing that cognitive skills are not important. What I am suggesting is that there is not only an affective dimension to education that schools have generally underplayed, but there is a social dimension that they have almost totally ignored. By this I mean that the school must take some responsibility for the attitudes of the rest of society toward youth. As long as students are locked off in the schools and not permitted or encouraged to provide services for society, the school is guaranteeing that the rest of society will underrate young people, no matter what the surrounding rhetoric. The school can only affect the way society regards young people by changing the real relationship between young people and the community.

Morisseau: How do we prepare the teacher of the future to function in this role? What are we not now doing in the training and preparation of teachers that we should be doing?

Toffler: I recognize that changes are taking place in the training of teachers. But I think that, to the extent individuals who wish to be teachers are still educated within tight disciplines, it is a mistake. To the degree that they are focused either entirely on the cognitive dimension or entirely on the affective dimension, it is a mistake. To the degree that they are focused on the past, as against the present and the future, it is a mistake. The education of teachers has to include such questions as: "How can we deal with the future in the classroom?" "How do we build an anticipatory consciousness among young people?" "How do we help young people examine the future consequences of decisions taken today, whether personal decisions taken by the student or political decisions taken by the system?"

At the same time, a very important component of teacher training is the question: "How does one deal with the future in the educational process?" By this I mean not just courses on the future and the development of curricular materials, but the changes in teacher behavior that will be required.

Morisseau: One last question: All of this says that the educational enterprise is going to operate very differently. It is going to be more fragmented in terms of its physical location, and administration is going to be more difficult. What about the people who manage the enterprise, the principals, the superintendents? We're going to need a different type of character here, aren't we?

Toffler: If we go, as I hope we do, to a more decentralized arrangement, then the system of organization is different and, therefore, the problems of administration are different. My guess is that we're going to have a much less pyramidal structure, or a flatter pyramid in any case. There will be fewer levels between the top of the system—the superintendent—and the bottom of the system—the classroom teacher.

Morisseau: The bureaucracy is going to shrink?

Toffler: That doesn't mean that less administration will be needed. It means that it's going to be done in different places and the distribution of the load is going to be different. Perhaps we will have fewer people who are full-time administrators and more who are part time.

Morisseau: You mean, teacher-administrators?

Toffler: Yes, teacher-administrators. And you know that might be a good thing. Like teachers, administrators need to be deprofessionalized. A survey of scientists some time ago indicated that the most creative, as rated by their fellow scientists, were those who did not limit themselves to the laboratory but were also active in administration or teaching or both. That seems logical inasmuch as creativity has to do with the crossover of knowledge, the ability to draw analogies from other fields—the cross-fertilization idea. It seems to me that we need to find a less top-heavy kind of administrative system for the public schools; more variety in what is going on at the lower level, less interchangeability. Maybe we will have "barefoot administrators."

Morisseau: It strikes me that if we're going to disperse the process, fragment it, meld it with the life of the community, whoever is on top of that pyramid is going to have one hell of a problem. Isn't he?

Toffler: Whoever is at the top *is* going to have a hell of a problem, but no more of a problem than whoever is at the top of the decentralized corporation of the future or the decentralized government agency of the future. One of the things we will need is a new approach to planning. Not just planning for longer periods of time, but a process that brings the community into planning at a much earlier stage. I think we may move toward a system of participatory planning in which representatives of the community work part time, for pay, with the "professional" planning staff of the school system.

The industrial society breeds the idea that things have to be done at the top, that some kind of superplan is going to save us. I'm not suggesting that we do not need some kind of coordinative planning at the higher levels. But that cannot take the place of micro-planning at the lower levels. Classroom teachers should be drawing up a plan of what ought to be taught five years from now, and that process ought to include students, in some capacity, as well as community people. The resulting plans will vary from classroom to classroom and from school to school. It is going to be very difficult to coordinate from the top.

I think we are going to be forced to—and ought to—move toward radical decentralization. This will be a very difficult process, and we will not do very well in coordinating it until we have had some experience. After a period of years, we should begin to develop a new kind of coordinative planning that will make it possible to pull everything together again. Meanwhile, we are going to go through a transitional period during which the old rules will no longer apply and during which only one prediction is absolutely safe: Administrators will suffer from more stress than ever before.

CONTRIBUTING AUTHORS

VICTOR H. BERNSTEIN works freelance as a writer on educational issues.

CHARLOTTE BURROWS is a reporter for *The Shreveport Times*.

R. FREEMAN BUTTS is William F. Russell Professor of the Foundations of Education at Teachers College, Columbia University. His latest book is *The Education of the West: A Formative Chapter in the History of Civilization*.

LAWRENCE CREMIN is Frederick A. P. Barnard professor of education and Director of the Institute of Philosophy and Politics of Education at Teachers College, Columbia University. He was recently appointed President of Teachers College. He is the author of *The Genius of American Education, The Transformation of the School,* and *American Education: The Colonial Experience*.

FRANK A. DONNELLY is an instructor in psychiatry (psychology) in the division of continuing education in psychiatry, University of Southern California School of Medicine.

JERRY FARBER is an English teacher at San Jose State College.

HARRY W. FORGAN is assistant professor of elementary education, University of Miami, Florida.

JAMES W. FRASER is a doctoral student at Columbia University and director of adult education at Church of the Covenant, Boston.

NANCY FRAZIER is a journalist who writes children's books and is active in the women's movement.

SUZANNE S. FREMON is the author of *Children and Their Parents.*

GORDON GAMMACK was a reporter for the *Des Moines Register and Tribune,* Iowa, until his death in 1974.

DICK GREGORY, first known as a comedian, is now prominent in the civil rights movement.

M. M. GUBSER is assistant dean of the College of Education, Tucson.

DON HAMACHEK is professor of counseling, personnel services, and educational psychology at Michigan State University.

CLIFFORD A. HARDY is associate professor of education, North Texas State University, Denton.

VIRGINIA HASH is assistant professor of education, University of Northern Iowa, Cedar Falls.

MARGOT HENTOFF writes for a number of publications, including *The New York Review of Books.*

IVAN ILLICH is director of the Center for Intercultural Documentation, Cuernavaca, Mexico, an educational organization devoted to improving the cultural and social environment of Latin American people.

ALVIN M. JOSEPHY, JR., is a vice-president and senior editor of American Heritage Publishing Co., Inc., and is the author of *The Indian Heritage of America* and *Red Power.*

MICHAEL B. KATZ is on the faculty of York University in Toronto. His publications include *The Irony of Early School Reform* (1968), *School Reform: Past and Present* (1971), and *Education in American History* (1973).

CHRISTOPHER LASCH is professor of history at the University of Rochester and is the author of *The American Liberal and the Russian Revolution, The Agony of the American Left,* and *The New Radicalism in America.*

DONALD H. LAYTON is assistant professor of education, University of California at Los Angeles.

DAVID LENDT is assistant to the vice-president for information and development, Iowa State University.

BETTY LEVY is an adjunct lecturer in the program in humanistic studies, College of the City of New York, and a doctoral candidate in educational psychology at Teachers College, Columbia.

GERALD E. LEVY is an instructor in the department of sociology at Adelphi University.

ROBERT W. LYNN is dean of Auburn Theological Seminary, New York City, and Professor at Union Seminary, New York City.

KIM MARSHALL is a teacher at the Martin Luther King, Jr., Middle School in Boston and is the author of *Law and Order in Grade 6—A Story of Chaos and Innovation in a Ghetto School.*

JUDITH MARTIN is a staff writer for *The Washington Post.*

MARGARET MARTIN is a reporter for *The Shreveport Times.*

PHILIP MEYER, former Nieman Fellow (1966–1967) and project director of the Russell Sage Foundation (1969–1970), is Washington correspondent for Knight Newspapers, Inc., and specializes in behavioral science applications to journalism.

PATRICIA MICHAELS is a member of the Bay Area Radical Teachers Organizing Committee.

JAMES J. MORISSEAU is a freelance writer who, for some years, was education writer for the *New York Herald Tribune* and later served as editorial associate for Educational Facilities Laboratories. He is the author of *Design and Planning: The New Schools.*

DONALD H. NAFTULIN is associate professor and director of the division of continuing education in psychiatry, University of Southern California School of Medicine.

JAMES NEY is a staff writer for the *Des Moines Register and Tribune,* Iowa.

ROBERT T. OLBERG is associate professor of education at Northern Illinois University, DeKalb.

FRANKLIN PARKER is Benedum Professor of Education at the University of West Virginia.

ROGER RICKLEFS is a staff reporter on the *Wall Street Journal.*

KEN RINGLE is a staff reporter on *The Washington Post.*

ROBERT ROSENTHAL is a professor of psychology at Harvard University.

MYRA SADKER is assistant professor of education at University of Wisconsin, Parkside.

JOEL T. SANTORO is co-chairman of the physical education department, Isaac E. Young Junior High School, New Rochelle, New York.

DAVID SCHIMMEL is professor of education at University of Massachusetts, Amherst. He is the author, with Louis Fischer, of *The Civil Rights of Teachers.*

CHARLES SILBERMAN is the author of *Crisis in the Classroom* and *Crisis in Black and White.*

ALAN A. SMALL was formerly assistant professor of education at Rockhurst College. He is presently residing in Thornbury, Ontario, Canada.

JOAN K. SMITH teaches educational foundations at Iowa State University, where she is a doctoral candidate in History and Philosophy of Education.

WELBY SMITH is a principal in Smith-Mattingly Productions, Ltd., and co-author of *Introducing the Single Camera VTR System.*

JUDITH STACEY was formerly an instructor, department of teacher education, Richmond College, CUNY, and is now a doctoral student in sociology at Brandeis University.

ALAN STANG is a contributing editor to *American Opinion* and is the author of *It's Very Simple* and *The Actor.*

MARK VAUGHAN is a regular contributor to the *Times Educational Supplement* (London).

JOHN E. WARE, JR., is assistant professor of medical education and health care planning, and director of research and evaluation, Southern Illinois University School of Medicine.

JOHN WESTERHOFF is editor of *Colloquy,* and a professor of religion and education at Duke University.

JOANNE ZAZZARO is features editor of *Nation's Schools.*

INDEX

A

Academic freedom, 78, 358–367
Academies, 370
Accountability, 106–110
Addams, Jane, 31
Administrators:
  functions of, 77–78
  attitudes toward drug abuse education, 119, 126
Aesthetic Education Program, The, 128, 137
Age of Jackson, The, 191
Alinsky, Saul D., 20
Alonson, Braulio, 22
Alpha One, 151
Alsop, Joseph, 213, 221
Alum Rock Union School District, 272
American Association of University Professors, 19
American education:
  purposes of, 37, 51 (*see also* such topics as Schools, Financing)
American Federation of Teachers (AFT), 14, 19, 80, 81, 269, 271
American Heritage, The, 137
American Jewish Congress, 271
American Philosophical Society, 99
Apollo School (Louisiana), 387–395
Applegate, Carol, 25
Aptheker, Herbert, 22
Arizona Citizens for Parental Rights, 109
Arizona Coalition on Educational Policy, 109

Aspira of America, 200
Association on American Indian Affairs, 191
Attitudes, schools' influence on, 109, 258
Ayers, Leonard, 255

B

Bain, Helen, 24
Banfield, Edward, 247
Banneker Project, 215
Barnard, Henry, 182, 252, 409
Baruch, Grace K., 158
Barzun, Jacques, 280
Battelle Memorial Institute, 270
Bean, Orson, 378
Behavioral objectives, 108
Belfrage, Sally, 23
Bell, Daniel, 247
Berg, Ivar, 262
Bessell, Harold, 131, 132, 133
Bilingual education, 196–200
Black education, 38, 43, 46, 214
  (*see also* Minority group education)
Black history, 23, 201–203, 214
Blaschke, Charles, 268, 269
Body Language, 112, 113
Boredom, 329
Bourgeoisie, 247
British infant schools, 383
Brown v. *Board of Education,* 182, 210
BSCS biology curriculum, 113, 114
Bureaucracy, 252–259, 268, 317, 447